PENGUIN BOOKS
JAMMU AND KASHMIR 1949–64

Dr Karan Singh was born heir apparent to the state of Jammu and Kashmir and served successively as regent, Sadar-i-Riyasat and governor. A Padma Vibhushan, Dr Singh has held the portfolios for tourism and civil aviation, health and family planning, and education and culture in the Indian government and served as ambassador to the United States. He has been chairman of the Committee on Ethics of the Rajya Sabha. As chancellor, he has been associated with the Jammu and Kashmir University, the Jawaharlal Nehru University and the Banaras Hindu University. He has chaired the Indian Board of Wildlife and the India International Centre.

Presently, Dr Singh is the chairman of the governing board of the Auroville Foundation and was India's representative on the UNESCO executive board for many years. Associated with several cultural and academic institutions, he composes and recites devotional songs in Dogri and is a connoisseur of Indian classical music.

Dr Singh's published works include his *Autobiography*, *Essays on Hinduism*, *An Examined Life*, *A Treasury of Indian Wisdom*, as well as his extensive correspondence with Indira Gandhi in *Kashmir and Beyond 1966–84*.

Dr Jawaid Alam teaches modern and contemporary Indian history at Jamia Millia Islamia, New Delhi. He was associated with the department of culture, Government of India, for ten years to edit the collected works of G.B. Pant and the selected works of Jawaharlal Nehru at the Teen Murti House. He worked as principal researcher and coordinator for collecting and scrutinizing relevant materials to create the high-profile museum at the Statue of Unity, Gujarat. He is the author of *Government and Politics in Colonial Bihar 1921–1937* and *Muslims in the Shaping of Modern India* (forthcoming) and co-editor, with Mushirul Hasan, of *Muslims and the Congress: Select Correspondence of Dr M.A. Ansari 1912–1936* (forthcoming).

JAMMU & KASHMIR
1949–64

Select Correspondence between
Jawaharlal Nehru
and **Karan Singh**

Edited by Jawaid Alam

Foreword by Sonia Gandhi

PENGUIN BOOKS
An imprint of Penguin Random House

PENGUIN BOOKS

USA | Canada | UK | Ireland | Australia
New Zealand | India | South Africa | China | Singapore

Penguin Books is part of the Penguin Random House group of companies
whose addresses can be found at global.penguinrandomhouse.com

Published by Penguin Random House India Pvt. Ltd
4th Floor, Capital Tower 1, MG Road,
Gurugram 122 002, Haryana, India

First published in Viking by Penguin Books India 2006
This edition published in Penguin Books by Penguin Random House India 2020

10 9 8 7 6 5 4 3 2

ISBN 9780143450511

Typeset in Bembo by Mantra Virtual Services, New Delhi
Printed at Repro India Limited

CONTENTS

FOREWORD

It gives me great pleasure to introduce *Jammu and Kashmir 1949-64: Select Correspondence between Jawaharlal Nehru and Karan Singh,* a compilation of extensive correspondence between Pandit Jawaharlal Nehru and Dr Karan Singh over a period of fifteen years.

Panditji was a master of the art of letter writing—an art that unfortunately is on the wane today. His letters reveal a deeply reflective mind, his enlightened and visionary thoughts on issues of national and international importance as well as his warm personality, his literary prowess and wide-ranging interests.

The correspondence spans a very eventful period in our history and will provide new insights into Panditji's views on Kashmir and many other matters of historical interest. I have no doubt it will be of great interest to scholars, historians as well as to the general reader and is a valuable addition to India's historical archives.

New Delhi
July 2006

Sonia Gandhi

PREFACE

For several years, friends have been urging me to get my extensive correspondence with Pandit Jawaharlal Nehru published in view of its considerable historical value. While some of his letters to me have been included in the multi-volume *Selected Works* being published by the Jawaharlal Nehru Memorial Fund, I felt that the entire correspondence should be available to historians as well as the general public. Our correspondence lasted fifteen years from 1949 when at the age of eighteen I entered public life as head of state in Jammu and Kashmir right up to Panditji's passing away in 1964. The select correspondence in this volume consists of 68 letters from him and 148 letters from me duly edited and annotated.

Panditji was my political mentor for those important years when I was regent, Sadar-i-Riyasat and then governor in Jammu and Kashmir during which period I also developed a keen interest in national politics. His guidance was a great source of strength to me in dealing with the many difficult situations that arose during this period. I will always treasure the memory of the affection with which he invariably treated me and I have taken the liberty of dedicating the book to his memory.

While looking through my papers I also came across a copy of the memorandum that my father Maharaja Hari Singh presented to the then president, Dr Rajendra Prasad, in August 1952. As far as I am aware, this document has never been published, and as it finds mention in our correspondence it is appropriate that this memorandum be included as an appendix to this volume.

I am grateful to Smt. Sonia Gandhi for writing the foreword to this book and to Penguin for publishing it.

All royalties from this book will go to the Jawaharlal Nehru Memorial Fund.

October 2006   Karan Singh

EDITOR'S NOTE

This volume is a collection of 216 letters and notes exchanged between Jawaharlal Nehru and Karan Singh covering the period from 1949 to 1964, a decidedly significant period in the history of the relationship between India and Kashmir. The whole body of correspondence has been streamlined, chronologically as well as grammatically. However, the appendix is not in chronological order as it contains various interrelated enclosures. Biographical and explanatory footnotes have been inserted in order to make the correspondence more useful. The original copies of all the correspondence included in this volume are in the possession of Dr Karan Singh.

Although the letters belong to a period now remote, they are still relevant as most of them have been thrown open to scholars for the first time and are rich in substance. Encompassing some of the most sensitive years of the lives of Jawaharlal Nehru and Karan Singh, they also shed light on a wide variety of events and issues of the contemporary history of Jammu and Kashmir.

The fondness that Nehru and Karan Singh shared is evident in these letters. During his formative years, contemporary political realities that were sweeping across the world made a deep impression on Karan Singh and convinced him that the system of feudal governance was on its way out. As a student at Doon School, he had developed great admiration for Nehru and was thrilled by his writings which provided valuable insights into the dramatic political developments of that era. Karan Singh writes to Nehru: 'I recall how avidly I used to read your books in my school days.' On 6 December 1947 Karan Singh met Nehru for the first time in Jammu and requested Nehru to autograph the *Autobiography* (Nehru's) which he was going through with great interest. Nehru wrote to Indira Gandhi on the same date saying, 'I met the Yuvaraj for the first time and liked him. He is a very bright boy . . .' It was at this stage that Karan Singh became an ardent admirer of Jawaharlal Nehru who was then shaping the political destiny of India as prime minister and began to look up to him as a role model and mentor.

Dr Singh was drawn into the political arena in June 1949 at the age of eighteen when he was appointed regent of the Jammu and

Kashmir state at the intervention of Nehru. Kashmir being the ancestral homeland of the Nehrus, Panditji took personal interest in its affairs and gave much administrative guidance and solace to Karan Singh.

At the outset, the correspondence highlights the closer links that developed between Nehru and Karan Singh. It also shows how Nehru provided liberal political training, personal guidance and abiding support to Karan Singh so that he would act as the representative of the people and bring about changes as desired by them. Karan Singh reciprocated accordingly. His letters reveal that he was very impressed by Nehru's efforts to facilitate democratic processes in the country and sought Nehru's assurance that Kashmir would be a part of that change.

Nehru's liking for Karan Singh increased consistently. He strongly urged Sheikh Abdullah, the most popular leader of Kashmir and a political adversary of the ruling family, to treat Karan Singh with 'courtesy and generosity' and utilize his services in the task of nation-building. Nehru wrote to Sheikh Abdullah: 'I hope you and your colleague will treat the Yuvaraj with friendship and understanding. He is a bright young boy, inexperienced but meaning well.'

During the last years of the 1940s and in the early 1950s the tempestuous phase Jammu and Kashmir had been passing through became an issue of international importance. Such developments became a cause of concern for Karan Singh's mother Maharani Tara Devi. She wrote an emotional letter to Nehru and sought his help and guidance for the Yuvaraj. He promptly conveyed to her that he could well understand a mother's concern and assured her saying: 'I have been seeing Tiger from time to time and have grown to like him very much. He is a fine young man and I think that his good qualities will enable him to face difficulties. I shall certainly help him and guide him in every way.' In their correspondence of this period, the Kashmir issue featured quite frequently and they subscribed to an independent posture in pursuance of certain well-defined and readily understandable national goals.

Karan Singh's letters of 1952 demonstrate that by this time he had acquired a mature perspective on national as well as international politics. Nehru's letters added considerably to his understanding. The question of an elected head of state and the framing of the new constitution find frequent mention in their correspondence. Regarding acceptance of the office of elected head of state, Karan Singh informed Nehru that, 'After the constitution is finalized, and I have studied it, I will be in a position to consider acceptance.' However, Nehru's assurance persuaded him to accept. Nehru also wrote to Sheikh Abdullah saying, 'the Yuvaraj had conducted himself well as constitutional Head Regent and therefore you would be in favour of electing him as the Head of State.'

On his election as the Sadar-i-Riyasat Nehru wrote to Karan Singh: 'This puts a great responsibility upon you, for you have not merely to follow an established convention but rather to help in making conventions for the future.' He added: 'You know that I shall often think of you and that you can always rely on such help and guidance as I can give.' Karan Singh acknowledged Nehru's assurance with an emotional touch: 'I need hardly express how greatly I value your guidance and advice.' And that, 'your assurance of future help and guidance gives me courage . . .' and 'I feel confident that despite my youth and inexperience I will be able to successfully fulfil my responsibilities.' Indeed, it marked the beginning of a new phase in the history of Jammu and Kashmir and Nehru himself admitted that it was 'a happy beginning'. Nehru put it in a more emphatic way in his letter to the chief ministers, whom he considered partners in the task of nation-building: 'This change-over appears to have been widely welcomed in Kashmir . . . Kashmir thus starts a new chapter in its history and is the first State to have an elected Head . . . This is a significant change which finally breaks with a past tradition. At the same time there is kind of continuation because the Yuvaraj was chosen as Sadar-i-Riyasat.'

Popular enthusiasm in Kashmir was, however, dampened by an aggressive agitation started by the Praja Parishad, a Jammu based communal organization closely allied to communal organizations in the rest of India. The agitation led to the polarization of politics on communal lines.

The year 1953 was a turbulent and eventful one in Kashmir politics. The correspondence indicates that the state became even more crucial in the calculations of Nehru and his comrades. Nehru noted that Karan Singh's 'own position becomes more and more embarrassing and he has continually to face the question as to whether and for how long he should continue where he is.' Karan Singh was, naturally, greatly worried at the turn of events. The situation, however, brought Karan Singh closer to Nehru. Initially, Nehru relied heavily on Sheikh Abdullah for his policies on Kashmir but now he increasingly looked towards Karan Singh and dubbed Sheikh Abdullah as a man who 'lacks political foresight and has a knack of saying the wrong thing.'

In the midst of a restive political situation Karan Singh rushed to Nehru in July and had a long talk with him. He recounts in his autobiography: 'I found Jawaharlal's attitude considerably changed. Not only did he not make any attempt to defend Sheikh Abdullah, he seemed to be as disturbed as I was about the way the situation was developing . . . As I took leave he put his hand on my shoulder and said, "Don't worry, do your best".' Indeed, the correspondence shows that serious differences arose in the Sheikh Abdullah cabinet and efforts by Karan Singh to explore the possibilities of securing a stable government failed. Thereupon, he dissolved the council of ministers and called Bakhshi Ghulam Mohammad to form a new cabinet. At this Nehru wrote to him: 'I quite realize the great strain which you must have undergone during the last few days. I think you have acted with wisdom and dignity.' Thus, despite his proximity to Sheikh Abdullah, Nehru showed great character by putting political rationality over personal affinities.

The correspondence of 1954 mainly deals with administrative matters of the state while that of 1955 focuses on international affairs and on the stand taken by Bulganin and Khrushchev on Kashmir during their visit to India. They also paid a visit to Kashmir at the request of Karan Singh and said, 'Kashmir is part of India and the people of Kashmir have themselves decided to be so.' In 1956, the correspondence deals with the question of the release of Sheikh Abdullah who had been in detention since 9 August 1953. Nehru was worried about such a prolonged detention as he felt that it would undermine India's position in the international arena, while Karan Singh's letters point out that after his release, 'he will immediately become the rallying point for all the disruptionist forces and disgruntled factions.' The new Constitution of Jammu and Kashmir was about to take final shape. Karan Singh made a comprehensive observation on it which was liked by Nehru.

In 1957 Nehru did not write to Karan Singh as he was engaged in election campaigns and in the formation of the government during the first four months. However, why he did not write again that year is not clear. Karan Singh wrote to him about elections and the formation of the new cabinet in Jammu and Kashmir. Similarly, they exchanged relatively fewer number of letters in 1958 but the note Karan Singh wrote for Nehru, reflecting on various issues of contemporary India which determined the moral and material creativity of post-Independence India is thought-provoking. In 1959 Karan Singh visited the Soviet Union and on his return wrote a note for Nehru which gives a vivid account of his trip. Nehru liked it and circulated it among his cabinet members. Likewise, in 1960, Karan Singh visited Nepal, the native country of his wife. He sent a confidential note to Nehru which evaluated the existing political situation in Nepal and the growing influence of China there. He had talks with various leaders of Nepal and gathered that they 'have genuine feelings of friendship and goodwill towards India but it was obvious that they were apprehensive of the growing might of the Chinese leviathan.'

The correspondence of 1961–62 concentrates on the internal dynamics of the politics in Jammu and Kashmir. The letters of 1963 shed light on the dramatic changes that took place in the state. Under the Kamaraj Plan, Bakshi Ghulam Mohammad resigned in October but wanted to play the role of kingmaker which led to the emergence of a fluid political situation. Karan Singh sought Nehru's guidance who tried to put things in the right perspective and suggested: 'All I can say now is that we have to watch developments and remain wide awake.' In 1964 there is only one letter which Nehru wrote to Karan Singh. In the appendix, the memorandum of Maharaja Hari Singh, submitted to the president of India, brings out various issues that came up and the rapid political developments that took place between October 1947 and August 1952.

In terms of style, language and historical significance, the letters are unique and impart much understanding to scholars as well the general reader. Above all, they are marked by intellectual brilliance and political acumen. They also bear witness to the fact that Jawaharlal Nehru had a special corner in his heart for Karan Singh.

I am grateful to Dr Karan Singh for the confidence he has reposed in me. I am much obliged to Professor Mushirul Hasan, Professor Bimal Prasad and Shri B.R. Nanda for their guidance and encouragement. I also owe special thanks to Ms Geeta Kudaisiya, Rajendra Prasad and Shyamal Roy for their help.

Teen Murti House   Jawaid Alam
25 September 2006

Srinagar
12 August 1949

My dear Panditji,

I have just returned from a tour of forward areas (Tithwal[1] etc.) with General Thimayya[2]. It was very interesting and I enjoyed seeing the troops and the country a lot. That part of the country is amazingly beautiful, especially the 10,000 feet Nashtachoor Pass[3], and it is a pleasure driving through it.

I shall be coming to Delhi within a few days, when I hope to have the pleasure of seeing you again. I shall only be staying in Delhi for a few days and then going on to Kasauli to visit my mother[4] or might go to Kasauli first and stop in Delhi for a few days on my way back.

I trust that this finds you and Mrs Gandhi[5] very well. I sincerely hope that we will have the pleasure of having you up here again soon.

With respectful regards,

Yours very sincerely,
Karan Singh

———————

1. A village situated between Muzaffarabad and Shalurah on the left bank of the Kishanganga river.
2. K.S. Thimayya (1906-1965); commissioned into the Indian army, 1926; commander, Indian troops in Kashmir, 1947-50; chairman, Neutral Nations Repatriation Commission in Korea, 1953-54; chief of army staff, 1957-61; died in an air crash when he was commander, UN Forces in Cyprus, 1965.
3. A pass leading to Tithwal.
4. Maharani Tara Devi (1910-1967); originally hailed from a Katoch family of Kangara district, Himachal Pradesh; a deeply religious lady, she had great concern for the poor; her work for War Aid during the Second World War earned her the coveted title 'Crown of India'.
5. Indira Gandhi (1917-1984); daughter of Jawaharlal Nehru, actively involved in the freedom movement during her childhood and founded *Bal Charkha Sangh* and *Vanar Sena* (monkey brigade) of children in 1930 to aid Congress agitational campaigns; joined Congress, 1938; married to Feroze Gandhi, 1942; imprisoned for thirteen months during the Quit India movement, 1942-43; worked in riot affected areas under Mahatma Gandhi, 1947; president, Indian National Congress, 1959; Union minister of information and broadcasting, 1964-66; prime minister of India, 1966-77 and 1980-84; awarded the Bharat Ratna in 1972; elected chairperson, Non-aligned Movement, 1982.

———— 2 ————

New Delhi
15 August 1949

My dear Tiger[1],
Thank you for your telegram of greetings today.

I received your letter today about your proposed visit to your mother. I hope you will remember that you have to stay with me when you pass through Delhi either way. Please let me know when you are expected here and who are accompanying you.

I shall be going to the United States early in October[2]. Before I go there I want to pay a brief visit to Srinagar, probably in the last week of September for two days[3].

Yours sincerely,
Jawaharlal Nehru

———— 3 ————

Srinagar
8 September 1949

My dear Panditji,
I suppose you have by now returned from your trip to Allahabad and Bombay. I do hope you found Mrs Gandhi very much better.

I have just returned form a three-day tour of Dras[4] with General Thimayya. We went through the Zojila Pass[5], over which the Indian Army so incredibly got tanks, and went on to Dras. We have all returned very badly chapped and sunburnt after the very hot and dusty jeep journey.

---

1. Karan Singh acquired the nickname 'Tiger' in his childhood when he entered the room where his father Maharaja Hari Singh and Maharaja Umaid Singh of Jodhpur were seated. Seeing Karan Singh, Umaid Singhji observed that, 'the boy is on all fours like a tiger'. Since then Karan Singh's father and his friends affectionately called him Tiger, so did Jawaharlal Nehru and others of his generation.
2. Nehru was on a goodwill tour of the USA from 11 to 22 October 1949 and then of Canada from 23 to 25 October. He returned to USA on 26 October and concluded his tour on 7 November 1949.
3. Nehru visited Srinagar on 24-25 September 1949.
4. Dras Pass lies along the valley of the Dras river.
5. It links the Kashmir valley with Ladakh.

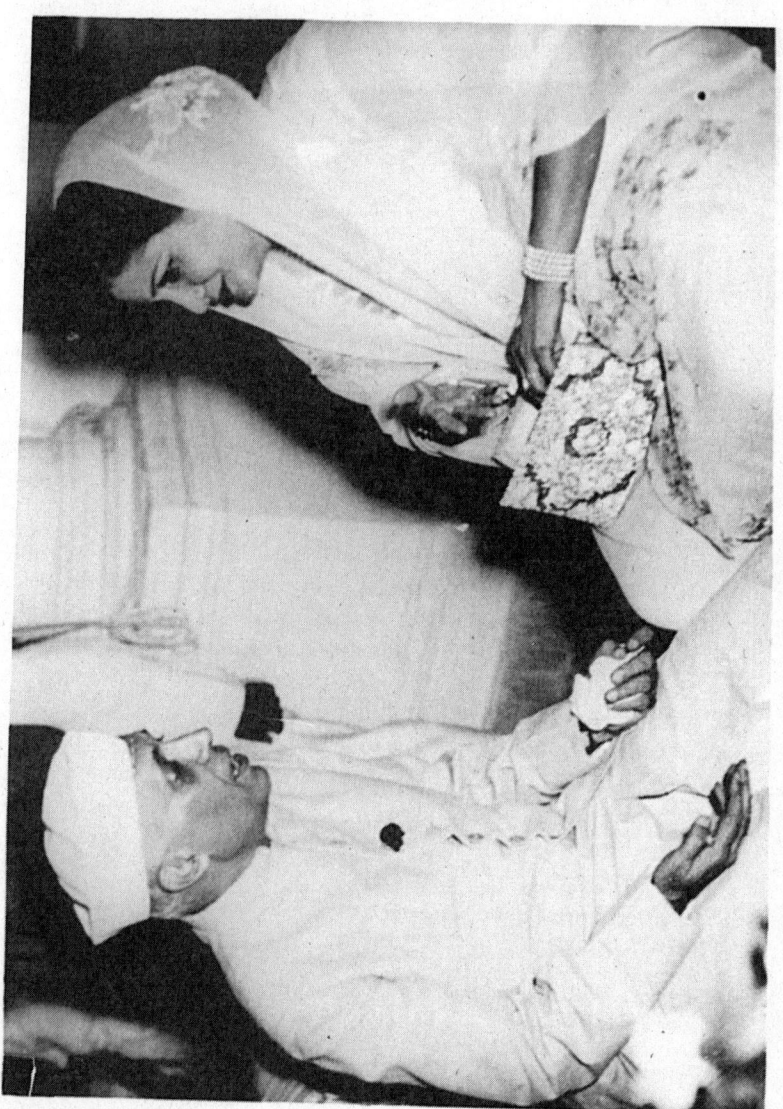

Maharani Tara Devi with Jawaharlal Nehru, New Delhi, 16 May 1949

I want to thank you very much for being so kind and putting me up in your house in Delhi. We are all looking forward to seeing you here on the 24th.

Hoping this finds you very well.

With deepest regards and respects,

Yours sincerely,
Karan Singh

———— 4 ————

New Delhi
11 September 1949

My dear Tiger,

Your letter of the 8th September has just reached me. Tomorrow morning Indira is going to Srinagar and I am giving this note to her. She is still very weak. But I hope that the air of Srinagar will make her strong soon. I am anxious that she should recover soon, as she has to leave for America early next month[1].

I am glad to learn that you went across the Zojila. I went to Dras on foot or riding in 1916, and that is a long time ago. But I still have the picture of that Pass impressed on my mind.

Sheikh Saheb[2] arrived here this evening and gave me a copy of the speech you intend delivering as Chancellor of the University.[3] I have just glanced through it and I find it very interesting. Surely you must be by far the youngest Chancellor that a University has had.

I hope to reach Srinagar on the 24th. It was my intention at first to go to Gurais.[4] But I think this will not be worthwhile during the

---

1. Indira Gandhi accompanied Jawaharlal Nehru on his tour of the United States and Canada.
2. Sheikh Mohammad Abdullah (1905-1982); campaigned for responsible government and founded Jammu and Kashmir Muslim Conference in 1932; later named it as National Conference in 1938; launched Quit Kashmir movement, 1946; prime minister of Jammu and Kashmir, 1948-53; detained for four and a half years from 9 August 1953; detained again in 1958 and released in 1964; chief minister, Jammu and Kashmir, 1974-82.
3. Karan Singh became ex-officio chancellor of Jammu and Kashmir University in June 1949. The university was established in 1948.
4. Gurais valley located in north Kashmir commonly referred to as 'Nanga Pahar' is considered to be amongst the finest scenery in Kashmir.

short time at my disposal. I shall therefore spend two days, the 24th and 25th in Srinagar. On the 26th morning I shall return with Indira and the children.[1]

The United Nations Commission[2] has given us a lot of trouble and taken up a great deal of my time.[3] I understand two[4] of them are coming here tomorrow.

With all good wishes,

Yours sincerely,
Jawaharlal Nehru

———— 5 ————

Srinagar
15 September 1949

My dear Panditji,

Thank you very much for your letter which Mrs Gandhi brought along with her. She arrived on the 12th, and I have put her up in Chashmashahi House.[5] I dropped in to see her the evening she arrived for a few minutes. I am sure the climate here will help her recuperate rapidly, and I sincerely hope that she will be quite recovered by the time you arrive.

---

1. Rajiv Gandhi and Sanjay Gandhi.
2. India and Pakistan approached the United Nations in January 1948 and urged the world body to mediate in their conflict over Kashmir. The Security Council passed a resolution on 17 January 1948 which asked both the nations to ease tension. In the negotiations that followed, both India and Pakistan accused each other of violating the provisions of the resolution. Finally, the UN Commission for India and Pakistan was constituted by a resolution passed on 21 April. The Commission started its work from 15 June 1948.
3. The UN Commission for India and Pakistan on 18 August 1949 cancelled the ministerial level meeting which was to be held in August to discuss the truce proposals as it felt that the divergent views of the Indian and Pakistan governments about the agenda of the meeting might not lead to positive results. Nehru's reaction to this was: 'It almost seems that they were not very keen on it.' Again on 29 August the Commission put forward the proposal for arbitration regarding the truce, with Admiral C.W. Nimitz as arbitrator. Nehru considered this behaviour as 'really odd'.
4. Oldrich Chyle, acting chairman of the UNCIP at this time and Alfredo Lozano, the Commission's principal representative.
5. A state guest house located near the Chashmashahi garden. It has become Raj Bhavan since 1967.

I am enclosing a revised copy of the address which I will deliver[1] on the 24th. The previous copy contained quite a lot of what I thought was superfluous and over-flowery. I went over it and cut it here and there, thereby, I think, improving it. Yes! I suppose I am the youngest Chancellor a University has ever had. It will be a great privilege for me to address such a distinguished audience.

I think that cutting Gurais out of your programme on this short visit was a very good idea. Otherwise, you would have been greatly over-rushed.

Hoping this finds you very well.

With respectful regards,

Yours very sincerely,
Karan Singh

———— 6 ————

Bombay
14 November 1949

My dear Panditji,

This is to wish you very many happy returns of the day and to convey my heartiest congratulations on your birthday.

I am sure you must have enjoyed your visit to America and Canada. While I was in America[2] I could feel the deep regard and respect the people there had for you and I am sure that your visit did more to create a better understanding between our country and their's than anything else could.

I am afraid I am in bed and in plaster again. I had a stroke of very bad luck. Last month I was going out for a shoot in Srinagar when our car collided with a lorry, with the result that I broke my left leg and cracked my right hip.[3] I was flown down here to Bombay so that I could have expert medical attendance. So I have ended up with

1. Karan Singh as the chancellor addressed the first convocation of the Jammu and Kashmir University on 24 September 1949 at Srinagar in an open park under chinar trees. After congratulating the students he advised them to continue the traditions of Jammu and Kashmir and to act as ambassadors of unity. Jawaharlal Nehru also addressed the convocation.
2. Karan Singh was in the USA from 31 December 1947 to 15 February 1949 for a special surgery on his left leg which was fractured in an automobile accident.
3. The accident happened on 29 October 1949.

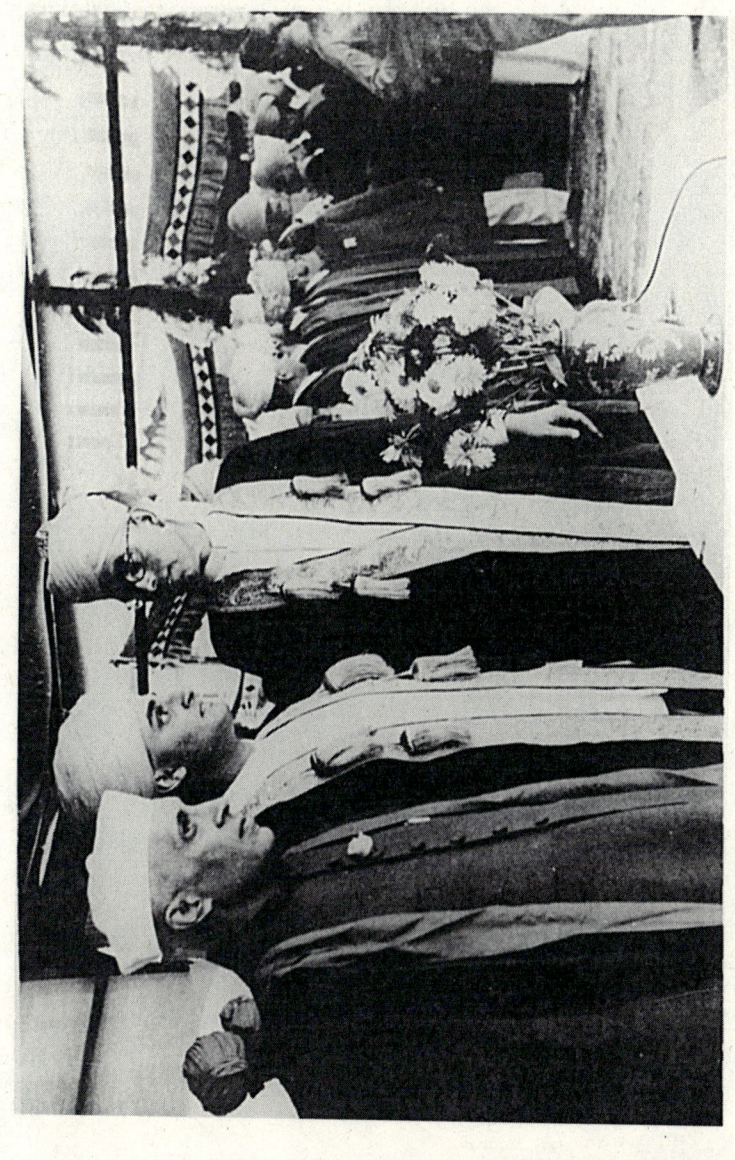

With Jawaharlal Nehru and Sheikh Abdullah at a convocation of the Jammu and Kashmir University in Srinagar, 24 September 1949

both legs in plaster again. However, the doctors say that in about six weeks I should be able to start walking again.

Hoping this finds you and Mrs Indira Gandhi very well. Please give my kindest regards to her.

With respectful regards,

Yours sincerely,
Karan Singh

——— 7 ———

Bombay
13 January 1950

My dear Panditji,
Thank you very much indeed for your card of good wishes for the New Year, which I sincerely reciprocate.

My leg was operated upon last month. Since then I have been progressing satisfactorily and, though still confined to bed, am hoping to be allowed up in about three weeks.

My marriage has, due to my accident, been postponed from the 15th of this month to the 5th of March.[1]

Hoping this finds you very well,

With respects,

Yours very sincerely,
Karan Singh

——— 8 ———

Srinagar
27 June 1950

My dear Panditji,
I am glad to hear that you are back from your highly successful tour of Indonesia and other countries.[2] I hope you enjoyed your trip.

---

1. Karan Singh married Princess Yasho Rajya Lakshmi, the daughter of General Sarada Shumsher and granddaughter of the last Rana prime minister of Nepal, Maharaja Mohan Shumsher. The marriage ceremony was performed at the Kutch Castle on Nepean Sea Road, Bombay.
2. Nehru visited Indonesia from 7 to 17 June 1950, Singapore and Malaya from 17 to 19 June and Burma from 20 to 23 June.

You may remember, during your last visit here, I had a talk with you about the Jammu and Kashmir State Forces. You then agreed with me, for reasons we discussed, that it would be advisable to keep these Forces as a separate entity.

I learn now that orders have been issued for the disbandment of the Headquarters of the Jammu and Kashmir State Forces.[1] I have no doubt you will agree that with the only coordinating agency (the Headquarters) gone, the Forces will no longer remain a compact unit. Besides, from the reports I have received it appears the news has had a very depressing effect on all ranks of the Forces. They are very perturbed that while their future is in the balance and insecure, the only agency which champions their cause and looks after their interests is being taken away. There are many other reasons which make me feel that the present decision is premature and requires reconsideration. I cannot put these reasons on paper, but some of these will be given to you verbally by the bearer of this letter, Captain Mohan Singh,[2] if you will kindly give him audience for five minutes.

In other State Unions, the Indian Army has deputed senior military officers to act as GOSC of the Union Forces. They control and administer the forces on behalf of the Indian Army, and provide the necessary liaison between the forces and the Army. Because of the peculiar circumstances prevailing here, I was hoping the same procedure would be adopted in respect of our Forces.

I have written this letter because it is possible that the decision may have been taken without your knowledge and that you may wish it to be revised. I feel that the Headquarters must remain and that they should be strengthened.

I expect to pass through Delhi, sometime in August, on my way back from Kasauli. I am looking forward to seeing you then.

With best regards from both of us,

Yours sincerely,
Karan Singh

---

1. It was later named the Jammu and Kashmir Regiment and placed under the Indian army.
2. ADC to Karan Singh, the regent, Jammu and Kashmir State.

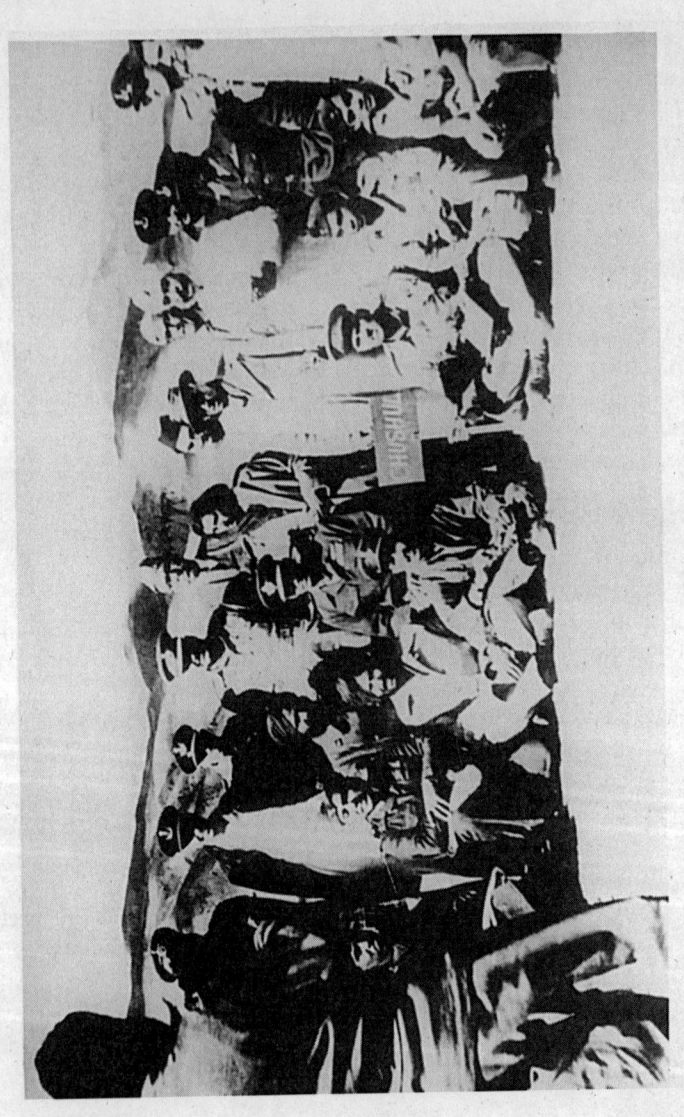

With Jawaharlal Nehru, Indira Gandhi, Sheikh Abdullah and others at Chushul, the world's highest airport, 14 May 1950

—————— 9 ——————

New Delhi
30 June 1950

My dear Yuvaraj,

Thank you for your letter of the 27th June which Captain Mohan Singh delivered to me.

I remember our talk, when I was in Srinagar, about the Jammu and Kashmir State Forces. I agreed with you then that these Forces should continue as a separate entity, at least for the present. So far as I know, this is the intention of our Defence Ministry also for a variety of reasons. Even their proposal in regard to the present administrative Headquarters was not meant to affect that separate entity. They considered it from the point of view of efficiency and economy. The point was whether the present administrative Headquarters of the Jammu and Kashmir State Forces should be fitted in some way with the appropriate organization of the Indian Army in Jammu.

I have referred the matter to the Defence Ministry and they are considering it. I shall write to you again after they have fully examined it.

I am glad to learn that you will be passing through Delhi some time in August. I shall be happy to see you then. You will, of course, stay with me when you are in Delhi. I hope your wife will be with you.

I had a most interesting time in Indonesia.[1] It is a beautiful country, but many places are beautiful. It is the people that attracted me, more especially in Bali. Indeed, I remarked there at a semi-public function that I had been more attracted by Bali than any other place with the sole exception of Kashmir.

Yours sincerely,
Jawaharlal Nehru

—————————————

1. During his ten-day visit to Indonesia, Nehru addressed the joint session of the Indonesian parliament, public meetings and the students of Gadja Mada University. He received a picturesque welcome there, more specially in Bali where he addressed the biggest meeting. He was widely cheered by the the people there as 'the Leader of Asia'.

——— 10 ———

Srinagar
3 July 1950

My dear Panditji,
Thank you very much for your letter which Captain Mohan Singh brought back to me. I am very grateful that you have referred the matter regarding the Jammu and Kashmir State Forces to the Defence Ministry, and I am looking forward to your letter after they have fully examined the question.

I can well imagine how beautiful Indonesia, especially Bali, must be. I am very keen on travelling, and hope, as soon as conditions here settle down, to visit several foreign countries. That is, of course, if we are not by that time in the midst of a world war.

Thank you very much for asking me to stay with you in Delhi. I shall most certainly avail of your kind hospitality.

It is fairly warm here nowadays. In Delhi it must be absolutely awful. I wonder when we will see you up here again?

With respectful regards,

Yours sincerely,
Karan Singh

——— 11 ———

Srinagar
5 August 1950

My dear Panditji,
I will be coming to Delhi on 13th of this month for about a week. I will be very pleased to avail myself of your kind invitation to stay with you. The Yuvarani[1] will be going straight on to Kasauli without stopping at Delhi.

We have been having amazing weather this year. The rains have been veritably monsoonish, and the temperature high. On the whole, it is very unpleasant for Srinagar.

———

1. Yasho Rajya Lakshmi (1937–2009), wife of Karan Singh; an eminent social worker; as president, Delhi Society for Welfare of Mentally Retarded Children (Okhla Centre), she built up an excellent institution in New Delhi which provides day care, vocational training and other facilities to the mentally challenged.

Looking forward to seeing you soon,
With respectful regards,

Yours very sincerely,
Karan Singh

——— 12 ———

Srinagar
23 October 1950

My dear Panditji,
Thank you very much for your letter.

I am delighted that you are coming up here for a couple of days.[1] I have spoken to Sheikh Sahib and asked him to refrain from cramming your visit with numerous engagements. He has promised to do so, and I hope you will enjoy a very restful two days. I wonder if Mrs Gandhi and your grandchildren are coming up with you?

Hoping this finds you well,
With kind regards,

Yours sincerely,
Karan Singh

——— 13 ———

Jammu Tawi
24 December 1950

My dear Panditji,
Thank you very much for your kind card of New Year greetings, which I heartily reciprocate. I sincerely hope that the new year will bring stability to our State, prosperity to our country and peace to the world, however unlikely these may seem at present.

It is very pleasant here in Jammu. I do hope you will find time if even a couple of days to visit us this winter. It will be a great pleasure if you will stay with me, and I assure you it will be almost as pleasant as Srinagar in spring. I do hope Mrs Gandhi will come with you here, along with your grandchildren.

———————

1. Nehru was in Srinagar on 28 and 29 October 1950.

With Jawaharlal Nehru during a boat procession on the Jhelum, Srinagar, 29 October 1950

I may be in Delhi soon, in which case I shall look forward to seeing you again.

With respectful regards from the Yuvarani and myself,

Yours very sincerely,
Karan Singh

P.S.

This year, as you know, we had the second Convocation of our University in November. The President kindly delivered the Convocation address.[1] I am enclosing a copy of a short address I wrote and delivered on that occasion, which might interest you.

After the great encouragement which we received from you last year in its first convocation, our infant University has been progressing steadily, and we hope, in due course of time, it will be able to fulfil all our hopes and aspirations.

K.S.

─────── 14 ───────

New Delhi
26 December 1950

My dear Tiger,

Thank you for your letter of the 24th.

I am sure it must be very pleasant in Jammu. It is pleasant enough here. I would like to visit Jammu this winter, but life is hard and time is difficult to find. Very soon I shall be going away to England[2] and shall stay there about two weeks. On my return I shall be immersed in my work again.

───────────

1. Addressing the convocation on 10 November 1950 President Rajendra Prasad said: 'The Jammu and Kashmir University should feel proud of its being a University which was born in free India. It is free from bad traditions of some of the older universities in India and I feel confident that in years to come this University will build of high traditions of imparting knowledge to the youths so that the people who leave the portals of this institution will prove useful citizen and show new light to the country'. Exhorting the students to serve their country, he said: 'You have to carry on the crusade against mass illiteracy, poverty and ill health in the country.'
2. Nehru visited England from 3 to 16 January 1951 for the Commonwealth Prime Minister's Conference.

I do not know when you are coming here. You will probably miss me, as I shall be in England. I am leaving on the 1st.

Yours sincerely,
Jawaharlal Nehru

———— 15 ————

Jammu Tawi
16 February 1951

My dear Panditji,
About a fortnight ago I was in Delhi for a couple of days, but at that time you were out, I think at Ahmadnagar.

I am sending a case of maltas from my garden, which I hope you will enjoy, and also some pork pickle made from a pig I shot.

I shall be in Delhi again within two or three weeks, at that time I am looking forward to seeing you again.

Hoping this finds you and Mrs Gandhi very well. We are still looking forward to a visit by you to Jammu.

With kind regards and respects,

Yours very sincerely,
Karan Singh

———— 16 ————

New Delhi
18 February 1951

My dear Tiger,
Thank you for your letter and for the maltas and the pickle.

I am sorry I missed you when you came here. I expect to be here now till the end of this month. On the 3rd March I shall be going away to Bombay for two days returning on the 5th. Lady Mountbatten[1] is expected to come here about that time.

With all good wishes to you,

Yours sincerely,
Jawaharlal Nehru

_____

1. Edwina Ashley, Countess Mountbatten (1901-1960); married to Lord Mountbatten, 1922; superintendent-in-chief, St John Ambulance Brigade, 1942; chairman, St John and Red Cross Society Hospitals, 1948.

——— 17 ———

New Delhi
19 March 1951

My dear Tiger,

I have received an invitation from you for a party. I am afraid I cannot come. But I am making a strenuous effort to go for two days to Srinagar. The two days are April 1st and 2nd. Very probably, Lady Mountbatten will accompany me and Indira. We intend starting at 9 a.m. on April 1st, Sunday, and returning at 9.15 a.m. on April 3rd from the Srinagar airfield.

My informing you does not mean that you should take the trouble to come to Srinagar for our sake. We are all tired out with our labours and want two days rest and not functions.

Our journey to Kashmir will, of course, depend to some extent on the weather.

With all good wishes,

Yours sincerely,
Jawaharlal Nehru

——— 18 ———

Jammu Tawi
27 March 1951

My dear Panditji,

Thank you very much for your letter. I am delighted to learn that you are coming up to Srinagar for a couple of days. I am sure you will have a pleasant rest. I would request you, if it is convenient, to please stop in Jammu for a few hours, either on your way up or on your return, and have lunch with us here. I do hope you will be able to do so. We will, if you prefer, have just a quiet lunch at which I will not invite any other guests.

I have just returned from a fortnight's visit to the Kangra Valley.[1] Mummy is at present staying there in a place called Alhilal—five hours drive from here. I do not know whether you have been there, but

---

1. Kangra valley in Himachal Pradesh extends from the foot of the Dhauladhar Range to the south of the Beas river. It is a strike valley.

With Jawaharlal Nehru, Sheikh Abdullah and Bakshi Ghulam Mohammad, Srinagar,

that part of the country is very beautiful, as a matter of fact very like Kashmir in places. While we were there we visited Jwalamukhi,[1] Chamunda,[2] Kangra and a few other places of worship which Mummy had been wanting to see for a long time, and also paid short visits to Mandi and Suket. As you know, the cultural ties and affinities of that part of country with Jammu are very close, and wherever we went we were accorded very warm receptions by the people. I also took the opportunity of visiting the Yole Refugee Camp,[3] which contains over 12,000 refugees from this State. They seemed very well looked after, and the Camp exceptionally clean and well run.

Hoping this finds you very well and looking forward to seeing you, Mrs Gandhi and Lady Mountbatten here in Jammu.

With respectful regards,

Yours very sincerely,
Karan Singh

———— 19 ————

Jammu Tawi
12 April 1951

My dear Panditji,
I hope you had a pleasant flight back to Delhi.

Newspaper reports of a speech Sheikh Sahib delivered[4] the other day, wherein he made certain reference to me, must have come to

———————————

1. Famous for the temple dedicated to Goddess Jwalamukhi, in the valley of the Beas river in Himachal Pradesh.
2. Known for the temple of Goddess Chamunda, in Himachal Pradesh.
3. Near Dharamsala in Himachal Pradesh where refugees from 'Azad Kashmir' were kept.
4. Sheikh Abdullah, at a public meeting on 9 April 1951 at Panthal, a village in Jammu, reportedly said that Yuvaraj Karan Singh was 'frequently conferring with the reactionary communal leaders who are plotting to bring back the Maharaja'. He added: 'I still hope that the young Prince will listen to better counsels. But if he persists in seeking the advice of the reactionaries and the communalists, I can tell him, for the time has come for plain speaking that his future will be not far different from that of his father. Let the Yuvaraj realize that the days of the Rajas and the Nawabs are past. Even in those places where monarchy is still tolerated, it is only subject to the will of the people which is supreme.'

your notice. In case you have not seen them I am enclosing two cuttings.[1]

I am very deeply hurt at Sheikh Sahib's making such remarks in public, particularly as they were not based on facts and were consequently highly misleading. I have written to him[2] in this connection, a copy of that letter I am also enclosing.

I am sure you will understand how grieved and insulted I feel. If it is convenient to you I would very much like to come down to Delhi for a day or two and talk this matter over with you.

Hoping this finds you very well and refreshed after your visit to Kashmir.

With kind regards and respects,

Yours very sincerely,
Karan Singh

———— 20 ————

New Delhi
15 April 1951

My dear Tiger,

I have your letter of the 12th April. I have also read the letter you wrote to Sheikh Saheb.

I am sorry that Sheikh Saheb made any reference to you in his speech and I am glad you wrote to him directly on the subject.

The position in regard to Jammu and Kashmir is, as you know, a very difficult one and we are up against Great Powers. This fact does not appear to be realized by many people. Oddly enough, those who are more opposed than any others to Pakistan's intrusion in the State, often act in a manner to help Pakistan. You will remember I spoke to you on this subject.

---

1. Karan Singh had enclosed the reports from the *Tribune* and the *Hindustan Times* of 10 April 1951.
2. Expressing his strong disapproval of Sheikh Abdullah's speech at Panthal, Karan Singh wrote to him on 12 April: 'I am sorry that this matter has arisen and that I have had to write to you about it. The reports of your speech, however, deeply hurt me and I thought it but fair to us both that I should either write or talk to you about this. I hope you will appreciate my frankness and take this in the spirit in which it has been written, and that there will be no misunderstanding'.

I shall always be glad to see you. Just at present I am terribly busy and not too well. Come a little later, if you like.

Yours sincerely,
Jawaharlal Nehru

———— 21 ————

Srinagar
13 May 1951

My dear Panditji,

I returned from Delhi with my mother, and on my way back spent a few days with her at Alhilal in Kangra. She was sorry that she was not able to see you while she was in Delhi, but she was not very well. The next time she is in Delhi, she is looking forward to seeing you again.

It was a very great relief to me to have met you in Delhi and to have talked to you. You have always been so good and kind to me. In the delicate position in which I am at present placed, your kind guidance is invaluable.

I have moved up here for the season. It is delightful here just now. It is cool and bracing and the spring flowers are in full bloom. My little garden is a mass of colour.

I hope this finds you very well. I wonder what you have decided about coming up here just now.

With very kind regards and respects,

Yours sincerely,
Karan Singh

——— 22 ———

New Delhi
17 May 1951

My dear Tiger,
Thank you for your letter of the 13th May. I was very happy to meet you for a short time here. I had a letter from your mother,[1] to which I sent an answer.[2] I am sorry I missed seeing her while she was here.

I wish I could go to Kashmir. But I cannot leave Delhi because of the Parliamentary session which goes on and on.[3]

Yours sincerely,
Jawaharlal Nehru

——— 23 ———

Srinagar
4 June 1951

My dear Tiger,
I am sending you a kind of a resume of my speech[4] at the Conference tonight. I thought it best to prepare this resume myself and give it to the Press in order to avoid misreporting. What I have said in connection with the Security Council and the Kashmir problem is of importance.[5]

---

1. In her letter of 5 May 1951 to Nehru, Maharani Tara Devi expressed concern for her son, Karan Singh who as the regent of the state was facing many ticklish issues and sought Nehru's help and guidance for him.

2. In his reply to Maharani Tara Devi on 13 May Nehru wrote: 'I have been seeing Tiger from time to time and have grown to like him very much. He is a fine young man and I think that his good qualities will enable him to face difficulties. I shall certainly help him and guide him in every way.'

3. The third session of the parliament continued from 5 February to 9 June 1951.

4. Nehru spoke at length at a session of the National Conference in Srinagar on 4 June 1951 on the Kashmir issue, the proposed election of the constituent assembly of Jammu and Kashmir and on the objection raised by Pakistan to it. For the full text of the speech, see *Selected Works of Jawaharlal Nehru* (second series), Vol. 16, Part I, pp. 383–393.

5. The Security Council Resolution of 30 March 1951 sought immediate demilitarization of Kashmir. On 4 June Nehru rejected it as 'totally unacceptable to a free and respectable nation' and added that while he wanted peaceful settlement of the Kashmir problem dictates of others were not acceptable.

With Jawaharlal Nehru, Yasho Rajya Lakshmi and General K.M. Cariappa in Srinagar, 28 August 1952

These two days in Srinagar have been busier for me than ever and I had not the chance, as I wanted, to have some real talk with you. On both these evenings the days have run late into the night. I shall write to you from Delhi in a few days time about certain matters which I consider important. But I might as well indicate them to you now.

I think that it is exceedingly important that your contacts with Sheikh Saheb should be almost continuous or, at any rate, very frequent. I think that you should have a good talk with him regularly once a week and, if necessary, oftener. This will enable you to keep in touch with what is happening and to take Sheikh Saheb's advice on many matters. If you have any difficulties you could then place them before him. I have mentioned this matter to Sheikh Saheb also and he fully agreed.

Apart from these direct contacts, there should be indirect but satisfactory contacts also. This can take place most conveniently by your having a Secretary of high standing and experience, who can continually act as a liaison between you and Sheikh Saheb. This man must be of superior quality who understands political questions and specially the situation in Kashmir. He should, of course, be one who has your confidence and fits in with your household. It is equally important that he should have Sheikh Saheb's confidence.

The normal practice for a head of a State is to have some such Secretary, sometimes more than one if necessary. Our President, Dr Rajendra Prasad,[1] has such a Secretary apart from Assistant Secretaries and the like. That Secretary advises him in regard to any matter coming up before him and keeps in touch with the Government. I am having almost daily references from the President about various matters, political, semi-political or even social. He refers them to me for my advice. Even his important engagements, which have any political significance or effect, are referred to me. The constitutional head of the State has a particular position. He should be in touch with all events. He can, whenever he chooses, offer his advice or his suggestions to Government. But the decisions in regard to those matters are these

---

1. Rajendra Prasad (1884–1963); eminent Congress leader from Bihar; joined Mahatma Gandhi during the satyagraha in Champaran, 1917; imprisoned several times during the freedom movement; president, Indian National Congress, 1934, 1939 and 1947-48; president, Constituent Assembly; president of India, 1950-62; publications include *Champaran Mein Mahatma Gandhi (Mahatma Gandhi in Champaran), India Divided* and *Autobiography*.

of Government or, usually, the Prime Minister. Because of this, the Head keeps in intimate touch with his Prime Minister.

We should try to follow this practice here also both because it is the right practice and because it is specially needed here. I am sure that many difficulties would be overcome if this practice was followed.

It may not be an easy matter to find a really suitable Secretary because he has to fulfil many qualifications. I suggest that you might have a talk about this with Sheikh Saheb. If my help is needed in this, or any other matter it will, of course, be available.

So far as the international aspect of the Kashmir problem is concerned, I have made our position clear. I have no doubts in my mind. We are not going to submit to any decision of the Security Council which is against our wishes. I am not worrying about this much. What I am anxious about is that the apparatus of Government here should function smoothly and efficiently and that the normal needs of the people should be satisfied and grievances removed as far as possible. Much has been done in this respect but the process must continue.

Yours sincerely
Jawaharlal Nehru

———— 24 ————

Srinagar
1 August 1951

My dear Panditji,
It was a great pleasure seeing you up here again. I am sure your short stay at Pahalgam gave you some much needed rest. It was a pity you could not stay on a few days longer.

You may be interested to know that I am considering donating the Gulab Mahal Palace to the University of Jammu and Kashmir. Our University, as you know, possesses no building of its own, nor has it the necessary funds to enable it to acquire or construct a suitable building. Gulab Mahal will, I am sure, be ideally suited for a university. It is a magnificent building, containing numberless rooms, several large halls and possessing lovely lawns. As a matter of fact, I am sure, with its delightful situation, it will be one of the most attractive University buildings in India. It would give me very great pleasure to see it transformed into a flourishing university, and I am sure this gift will go a long way in enabling our University to achieve its lofty ambitions.

Our private property is, however, under the direct control of His Highness.[1] He has just returned from Paris and I have sent him a message requesting him to allow me to donate the building. I am expecting a reply from him soon.

We all deeply appreciate your strong and forthright stand vis-a-vis the hostile and outrageous war propaganda and hysteria which is sweeping Pakistan.[2] I sincerely hope that your clear statements[3] will make them see sense, and that your repeated declaration that India will strongly resist any aggression on her territory, including our State, will make them desist from their insane policy which seems to have

---

1. Maharaja Hari Singh (1895-1961); son of Raja Amar Singh and great grandson of Maharaja Gulab Singh; educated at Mayo College Ajmer; received military training at Imperial Cadet Corps, Dehradun; became commander-in-chief of Jammu and Kashmir State Forces in 1915; became Maharaja on 23 September 1925; paid much attention to the promotion of agriculture, education, medical facilities; abolished forced labour, infanticide and untouchability; allowed harijans to visit all temples; acceded Jammu and Kashmir State to the Indian Union in October 1947.

2. Propaganda against India and threats of war over Kashmir in the Pakistan press had been continuing for several months. For instance on 10 January 1951 the *Pakistan Times* published the statement of Sardar Abdur Rab Nishtar, governor of west Punjab: 'So long as a single Pakistani is alive, nobody dare snatch Kashmir from Pakistan by force…. if the problem was not settled immediately, the whole of Asia would be engulfed in the flame of war which might lead to a world conflagration.' On 14 June 1951, the *Dawn* published the statement of Sir Muhammad Zafarulla Khan, Pakistan's foreign minister: 'I say this with full responsibility that India has now over several months taken up the attitude with regard to Kashmir which deliberately blocks progress along peaceful lines. What does India desire? It has no right to complain if it gets something else.' Similarly, on 15 July 1951, Liaquat Ali Khan, the prime minister of Pakistan, said at a press conference in Karachi that ninety per cent of the Indian army had been concentrated within striking distance of the borders of West and East Pakistan, constituting a grave threat to Pakistan's security, the interests of neighbourly relations between the two countries and to international peace.

3. At a National Conference session on 4 June 1951 in Srinagar, Nehru said that if Pakistan 'undertake *jehad*, they will be answered in kind and will be defeated.' Further, he added: 'if there is another attack on Kashmir by Pakistan, we will not stop our armed forces once again, as we did once earlier, from crossing the border into Pakistan.' Similarly, on 16 July at a public meeting in Bangalore, he declared: 'It is intolerable for continuous propaganda for *jehad* to be carried out in Pakistan, month after month without check or hindrance…. we want good neighbourly relations but not at the price of aggression, insult and calumny and continuous threat of war.' He also stated that, 'if Pakistan attacks any part of the Indian territory we shall repel this attack with all our strength.'

as its goal the plunging of the two countries into a tragic and disastrous war. I am sure, however, that under your leadership this danger will, in due course, be averted.

I hope this finds you very well.

With very kind regards and respects,

Yours sincerely,
Karan Singh

———— 25 ————

New Delhi
3 August 1951

My dear Tiger,

I have just received your letter of the 1st August. Thank you for it.

I am very glad to learn that you intend donating the Gulab Mahal Palace to the University of Jammu and Kashmir. That is the very best use you can put that building to and I am sure it will be greatly appreciated by the public. We have ourselves been handing over our old Government Houses to Universities and other public institutions. In Poona there was a very fine Government House with a park attached to it. This has now become the headquarters of the Poona University.

We are living in critical times and the situation vis-à-vis Pakistan difficult and delicate. I do not know how things will turn out in the end. But I doubt very much if there will be war. Yet we cannot be sure and we have to take all precautions.

Perhaps, you know that the King[1] of Nepal's daughter, the Princess Vijaya Lakshmi, is going to Kashmir for a two-month stay. She has not been keeping well, although lately she has progressed greatly. I believe arrangements are being made for her stay in a house at Tangmarg. She will probably go to Kashmir on the 17th August.

The King of Nepal is coming here[2] to see her before she goes and also to have some consultations with me. There is just an odd possibility that he might like to accompany his daughter to Kashmir and stay there for about two days and then return. I am merely warning you and I am not at all sure about it.

———

1. Tribhuvan Bir Bikram Shah (1906-1955); king of Nepal, 1911-50 and 1952-55.
2. King Tribhuvan was in India from 13 to 21 August 1951.

The King is coming here with a fairly large party—his two Queens, his three daughters and a number of others.

Yours sincerely,
Jawaharlal Nehru

———— 26 ————

Srinagar
17 August 1951

My dear Panditji,
Thank you very much for your letter of the 3rd August. His Majesty and party were to have arrived here today, but due to bad weather they have not been able to come. I do hope they are able to get through tomorrow. I wonder when we will have the pleasure of seeing you up here again. Our University Convocation has been fixed for the 1st of September. Rajaji[1] has very kindly consented to come up and deliver the address.[2] We are looking forward to his presence on the occasion and to the illuminating address which I am sure he will deliver.

I hope this finds you and Mrs Gandhi very well.
With very kind regards and respects,

Yours sincerely,
Karan Singh

---

1. C. Rajagopalachari (1878-1972); lawyer from Salem (Madras Presidency), joined the non-cooperation movement, 1920; member, Congress Working Committee, 1922-42, 1946-47 and 1951-54; chief minister, Madras, 1937-39 and 1952-54; left Congress in 1942 but rejoined in 1946; governor, West Bengal, 1947-48; governor general of India, 1948-50; Union home minister, 1950-51; founder of Swatantra Party.
2. In his address Rajagopalachari said: 'The future of our country lies in the Universities whatever might be the form of the democratic institutions that we set up.' He added: 'The success of democracy depends on the availability of sound leadership. The screening and training necessary for sound leadership has to be done in the universities.'

——— 27 ———

Srinagar
4 November 1951

My dear Panditji,
I have just finished my B.A. examinations. I intend soon to start studying for my M.A. in Political Science.

You must be in full touch with the proceedings of our Constituent Assembly.[1] There was no inauguration by me, but I sent a message of goodwill, a copy of which I am enclosing.

I wonder whether we shall see you up here again this season. I expect to go to Delhi soon after we move down to Jammu by the middle of the month and look forward to seeing you then.

It is still very pleasant here. Delhi just now must be very nice.

I hope this finds you in the best of health.

With very kind regards and respects,

Yours sincerely,
Karan Singh

——— 28 ———

Jammu Tawi
26 December 1951

My dear Panditji,
Thank you very much for your card of season's greetings, which I warmly reciprocate. You may be interested to hear that I have passed the B.A. examination for which I appeared in Srinagar, securing good marks. I may be in Delhi again soon, in which case I shall look forward to seeing you.

I hope this finds you very well, and not too tired by your strenuous election tours.[2]

With very kind regards and respects,

Yours sincerely,
Karan Singh

---

1. The Constituent Assembly of Jammu and Kashmir at this time considered four main issues: (i) the future of the ruling dynasty, (ii) payment of compensations for land transferred to cultivators in the Big Landed Estates Act, 1950, (iii) ratification of the state's accession to India and (iv) the framing of the constitution of the state.
2. In connection with the Congress campaign for the first general elections, Nehru toured various parts of the country from 15 November 1951 to 21 January 1952.

——— 29 ———

Camp: Hazaribagh
2 January 1952

My dear Tiger,
Thank you for your letter of 26th December which has followed me on tour.

I am very glad to know that you have passed your B.A. Examination. I have been told that you did very well in it.

If you come to Delhi I should of course like to meet you. But for another two or three weeks I shall be mostly on tour. I expect to be in Delhi from the 11th to the 14th. After that I shall go out again till the 20th. That will be the end of my election tour.

With all good wishes for the New Year,

Yours sincerely,
Jawaharlal Nehru

——— 30 ———

Bombay
16 February 1952

My dear Panditji,
Many congratulations upon your being returned to the House of the People with such a huge majority.[1]

We have just returned from a short trip to Jamnagar, which we enjoyed a lot. I do not know whether you have been there. It is a very nice open town, and the climate just now was very pleasant. Next week my wife and myself are going on a trip to see the Ajanta[2] and Ellora[3] caves. We have heard a great deal of their wonderful beauty,

---

1. In the first general elections to the Lok Sabha, which were held from 25 October 1951 to 10th February 1952, the Congress party won 362 seats out of 489. Nehru won the election from Allahabad by a margin of 173, 929 votes.
2. Site of world famous cave temples and monasteries in Maharashtra, containing sculptures and fresco-painting executed by the Buddhists between second century BC and seventh century AD which depict episodes from the life of the Buddha.
3. In Maharashtra, the Ellora is famous for rock-cut temples. These are divided into three separate groups. The right side contains Buddhist Chaitya halls and the extreme left is occupied by the Jain caves. The centre is occupied by Hindu temples. These temples were built between the seventh and eleventh centuries.

and expect to have a very pleasurable time seeing them.

I was very perturbed and distressed to hear and read of the recent disturbances in Jammu.[1] I was in touch both with Bakshi Ghulam Mohammad[2] and Shri Ayyangar,[3] and they both said that the situation was completely under control and did not necessitate cutting short my trip and returning.

I was sorry that I just missed seeing Sheikh Sahib here, as he left yesterday morning a few hours before I got back from Jamnagar. By now, of course, he must have seen you in Delhi.

Bombay is still quite pleasant, though it is warming up. I expect to return to Delhi within about a fortnight, and shall look forward to seeing you then.

Hoping this finds you very well,

With respectful regards,

Yours very sincerely,
Karan Singh

---

1.   At an official function on 15 January 1952 in the Gandhi Memorial College in Jammu, the National Conference flag was hoisted alongside the Indian flag. Some students protested against the flag of the National Conference for which they were penalized. On 8 February, a procession was taken out to demonstrate sympathy with the students. But the processionists became violent as a result of which the military was called in and a seventy-two hour curfew was imposed in Jammu. The students were released but several of the Praja Parishad leaders including its president, P.N. Dogra, were taken into custody.

2.   (1919-1971); member, Kashmir National Conference; member, Jammu and Kashmir Assembly, 1951-67; prime minister, Jammu and Kashmir, 1953-63; member, Lok Sabha, 1967-71.

3.   N. Gopalaswami Ayyangar (1882-1953); served in the Madras Provincial Services ; dewan (prime minister) of Kashmir 1937-43; member, Council of States, 1944-46; member, Constituent Assembly of India; Union minister without portfolio, 1947-48, minister for railways and transport, 1948-1952, minister of states, December 1950-May 1952 and defence, 1952-53; leader of the Indian delegation to the United Nations, 1948.

——— 31 ———

Srinagar
5 May 1952

My dear Panditji,
As you may have read in the papers, I addressed this morning the first meeting of the State Legislative Assembly.[1] I am enclosing a copy of my speech in Jammu and Kashmir Legislative Assembly, which you might be interested to glance through.

It was a great pleasure seeing you when I was in Delhi last, and dining with you. I do not know when I shall be in Delhi next, but I expect I may have to go down again within a month.

The weather up here is rather remarkable. It has rained fairly heavily during the last few days and has got quite cold. This morning the tops of the mountains I overlook from my house were covered with snow. Delhi must be really hot by now.

I hope this finds you very well. I expect you are very busy due to the approaching session of Parliament.

With deep regards and respects,

Yours very sincerely,
Karan Singh

P.S.
My very kind regards to Mrs Gandhi.

K.S.

———

1. In his address as the regent, Karan Singh said: 'The secular ideals, I am glad to observe, has taken firm roots in our land and Kashmir stands as a living symbol of communal harmony and concord.' He also referred at length to 'the transition period that followed the invasion of 1947 which had been full of trials and tribulations for the State and its people. The State witnessed loot, arson and savagery of raiders, who had been equipped and instigated by Pakistan, and also the gruesome happenings in certain parts of the State, which were the result of the activities of certain anti-national elements. However, with the magnificent help and sacrifices of the Indian Army, along with our own resources, law and order was completely restored here.'

———— 32 ————

New Delhi
26 July 1952

My dear Tiger,

I have been wanting to write to you for some days, but have been so terribly busy that I could not find the time. You have however been very much in my mind.

You must have read a report of the long speech I delivered in Parliament about Kashmir.[1] A very great part of it, of course, dealt with past events. Towards the end, I indicated the broad lines of the agreement reached between us and Sheikh Abdullah and his colleagues who had come here.[2]

Our discussions were prolonged and we sat for many hours day after day. It was an exhausting business. We had to keep in mind all the aspects of this complicated matter. There were the legal and constitutional aspects, and there were the other aspects which were at least, if not more, important. I think that the agreement we arrived at was a satisfactory one. Apart from its contents, it brought about good feeling and put an end to the tension that has existed for some time past. The best part of this agreement was this psychological atmosphere

---

1. Nehru delivered this speech in the Lok Sabha on 24 July 1952. It has been reproduced in the *Selected Works of Jawaharlal Nehru* (second series) Vol. 19, pp. 219-38.
2. The agreement regarding constitutional relationship between India and Kashmir was announced on 24 July 1952. Its salient features were: (i) the head of the state of Jammu and Kashmir would be a person recommended by the state legislature and recognized by the president of India; (ii) the Indian flag would have the same status in Kashmir as in any other part of India but the Kashmir state flag would be retained; (iii) citizenship would be common in two parts of the country but the state legislature would have power to define and regulate the rights and privileges of the permanent residents in Kashmir; (iv) the fundamental rights as laid down in the Indian constitution would be extended to Kashmir, but these would not come in the way of the State's programme of land reforms; (v) power to reprieve or commute death sentences would belong to the president of India; (vi) the Indian president's power to declare a state of emergency in case of external danger or internal disturbances would be extended to Kashmir, but in regard to internal disturbances it would be used only at the request of the state government; (vii) residuary powers would be retained by the state but the state could transfer more rights to the Union; (viii) the Supreme Court could adjudicate in regard to disputes between the state and the central and other provincial governments and on fundamental rights agreed to by the state; and (ix) the details of the financial arrangements would be further considered.

of friendship and cooperation.

Many things were decided by this agreement which knit the Jammu and Kashmir State closer to India and which make our Constitution applicable in a greater measure to the State. At the same time, we recognized the special position of the State and gave it greater autonomy in many matters than our other States of the Indian Union possess.

You will, of course, be chiefly interested in the decisions arrived at in regard to the Head of the State[1]. Perhaps, you may not like some part of them, but I had indicated to you, in the course of our talks when you were here, that it seemed inevitable to me that some such change must take place. Circumstances had so developed and they could not be denied without causing injury to all concerned and the cause we have at heart. I think that the decision and the form of words we have used are satisfactory and a fair compromise. Whatever law or Constitution might say, in the last analysis, we have to pay heed to the wishes of the people. That indeed had often been declared by us in regard to the Jammu and Kashmir State. But really the principle applies everywhere in India. When this question was raised positively, in the manner it had been raised, it became impossible to bypass it or to postpone it for long. It was better to face it and come to a decision than to leave a feeling of uncertainty and doubt in people's minds and thus not even have the great advantage of a settlement by agreement with all the psychological consequences of friendly feeling that this produced.

In effect now, this means that at the proper moment the Constituent Assembly of Jammu and Kashmir State will make a recommendation to the President by election of a person who is to be the Head of the State. Although this is called a recommendation, the President will naturally agree. There is no doubt that your name is going to be recommended.

The period is five years. It is quite likely that at the end of the period, you might be re-elected. That is at any rate the present intention of the Kashmir leaders and, of course, we would very much welcome it. But any attempt to force the pace or to try to have a longer period, would have defeated the real purpose in view.

---

1. According to the Delhi Agreement, the head of the state would be a person recognized by the president of the Union on the recommendation of the legislature of the state, holding office at the pleasure of the president for a term of five years.

As a matter of fact, in the world today, five years is a long time. Only this evening we have had the news of the sudden changes in Egypt[1] and the forcible abdication of King Farouk[2] of Egypt and his sudden departure for America. For any of us to think in static terms of continuing things as they are, is to misunderstand this changing and dynamic world. We have to understand this world and adapt ourselves to it.

I am sure you will appreciate what I am writing. I need not tell you that now and later, you will be in my mind and you can always come to me for advice or any help that I can give you. The best advice is to accept cheerfully and willingly the changes suggested and thereby to put yourself in the forefront of them, instead of appearing as if you unwillingly agreed to something that you disliked. If we have to do something, we should do it gracefully and thereby gain the goodwill and respect of others.

I hope, therefore, that you will make it clear to Sheikh Abdullah and others that you willingly accept the changes suggested by agreement with the Government of India and that you will abide by any decisions that the Constituent Assembly of the Jammu and Kashmir State takes. Thus you will strengthen not only your position but the affection that people have for you in the State.

I am feeling terribly tired after many months of continuous hard work. I want very much to go to Kashmir for a few days. It is difficult to be certain about my future programme, but I hope to be able to go to Srinagar on the 18th August or thereabouts. If I can manage it, I shall go on a short trek, probably in the Gurais Valley.

Dr Graham[3] has suggested a meeting at ministerial level at Geneva.[4] We wanted this meeting to be at Delhi, but this was not agreed to by the other people. So we have agreed to Geneva. I have suggested the

---

1. In Egypt on 23 July 1952, King Farouk was forced to abdicate by General Neguib in a military coup.
2. Fouad Farouk (1920-1965); last reigning king of Egypt from 1936 till his abdication in July 1952.
3. Frank P. Graham (1886-1972); president, University of North Carolina, 1930-49; appointed UN mediator for India and Pakistan in relation to the Kashmir dispute on 30 April 1951.
4. The ministerial level conference was held in Geneva from 26 August to 10 September 1952. Its object was to evolve a workable plan for demilitarization of Jammu and Kashmir and to prepare the ground for the appointment of a plebiscite administrator. India was represented by Gopalaswami Ayyangar and Pakistan by Zafrulla Khan.

date as August 25th. If this is agreed to, I am requesting Shri
Gopalaswami Ayyangar to go there on our behalf. I am reluctant to
give him this trouble, but he is obviously the best person to go and I
am glad to say that he has agreed to do so. Probably the Geneva
meeting will last about a week.

With all good wishes,

Yours sincerely,
Jawaharlal Nehru

———— 33 ————

Jammu Tawi
3 August 1952

My dear Panditji,

Thank you very much for your letter to me dated 26th July 1952.

Before I proceed, I would like to express my deep gratitude to
you for the kind and sympathetic interest you have been taking in my
affairs during the last three years or so since I became Regent.[1] I need
hardly express how greatly I value your guidance and advice.

As regards the question of whether I should or should not accept
a five-year elected term as Head of State, I have—since your speech
in Parliament was delivered about ten days ago[2]—been giving the
matter my most thorough consideration from all its various aspects.

My highest ambition is to be able to serve effectively the people
of my country, and any position which gives me that opportunity will
naturally be welcomed. However, in the present circumstances, I feel
that it is not possible for me to come to any decision until the new
Constitution for Kashmir emerges in its final shape from the
Constituent Assembly and receives the approval of the Government
of India. I am sure you will appreciate that it is hardly possible for me
to accept a position without knowing exactly and clearly the duties
and functions which attach to it, the responsibilities which I will have

---

1. Karan Singh was appointed regent by his father, Maharaja Hari Singh at the
    intervention of Jawaharlal Nehru on 20 June 1949.
2. On 24 July 1952, Nehru made a detailed statement in the Lok Sabha on the Delhi
    Agreement in regard to Jammu and Kashmir State. Among other things, he declared:
    'the accession is complete in law and, in fact, Jammu and Kashmir State is a constituent
    unit like any other.'

to shoulder and the conditions under which I will have to work.

If the Indian Constitution was going to be accepted in toto by Kashmir, the position would have been quite clear. But as you said in your speech the situation in Kashmir differs from that which obtains in other States of the Union, and the Kashmir Consembly may draft a Constitution along lines which differ from the Indian. As a matter of fact I do not think anyone, even Sheikh Sahib, is in a position to say definitely at this stage what exactly the new Constitution will be like.

As Head of State I will have important responsibilities to fulfil, and, as Sheikh Sahib is reported to have reiterated in some of his recent speeches, if I fail to fulfil them satisfactorily I will even be liable to impeachment.[1] I therefore, strongly feel that I should be very clear as to what my exact position and responsibilities are going to be, and also as to the nature of the Constitution over which I shall have to preside. If I accept anything without being absolutely clear I will be being unfair not only to myself but also to all those with whom I shall have to work and come into contact and, in the larger context, to the people of the State.

Regarding my tenure of office, as I indicated to you personally, I would much prefer, if I am to serve as Head of State, to do so for more than the very limited term of five years. I would be very much happier if no time limit is imposed. If, however, political considerations make it imperative for a fixed term to be incorporated in the Constitution (although personally I do not think such overriding considerations exist, particularly when weighed against the political advantages flowing from the opposite course of action), I am somewhat reassured by what you say in your letter with regard to my future re-election. I am still very young, and have to plan for many years ahead, not only for five. May I feel confident that in the event of my becoming Head of State, both the Government of India and the Jammu and Kashmir Government will see that I am able to continue for much longer than just a five year period? I need hardly add that this will be subject to the condition that I perform my duties to the satisfaction of the Government of India. All I can assure you is that if I do take up the position, I will sincerely and honestly work to the very best of my

---

1. In fact, the impeachment provision did not rest with the constitution of Kashmir, while Sheikh Abdullah wanted to include this.

ability to make it a complete success, as I have done in the three years I have acted as Regent.

I was rather surprised at press reports which I brought to your notice when I saw you in Delhi a few days ago—that the Consembly was making preparations to swear in new Head of State within a very few days. I think, to say the least, that it is rather unusual that an office is sought to be filled before it even exists constitutionally and before its duties and functions have been clearly defined. I would suggest that the matter be only taken up after the new Constitution for Kashmir has been finally prepared.

After the Constitution is finalized, and I have studied it, I will be in a position to consider acceptance. But I am sure you will appreciate my view that until that time it is not possible for me to come to any decision.

With very kind regards and respects,

Yours sincerely,
Karan Singh

——— 34 ———

Jammu Tawi
3 August 1952

My dear Panditji,

I am writing to you from Jammu, where I am spending a night on my way back to Srinagar. I had intended to stop in Delhi for a day or two on my return, but I received an urgent message from Sheikh Sahib saying that he wanted to have some consultations with me as soon as possible and am therefore returning direct to Srinagar.

I was very pleased to have been able to talk to you the other day in Delhi. I have been giving the matter my thorough consideration, and am enclosing a letter in reply to yours dated the 26 July.

I do hope we shall see you up in Kashmir on the 18th, and that you will be able to get away for a few days rest and relaxation from the tremendous pressure of work upon you in Delhi. We may also be fortunate enough to have you witness and perhaps address our Convocation[1], which is also on the 18th.

With very kind regards and respects,

Yours sincerely,
Karan Singh

---

1. Nehru did not attend the convocation of the Jammu and Kashmir University.

—————— 35 ——————

Srinagar
7 August 1952

My dear Panditji,

I am sending this letter to you by hand of my ADC, Captain Kohar Singh. He is returning here on Saturday morning, and will bring back with him any reply you may be pleased to send.

By now you must have received the letter I wrote to you from Jammu on the 3rd. I was delayed en route for a day due to heavy rain, and arrived here on Tuesday evening. Sheikh Sahib came to see me yesterday afternoon, and I had a long talk with him. In the course of our conversation I dwelt at some length on the two points which had formed the basis of my letter to you, namely, the question of tenure and re-election, and the fact that I could not come to any decision until the Constitution for Kashmir had been finalized. I particularly stressed the latter point which, to my mind, is the more important and significant of the two.

In reply to the question of re-election, he said that it was not possible for him to give any assurance, as he did not know what the circumstances would be after five years. To the second point he said that he could not wait until the new Constitution was finalized to elect the Head of State.[1] He did not give me any convincing reason as to why he was in such a desperate hurry, and merely said that the new Constitution might take a considerable time in the drafting and that he was not prepared to wait until then.

I tried to persuade him to understand that it was just not possible for me to say anything until the new Constitution was completed and I knew exactly what my duties and position would be, and that anyhow the question of choosing a Head of State would only arise after that. He was, however, very adamant that the matter would be taken up by the Consembly on Monday the 11th August, and asked that I should make up my mind and let him know my decision as soon as possible before that date.

I remember your saying when we met in Delhi recently that it

—————————————————————

1. On 14 November 1952, Karan Singh was elected the first head of the state and was called Sadar-i-Riyasat while the constitution of Kashmir was adopted on 17 November 1956, fixing 26 January 1957 as the date for its commencement.

would not be proper or possible for the Consembly to proceed in the matter until the Indian Constitution had been suitably amended, either directly or by a Presidential Order. In addition, I am sure you will appreciate the reasonableness of my point of view, and of the contention that the only proper time for the new Head of State to be chosen is after and not before the Constitution of which he is the creation and under which he has to function has been finalized.

Under the circumstances I would request you to use you great influence with Sheikh Sahib and his colleagues to persuade them to take a more reasonable view of the matter and to adopt what I feel, and what I am sure you will agree, is the only logical and constitutional line of action, viz., complete the framing of the new Constitution before taking up the question of the Head of the State. If he insists on going through with his present scheme, the only answer I can give him at this juncture is to repeat that I am not able to say anything until the new Constitution is prepared in its final form.

I am sure, Panditji, you know me well enough to see that it is no outmoded conception of absolute monarchy or autocracy or anything of the sort that prompts me to take up this attitude. It is purely that I am not prepared to accept a responsible position until I know clearly what it entails, especially under the peculiarly delicate and difficult situation that exists here.

I have put my point of view frankly and clearly before you, in the earnest hope that it will meet with your sympathetic consideration. It is now entirely up to you to decide whatever action—if any—you deem it necessary to take.

With respectful regards,

Yours very sincerely,
Karan Singh

——— 36 ———

New Delhi
8 August 1952

My dear Tiger,
I have received your two letters, one from Jammu dated 3rd August and the other from Srinagar dated 7th August.

2. In the course of the last two days, I have also heard from Sheikh

Abdullah and Deputy Minister, D. P. Dhar[1] has come here to explain certain proposals[2] which were being considered for the Constituent Assembly.

3. I have unfortunately not been keeping very well owing to a slight accident. The accident was not much, but an anti-tetanus injection that was given to me produced powerful results and all my body swelled up and caused a great amount of trouble. In spite of this, I had to carry on in Parliament because of urgent work. Part of this work indeed was due to resolutions in regard to Jammu and Kashmir State, which were moved by me in the Council of States[3] and the House of the People.[4] There were long debates and I spoke at some length. You will no doubt have seen the reports of these debates. As a result, the resolutions embodying the points of agreement[5] arrived at here, when Sheikh Abdullah and his colleagues were here, were accepted by Parliament.[6] In fact, our general policy in regard to Kashmir was approved of. Our Government is, therefore, clearly committed to that policy.

4. In spite of my indifferent health and the heavy pressure of work on me, we have given a good deal of thought to the reports we have received from Srinagar and to your letters. I have written to Sheikh Abdullah myself at some length twice since day before yesterday. I have naturally consulted Maulana Azad,[7] Mr Gopalswami Ayyangar

1. Durga Prasad Dhar (1918-1975); deputy home minister, Kashmir government, 1948-57; minister in the Kashmir government, 1961-68; ambassador to USSR, 1969-71; chairman, Policy Planning Committee, minister of external affairs, August 1971-July 1972; Union minister for planning and deputy chairman, Planning Commission, 1972-74; member, Rajya Sabha, 1972-75.
2. These were related to the position of the head of the state and the provision for his impeachment.
3. On 5 August 1952.
4. On 7 August 1952.
5. See *ante*, p. 34.
6. On 7 August 1952.
7. Maulana Abul Kalam Azad (1888-1958); scholar and eminent leader of the Congress; founder-editor, *Al-Hilal* and *Al Balagh* (Urdu weeklies); imprisoned several times during the freedom movement; president, All India Khilafat Committee, 1920, Unity Conference, 1924, and Nationalist Muslims Conference, 1928; president, Indian National Congress, 1923 and 1940-46; Union minister of education, 1947-58; publications include *Tarjuman al-Quran, Tazkira, Gubar-i-Khatir* and *India Wins Freedom*.

and Dr Katju.[1] This afternoon all of us had a talk with D. P. Dhar and explained to him what our views were as to the steps that should be taken in furtherance of agreement arrived at. He is returning early tomorrow morning to Srinagar and will no doubt communicate our advice to Sheikh Abdullah.

5. Some drafts were shown to us by D. P. Dhar. We did not like these drafts or much that they contained and we have made suggestions for considerable changes in them.

6. I can very well understand your anxieties and difficulties in this matter. To a large extent, I share them with you, and I have not liked much that has happened. But, in dealing with public matters, one has to take a dispassionate view and not allow oneself to be governed merely by likes and dislikes.

7. I quite agree with you that this business of hustling through a part of the Constitution is neither normal nor ordinarily desirable. The proper course would have been to pass the full Constitution and then give effect to it. But this matter was discussed by us at very great length when the Kashmir delegation was here and ultimately we came to the conclusions which were embodied in the points of agreement.[2] It serves little purpose to go back on them and renew the old argument. Much has been done which cannot be undone at the present stage and any attempt to do so would only produce further complications. Therefore, we have to accept the present position as it is. That is to say that a part of the Constitution dealing with the Head of the State, in the form agreed upon, should be adopted first.

8. You will have noticed that several other important matters were agreed to between us. This whole picture has to be seen together. Some of these other points bring the Jammu and Kashmir State closer

---

1. K.N. Katju (1887-1968); lawyer and Congressman from Allahabad; minister in the UP government, 1937-39 and 1946-47; member, Constituent Assembly, 1946-47; governor of Orissa, 1947-48 and of West Bengal, 1948-51; Union minister for law, 1951-52, for home affairs, 1952-55 and for defence, 1955-57; chief minister, Madhya Pradesh, 1957-62.

2. Regarding head of the state, the following points were agreed upon: (i) the head of the state shall be the person recognized by the president on the recommendation of the legislature of the state; (ii) he shall hold office during the pleasure of the president; (iii) he may, by writing under his hand addressed to the president, resign his office; (iv) subject to the foregoing provisions of this Article, the head of the state shall hold office for a term of five years from the date he enters upon his office, provided that he shall, notwithstanding the expiration of his term, continue to hold office until his successor enters upon his office.

to India and to our Constitution. If all this is given effect to then the other remaining provisions need not make much difference. In a sense, we get a broad framework of the Constitution in its relation to India. The details can be filled in later. In filling in these details also, of course care should be taken.

9. Our Parliament has accepted this broad framework. It is desirable and necessary that the Constituent Assembly of the Jammu and Kashmir State should do this also, that is to say, it should adopt a similar procedure and, by resolution, accept the points of agreement, as we have done here.

10. This is our first and basic suggestion to Sheikh Abdullah. Having done this, the Constituent Assembly can proceed to consider the other important matter, namely, that relating to the Head of the State. We have suggested that the identical language used by us and agreed upon should be used. Some minor ancillary provisions might be added. To this might be added that the Government of Jammu and Kashmir State be authorized to forward the decision of the Constituent Assembly to the President of India and should further be authorized to take such other steps as may be necessary to implement that decision.

11. I am not giving the exact language of the resolution and I am writing from memory. Shri Gopalswami Ayyangar is giving a note on this subject to D. P. Dhar.

12. This procedure thus gives time for the consideration of what other steps should be taken and how all this should be done. It gives time for the President of India also to issue such notifications as may be necessary.

13. In the draft proposal sent to us, there was a good deal of detail. There was reference also to possible impeachment for grave misconduct etc. We thought all this is wholly unnecessary. Of course, a full Constitution deals with such matters just as our Constitution lays down a certain procedure for the impeachment of the President. The question does not arise, so far as we are concerned, in regard to Kashmir, because the Head of the Jammu and Kashmir State will be formally recognized by our President and will hold office during the pleasure of the President.

14. Thus what we have suggested is a simple form to be passed now with authority given to work it out later for purposes of implementation. This does not mean that there will be great delay or that we shall wait for the full Constitution to take shape. It does mean

that we shall have some leisure to think out various consequences and decide on the procedure to be adopted.

15. In your letter you lay stress on two points. One is that the whole Constitution should be framed before the question of the Head of the State is taken up and secondly, the question of tenure and re-election. As for the first point, I have already said that we discussed this matter at length and decided ultimately not to press it. Events had gone too far to be reversed. As for the tenure and re-election, re-election there can always be and I am told that this is the present intention. But in the nature of things it is hardly possible for any person to guarantee it. I told you when you were here that the next five years would very probably see the end of the present system of Rajpramukhships for life. Indeed, I think that a change is likely to occur long before those five years are over. Already people are beginning to talk about it and press for it.[1] It is true that the developments in Kashmir have made people think of this more than they might have done at present.

16. Personally, I do not think it at all wise to ask for a longer tenure than five years to begin with. Even if this was agreed to, it would have little meaning in this changing world and pressing for it rather takes the grace out of it. Normally speaking, if you accept this for five years, conditions are such that you will continue. But no present guarantee will make that more assured and your asking for it does not appear to me to be right.

17. I can well understand your doubts and hesitations. The real answer to them is that nobody can compel you to stay on if, at any time, you feel like quitting. That decision no one can take away from you. To quit now, unless there are present any adequate reasons, is merely to do so for fear of a future contingency which may or may not arise.

18. I have thought about this matter not only from your personal point of view but also from the larger point of view of the State. Grave decisions are being taken which will naturally affect the future of the State. I think that from this larger point of view, it is highly desirable that you should undertake this responsibility. For you not to do so now would create grave difficulties for the State. As I have said above, even after taking this responsibility, you are not bound down

---

1. In July 1952 a conference of the representatives of Part B States, held in Kashmir, urged abolition of the system of Rajpramukhs.

to it whatever happens. You retain your freedom of action to a large extent.

19. I would, therefore, advice you that if Sheikh Abdullah and his colleagues accept our advice in this matter and follow the procedure we have recommended to them, then you should accept the offer made to you. Before you finally make up your mind, you might observe how these developments take place in the course of the next few days. After that, according to our suggestion, the details and the procedure will have to be worked out and naturally this should be done with propriety to all concerned.

20. The alternative to your not accepting this will not only be bad for the State but will be of no advantage to you at this stage. You mentioned to me your desire for education abroad. A year or more abroad may do you good no doubt. But we learn more about life and its problems by facing them than by mere changes in geographical environment. You are likely to have a fair amount of time at your disposal for study. You are attracted to it and you can thus prepare yourself in many ways better in the State than if you went abroad. Most foreign countries today are full of the noise of war and its preparations and are not very pleasant places to go to except for brief visits.

21. I feel, therefore, that it would be the right thing for you to accept the offer in the manner I have suggested and thereby put yourself right with your people and do them much service in many ways which may not be so obvious and yet which are important. And then, after all, you retain your freedom of choice at any later moment, should occasion so demand.

22. Owing to my injury and subsequent happenings, I fear I must give up the idea of the trek in Kashmir. But I still hope to go there for a few days. I am sorry I shall not be able to go for the Convocation. I might come on the 21st of August.[1]

Yours sincerely,
Jawaharlal Nehru

---

1. Nehru visited Kashmir from 21 to 30 August 1952.

——— 37 ———

Srinagar
10 August 1952

My dear Panditji,
Thank you very much for your letter dated the 8th August, which my
ADC[1] brought back with him.

I have gone through the letter carefully, and am giving the matter
my closest thought and consideration. I am very pleased that you
understand my difficulties and anxieties, and realize the very difficult
position in which I am placed.

Sheikh Abdullah and his colleagues are doubtless considering the
suggestions you sent them through D. P. Dhar. I have not heard from
Sheikh Abdullah since he saw me last. After he has decided what line
of action he intends to take in the light of your suggestions he will
probably contact me again. I will ask to see the concerned draft
resolutions, so that I can study them before coming to any final
conclusion.

I was very sorry to hear of your accident and subsequent
indisposition. I hope you are quite recovered now. We are all very
sorry that you will not be here for our Convocation. I do hope,
however, that you will be able to come a little later.

With very kind regards and respects,

Yours sincerely,
Karan Singh

——— 38 ———

Srinagar
14 August 1952

My dear Panditji,
Since I wrote to you last I have been considering the question carefully,
and have had another talk with Sheikh Abdullah.

There are some important aspects of the situation which I would
very much like to talk over with you personally. Our Convocation is
on Monday (18 August), and I shall come down to Delhi immediately

---

1. Captain Kohar Singh.

after that, on Tuesday (19 August).

I hope this finds you now very well. It has rained here and is now delightfully pleasant.

With respectful regards,

Yours very sincerely,
Karan Singh

——— 39 ———

Srinagar
1 September 1952

My dear Tiger,

I was surprised to see in today's paper that some of the persons you had invited from Jammu had refused to meet you.[1] I was also surprised to see that Dhanwantri, the Communist leader had also been invited.[2] However, that does not matter much.

But the refusal to come by Girdharilal Anand, the President of the Chamber of Commerce of Jammu, as reported in the press cutting attached, is not only a discourtesy to you but an insult to both you and even the Government of India. Mr Girdharilal Anand, by his refusal, has put himself outside the pale. In future there can be no dealings with him and he must be made clearly to understand this. Certainly, I will not meet him or any of his crowd in future, even if I go to Jammu. I do not think you should meet him either in Srinagar or Jammu in future. He should be made to understand that his behaviour, quite apart from politics, is highly objectionable and there can be no dealings with him or even with the Jammu Chamber of Commerce in future so long as he is connected with it. It is really extraordinary that any person should have the temerity to behave in this manner to the acknowledged Head of the State. This shows the mentality of some of these people in Jammu who are shouting such a lot. If they think that they are going to gain their objective by insulting both the Kashmir

---

1. See the succeeding item.
2. Dhanwantari had been deputed by the Communist Party of India to Kashmir to settle the differences among the ministers in the Kashmir cabinet who had leftist leanings. However, he formed a liaison with the Praja Parishad leaders and his stand was contradictory to his party's appreciation of the Kashmir policy of the Union government.

Government and the Government of India, they are very much mistaken.

Yours sincerely,
Jawaharlal Nehru

———— 40 ————

Srinagar
4 September 1952

My dear Panditji,

Thank you for your letter. I must say that the manner in which Mr Anand[1] has acted has been highly objectionable, and there is now no question at all of my meeting him, either here or anywhere. He has displayed remarkable stupidity and ill grace which, as you say, has put him outside the pale. I had invited him and even the Communist leader Dhanwantari because I wanted to gain the view of all sections of opinion so that none could say that they were ignored. By not coming they have put themselves and their groups entirely in the wrong.

Pandit Prem Nath Dogra[2] and some of his colleagues have been here for the last few days, and we have had several long meetings which have throughout been frank and cordial. The meetings are continuing, and I shall write to you at their conclusion within a few days.

It was a great pleasure having you up here, and I was very happy to have been able to talk to you at some length. I also enjoyed immensely the flight to Eastern Ladakh over that magnificent mountain scenery. I hope your stay here gave you the rest you so badly required, and that you returned to Delhi refreshed.

It continues to be lovely here. Summer is over, and Autumn is imperceptibly asserting its sway.

I hope this finds you very well.

With very warm regards and respects,

Yours sincerely,
Karan Singh

---

1. Girdharilal Anand, president Chamber of Commerce Jammu, had refused Yuvaraj Karan Singh's invitation to meet him in Srinagar to discuss the question of the elected head of the state because he considered that, 'The present Kashmir Government as well as the Constituent Assembly have by their action shown scant regard for the opinion of Jammu people.'
2. (1882-1972); a leading RSS worker in Jammu and president of the Praja Parishad.

——————— 41 ———————

Srinagar
8 September 1952

My dear Panditji,

As you know, I have been having a series of meetings with political leaders from Jammu, mainly belonging to the Praja Parishad Party.[1] These meetings ended yesterday.

The talks were fairly comprehensive, as the invitees took the opportunity of discussing with me a range of current problems in addition to the specific question of the Headship of the State. On the whole they did not take an entirely one-sided view, and I think my talks with them will prove to be useful.

The Jammu people do, however, feel distressed and injured for several reasons. They say that they have neither any voice in the State Assembly (which they hold they boycotted under protest, and which contains representatives of only one party), nor in the State Government and nor again in the Indian Parliament, because the members from our State were nominated and not elected.[2] They, therefore, feel extremely frustrated, as they hold that there is no one who can effectively voice their grievances and demands, and see that justice is done to them. They have several important demands—into which I need not enter here—which they strongly feel deserve sympathetic consideration. The proposed ending of the ruling dynasty has upset them immensely, not because of sentimental attachment alone but because they feel that this step will break the only link which bound them to Kashmir, and that unless it is followed by complete accession to India their position will be even more precarious than it has been for the last five years.

Their basic demand, as you know, is full accession of the whole State to India. Although I myself would very much like a closer

1. The Praja Parishad Party of the Jammu Hindus was formed in November 1947. The Party gained much strength under the leadership of Prem Nath Dogra in the 1950s. Its main object was 'to achieve full integration of Jammu and Kashmir State with the rest of India like other acceding states and safeguard the legitimate democratic rights of the people of Jammu from the Communist dominated anti-Dogra Government of Sheikh Abdullah'.
2. Members of the Lok Sabha representing Jammu and Kashmir were nominated upto 1957. From 1967, election of the members started.

association of this State with India, it seems clear that the Government of India is committed—at least for the time being—to limited accession, and the alternative of Jammu breaking away from Kashmir will also, at this stage, be disastrous to India, Kashmir and to Jammu itself.

Nevertheless, I feel that everything possible should be done to redress the legitimate grievances of the Jammu people, because this internal discord and disharmony is to my mind most unfortunate. It is rather tragic irony, I think, that those who want complete accession to India should be proving a source of embarrassment to India and should feel unhappy and oppressed. As I have mentioned to you personally several times, I feel that the Jammu situation has not been handled as well as it might have been. My sincere desire is that this unfortunate state of affairs should be ameliorated, and, if the State is to remain as a single unit, the maximum amount of cooperation and goodwill should be sought from all sections.

When you were here you mentioned that you would not be averse to meeting these Jammu leaders of the Praja Parishad. Maulana Sahib[1] specifically asked me to tell them that the Government of India would always be pleased to meet them and talk to them. Pandit Prem Nath and his colleagues have expressed a great desire to meet you and other concerned Ministers of India with a view of placing before you their difficulties and demands. I would strongly urge that they be given a sympathetic hearing, as I feel that much good can come of such a meeting. Of course, you are very busy, and might only be able to see them for a short while. But I feel that Maulana Sahib, Shri Ayyangar, Dr Katju and perhaps Dr Radhakrishnan could talk to them at some length. Now, I think it would be very desirable if one or two members of the Kashmir Government were also present, so that controversial matters could be thrashed out on the spot, and the clouds of misunderstanding and animosity could perhaps be lifted to some extent. I do not know, however, what Sheikh Sahib's reaction to this idea will be, as I have not mentioned it to him. I thought that if you approved of the idea of a member or two of the Kashmir Government perhaps someone like D. P. Dhar—being also present, you might drop a line or talk to Sheikh Sahib about it. I do not think he will be averse to the idea, as I am sure he is as keen as we are that the internal difficulties of the State be resolved.

---

1. Maulana Abul Kalam Azad.

I am enclosing a copy of a statement which Pandit Prem Nath Dogra issued yesterday at the conclusion of the talks, in which he sets out his Party's attitude.[1] I have decided to issue no statement yet.

I have been waiting to hear from Dr Katju as what he has settled with His Highness.[2] In the meanwhile I saw in the papers that His Highness has sent a long memorandum[3] to the President,[4] which is now receiving the consideration of your Government. I have not received a copy, so I do not know the contents. The papers, however, say that he has asked for a referendum in the State upon the issue of the retention or otherwise of the dynasty.

I wonder what your view about this is. If it is possible to have a referendum and I do not see why it should not be—I feel it would be a good thing, as it would give the people of the State a fully democratic method of expressing their decision as to whether they would like a member of the dynasty to be their Constitutional Head or would prefer to elect someone periodically. Thus no section or group will feel that its views have been ignored in coming to a decision on this important question. I must add that from indications both in Jammu and the Valley I feel that the result of such a referendum is by no means a foregone conclusion.

I hope this finds you very well.

With warm regards and respects,

Yours very sincerely,
Karan Singh

---

1. While reiterating the demand for complete accession, Prem Nath Dogra declared that, 'so long as the question of the Maharaja's abdication or withdrawal of his recognition as "Rajpramukh" is not finally decided by the Government of India, and till the new Constitution for the State assumes a concrete shape, it would be premature to give any definite opinion on this single issue of accepting or rejecting the office of the Head of the State by Shree Yuvaraj Bahadur.'
2. Maharaja Hari Singh.
3. See Appendix.
4. Rajendra Prasad.

——— 42 ———

New Delhi
9 September 1952

My dear Tiger,

I have just received your letter of the 8 September.

I have no doubt that the Jammu people have a number of grievances and feel rather frustrated. Some of these grievances have, I believe, justification. Indeed, both Sheikh Saheb and Bakshi Ghulam Mohammad mentioned to me some of the disabilities that Jammu Province was suffering from and their desire to remove them. At the same time they pointed out to me certain difficulties. Thus, for instance, the lack of water in Jammu is a very serious handicap.

The Praja Parishad people have largely to blame themselves for the plight they have landed themselves in. Others may also be to blame. But, consciously or unconsciously, the Praja Parishad in Jammu has acted in a manner which has been quite deplorable and excessively stupid. It is not that they have not had a chance of meeting other people and discussing affairs with them. They have met them. As you know, I met Pandit Prem Nath Dogra and had a fairly long talk with him. In the course of our talk he agreed almost entirely with what I told him. Soon after he made public statements exactly contrary to what he had said to me and embarrassed me greatly. I found him and his companions completely irresponsible.

The kind of agitation they have been carrying on in the past in Delhi[1] itself, apart from what they have done in Jammu, has been pernicious in the extreme. They have sided with the most communal elements[2] in Delhi and attacked the Government of India in every way. If a person is to be known from his associations, then the Praja Parishad's associations were the most undesirable in Delhi or the

---

1. In the third week of June 1952, the Praja Parishad leaders submitted a memorandum to President Rajendra Prasad, in which they demanded full application of the Indian constitution to Jammu, extension of the jurisdiction of the Supreme Court, acceptance for Jammu of the fundamental rights of the Indian constitution and of the national flag of India. On 26 June, a big demonstration was staged outside the parliament to reinforce the Parishad demands.
2. S.P. Mookerjee, V.G. Deshpande, U.M. Trivedi and Ram Narayan Singh, members of parliament who had visited Jammu and Kashmir, said in a statement on 12 August 1952 that the people of Jammu were not prepared to be tagged on to the Kashmir valley unless the principle of full integration with India was accepted.

Punjab. Their activities did more harm to the Kashmir issue, from our point of view than anything else that has happened in recent years. As a result, they received the greatest publicity in Pakistan.[1]

There is a certain looseness in the use of language in regard to accession. Kashmir has fully acceded to India. It is true that, because of international complications, there was a loophole and a vague possibility of a change, but that did not affect the fullness of the accession. There is a difference between full accession and full integration. It is that integration that has not been full, although accession has been complete.

As the position is, any attempt to give effect to their demand would not only fail in itself, but might put an end to even the present accession. I explained that to you.

The Parishad people have been a disruptive influence[2] at a time when it was most important to lay stress on unity. Their influence has been disruptive not only in the Jammu and Kashmir State, but indirectly in the whole of India. The forces in India which we consider most harmful have been encouraged by the attitude of the Praja Parishad of Jammu.

I do not like being exploited and treated with discourtesy by any one in my official capacity. The Praja Parishad people have done that and, normally, they would have scant courtesy from me. But I have no objection to meeting them should you so desire. I am sure Maulana Saheb would also be prepared to meet them. So also Dr Katju and Shri Gopalaswami Ayyangar. But, it would be improper for all of us to meet them together and to hold a kind of a conference. They will have to meet people individually and separately. I do not think that Dr Radhakrishnan should be dragged into this particular picture. As a matter of fact, he is soon going away to Europe. D. P. Dhar might be present when one of us meets the Praja Parishad people. I shall mention this matter to Sheikh Saheb. He is coming here tomorrow to accompany me to our Congress meeting in Indore.

I do not like the statement issued by Prem Nath Dogra after the

---

1. The press in Pakistan portrayed the Praja Parishad leaders as being regarded 'the Heroes of Jammu' by the Hindus.
2. Some leaders of the Praja Parishad were opposed to the idea of accepting the office of elected headship of the state by Karan Singh. They opined that he should not accept Sheikh Abdullah's offer in its vague form.

conclusion of his talks with you.[1] It might, of course, have been worse. But it might have been better also. In any event, you should not issue any statement about these talks. If you see Sheikh Saheb, of course, you should tell him briefly what the nature of the talks was.

I have seen the long memorandum which your father has sent to the President. There is no reference in it to a referendum. The memorandum is rather an angry and tendentious document. Your father does not seem to realize at all that the world has changed and is changing rather rapidly. It was Dr Katju's intention to send the States Secretary, Venkatachar,[2] to Poona to see your father, but just as he was on the point of going, a telegram came that your father was not feeling quite well. So, Venkatachar's visit has been postponed for two or three days.

I am rather surprised at your reference to the referendum. This is not at all possible either from the local or from the international point of view. We have been talking about the plebiscite over other issues and even this cannot come off because there is no agreement. If the question of a referendum on a limited issue was raised, this would immediately lead to all kinds of international complications and the demand for a plebiscite immediately over the wider area. Even this referendum, it would be said, if held at all, should be over that wider area, including that part which is held by Pakistan. Within the present boundaries of the State under our control the referendum issue would, naturally lead to bitterness and controversy and in effect tend to split up the State, regardless of the final issue. Indeed, I think that such a proposal is completely out of court in present circumstance. Pakistan would, no doubt, profit by it, but no one else.

I am going day after tomorrow to Indore and I shall be away for five or six days. Dr Katju is going with me. Gopalaswami Ayyangar intends returning here on the 13th or 14th of this month.

All good wishes and affection,

Yours,
Jawaharlal Nehru

---

1. See preceding item.
2. C. S. Venkatachar (b. 1898); joined the ICS 1922; served in various capacities in the United Provinces and Central Indian States 1923-37; agent to governor-general of India in British Malaysia, 1937-41, commissioner of Allahabad division, 1941-46; prime minister, Jodhpur, 1946-47; secretary, states ministry, 1951-55; secretary to the president of India, 1955-58; high commissioner to Canada, 1958-61.

——— 43 ———

Srinagar
13 September 1952

My dear Panditji,

Thank you very much for your letter dated the 9th September.

I quite realize the manner in which the Parishad activities have been proving a source of embarrassment in the context of the Indo-Pakistan situation in Kashmir. I also realize—as I said in my last letter—that any attempt substantially to alter at this stage the quantum of integration might have highly harmful results.

Nevertheless, a lessening of our internal difficulties will make the task both of the Government of India and of the State Government easier, and will also bring a measure of relief to the unfortunate inhabitants of the State who have suffered so much over the last few years. It was with this in view that I suggested your granting an interview to the Parishad leaders, and I greatly appreciate your willingness to do so. I am also glad that you appreciate my suggestion regarding D. P. Dhar. I sincerely hope that this will result in the long run in real benefit to the people of the State, and in smoothening the way for our progress towards stability and prosperity. That is my fundamental interest in this whole affair.

I was interested to read what you say about His Highness's representation to the President[1]. I am surprised that [the] numerous newspaper reports about the proposed referendum were completely without foundation. Of course, under the present circumstances a referendum of this sort would be rather difficult to have, although as a method of directly and clearly ascertaining public opinion on an important issue it has much to commend itself. My remarks were merely to convey to you my personal feeling that despite all that is said, the result of such a referendum, if held, can hardly be predicted in advance.

I have decided to go on my visit to Ladakh next week. My trip was, as you know, postponed in July due to a spell of continued bad flying weather. The weather now is very favourable, and if I wait too long it will get unpleasantly cold there. I shall spend a few days at

———

1. See Appendix.

Leh, visit the Hemis Gumpa,[1] and on my return pay a short visit to Kargil.

The Yuvrani is accompanying me on this trip.

Mr Venkatachar must have met His Highness by now.[2] Dr Katju will doubtless communicate with me whenever anything conclusive has been settled with him.

With deep regards and respects,

Yours very sincerely,
Karan Singh

——— 44 ———

New Delhi
23 September 1952

My dear Tiger,

Thank you for your letter of the 13th September. I am glad you went to Ladakh and took your wife with you.[3]

You write to me about Jammu Parishad leaders. I read two days ago another statement by them.[4] They have a peculiar knack of saying the wrong thing and saying even that in the wrong way. They are all the time issuing an ultimatum. If a great power like the USA or the UK addressed my Government in this way, our reply would be expressed in the strongest language. But the Praja Parishad leaders evidently have got such an idea of their high importance that they presume to speak as if they could dictate terms. I am not used to this manner of speaking or being addressed. All that they will do is to injure themselves in this process.

As I have told you, I am prepared to see them in the normal course if they apply for an interview and when I have time. But I confess that the more I learn about them, the less I like them. It is quite possible

1. Main Buddhist temple in Ladakh.
2. C.S. Venkatachar, secretary of the state ministry, met Maharaja Hari Singh in Bombay during the first week of October and discussed the matters which the Maharaja had raised in his memorandum.
3. Karan Singh visited Ladakh from 19 to 22 September and presented to the head lama of Ladakh a 400 year old image of Lord Buddha.
4. On 20 September 1952, the Praja Parishad leaders threatened to launch civil disobedience if their demands were not fulfilled.

that when they come to see me they will hear something from me, which they will not like. They have done enough mischief already and I wish to make this clear to them.

D. P. Dhar has not returned yet, as he fell ill in Paris. I am going to Hyderabad tomorrow morning for about a week.

Yours sincerely,
Jawaharlal Nehru

——— 45 ———

Srinagar
24 September 1952

My dear Panditji,

I have just returned from a most interesting four-day visit to Ladakh.[1] We stayed at Leh for four days. In the course of which we visited many lovely Gumpas,[2] including the one at Hemis. Some of those Gumpas are truly marvellous, specially the one at Shay with huge forty-foot metal image of Lord Buddha. We also saw ritualistic lama dances in their colourful masks and costumes, and many local dances. The people of Ladakh are really most charming. Despite their poverty they are always smiling and cheerful, and are very affectionate and friendly. I thoroughly enjoyed myself there. While I was there, gifts which I had taken up for the people, including about twenty five thousand yards of cloth, needles, thread, etc. were announced.

On our flight back we broke journey for a few hours to visit Kargil. The warmth and enthusiasm with which the people greeted me at both places was really most gratifying. They seemed genuinely delighted to see me, and for my part I was very happy to see them and their picturesque country.

During this visit I took the opportunity of seeing things for myself, and of acquainting myself with the true conditions, both by personal observation and by talks with Kushak Bakula[3] and others. As you

1. This was the first time that the head of the state visited this area.
2. Buddhist temples.
3. Kushak Bakula (1917-2003); head lama of Ladakh; president, National Conference, Leh, 1949-53; member, Jammu and Kashmir Legislative Assembly, 1951-67; minister of state for Ladakh affairs and trade agencies, Jammu and Kashmir government, 1957-62, for health, local self-government, Ladakh affairs and trade agencies, 1964-67; member, Lok Sabha, 1967-76.

know, the question of Ladakh has been troubling us for the last few years, and no satisfactory solution has yet been arrived at.[1] The result is that the Ladakhis feel very distressed, insecure and unhappy, and this atmosphere makes the situation liable easily to be exploited by mischievous elements. I feel it is my duty to acquaint you with my views on the matter after my recent visit. I hope you will give full and careful consideration to my analysis of the situation and suggestions which I have set out in the attached secret note.[2] I strongly feel that something should be done very soon to remove the difficulties and disabilities of those simple people, whose guiltlessness and sincerity are matched only by their poverty and backwardness.

It is very pleasant in Srinagar, and must now have got fairly pleasant in Delhi also. I hope this finds you in very good health.

With very warm regards and respects,

Yours sincerely,
Karan Singh

46

Situation in Ladakh[3]

As you know, the people of Ladakh form a distinct cultural unit in our State. Their social set up, customs, language and local conditions are entirely different from those existent in other parts of the State. Ladakh was a conquered territory,[4] and now with the ending of the dynasty they strongly feel that they have the right of self-determination.

From talks with the Head Lama, Kushak Bakula, and others at Leh I have gathered that they are feeling most uneasy over their present

---

1. Resource crunches and stepmotherly treatment in the matter of development in Ladakh by the Jammu and Kashmir government made people discontented and frustrated. Expressions of these were be seen in agitations, demonstrations and violence. The Ladakhis started drifting away from the state and the ideas of the centre taking over the region began to appear. They began to assert that the Ladakhis were free to choose their own course.
2. See the succeeding item.
3. Note for Jawaharlal Nehru, Srinagar, 24 September 1952.
4. Ladakh was annexed to Kashmir in 1846.

position, which they feel is very unsatisfactory. Their demands can be grouped into three categories: Firstly, they feel that with only one member in the State Assembly (which is all they are entitled to on the basis of population) they have absolutely no effective voice in legislation, including legislation which vitally affects the interests and internal conditions of Ladakh. Being a distinct unit with their own peculiar conditions and problems they feel that they should have an effective voice in managing the internal affairs of their district, as the Legislative Assembly cannot be expected to be acquainted with local conditions and needs.

They, therefore, want a statutory Advisory Committee[1] to be established in Ladakh (excluding Kargil which, it seems, is content to remain in the present position). This Committee would be elected on the basis of full adult franchise, and would consist of five or seven members. It would be obligatory for the State Assembly to refer all legislation which vitally affects Ladakh to this Committee for its views and approval. In this manner they feel they will gain an effective role in managing their internal affairs, as the Committee would also be able to exercise general supervision and give advice as regards internal administration, and also to voice the necessities of the Ladakhi people.

Secondly, they feel that the Zanskar district, which is at present with Kargil tehsil, should be joined with Leh. This district is predominantly (over 95% I believe) Buddhist, and is also economically linked with and geographically contiguous to Leh tehsil. The inhabitants of that district have been suffering considerably during the last few years, and it is reported that they are almost on the point of migrating en masse if they are not joined with Leh. They are predominantly in favour of joining Leh, and this can, if necessary be verified by sending a committee consisting of Kushak Bakula, the Kargil representative, Ibrahim Shah, and a third impartial person to investigate and ascertain the wishes of those people. The joining of that area with Leh will make the cultural group more homogeneous, and prove to be greatly helpful to the people of Zanskar.

Thirdly, as regards the administration of Ladakh, they wish that

---

1. The central committee of the Ladakh National Conference at an extraordinary meeting in August 1952 adopted a resolution demanding an elected advisory committee for the region.

an Administrator for them be sent from India, if necessary on loan to the State Government. If I remember rightly, this matter was discussed between Shri Gopalaswami, Sheikh Abdullah and Kushak Bakula in Jammu, and all parties agreed that a person would be sent from India.

In addition, the system of local administration would have to be adapted to suit the peculiar local conditions. In this connection an impartial person from India could be sent to look into local conditions and report to the State Government and the Government of India as to what form of local set up would best suit the circumstances. In the meantime, they would also prepare draft schemes for submission to the Government.

These are the main points which they put before me, and my personal feeling is that they are not unreasonable, and that if conceded they will greatly better the morale and condition of those people.

Kushak Bakula, who I observed is held in tremendous regard by all people there, repeatedly requested me to convey to you that there is no question at all of their having communist sympathies and wanting to join Tibet, as some have alleged. He said that the people of Leh were genuinely and fervently desirous of having the closest possible union with India, and had the highest love and regard for your person. As a matter of fact they were pressing that India should directly take over the administration of Ladakh, but I explained to them that in views of the present conditions, national and international, that would not at this stage be possible. Incidentally, while I was in Leh, Kushak Bakula urged me to accept the office of Head of State.

Personally, I do not doubt their bona fides. They are a simple people, with a distinctive if rather quaint, culture. With the recent political changes in Tibet, I feel there is a distinct possibility of attempts being made to win the sympathy of the Ladakhis away from India and towards Communism. The best safeguard against this is a happy and contented Ladakh, and that I feel, can only be achieved by a sympathetic consideration of the points raised by them. If the matter is handled in an understanding manner by the State Government I see no reason why matters should not be smoothly settled to the satisfaction of all concerned. I have not seen Sheikh Abdullah yet since I refused but I hope to do so soon and I shall talk to him about this.

My purpose in writing to you in this connection was to lay before you what I gathered on my recent visit, and to urge that sympathetic consideration be given to the requests of the Ladakhis. Ladakh is strategically very important, more so for India as a whole even than for the States, and it will be a tragedy if for lack of an accommodating spirit the people of Ladakh remain unhappy and discontented, and thus an easy prey to all sorts of exploitation, both communalist and communist. I would also add that if the Government of India decides to advise Sheikh Sahib to agree to these proposals of the Ladakhis, they should be put into effect as soon as possible, preferably before this winter sets in. To waste any more time than is necessary will not be without danger.

I do hope that by writing this to you I have not overstepped the propriety of my Constitutional position, but when there is a situation which I feel needs remedying I consider it my duty to acquaint you with my views and what I feel is the true state of affairs. As a matter of fact, I feel that this is one of my more important functions, in addition to the purely formal duty of affixing my signature to official documents.

Finally, I would again urge that you give this note careful consideration. No doubt you are already well informed about the Ladakh situation, but nevertheless, an impartial and independent opinion might prove of value to you in coming to a decision on this matter.

——— 47 ———

New Delhi
2 October 1952

My dear Tiger,

Thank you for your letter of the 24th September and for your note on Ladakh.

The points you have mentioned in the note are well known. I have discussed these matters with Sheikh Sahib on several occasions. His attitude has been a favourable one. Some of these matters can easily be taken up in the framing of the new Constitution in the Constituent Assembly.

The real difficulty about Ladakh is its terrible economic

backwardness and the Kushak Lama[1] has no remedy for that at all. He can hardly be expected to suggest anything. The very straightened finances of Kashmir State have made it difficult for much money to be spent there. We are, however, having a Community Centre there for which we shall be directly responsible. We are also considering other economic projects. I believe that something has been included in the Kashmir five year plan[2] which we have largely approved of.

We should like to make a road to Leh from Kulu Valley, but this is a very expensive undertaking and, for the present, it is difficult to take it up. That road will open out the mineral deposits of Ladakh and will bring a certain measure of prosperity to that region.

Thank you for your telegram.

Yours affectionately,
Jawaharlal Nehru

--------- 48 ---------

New Delhi
30 October 1952

My dear Tiger,
Thank you for your message of good wishes on the occasion of the Diwali.

I have recently returned from a visit to the North East Frontier of ours.[3] I spent a week there and travelled widely in various States and

---

1. Kushak Bakula, the head lama of Ladakh, found little difference between Abdullah's revolutionary programme of land reform and communism, and desired autonomy for Ladakh within the Indian Union. In a memorandum to Sheikh Abdullah, he demanded, 'a statutory provision in the future Constitution of the State under which the province of Ladakh would become a federating unit of Kashmir as long as the accession of the State to India endures.' Bakula, however, pointed out that if his plan was 'feasible just now', a statutory advisory committee elected by a joint electorate could be set up for Ladakh districts and no measure affecting the economic, political and religious life of Ladakh should be passed by the state constituent assembly or the government without the approval of the committee.
2. In March 1952, the Kashmir government drafted a five year plan for the state envisaging expenditure amounting to Rs 13 crores. The central government agreed to make available Rs 7 crores for the capital requirement.
3. Nehru, for the first time, visited the tribal areas in Assam, NEFA, Nagaland, Manipur and Tripura from 19 to 25 October 1952.

tribal areas. I found this visit exceedingly interesting. I like the people very much.

As you know, we have had repeated discussions with Sheikh Abdullah and his Advisers about the legal formalities to be gone through to bring about the changes desired in the Jammu and Kashmir State, more particularly those relating to the Head of the State. We have consulted our Law Ministry, Attorney General[1] and others. At long last these matters have been finally settled and it has been agreed that the President should act under Article 370 of the Constitution and vary the explanation given there in regard to the Head of the State. Other procedural details have also been settled.

This matter has long been pending and it is desirable that it should be settled at an early date. Otherwise, needless uncertainty continues and gives rise to agitation. It is proposed, therefore, that the necessary steps should be taken roundabout the middle of November—say 16th or 17th—while the Constituent Assembly is sitting in Srinagar. It is better to finalize this at this stage than to postpone it. Sheikh Abdullah will, no doubt meet you and speak to you in order to fix up details. I hope that you will agree to the steps we have suggested. That is the only course that is open to us now and we should not hesitate to take it. Any other course or an attempt at postponement will only lead to difficulty and trouble.

I am afraid your father, the Maharaja, has not been very cooperative. We have tried to explain matters to him and to help him as far as possible. But he appears to be totally unaware of the changes that have taken place and are taking place in the world and puts forward some pleas which have no application in the present. The Home Minister, Dr Katju, is in correspondence with him. We cannot obviously wait indefinitely for the conclusion of this correspondence and we have to take action in any event.

You will remember suggesting to me that I should meet the president or some others of the Praja Parishad of Jammu. In deference to your wishes I had said that I was prepared to do so if they asked for an interview, although I had an unfortunate experience previously about such interviews. Since then I have not only not had any such request, but I have noticed a deliberate attempt on the part of the Praja Parishad to carry on an aggressive and threatening agitation not

---

1. M. C. Setalvad.

only roundabout Jammu, but in other parts of India. I confess I do not understand this except on the supposition that the Praja Parishad is functioning completely on the lines of the RSS Organization and its chief aim is to give trouble to our Government. We do not deal with communal organizations as such, and, apart from this, an organization that is issuing threats to us and behaving most irresponsibly cannot be encouraged in any way. I know the kind of persons the Praja Parishad people meet in Delhi and elsewhere. We have full reports of that. These persons are continually giving us trouble in various ways. I shall, therefore, have to take up a fairly strong line with these Praja Parishad people. I am not prepared to meet them now. Any such meeting will only be exploited by them.

I had hoped to be able to visit Kashmir for a day or two sometime in November. But I find that this is not possible as I am far too full up during that month. I am vaguely thinking of paying a brief visit to Jammu sometime in December.

With all good wishes,

Yours sincerely,
Jawaharlal Nehru

——— 49 ———

Srinagar
31 October 1952

My dear Panditji,
I have been reading with great interest about your visits to various parts of the country, which have had an invigorating and heartening effect upon the people.

I am enclosing a copy of a letter I have written to Dr Katju.[1] As you are so busy I did not want to trouble you with a long and detailed letter, and therefore, addressed it to the States Minister.

---

1. In his letter of 31 October to Dr K.N. Katju, Karan Singh referred to the newspaper reports that the constitutional details with regard to electing the Sadar-i-Riyasat had been worked out between the representatives of the state government and the government of India and also between the government of India and Maharaja Hari Singh. He added that before he would finally announce his decision regarding acceptance or otherwise of the office, he would like to know 'the details of the agreement which you have concluded with His Highness, with special reference to my future position, privy purse, private property, privileges etc.'

It is perfectly delightful in Kashmir nowadays. Although the mornings and evenings have got quite chilly, the mellow daytime sunshine is glorious. I think, this is the best time of year here, second only perhaps to early spring. Delhi must also be quite pleasant now. I may be down there soon, and look forward to seeing you then.

I am sending some apples from my own orchard.

With warm regards and respects,

Yours very sincerely,
Karan Singh

——— 50 ———

New Delhi
2 November 1952

My dear Tiger,

I returned today from my visit to Wardha, Sevagram, etc. Just before I went, I wrote to you. This afternoon Dr Katju showed me a letter that you had written to him.[1] He will be replying to you,[2] but I am supplementing that briefly.

In all these matters that we have been considering, it is always better not to appear to bargain about things. Ultimately, it is not assurances and promises that count in a democratic set up but the relationship and the personal element. I would, therefore, advise you not to pay too much attention to the various matters that you have raised. The principal one is about the entire Constitution and waiting for it to be finalized. Obviously, this question does not arise at this stage. We have discussed it enough and come to certain conclusions.

As for your freedom to resign at any stage, surely every individual has that freedom. To lay stress on it would mean that you are already thinking of resigning at some later stage. That is hardly a good beginning.

---

1. Dated 31 October 1952. See the preceding item.
2. Dr Katju informed Karan Singh on 4 November 1952, that C.S. Venkatachar, secretary, ministry of states, had discussed the whole matter with Maharaja Hari Singh who 'raised many matters relating to his own position and status'. Katju added that, 'so far as his privy purse is concerned it was agreed that out of Rs 10 lakhs, Rs 5 lakhs would be assigned to His Highness, Rs 1 lakh to your mother and Rs 4 lakhs to yourself... when occasion arises these portions of the privy purse assigned to His Highness and to your mother would devolve upon you.'

Again, your desire to go abroad occasionally is something to which there should be no bar. But long visits abroad would obviously be undesirable. Indeed, apart from other considerations, the question of exchange comes in.

Then there is the possibility of some provision about impeachment in the Constitution. This has to be looked at not from a personal point of view but as something which is desirable or not. I would have preferred to have no such provision, but really it is not a very important matter.

This whole business depends on a number of factors, the principal one being the relationship of Kashmir State to the Indian Union. If that breaks down in any way, then of course, all kinds of difficulties come in. In the nature of things, however, this is exceedingly unlikely and hardly conceivable. One should, therefore, proceed on that assumption. If anything big happens, then of course, we have to adjust ourselves accordingly. If that relationship persists, as it must as far as I can see, then these speculations have no force or importance.

You mention the flag. Personally, I think that the Head of the State should have a personal flag. Our President has a personal flag. Our Governors have their own personal flags.

If you have to start a new relationship, it should be under as favourable auspices as possible and with goodwill. That is a stronger guarantee than anything else.

Yours sincerely,
Jawaharlal Nehru

——— 51 ———

New Delhi
15 November 1952

My dear Tiger,
I am sending you separately a semi-formal letter of congratulation and good wishes. I did not quite know how to address such a letter. You know that I shall often think of you and that you can always rely on such help and guidance as I can give.

Yours sincerely,
Jawaharlal Nehru

——————— 52 ———————

New Delhi
15 November 1952

My dear Yuvaraj,

I write to congratulate you on the high honour that has been conferred upon you by the people of Jammu and Kashmir State on your election as Sadar-i-Riyasat[1]. I should like to congratulate the people of the State also on their wise choice. This puts a great responsibility upon you, for you have not merely to follow an established convention but rather to help in making conventions for the future. You know how dear the future of the State is to me. It is dear to me because of my own intimate relationship with Kashmir and it is dear to me also because of the numerous ties that bind the State to India. Our future is linked together and we have to face good fortune and ill-fortune alike together.

A new chapter opens now in the Jammu and Kashmir State. And yet, although it is new, it is a continuation of the old but in a different form. The processes of life, whether that of an individual or of a nation, are both a continuation and a continuous change.

I earnestly hope that the changes that have been brought about in the Constitution of the Jammu and Kashmir State will lead to the greater prosperity and happiness of the people of the State and will bring them even closer to India, of which they are such an intimate part.

To you, who have to shoulder this burden and this responsibility at such an early age, I send all my good wishes and my affection.

Yours sincerely,
Jawaharlal Nehru

———————

1. On 14 November 1952, Karan Singh was elected Sadar-i-Riyasat.

Affixing signature to the oath after election as Sadar-i-Riyasat,
Chief Justice Janki Nath Wazir looks on, Srinagar, 17 November
1952

——— 53 ———

Srinagar
18 November 1952

My dear Panditji,

Thank you very much indeed for your kind letters[1] in connection with my having been elected Sadar-i-Riyasat.

Since June 1949, when I first assumed the duties of Regent, down to the present day I have been faced from time to time with several difficult situations. Without your constant help and encouragement— the appreciation and gratitude for which it is hard for me to express— I would not have been able to achieve the measure of success which had up till now crowned my efforts. Your assurance of future help and guidance gives me courage to face with confidence the new responsibilities which I have now assumed.

I am aware of the great confidence which the people of the State have reposed in me, and also of the fact that there are many difficult and serious problems which confront us. I can assure you that my efforts will always be towards serving in whatever manner I can the people of this State and, in the larger context, the people of the rest of our great country. With your good wishes and affectionate guidance I feel confident that despite my youth and inexperience I will be able to successfully fulfil my responsibilities.

The oath-taking ceremony took place yesterday morning in the Rajgarh Palace. I enclose a copy of a short speech I delivered on that occasion.[2]

Thanking you again for your good wishes, and with deep respects and regards,

Yours very sincerely,
Karan Singh

---

1. See preceding items.
2. In his speech Karan Singh told the gathering in the assembly hall: 'In this land of colour and beauty, men of different faiths and creeds live as common inheritors of a great past and culture. It is our task now to forge greater unity among them as joint architects of their future. Such abiding unity cannot be imposed from above, but has to be based upon interests of the common man.' He described the division of Kashmir into two parts as the 'direct consequence of wanton aggression. Any attempt to impose an arbitrary solution seeking to circumvent this fundamental aspect of the situation cannot be acceptable to us.' He further said: 'Now that we are intimately associated with the Republic of India, we can look forward to a bright and prosperous future.'

———— 54 ————

New Delhi
21 November 1952

My dear Tiger,
Thank you for your letter of the 18th November. I am happy that
everything passed off well. The speech you delivered on the occasion
of your installation was excellent.

Yours sincerely,
Jawaharlal Nehru

———— 55 ————

New Delhi
24 November 1952

My dear Tiger,
I am very grateful to you for your message of good wishes on the
occasion of my 63rd birthday. To be remembered with affection by so
many friends all over the country and abroad is rather an overwhelming
thought. At the same time it strengthens, for one has the feeling of a
common purpose animating so many of us. I hope that all of us,
wherever we might be, will engage ourselves in this common purpose
of serving India and humanity to the best of our ability.

Yours sincerely,
Jawaharlal Nehru

———— 56 ————

Jammu Tawi
26 November 1952

My dear Panditji,
You must have received my letter dated the 18th November.
During the week I spent in Srinagar after my inauguration[1] I was
extremely busy with numerous parties and public functions, all of
which went off very well. On the whole the public opinion in the
Valley seems to be very favourable. The same is the case in Ladakh

---

1. As Sadar-i-Riyasat.

because, as I had written to you, Kushak Bakula had urged me to accept the office. In Jammu, of course, it was expected that there would be some resentment, but the Government seems anxious to solve the genuine difficulties of the Jammu people, and I am sure that the situation will improve. There is, as you know, a flag controversy here.[1] No flag has yet been hoisted upon the Jammu Secretariat because the Government offices have not yet opened here. My suggestion to Bakshi Sahib and others has been that the Indian Flag should be hoisted upon the Secretariat and should continue to fly there along with the new State Flag.[2] As we are an integral part of India this will be the correct thing to do, and what is more it will at the same time take the wind from the sails of those who are attempting to mislead the people in the name of India. The matter is being considered, and I hope my suggestion will be accepted.

I arrived here in Jammu on the 24th November. The Government had arranged an elaborate reception, and I drove in a procession from the airport to the Palace in an open jeep, with Bakshi Sahib sitting with me. As you might have seen in the papers, the Praja Parishad staged a black-flag demonstration as a protest against the recent changes and my accepting the new office.[3] About two hundred young boys took part in the demonstration, waving paper flags and shouting slogans. It seems that the saner section of opinion, even within the Praja Parishad party itself, had opposed this sort of behaviour but the more extreme group which in trying to force the issues—had its way. Uptil now, despite provocation the Government did not take any strong measures and showed admirable patience. Today, however, as demonstrators were continuing to defy the law, some arrests have been made.

---

1. The Praja Parishad during its civil disobedience campaign in Jammu on 23 November 1952, demanded the use of the national flag of India only and the exclusion of the state flag.

2. On 10 June 1952, the Kashmir constituent assembly adopted a resolution for having a new state flag. It was decided in the Delhi Agreement that the national flag would have the same status and position in Jammu and Kashmir as in the rest of India. The state flag was in no sense a rival to the national flag. However, for historical and sentimental reasons, connected as it was with the freedom struggle in Kashmir, it was agreed upon to continue this symbol.

3. The Praja Parishad mobilized some people to boycott the reception of the Sadar-i-Riyasat and to observe hartal. The demonstrators threw stones on the cars following the Sadar-i-Riyasat's car, defied authority in various ways and made provocative speeches.

After the rather uncomfortable cold of Srinagar the mellow weather here in Jammu is a welcome change.

We are all watching with keen interest and admiration your attempts to bring an end to the Korean conflict.[1] I sincerely hope that they are successful, because if they are, it will not only be saving Korea from further total devastation but also the world from imminent danger of a mass conflagration.

I hope this finds you very well.

With deep regards and respects,

Yours sincerely,
Karan Singh

——— 57 ———

Jammu Tawi
1 December 1952

My dear Panditji,

I have been here for about a week and have had the opportunity of studying the situation at close range. The situation is serious, not in any military sense but in the sense that an overwhelming majority of the Jammu Province seem to be emphatically in sympathy with the agitation. Fundamentally responsible for this, I feel, are several deep-seated and genuine economic and psychological reasons, and I do not think it will be a correct appraisal to dismiss the whole affair as merely the creation of a reactionary clique. It is no doubt true that this element is playing an important role, but it is deriving its strength from the fact that the people at large are feeling extremely wounded and frustrated. As a matter of fact this frustration is fast becoming desperation and unless speedy measures are taken to tackle the fundamental causes there is danger of the situation deteriorating considerably.

I am in touch with the situation and am trying together authoritative information as to the genuine remediable difficulties of the people. I am also in close touch with Bakshi Sahib and other ministers who are

---

1. The Korean war broke out on 25 June 1950 when the North Korean forces invaded South Korea and finally came to an end on 27 July 1953. Nehru raised the issue at the Commonwealth Prime Ministers' Conference and at the UN and played an important part in bringing together the hostile groups.

here. Sheikh Sahib has not yet come down from Srinagar. Within a week or ten days I would like to make a short trip to Delhi[1] so that I can place the whole situation before you personally. Frankly, I am not happy at all about the present state of affairs.

Today the new State Flag was hoisted upon the Secretariat here, but I am afraid my suggestion about also hoisting the Indian Flag has not been accepted. I feel that would have been a graceful and becoming gesture, which might have had a very healthy psychological effect, and would have forestalled much trouble.

With respectful regards,

Yours very sincerely,
Karan Singh

———— 58 ————

New Delhi
22 December 1952

My dear Panditji,

With reference to my conversations with you, I am enclosing a note on the Jammu situation. It contains an analysis of the situation and also some concrete suggestions for bringing about a satisfactory solution. As I mentioned personally I fear that lack of effective action might lead to a considerable deterioration of the situation, with all the attendant dangerous and harmful repercussions. Being so intimately in touch with the situation, and in view of the confidence and affection you have always shown for me, I have felt it my duty to put my views before you as frankly and clearly as I can.

I feel that if Sheikh Sahib and his colleagues were to come down to Delhi, or perhaps meet you in Hyderabad, and you were to talk to them personally in this connection it might have an effective and favourable result.

My abiding interest is that this matter should be settled in a manner which not only bring about harmony and cohesion within the State but also strengthens our bonds with the rest of India. And my greatest desire is to be of use in bringing about this consummation.

With respectful regards,

Yours very sincerely,
Karan Singh

———————————

1. Karan Singh was in Delhi from 20 to 22 December 1952.

——————— 59 ———————
Situation in Jammu[1]

The situation in Jammu is serious, not in a military sense but in the sense that an overwhelming majority of the people of Jammu province seem to be actively in sympathy with the present agitation. It will not be a correct appreciation of the situation to dismiss it as merely the work of a reactionary clique. This element is no doubt playing its role and trying to exploit the situation for its own ends, but it bases its strength and appeal upon the fact that the large mass of the people are feeling genuinely injured and very frustrated. This frustration has now begun to turn into desperation, and this dangerous trend must be prevented by taking speedy measures to tackle and remove the genuine grievances and difficulties of the people.

At the root of all this trouble are certain deeply felt psychological and economic factors. The fears, suspicions and general feeling of resentment which the people of Jammu have been feeling over the last five years have now been crystallized into stubborn and widespread resistance by the recent acts of the State Government in pushing through the questions of the ruling family and the State Flag. As it was, the Indo-Kashmir agreement did not satisfy the Jammu people, who are for full and unlimited integration, but the manner in which these two matters—upon which they had the deepest emotional and psychological attachment—have been rushed through without touching at all upon any of the other basic problems covered by the agreement has caused very great resentment. The people feel that they have not only been treated with scant regard, but that consistent and vindictive efforts have been made to ruin them economically over the last five years and to outrage their deepest and most cherished sentiments, without giving them the compensatory satisfaction of becoming wholly integrated with India. They would not have minded the abolition of the old State Flag if they had seen the State Government adopting the Indian National Flag, and they would not have minded the abolition of hereditary rule if a system of Rajpramukh—as in other Part B States—had been introduced. What has caused great resentment is that while their deeply cherished flag and rule have

———————————————————

1. Note for Jawaharlal Nehru, New Delhi, 22 December 1952.

gone, in their place they have not been given what has been given to the rest of the Part B States and that a new flag and a new kind of Head of the State has been foisted upon them against their will.

Up till now the movement has been basically peaceful, despite a few unpleasant incidents. But a situation of this kind is liable to take an ugly turn at any time, causing considerable loss of life and widespread suffering. For this reason, and also for the fact that the agitation is not only disrupting the smooth functioning of the administration but is also being fully exploited by Pakistan and is likely to have undesirable international repercussions, it is very essential that conditions be speedily created in which this agitation can be called off, or at least lose its appeal with the masses, and the people of Jammu be made to feel that their rights, culture and interests are safe and that they are not being treated in a discriminatory manner.

Stripped of all its non-essentials, the situation is that whereas Jammu and Ladakh strongly desire complete integration with India, Sheikh Sahib and his colleagues are extremely insistent upon the limited nature of the accession and are not prepared to agree to complete integration. In view of these basic facts, unless Sheikh Sahib can be made to agree to full integration, there seem to be only three alternatives:

A) Jammu and Ladakh separate from Kashmir: Under the present international complications, this will be a very undesirable and dangerous development, as it is likely to have the effect of pushing the Kashmir Valley into the hands of Pakistan. That, of course, will be the most tragic and unfortunate consummation conceivable. It is no doubt true that the people of Jammu are culturally and linguistically much more closely allied with the Dogra areas of Kangra and Himachal Pradesh, and also geographically contiguous to them. But as I said any realignment at this stage is likely to prove disastrous.

B) The present status quo as regards the internal and external relations of the State be maintained: This also will not be satisfactory, as in the ultimate analysis the three units of the State can remain together only by common consent, and if the present unrest and discontent continues there is a strong possibility of the situation deteriorating considerably. It is clear that forcible repression can at best act merely as a palliative, and a very temporary one at that. At worst it can sow such seeds of hatred and resentment as will completely inhibit any solution or settlement for many years to come. It will also be very unfortunate, and not free from grave risks, if the Indian Army or the Indian Police are called upon to fire on processions carrying the Indian flag and portraits of the Indian President. As I said this movement is very widespread and needs to be tackled in a sympathetic and understanding manner. Our attitude, therefore, while dealing adequately with violent elements, should be one which is conducive to arriving at an amicable and mutually satisfactory solution.

C) A formula is evolved whereby, while remaining with Kashmir as one unit, the people of Jammu and Ladakh are made to feel happy and contented: This to my mind is the only satisfactory solution possible under the circumstances. For its attainment, however, it is very necessary that certain measures be swiftly adopted. I feel that if the measures suggested in this note are specially implemented, and full efforts are made to consolidate the goodwill and confidence they are bound to generate, the whole problem can be peacefully and satisfactorily settled within a short time.

Measures which should be taken to deal with the situation

The measures required to be taken fall broadly into two categories, Political and Economic.

a) Political

1. The speedy implementation of the Indo-Kashmir agreement, which will form the basis of the new Constitution for the State. This agreement has been approved not only by the Government of India and the State Government, but by the Indian Houses of Parliament and the State Constituent Assembly. There is, therefore, no conceivable reason why it should not be implemented without delay. It is now over half a year since the agreement was reached, and the delay in implementing it fully—especially after going through with the questions of the Headship and the Flag is causing extreme resentment and has sown a distrust of the bona fides of the State Government in the hearts of the Jammu people. The Constitution, if properly drafted, will prove to be a great source of strength for the State, and there is no reason why it should not be taken full advantage of as soon as possible.

The Assembly should waste no time in drafting the Constitution which I feel should be ready if possible by the 1st Baisakh (our New Year in the State, equivalent to April 13th.) At any rate some time limit should be fixed for drafting and putting the new Constitution into effect. This Constitution will naturally, deal with such important and basic questions as fundamental rights, jurisdiction of the Supreme Court, emergency powers of the Indian President, exact functions and position of the Sadar-i-Riyasat, provincial autonomy etc.

With particular reference to the Jammu problem, very close attention must be paid to framing this Constitution in a manner in which all sections of the State feel secure that their culture, rights and interests are fully safeguarded, and that there is absolutely no chance for the exploitation of one area or people by another. This is the clearly expressed and oft-repeated intention of Sheikh Sahib and must be practically put into effect by working out a satisfactory system of provincial autonomy. As I have said before, the regions can remain together ultimately only by common consent, and therefore all possible steps should be taken to secure that happy and willing consent.

2. Immediately, the Indian National Flag should be hoisted and should continue to fly side by side with the State Flag over at least the Secretariats in Jammu and Srinagar. This will not only be the correct thing to do but will also have a very healthy effect upon public opinion both within the State and in India.

At present, to the best of my knowledge, there is not a single building in the whole of the Jammu and Kashmir State upon which the Indian Flag is flown. This is not at all proper, and the view that it will be flown only on our National days is not satisfactory. As the Government is at present in Jammu the Flag should at least be flown there, and it can be raised on the Srinagar Secretariat when the Government moves up next season.

3. A very important and almost universal complaint is the widespread corruption in the working of Governmental machinery, especially on the lower levels. This was very noticeable in the implementation

of the Big Landed Estates Abolition Act[1]. On paper the tenants did not have to pay any compensation. In fact, however, they did pay it: not to the landholder but in the form of bribes to the *patwaris, girdawar* and *tehsildars* who were responsible for the actual land transfers. A very thorough drive must be instituted against corruption, and exemplary punishment be meted out to all against whom dishonesty can be proved, regardless of how high up or highly connected he may be. This will remove the widespread conviction that favourites have been let loose upon the people, and will restore confidence in the working of the Government mechanism.

Party influence in the day to day administration, often amounting to interference, has also become widespread and should be effectively rooted out as it is having an unfortunate effect upon the public as well as upon the efficiency of the administration.

4. As regards education in the Jammu Province, there are several steps which must be of great use in helping the people and creating a better atmosphere:
   a)   Announcement of the decision (which I believe has already been taken) to introduce Dogri as the regional language—in the same manner as Kashmiri has been introduced in the Valley—and its actual introduction from 1st Baisakh.
   b)   Setting up a separate girls' college in Jammu city, and Intermediate colleges in Udhampur and in Samba or Kathua.
   c)   Revision of Hindi textbooks to simplify the language and standardize it on the same basis as in India. At present there is a great complaint that these books contain many Urdu and even Persian words, merely written in the Devanagari script, and that their content is also not very desirable.

5. In general the leaders of the Government and the party in power should be very careful in their public and private utterances not

---

1. Under the Big Landed Estates Abolition Act, 1950, 450,000 acres of land were acquired from the landlords out of which 230,000 acres were transferred to tillers. A big slice of the rest was taken over by the collective farms run by the government. The ten man committee of the Constituent Assembly of Jammu and Kashmir was assigned to decide the issue of compensation which on 27 March 1952 recommended abolition of feudalism without compensation. The Assembly adopted its recommendation on 31 March.

to say anything that may give the people the impression that they are anti-Dogra or anti-Jammu, and their whole attitude should be such as to instil into the people of Jammu a sense of confidence and trust in them.

b) Economic

1. The question of financial integration, which was left open in the Indo-Kashmir agreement, will have to be taken up in the framing of the new Constitution. Such integration is greatly in the interests of the State and as such the State Government should accept it willingly. One point which is of very great significance, however, regardless of the technical details of the financial agreement, is the abolition of the State Customs Duty. This is the most important both from the economic and the political standpoints, as it will bring immediate substantial relief to all the people of the State, especially the poor, and will also give a great impetus to trade and commerce between the State and the rest of India.

In this connection a resolution tabled by some National Conference workers in the Valley recently requesting that the Rawalpindi road be opened as it would help their trade, is a stern reminder of the necessity of encouraging trade and bringing swift economic relief to the people. Now that they are a part of India, the people of the State should at least get the tangible benefits of this association. I would make a very strong plea to the Government of India, which is spending so much upon Kashmir as it is, to agree to make up the deficit without setting a fixed time limit until the State can increase its revenues to the present level by exploiting other sources of income. I am sure that the liability (which I believe the Government of India is even now prepared to take upon itself for ten years) will be more than offset by the very substantial economic and political benefits which will accrue from the abolition of the Customs Duty. This is one of the important matters which can be brought into effect almost immediately and need not await the completion of the Constitution. The sooner this is done the better, I feel, will it be.

2. The Big Landed Estates Abolition Act has unfortunately not proved satisfactory in the Jammu Province. The flat rate of 182 kanals, regardless of the productivity and fertility of the land, does not in many areas of the Jammu province constitute an economic holding at all. There is a tremendous difference between the produce of

182 kanals in the Kashmir Valley and in the Kandi and Pahari areas of Jammu. This was unfortunately not kept in mind by the framers of the Act, with the result that not only have they been accused of sinister motives, but it has caused very great distress in large areas of the Province. Then even the 182 kanals (about 23 acres) unit is not a freehold, and cannot be cultivated by the landholder himself. And to add to the trouble the tenants often do not even pay the landholder his share of the produce, and there is strong complaint that in such cases, the Government policy has been to back the tenant whether he was right or wrong. The result is that those who owned land have been completely ruined. They have not been paid any compensation whatsoever, and in effect they have been left with no land upon which even to feed their families. The small landowners, mostly Rajputs, have been the hardest hit as they did not have any savings and lived entirely on the land.

This state of affairs must be remedied. If the criterion fixed by the framers of the act had been upon the basis of land produce, or land revenue it would have been equitable. I feel that a new criterion upon one of these bases should be fixed for the Jammu Province, where the productivity of the land varies a very great deal. Failing this the dispossessed landholder should be given his 182 kanals for self-cultivation so that he can become self-supporting. In the course of land transfers a lot of land is escheating to the Government. This can be given to the tenants of the 182 kanals or alternatively to the landholder himself.

This should also apply to some very small *jagirdars* who depended for their living solely upon their tiny *jagirs*. In the act abolishing *jagirs* there was a clause which said that while no compensation would be paid whatsoever the Government would give appropriate help to those who have no other means of support. Such deserving cases should be looked into and be given some help, either in the form of employment or, some Government land. These *jagirdars*, incidentally, have not even been left with 182 kanals.

3. The unemployment problem in the Jammu Province has reached alarming proportions, and was greatly worsened by the breaking up last year of three of our State Force Units, by which over 3,000 men—mostly Rajputs and Brahmins—were rendered unemployed. Counting their dependents this left about 20,000 people without adequate means of support. The Jammu people

do not have any sidelines of income such as handicrafts, tourist traffic etc. Their only sources of income are either agriculture or service employment.

To solve the unemployment problem two measures can prove helpful. Firstly as many of these retired soldiers as possible should be re-employed in the Militia, Home Guards, Police etc. Secondly, the Government should set up an unemployment commission to study the extent and causes of unemployment and to suggest short and long term measures for its removal. This will not only be helpful to the Government but will encourage the people.

4. Concentration upon long term planning to remove the basic economic difficulties of the people. This has been tackled to some extent in the State Five Year plan, but I feel more needs to be done. The greatest single problem in Jammu is that of supplying water to the Kandi areas, and if a dam could be constructed on the Tawi it would revolutionise the life of the people. In this, of course, the Government of India will have to give financial assistance.

The revision of the Rivaz Award to enable the Ravi water to be used for irrigation purposes within the State will also be very helpful. Short term measures are also required to bring some immediate relief to the people until the longer plans materialize. If something can be done to help the Kandi area this summer it will create a very favourable atmosphere.

In addition to the water problem, the cottage industries of the Province should be encouraged and the potentially promising tourist resorts should be developed.

5. There is a frequent complaint about the State Government having taken to itself the virtual monopoly of transport in the State (which it is said to be enforcing through continued petrol rationing). This is alleged to be not only ruining the transport companies and reducing yet another avenue of employment, but also of keeping the cost of transport artificially high due to the absence of effective competition. It should not be necessary for the Government to take the monopoly of the transport of goods except of course to those areas where normally transport facilities are not available such as Ladakh and Kishtwar.

The announcement and speedy implementation of these measures will, I feel, take the wind out of the sails of the agitation as they will remove some of the most important difficulties and grievances of the people. This might be followed by a general amnesty freeing the people arrested during the agitation, and sincere efforts should be made by the State Government to create an atmosphere of cordiality and understanding which, ultimately, can be the only basis for a peaceful and satisfactory settlement.

———— 60 ————

New Delhi
27 December 1952

My dear Panditji,

Thank you very much for your card of New Year greetings, which I warmly reciprocate.

I have been having a very busy time since I last saw you at the Asian Students' party.[1] Those students cornered me there and got me to address their plenary session. We also went and saw the Moral Rearmament[2] play, 'The Forgotten Factor', to which you very kindly gave us tickets. We enjoyed it very much indeed, as it was excellently acted and had a very interesting and thought-provoking theme. I also met Dr Buchman[3] who happened to attend the performance that day. This morning I visited the National Physical Laboratory, which Dr Krishnan[4] kindly showed me around. It is a really wonderful place, and it makes one proud to see that we have such institutions in our country.

Yesterday we paid a visit to Agra, where we gazed in wonder and admiration at the inimitable Taj and the other Mughal buildings.

We are leaving Delhi tomorrow. On my way back I shall drop in for a few days at Kangra to see my mother, as I have not seen her now

1. The UN Asian Students Convention was held on 20 December 1952 at the Delhi University.
2. The Moral Rearmament (MRA) movement, also known as the Oxford Group or the First Century Christian Fellowship which was started in 1938 by Dr Frank Buchman, advocated character building. It became an international movement and propagated the ideal 'world changing through life changing'. It was alleged that the movement took in only the rich and the influential in its fold.
3. Frank Nathan Daniel Buchman (1878-1961); American evangelist; head of religious work at Pensylvania State College, 1905-15; founded at Oxford the 'Group Movement' in 1938 later known as Moral Rearmament (MRA); extensively toured and gave lectures for Hartford Theological Foundation.
4. K.S. Krishnan (1898-1961); Fellow of the Royal Society; professor of Physics, Allahabad University, 1942-47; director, National Physical Laboratory, Delhi, 1947-61.

for over four months.

With deep regards, and wishes for a very happy and dynamically constructive New Year,

Yours very sincerely,
Karan Singh

———— 61 ————

Jammu Tawi
4 January 1953

My dear Panditji,

After leaving Delhi I went to visit Her Highness, my mother at Kangra, but the day after I arrived there I heard the distressing news of the police firing at Sunderbani which resulted in some deaths.[1] As I had already been away from Jammu for a fortnight I did not think it desirable to prolong my absence and therefore returned here immediately.

Since I returned I have had a long talk with Sheikh Sahib and also with other Ministers, officials and non-officials here. As I feared, the situation is drifting from bad to worse, and if we are to prevent complete disaster we must arrest this deterioration. I have read the long letter which Sheikh Sahib wrote to you[2] in reply to yours.[3] But

1. The police fired on the Praja Parishad processionists on 28 December 1952 at Sunderbani who were protesting against the alleged harsh treatment to satyagrahis in different police lock-ups and sub-jails. In protest, the Praja Parishad observed hartal on 30 December in Jammu city.
2. Sheikh Abdullah wrote to Nehru on 23 December 1952 justifying the stand of his government on the Praja Parishad agitation. He described the whole Jammu problem as the work of communal organizations and characterized it as 'a violent reaction on the part of Jammu landlords and other upper classes'. He added: 'The real problems of Jammu do not relate to the completion of its association with India and Kashmir nor to the propriety of this or that symbol. These problems are colossal in magnitude and need the active participation of every man and woman so that the wretchedness, poverty and degeneration of the vast masses of Jammu people are vanished.'
3. Nehru wrote to Sheikh Abdullah on 14 December 1952 that Praja Parishad had 'for the moment got the sympathy of a large number of people. There does appear to be a widespread feeling of frustration in Jammu. Some of it may have legitimate causes, some may be wholly unreasonable. But there is a grave feeling of dissatisfaction and frustration. I get the impression that the Jammu people feel that all importance is attached to Kashmir in the State and they are ignored. Not only are they ignored but they are often condemned as a bad lot.'

that letter contains only an analysis of past developments, an analysis—
I may add—which is not complete in all respects. It contains nothing
constructive for the future, no indication of what steps will be taken
to meet the situation as it is. When one is wounded by an arrow it is
not much use sitting down and conjecturing or arguing as to where
the arrow could have come from. It is much more important to see
immediately that the injured person does not succumb to his injuries.
It is now over a month and a half since this agitation began on the
14th November, but I am afraid that during this period nothing positive
or concrete has been done by our Government. We have taken police
measures, of course, but these are at best negative measures and cannot
at all strike at the root of the problem which is to recreate a sense of
confidence in the minds of the masses of Jammu.

A view which seems prevalent among Government circles here is
that if Jammu wants to break away from Kashmir they will not stand
in its way, except that only the Hindu majority areas of the Jammu
province will be allowed to break. This is an extremely negative and
defeatist attitude. Why should we not take active and positive steps to
prevent a break? If we just sit back and do nothing then, of course, we
might drift into the very break up we so dread and which will be so
disastrous. But I am confident that this can still be avoided if we act
correctly and fast.

As I stressed when talking to you personally and in my note, there
are two major things which must be done immediately by the State
Government or at least announced and actively begun. These are firstly,
the implementing of the remaining provisions of the Indo-Kashmir
Agreement[1] and reducing them as soon as possible to constitutional
form, and secondly, the granting and working out of a system of
provincial autonomy. These must not and need not be delayed any
longer at any cost, particularly as the National Conference is clearly
and firmly committed to both of these steps. At the same time, of
course, active measures must be taken to relieve economic distress in
Jammu.

Then there is another point which I would like to submit. Sheikh
Sahib reiterates, and probably correctly, that the control and direction
of this movement is from outside the State in India.[2] If that is so then

1.   For provisions of the agreement, also known as the Delhi Agreement, see ante, p. 27.
2.   The Hindu communal parties like Jana Sangh, Ram Rajya Parishad and the Hindu
     Mahasabha were controlling and guiding the Praja Parishad agitation in Jammu.

we should tackle those factors if we wish to solve the problem, and to end the present deadlock which in addition to the internal disruption in Jammu is having an unhappy effect upon Indian public opinion and also upon opinion in the Valley.

The initiative in this respect can lie in your hands alone, and I would earnestly and sincerely request you, for the sake of the State and the tremendous stake India has in it, to make a decisive move to end this unhappy deadlock. I feel sure that if the leaders of the main political parties in India are explained how this agitation is affecting the interests of India which they all profess to serve, they will help in settling the problem. If Sheikh Sahib attends the Hyderabad Congress Session,[1] as I have urged him to do, that will be an opportunity for him to get into direct contact with these people. And if he simultaneously makes a definite and uninhibited move to implement the agreement fully and also agrees in principle to provincial autonomy for Jammu (the details, of course, will have to be carefully worked out later in consultation with those vitally concerned) I am sure that with your immense prestige you will succeed in getting the agitation called off. This is a suggestion I have made bold to make only because I feel so keenly the imperative necessity for preventing our inexorable drift towards the precipice. If I can personally be of any use in this connection I will be ready to do all I can in whatever way possible.

I feel, and this feeling is shared by a large section of thinking people here, that the time has come for the Government of India and yourself in particular to take a direct hand in stabilizing this deteriorating situation. I have felt it my duty to convey this to you, in the anxious hope that it will receive at your hands close and sympathetic consideration.

With respectful regards,

Yours very sincerely,
Karan Singh

6. The 58th session of the Indian National Congress held in Hyderabad from 15 to 18 January 1953. Sheikh Abdullah also attended the session.

——— 62 ———

Jammu Tawi
7 January 1953

My dear Panditji,
I hope you have received my letter of the 4th.

I was extremely surprised when a news item in an Urdu paper from Jullunder was brought to my notice this morning, containing a report said to emanate from United Press of India publishing some of the contents of the letter I wrote to you regarding certain aspects of the Jammu situation. There could not possibly have been any leak from my side, because I typed that letter and note[1] with my own hands and delivered it personally at your house. I am therefore, completely at a loss to understand how this could have happened. I feel, I should bring the matter to your attention immediately, and am enclosing the cutting from the Urdu paper *Hind Samachar*. We did not get any English papers today because I think, the plane did not come in, so I do not know whether they have also published the report or not.

This is rather a regrettable incident as it may put me in a somewhat embarrassing position. I can assure you that it is due to no negligence on my part, as the file containing the letter remains under lock and key.

With respectful regards,

Yours sincerely,
Karan Singh

——— 63 ———

New Delhi
7 January 1953

My dear Tiger,
Thank you for your letter of the 4th January.

I can quite understand your great concern over the developments in Jammu. I am naturally also very much concerned and I have followed them closely. I entirely agree with you that while police measures are, of course necessary, that is only a negative way of dealing with the situation. A positive approach is always necessary. For your personal

---

1. For the letter and note dated 22 December 1952, see *ante*, pp. 66-74.

information, I might tell you that I have, written at some length to Sheikh Saheb on this subject.[1] I hope that he will come to Hyderabad for the Congress session and I shall certainly discuss these matters with him fully. And so with others. On my return from Hyderabad, I shall take such further action as might appear proper then. Perhaps, I might come to Jammu myself.

I agree with you also that a negative and defeatist attitude is all wrong. To talk about the Jammu Province, or part of it, breaking away from the rest of the State is folly. It is wrong for the Praja Parishad people as well as some of their supporters in India to talk of this. It is equally wrong for others to say that if Jammu wants to break away from Kashmir, it can do so. This defeatist tendency must not be encouraged.

I have seen a cutting from a Hindi newspaper in Delhi called *Veer Arjun* dated 6th January. In this it is stated that you have written a letter to me about the Jammu agitation and made various suggestions. The details given in the *Veer Arjun* are not wholly correct. But, evidently, some one who had access to your papers has got into touch with them. This is unfortunate and I hope you will take care to prevent this kind of thing happening.

I shall be leaving Delhi on the 13th January morning for Bombay and I shall reach Hyderabad on the 14th morning. I am likely to be away for about 9 days.

The situation in Jammu is serious enough to deserve our fullest consideration and such positive action as may be considered necessary. At the same time, one has to view these matters, as all other important matters, coolly and dispassionately.

I am terribly busy at present. That is my usual fate, but work and responsibility grow as India plays a more and more important role in the world. We have all kinds of conferences and seminars here drawing important people from other parts of the world.

With all good wishes,

Ever yours,
Jawaharlal Nehru

---

1. On 5 January, Nehru wrote to Sheikh Abdullah: 'I have tried to study the situation in Kashmir and Jammu with all the data available to me, and that is a good deal, from all sources. But what is more, I have approached this question with certain receptiveness which is so necessary to understand any problem. Kashmir has been for me some thing much more than a political issue, as you know.' For complete text of the letter see *Selected Works of Jawaharlal Nehru* (second series) Vol. 21, pp. 172-76.

——— 64 ———

Jammu Tawi
9 January 1953

My dear Panditji,
I am very grateful for your letter of the 7th.

You must have received my letter of the same date, which evidently crossed yours. In continuation of that I am enclosing a copy of a letter I received from Sheikh Abdullah this morning and of my reply.

With respectful regards,

Yours sincerely,
Karan Singh

——— 65 ———

Jammu Tawi
11 January 1953

My dear Panditji,
In this morning's *Tribune* I was astounded to read about an interview which I am supposed to have given in Kangra regarding the present controversy.[1] I am enclosing the cutting. Needless to say the report is entirely without foundation and I am really amazed that Kashmir Government Press Information Bureau should have circulated a report pertaining to me appearing in some unknown Kangra paper without first checking with me and getting the report confirmed.

In view of this, and the previous incident, I have today issued a

---

1. On 11 January 1953, the *Tribune* carried a report under the caption 'Yuvaraj Condemns Parishad Movement' and quoted Yuvaraj Karan Singh: 'The Parishad agitation is not only detrimental but even dangerous for India particularly Kashmir. The sooner it ends the better... The basis on which the agitation has been started is absolutely wrong. The National Flag has the same importance in the State as in India. The same is the position of the Indian Constitution. The State has, however, under the plan of "New Kashmir" made greater progress than India in several respects, such as abolition of landlordism without compensation. There is also no difference between a Sadar-i-Riyasat or a Rajpramukh. Moreover, I have not accepted office under duress.'

short Press Note,[1] a copy of which I enclose, which I hope will put a stop to these attempts to drag me into the present controversies within the State.

I am very sorry to bother you with these letters, but I feel that I should keep you informed about these developments, minor as they are.

Sheikh Abdullah saw me for a short while before he left for Delhi this afternoon. He did not seem to be in a very happy or constructive mood.

Yours respectfully,
Karan Singh

———— 66 ————

Jammu Tawi
17 January 1953

My dear Panditji,

I hope the Hyderabad Session of the Congress proved to be a complete success. I am sure that under your dynamic guidance this organization will rise equal to the tremendous tasks and responsibilities which lie before it, and will be able to fulfil the historic role which it is destined to play in the future in the same manner as it has fulfilled its past role.

Sheikh Abdullah must have given you his appraisal of the situation in Jammu, and I hope he has put forward a constructive line of action which will provide a solution to the present unhappy trend of events.

It is about a fortnight since I wrote about the situation here. Since then, there appears to have been further deterioration. Sikhs[2] are reported to have joined the movement for the first time, and there are

---

1. The press note said: 'Attempts have been made recently in some sections of press to involve Yuvaraj Karan Singh in the present controversies within the State. The Yuvaraj deprecates such attempts and wishes to make it clear that no press interview has been given by him within the State or elsewhere in India in this connection. As head of the State he does not wish to be dragged into any controversy in this manner. Of course, the welfare of the State and its people are his primary concern and his efforts consistent with his constitutional position, are always directed towards that end.'

2. The Akali Dal had thrown its full weight to support the Praja Parishad agitation in Jammu. Master Tara Singh attended the joint meeting of the Jana Sangh, the Hindu Mahasabha and the Ram Rajya Parishad held in Delhi on 10 January 1953 wherein it was resolved to work unitedly.

apprehensions that the Communists are likely to exploit the growing bitterness for their own ends.

The police have resorted to lathi charges and tear gas on many occasions, and have also had to open fire several times. As a result, several lives have been lost and many people have been injured. This has given a greater momentum to the agitation, which has enlisted the support and sympathy of even those sections of the people who had so far remained detached. Even women and boys are taking an active part, and police measures against them have generated increased resentment and bitterness and given the agitation further impetus. A serious feature, which is daily becoming clearer, is that the movement has been able to enlist widespread support and strength from the rural areas of the province.

May I, at this stage, offer a suggestion for your consideration? I feel it may be useful to you, in order properly to appraise the situation, to depute some persons of high standing on behalf of the Government of India to spare a few days to come to Jammu in order to study the situation on the spot. In this connection, if you will permit me to offer a personal view, the names of Dr Radhakrishnan and Maulana Azad appear to me to be most suited. If possible they may be armed with necessary authority to take whatever steps may appear to them to be appropriate for clearing the atmosphere of the existing friction and bitterness. This will, incidentally, save you the time and the strain of personally coming over at this juncture when other important work and problems await your attention in the Capital.

Both Dr Radhakrishnan and Maulana Sahib command great personal respect, and I have great faith that their presence here may well succeed in bringing this unfortunate state of affairs to a close. It is over two months now that the agitation started, and the consequences of its continuing and gaining further strength will obviously be very undesirable.

It is very necessary that conditions be created in which the people of Jammu and Kashmir can mutually adjust themselves to secure a harmonious and integrated existence, and further estrangement can be prevented. It is with this in view that I have proffered the suggestion made above.

We have had three days of rain here which, in addition to being of great value for the crops, has made the weather delightfully pleasant.

With respects and deep regards,

Yours very sincerely,
Karan Singh

——— 67 ———

Jammu Tawi
29 January 1953

My dear Panditji,

I received your message,[1] and you must have got my reply saying that I will certainly attend the Conference. I am planning to arrive in Delhi on the 3 February. The President[2] has very kindly invited me to stay at Rashtrapati Bhavan, and I shall stay there till the 6th.

I have also received your kind invitation to lunch on Wednesday the 4th, which I shall attend with pleasure. My wife will not be able to come with me to Delhi this time.

On Republic Day I took the salute at a March Past of some Army detachments followed by about 1500 school and college students. I also unfurled the National Flag on that occasion. The National Flag was flown upon the Secretariat and other buildings in Jammu on that day, but I was disappointed to see that it has been taken down from the Secretariat. I was hoping that this opportunity would be taken to keep the Flag flying at least upon the Secretariat along with the State Flag, and as a matter of fact had suggested this to Bakshi and others. Bakshi has agreed with me, but it seems that he has been overruled.

I look forward to the pleasure of seeing you in Delhi soon.

With deep regards,

Yours very sincerely,
Karan Singh

——— ———

68

New Delhi
14 February 1953

My dear Panditji,

I am returning to Jammu tomorrow. It was very kind of you to have had me over for lunch and dinner. I am trying to get a small plot of land in the New Diplomatic Enclave so that I can build myself a small

---

1. Nehru informed Karan Singh on 25 January by telegram that the president had invited him to the Conference of Governors and Rajpramukhs, which was to be held on 4 February 1953.
2. Rajendra Prasad.

house here. When it is ready I hope I shall some day have the privilege of your having an informal meal with me there. Considering that I come to Delhi so often I feel it will be very convenient to have a small house of my own. Hotels, be they the Ambassador, the Imperial or any other, are fantastically expensive and not merely as comfortable as a private house.

I was happy to have attended the Conference of Governors and Rajpramukhs, from which I feel I have profited considerably.

As regards the unfortunate situation in Jammu I have put my views before you and, of course, even otherwise you are fully informed about the true state of affairs. I am sure the matter is receiving your close personal attention, as the welfare of our State and its people has been always as dear to you as it is to any of us. I am sure that with your statesmanship an honourable and satisfactory solution can be found, and I may say must be found if further deterioration is to be prevented.

I shall, of course, discuss the matter at some length with Sheikh Sahib when I get back. I only hope that his attitude is not defeatist, and that he views the matter without unnecessary inhibitions and with a strong desire to actively set about putting things right. Given that, I feel there is no insuperable difficulty in bringing this regrettable episode to a speedy and mutually satisfactory close.

I shall, of course, if I may say, keep writing to you off and on from Jammu about how things are shaping.

With deep regards and respects,

Yours very sincerely,
Karan Singh

———— 69 ————

New Delhi
14 February 1953

My dear Tiger,
Thank you for your letter of today's date.

I am glad you propose to build a small house here in Delhi. That will undoubtedly be convenient for you.

The Jammu situation is very much before me and I am giving constant thought to it. As a matter of fact, it is no longer a Jammu situation, but an all India situation in which, unfortunately, several communal organizations in India[1] are taking an important part. Therefore, we have to pay a great deal of attention to it. Indeed, we are threatened with an all India agitation. Therefore, in considering this matter we have to keep this in view.

I am keeping in fairly close touch with Sheikh Abdullah by correspondence. I have had some correspondence also with Dr Syama Prasad Mookerjee[2] and Mr N.C. Chatterjee.[3] The letters they wrote to me were similarly unhelpful and to some extent rather irritating.[4] The speeches they delivered here last Sunday[5] were highly

---

1. The agitation in Jammu started by the Praja Parishad had been openly supported by the Jana Sangh, the Hindu Mahasabha and the Ram Rajya Parishad. The RSS also lent quiet support to it while Tara Singh of the Akali Dal promised support in the joint meeting of these organizations in New Delhi on 9 February 1953.

2. (1901-1953); vice-chancellor, Calcutta University, 1934-38; member, Bengal Legislative Council, 1929-37; member, Bengal Legislative Assembly, 1937-47; minister of industry and supply, government of India, 1947-50; founder-president, Bharatiya Jana Sangh, 1951, member, Lok Sabha 1952-53.

3. (1895-1972); a prominent leader of the Hindu Mahasabha, councillor, Calcutta Municipal Corporation, 1940-44; judge, Calcutta High Court, 1948-49; senior advocate, Supreme Court, 1952-57; president, All India Hindu Mahasabha, 1952-55; member, Lok Sabha, 1952-57 and 1963-72.

4. In his letter of 3 February 1953, S.P. Mookerjee wrote to Nehru that, 'It is through your mistaken policy and your failure to understand the viewpoints of those who differ from you, that the country is being brought to the brink of disaster.' Again on 8 February, he wrote that Nehru 'could not reply to arguments with arguments but had only to cast motives upon and made wild aspersions against those who differed from his official policy.' Further on 12 February, he wrote to Nehru asking if the constituent assembly of Jammu and Kashmir could not pass a resolution accepting final accession, 'what is your alternative proposal for finalizing accession?' Similarly, N.C. Chatterjee in his letter of 9 February 1953 warned Nehru that if the government of India would not intervene in the Jammu and Kashmir affairs 'before it is too late, the agitation will take the shape of an All-India movement and the repercussion will be serious.' On 12 February, Chatterjee again wrote to Nehru that it was difficult for him 'to appreciate that difference in outlook and approach between them is so fundamental that it is not possible to come to a reasonable understanding.'

5. On 9 February 1953, at a public meeting in New Delhi, S.P. Mookerjee warned the government that if, within the next three weeks, it did not 'explore the possibility of a peaceful settlement of the Praja Parishad agitations, it would spread to other parts of the country. The only way of achieving a settlement was by a round table conference between the government and the leaders of the Parishad, who should be released for the purpose.' During the period of these negotiations, the Praja Parishad would suspend the movement. N.C. Chatterjee said at the same meeting that there should be no difficulty for the government to call the Praja Parishad leaders to a conference to thrash out issues. He also said that the arrests of the Punjab leaders had been unprovoked and unjustified.

objectionable. We cannot permit this aggressive communal approach to prevail in India. I think, they realize this and are therefore toning down. If they start any agitation, we shall have to take all necessary measures to meet it. That is clear. I hope, however, that they will see wisdom.

So far as the Jammu situation is concerned, I think that it will improve. What I am concerned with is not merely the immediate situation but, looking ahead, the avoidance of trail of bitterness. I shall do my utmost to avoid this.

All good wishes,

Yours sincerely,
Jawaharlal Nehru

———— 70 ————

Jammu
23 February 1953

My dear Panditji,
Since I returned from Delhi I have had talks with Sheikh Abdullah and Bakshi Ghulam Mohammad. I have also been following with close interest the debate in Parliament concerning the Jammu situation[1] and particularly your speeches[2] in this connection.

Here at present there is a lull as far as the active agitation, processions and the like go. It is said that the local leaders of the Praja Parishad have issued a directive for this phase of inactivity so as to facilitate the high level consideration of this issue which everyone believes is being carried on in the capital. The people, however, continue to be sullen and resentful and the lull can hardly be interpreted to mean that they have been won over to the Government's viewpoint.

For some time now there has been a stream of reports about alleged police excesses, specially in the villages. These are said to take the form of vindictive and wide scale beatings, looting of houses and livestock, and even molestation of women. How far these reports are

1. The Jammu situation dominated the debate on the address by the president in the Lok Sabha from 13 to 18 February 1953.
2. Nehru declared that the grievances and demands of Jammu people would be considered carefully, 'but so far as the Praja Parishad agitation is concerned it is clearly communal and is intended to disturb the Government of India.'

accurate I am not in a position to say, although I would not be surprised
if they have some basis in fact. I have talked to Bakshi Sahib about this
and have also sent on to him certain detailed written reports which I
have received in this connection. I impressed upon him that this sort
of repression if indulged in creates more problems than it solves, and
that if the police or militia is indulging in any highhandedness it
should be stopped immediately and severe disciplinary action be taken
against the offending persons. Violence and hooliganism have, of
course, to be dealt with, with a firm hand, but such unwarranted
behaviour only spreads unnecessary resentment and bitterness and,
while making a difficult situation all the more intractable, brings
discredit upon the Government.

To return to the political situation, I must say I was quite favourably
impressed by the general tone of Dr Mookerjee's[1] and other
opposition speeches in Parliament regarding Jammu. It seems that
they realize the dangers and are now becoming really keen to see an
end of this unhappy episode. If this is true then I feel that there is
hope that things can be cleared up. The UN negotiations seem to
have broken down for the time being[2] and we have some breathing
space there. Here in Jammu, as I said, there is also a lull. I feel,
therefore, that this is as favourable a juncture for the State Government
to act as any.

Sheikh Sahib in his conversations lays great stress upon the 'absolute
impossibility' of his meeting or having anything to do with the leaders
of the Praja Parishad.[3] Although I can understand his basic sentiments
I confess I cannot quite appreciate this attitude of his. After all, if these
leaders had been in the State Assembly—as they very likely would
have been if they had not foolishly boycotted the elections—then
Sheikh Sahib whether he liked it or not would have had to discuss

---

1. On 17 February S.P. Mookerjee of the Jana Sangh offered in the Lok Sabha to
   withdraw the Praja Parishad movement provided the Kashmir government undertook
   the release of the arrested Parishad leaders and asked them to attend a round table
   conference to discuss the matter.
2. Anglo-US draft which asked India and Pakistan to enter into negotiations on the
   quantum of forces in Kashmir was debated on 23 December at the UN General
   Assembly. India had rejected the draft even before it was debated. USSR termed it
   an imperialist design to impose colonial domination in Kashmir and abstained from
   the voting. This caused a breakdown in the negotiation for sometime.
3. Sheikh Abdullah was reportedly not ready to call the Praja Parishad leaders for talks
   unless the agitation was withdrawn.

matters with them upon the floor of the House. In that event it would not have been possible for him to say that he would not talk to them nor sit in the same room with them. Also, I am sure that your dislike of communalism is no less than that of Sheikh Sahib's, yet in a democratic Parliament you sit and debate with members belonging to all shades of political opinion. And finally, in a matter in which the whole future of the country is involved I feel that we should rise above our personal predilections in order to serve the interests of the country. If Sheikh Sahib would call the Parishad leaders, not with a view to surrendering to them but only with a view to explaining matters to them, I feel this whole unhappy situation would have a much better chance of an amicable settlement. Your assurance that you are perfectly prepared to explain things to any person and dispel their fears contrasts greatly with Sheikh Sahib's rigid and I may say somewhat unrealistic attitude.

Merely meeting, however, will not be enough. I feel that certain concrete steps need to be taken by the State Government. These might be along the following lines:

1. Announcement of a period within which the Constituent Assembly will complete and put into effect the new Constitution for the State. This will, of course, be framed in the light of the Indo-Kashmir agreement. I feel that three months should be ample for completing this work, but if the Legislators require some more time they should not, of course, be rushed. I have suggested a voluntary time limit because that will have a reassuring effect upon the people, who have become rather sceptical of the real intentions of the party in power.

2. Simultaneously a committee, consisting mostly of people from Jammu, should be set up to study and work out a system of provincial autonomy for Jammu. This committee should issue a questionnaire and should attempt to elicit and associate as wide public opinion as possible. It should contain some public men in whom the people of Jammu have confidence, and not be a purely Government committee. A date, which I think need not exceed two months, should be set for the report of this committee which will be put before the Assembly and should become the basis of the clauses regarding provincial autonomy in the Constitution.

3. It might also be announced that after the Constitution is framed and put into effect there will be fresh elections, as the work of the Constituent Assembly will then be over. Before it dissolves it might,

if you consider it desirable, pass a resolution confirming and finalizing the accession of the State to India.

4. An important step which will go a long way in creating a better atmosphere here will be the appointment by the State Government of an impartial investigation committee to look into the various cases of firing that have taken place in the Province. This was the practice even in the old days, and many times eminent Englishmen and Indians were imported from British India to enquire into firings in the valley and once even in Jammu city. This step will have several advantages. First it will raise the prestige of the Government and will have the effect of somewhat soothing and calming the resentment which these firings generated. Then it will also clear the position of the Government. What has happened is that whereas according to Government figures the deaths in all the firings account to only 11, the widespread conviction is that they are really much more. Estimates vary, but almost everyone in Jammu is convinced and openly asserting that at least 30 peoples have been killed and many more injured. Hence an impartial enquiry will be in the interest of the Government as it will not only authoritatively give the figures of those dead but will also be able to say whether the firings were justified. The Government holds that they were justified and hence have nothing to fear.

The personnel of the enquiry committee, however, must be really impartial if it is to have any utility at all. Several weeks ago a sub-judge was sent to enquire into Sunderbani incident, but the people can hardly be expected to have confidence in his impartiality vis-a-vis the Government. I would think that one or two retired, or if possible serving, High Court judges from India would be very suitable, along with perhaps one judge from our High Court here.

This demand for an impartial enquiry has at present overshadowed all others here, and it is desirable that it should be met soon. It is very important that the enquiry is allowed to be conducted in a free and unfettered manner and that the members be allowed free access to those who can give evidence, wherever they may be.

If these measures are taken as soon as possible, I feel that they will greatly improve the situation. Whether they can become the basis for the agitation being called off,[1] I cannot say as I do not know the

---

1. On 3 July 1953, Nehru appealed for the withdrawal of the agitation 'completely and then deal with any grievances that may exist'. As a result of it the agitation was called off on 7 July by the Praja Parishad and the Jana Sangh.

minds of the Parishad and their supporters in India. I am sure, however, that if these steps are taken it will greatly improve the atmosphere and there will be a very much better chance of a settlement. If the movement can be called off that would create a much better atmosphere and the advantages and significance of these steps will greatly increase. If that is done then I think, the Government should declare an amnesty and free all prisoners connected with this movement.

As regards economic difficulties and grievances they must be looked into carefully. Once our development projects get moving they will help greatly. Some specific problems have already been given to the Wazir Committee.[1] I feel that the terms should be widened to allow the committee to examine the working of land reforms in the whole Province, and not only in the *Kandi* areas. The produce all over Jammu is much lower than in the Valley. This is, of course, more so in the *Kandi* area, but the rest of the Province should not be left out of the enquiry.

It would be a becoming gesture if the State Government decides to fly the National Flag upon the Secretariat in addition to the new State flag.[2] Your words in Parliament regarding the situation here, especially about the necessity for removing genuine grievances wherever they exist and about repression not being able to solve the problem, have given fresh hope to people here, who now look forward eagerly to some speedy and satisfactory solution. If the initiative, as you said in your speech, must lie with the State Government and if it is not possible for the Government of India to openly or actively intervene, then some of the concrete steps I have suggested in this letter might be taken from here. It will be an immense tragedy if the situation is allowed to drift into further violence, bitterness and disruption.

With all your tremendous preoccupations, I feel very reluctant to

---

1. In January 1953, the government of Jammu and Kashmir constituted an enquiry committee under the chairmanship of Justice Janki Nath Wazir to enquire into the alleged malpractices with regard to the land settlements and other economic issues. The committee recommended that in case of any soil the limit of land ownership should be raised to thirty-eight acres in Jammu and twenty-eight acres in Kashmir and *Mujawaza,* a tax on food grains be abolished.
2. The Constituent Assembly of Kashmir adopted a resolution on 10 June 1952 for having a new state flag.

impose these lengthy letters upon you, but I, and I am sure most people in Jammu look up towards you to help us out of our difficulties and troubles. I trust, therefore, that you will forgive this imposition and give, as you have always done, sympathetic consideration to the points which I have made in this letter.

With respectful regards,

Yours sincerely,
Karan Singh

––––––– 71 –––––––

Jammu
16 March 1953

My dear Panditji,

I hope you have received my letter dated the 23rd February.

In the middle of July this year quinquennial Congress of Commonwealth Universities[1] is being held in Cambridge. This will be attended by representatives from all the Universities in the Commonwealth. The Syndicate of the University of Jammu and Kashmir has requested me to represent the University on this occasion. I have talked to Sheikh Sahib about this and he is very keen that I should go. I also feel that it will be a pleasant and educative opportunity for me and my wife to go abroad for a short while.

I am planning to be away for about six weeks. I will spend a fortnight in England—four days at Cambridge and the rest at London. The remaining time I wish to spend on the Continent. I am particularly keen to visit my birthplace in Cannes, in the south of France. I came back to India when I was a few weeks old and have never been able to visit there since. If, God forbid, there is another war then I may never be able to go there. I also want to spend a week or so in Switzerland as I have heard that is perhaps the only place in the world which can rival Kashmir in natural beauty, although, of course, it is incomparably better developed.

––––––––––––––––––

1. The Congress of Universities of the Commonwealth was held in Cambridge from 13 to 17 July 1953. The Congress was the seventh of the series organized at quinquennial intervals since 1912 by the Association of Universities of the British Commonwealth formerly known as the Universities Bureau of the British Empire.

The Budget Session of the Legislative Assembly begins on the 25th, and on that day I will address the Assembly.

With respectful regards,

Yours very sincerely,
Karan Singh

———— 72 ————

New Delhi
21 March 1953

My dear Tiger,

I have your letter of March 16. I also received your previous letter. Bakshi Ghulam Mohammad was here for some days and I had some talks with him. He informed me of the discussions they were having in Jammu and the steps they propose to take, more especially, in regard to the implementation of our Agreement.

I like the idea of your going to the Commonwealth Universities Congress to be held at Cambridge next July. This visit will be good for you in various ways and will give you a breath of fresh air. I do not think there is chance of a war in the near future.

When you draw up your programme, please send it to us so that we can send word to our missions abroad, that is to the places where you are likely to visit. In your letter you mention England of course, and France and Switzerland. Is there any other country in Europe you are likely to visit?

Have you got a proper passport, etc.?

Yours sincerely,
Jawaharlal Nehru

———— 73 ————

New Delhi
22 March 1953

My dear Tiger,

I sent you a brief letter the other day about your going to Europe.

I received your letter of the 23rd February long ago. I did not answer it then because there was not much to answer. Since then I have had long talks with Bakshi Ghulam Mohammad and Girdharilal

Dogra,[1] who came with him, and he has informed me what they are discussing and proposed to do. I need not go into that either here except that, as far as I can see, they are moving in the right direction. They are likely to have a good many difficulties of their own and my direct interference is not desirable. Later Sheikh Saheb is likely to come here.

There are one or two matters which I should like to mention to you. You refer to police excesses. Probably, there had been excesses and undoubtedly where such excesses take place, they should be dealt properly. On no account must there be any vindictiveness on the part of the police. But the kind of reports that are circulated by the Praja Parishad are, on the face of it, so wildly exaggerated and often without foundation that hardly any credit can be attached to them. Many of these reports here emanate from the Pathankot office of the Praja Parishad. Every wild rumour is put down without the least attempt at verification.

As you know, the Jammu situation is hardly a Jammu situation now and Dr Syama Prasad Mookerjee and others have tried to make it an all India affair. In Delhi they carry on some kind of satyagraha, as they call it. This usually means some violence also in the shape of stoning the police. The Delhi people have kept quite apart from this, except for groups of RSS boys. The so-called stayagrahis are drafted from other parts of India, Kanpur, Gorakhpur, etc., and are very poor lot as a rule. The whole thing is completely artificial and has created practically no effect in Delhi. Of course, this kind of thing can be carried on for some time, so long as somebody provides the funds for it.

There is general realization in Parliament as well as outside that, whatever the nature of the Jammu situation, the steps that Dr Syama Prasad Mookerjee and other have taken here are so much utterly wrong and so harmful to India's interests that it is astonishing that any intelligent person could have acted in that way. There is no doubt at

---

1. Girdharilal Dogra (1915-1987); a close associate of Sheikh Abdullah who later became hostile; member, Constituent Assembly of Jammu and Kashmir, 1951-57; member, Legislative Assembly, Jammu and Kashmir, 1957-January 9, 1980; finance minister of the state, 1948-57; chairman, Kashmir Constitution Drafting Committee, 1951; opposed Sheikh Abdullah in 1953 and joined Bakshi Ghulam Mohammad's cabinet; minister of law, finance and industries, 1964-67, of revenue rehabilitation, food and supplies, 1967-69; of finance, planning and labour, law and tourism, 1970-75; member, Lok Sabha, 1980-84

all that the Praja Parishad and Jan Sangh agitation had made our situation in regard to Kashmir very difficult, national and international. Jammu and Kashmir have just been exploited merely to discredit our Government here.

You refer to Dr Mookerjee's speech in Parliament. It is true that his speeches are somewhat weaker than they were previously. The fact is that he realizes completely how wrong he has been. Among themselves, that is, as between Syama Parasad Mookerjee and Chatterjee[1] and Nandlal Sharma,[2] there is conflict and disagreement. Each is blaming the other. There is no doubt that they want a way out to withdraw this agitation. I would welcome the withdrawal. But I just do not want them to put it across to the people that they are the peace makers and that their viewpoint has prevailed. I am always prepared to see Dr Mookerjee as an MP. But I do not propose to give any encouragement to the Praja Parishad or the Jana Sangh as such.

Only today Pandit Govind Ballabh Pant came to see me. He is, as you know, very gentle in his approach. He insisted that we should not have any dealings with the Jana Sangh or the Praja Parishad people. In my view what these people have done is little short of treason of the country and the people should realize it.

We see what has been happening in Pakistan because of the anti-Quadiani agitation.[3] That is the sort of thing that might well grow in India if the Jana Sangh had its way.

I think, therefore, that we should proceed a little cautiously in this matter and not take a false step which might lead to greater difficulties in the future.

Yours sincerely,
Jawaharlal Nehru

1. N.C. Chatterjee.
2. A leader of the Ram Rajya Parishad.
3. There was a widespread agitation in Pakistan against the Quadianis, the followers of Mirza Ghulam Ahmad of Quadian (Punjab) who claimed in 1889 to be the Mahdi or Messiah. The agitationists refused to consider the Quadianis as Muslims because of certain doctrinal differences. They proposed that the Quadianis should be considered a community and not Muslim.

————— 74 —————

New Delhi
23 March 1953

My dear Tiger,
I enclose a copy of a letter[1] from Dr Kosambi,[2] which will explain itself.

I understand that this matter was first raised some time back and the States Ministry tired to persuade your father to send the manuscripts out of Jammu. Your father, however, was not willing to do so.

I think this is a pity. The manuscripts, if sent, will of course, be taken full care of and then returned. Could you please look into this matter and let me know if anything can be done.

Yours sincerely,
Jawaharlal Nehru

————— 75 —————

Jammu
27 March 1953

My dear Panditji,
Thank you very much for your kind letters.

Day before yesterday I delivered an address to the Legislative Assembly on the opening of its Budget Session, a copy of which I enclose.[3] I would have been happier if the speech had made a more

1. In his letter of 19 February D.D. Kosambi urged Nehru 'to intercede for a loan of five Bhartahari Manuscripts at the Raghunath Temple Library in Kashmir (Stein's Catalogue 559, 4016, 980, 1037, 229) on loan through the Bhandarkar Institute.'

2. D.D. Kosambi (1907–1966); mathematician and historian from Maharashtra, educated in USA; taught in Banaras Hindu University, Aligarh Muslim University, Fergusson College, Pune; works include. *An Introduction to the Study of Indian History*, 1956, *Myth and Reality, Studies in the Foundation of Indian Culture,* 1962, and *The Culture and Civilization of Ancient India in Historical Outline,*1965.

3. In his address on 25 March as the first Sadar-i-Riyasat of the state, Karan Singh declared that, 'the entire country has to be alert against any internal weakness which might make it possible for external pressure to succeed to our disadvantage.' He spoke at length on the Jammu agitation and observed: 'In view of the undesirable repercussions of such an agitation it is hoped that it will be called off forthwith.' He

positive approach to the difficult problem which is facing us in Jammu, but naturally as Constitutional Head I had to read the speech prepared by the Government. The most I could do was to offer some suggestions. As a matter of fact when Sheikh Abdullah came to see me a few weeks ago I mentioned that this speech would be a very good opportunity for the Government to make a fresh and positive approach to this unhappy problem. He agreed with me, and asked me to jot down the points which I felt might be incorporated in the speech. I did so, and sent him a short note, a copy of which I enclose. In drafting this I aimed at a speech which, while not deviating one iota from the principles of secularism to which we are pledged, would nevertheless have substantially counteracted the thickening atmosphere of distrust and suspicion here and might well have won away a very large section of the following of the agitation and subsequently perhaps have led to the end of the agitation itself. I do not think the same can be said for the speech which was finally delivered.

I have read your letter carefully and have also been following your speeches in Parliament.[1] I think, I have been able to understand your views on this question and I am grateful for the trouble you have taken to clarify them for my benefit. What really disturbs me is the fact that the gulf between Jammu and Kashmir has widened tremendously over the last few months, and that the breach instead of being bridged seems to be steadily widening. Neither of the parties seem to quite realize the implications of this, and I fear that we may reap a very bitter harvest in years to come. Hence it is that I feel that only from a person of your unique stature and influence can true and correct guidance come.

My sole desire is to see an end of this unhappy chapter and to witness the progress towards true democracy and economic emancipation of the people of our State as a whole. The key to this at present seems to be the speedy framing and implementation of our proposed Constitution which will on the one hand deal with the relationship of our State with the Centre (which, it seems to me, will necessarily have to intimate) and on the other with our internal set

---

also said: 'It is with much concern and pain that the Government has been called upon to deal with an aggressive, misguided and mistaken agitation in Jammu which while professedly seeking to strengthen the kinship and association of the State with Indian Union, in actual practice, constitutes a grave danger to this relationship.'

1. See *ante*, p. 95.

up including the very important question of provincial autonomy. I am told that the work of constitution-making will soon be taken in hand. It is already long overdue and I always try and impress upon Sheikh Abdullah and others that it should be expedited.

Regarding police excesses I quite agree with you that there might be many exaggerations, but the situation demands that all concrete cases should be dealt with speedily and impartially by the Government. That will go a long way in recreating a sense of confidence in the people. Unfortunately, this does not seem to have been done yet and this has led people to believe that the Government is deliberately perpetrating the repression in order to break their spirit and crush all opposition. This is a most unfortunate feeling, and at present, while the agitation seems to have toned off, the people continue to remain bitter, sullen and unreconciled. It is in order to counteract this that I had suggested an impartial judicial enquiry.

I am so glad that you approve of my proposed visit to Europe. It is very kind of you to say that you will send word to the Missions abroad. I am drawing up a detailed programme, and in the mean time we are writing to the States Ministry regarding passports, visas, courtesy certificates, foreign exchange and the like.

In this connection there is one problem which I would like to bring to your notice. Considering that I will be away from the country for some time, should I formally ask the President for leave? And if so, who will officiate as Sadar during my absence? I presume that the President will have to recognize someone before he can officiate and he will have to be duly sworn in. I would be most grateful if you could tell me what should be done.

I am in receipt of your letter regarding the manuscripts. I am examining the matter and will write to you as soon as possible.

Some time ago I mentioned in one of my letters that I want to build a small house in Delhi, and you approved of the idea. I submitted an application to the Ministry of Works, Housing and Supply several months ago for a plot of land at a fixed rate in the Diplomatic Colony, but I have not been allotted a plot yet. When I was in Delhi last I made enquiries but learnt that the matter had gone up to the Cabinet for sanction.

Most unfortunately there has been prolonged drought here as a result of which a large portion of the crops in the *Kandi* area have been completely ruined. This will add to the distress of the people living in those areas. Sometimes it seems that even nature is against us.

I have just finished rereading with great interest your *Autobiography*. I read it first many years ago before I had had the privilege of meeting you. I was then in my middle teens, and it had a powerful effect upon me. Since then perhaps the most rewarding and encouraging aspects of my career has been my close association with you and your continued kindness towards me.

With respectful regards,

Yours very sincerely,
Karan Singh

——————— 76 ———————

Jammu Tawi
30 March 1953

My dear Panditji,

Sometime ago I addressed a letter to the Minister for States regarding continuance of the guards which are at present deputed from the State Forces on duty with me and my mother. The State troops are already on the move, and I am very anxious that orders are issued for the existing arrangements of guards from State Force units to continue.

We want these guards not for ceremonial purposes at all, but only for protective purposes, in view of the very tense internal and external conditions that we are facing. As you know the place where my mother stays is several miles, from the nearest police station, and without a military guard I do not feel that her person or property are at all safe.

I am enclosing for ready reference a copy of the letter I wrote to Dr Katju. I am very sorry to bother you with this small matter, but as it is of considerable personal importance to me I take the liberty of putting it before you for consideration.

With respectful regards,

Yours sincerely,
Karan Singh

——— 77 ———

Jammu
1 April 1953

My dear Panditji,

I am writing this to you in connection with the future of the Jammu and Kashmir State Forces.[1] The decision regarding their integration is being implemented and those who have been in the front lines continuously for nearly six years are now being transferred to peace time stations. Integration was inevitable, but there are certain problems arising there which deserve sympathy and consideration.

Sheikh Sahib, I understand, has already addressed a letter to you representing the Government's views in this matter. I believe it conveys the political and economic aspects of this development. I need not go into details except to emphasize one or two points. In view of the peculiar political and strategic significance of the areas to which these men belong, it will be a great appreciation of their work and evoke a loyal response if the units and their personnel are maintained intact and these men, whose record of service has earned them fame and respect in various theatres and from reputed Commanders, are exempted from the process of screening. Their unique record of service over the last six years in which they have worked shoulder to shoulder in the defence of the nation as an integral part of the Indian Army singles them out for special treatment. Their case does not deserve to be treated on the analogy of other State troops.

Apart from the necessary undesirable political repercussions of further pruning and disbandment, the economic distress that such an action will bring about will be neither fair to the Government nor the people who are facing real political and economic difficulties of a border State, coupled with the agonizing uncertainty of their national future. The earlier disbandment of over 3000 men caused acute economic distress and has left sore wounds behind in this land where military service is not only considered the highest ideal of national service, but also provides an extremely important basis for economic existence. There will, I feel, be considerable opposition to their absorption and seniority in the cadres but it will be a pity if such considerations were allowed to create distress and dismay in the hearts

---

1. Finally, the Jammu and Kashmir State forces were made part of the Indian army and named JAK Regiment. Its headquarters are located in Jabalpur.

of thousands of men and their dependents to whom loyalty to India is dearer than their lives.

The uncertainty regarding their future has naturally caused some anxiety among the State Forces, but they, one and all, have confidence that you will see that they get a fair and generous deal. In my conversations with many of the men and officers I have noticed this, and they all look up towards you to safeguard their interests, particularly as you also now hold the Defence portfolio. They have been actively and loyally serving their motherland for the last six years, and I am sure that their case will receive at your hands the favourable consideration which I strongly feel it deserves.

With respectful regards,

Yours sincerely,
Karan Singh

———— 78 ————

New Delhi
6 April 1953

My dear Tiger,
I returned last evening from a tour in the Indo-Burma frontier[1] and received your letter of April 1st.

About the Jammu and Kashmir State Forces, the decision we have taken is that this matter should be proceeded with slowly and, as far as possible, without upsetting anything. Further that care should be taken that any person who is demobilized is to be provided for elsewhere. I am enquiring further into this matter and shall keep in touch with developments.

Yours sincerely,
Jawaharlal Nehru

---

1. Nehru was on a tour of the Indo-Burma border from 29 March to 4 April 1953.

——— 79 ———

New Delhi
6 April 1953

My dear Tiger,

Your letter of the 27th March.

I think you should write formally to the President about your proposal to visit Europe to attend the Commonwealth University Conference at Cambridge. I am, of course, keeping him informed.[1] I am writing to Sheikh Saheb also about the selection of some one to officiate on your behalf during your absence. I think that his name should be communicated to the President. He will, of course, have to be sworn in.

I am enquiring about the plot of land which you want in Delhi.

About the other matters to which you have referred in your letter, I am having them in mind and am constantly thinking about what steps should be taken.

On my return last night from my tour in the North Eastern frontier, I find myself overwhelmed with work. Very important international developments have taken place which require constant attention. Also my old friend and colleague, Asaf Ali[2] died suddenly at Berne. I was greatly looking forward to meeting him in June next. His body is arriving here this evening and the funeral will take place tomorrow.

Yours ever,
Jawaharlal Nehru

1. Nehru wrote to Rajendra Prasad on 6 April 1953 regarding this.
2. (1888-1953); prominent Congressman from Delhi; secretary, Congress Parliamentary Board, 1934; member, Congress Working Committee, 1940-42; took active part in the freedom struggle and was imprisoned during 1942-45; deputy leader, Congress party in the Central Assembly, 1945; member, interim government, 1946-47; India's ambassador to the USA, 1947-48; governor of Orissa, 1948-52; ambassador to Switzerland, 1952-53.

——— 80 ———

Jammu
9 April 1953

My dear Panditji,

Thank you very much for your two letters dated the 6th April.

In the middle of this month I am visiting Delhi with my mother, who requires some medical treatment there. I look forward to the pleasure of meeting and talking with you then.

The death of Mr Asaf Ali was indeed very sad. It must be very distressing to lose an old and valued colleague.

I was following with great interest news reports of your tour of the Indo-Burmese border with the Burmese Prime Minister.[1] Let us hope that circumstances will in due course lead to our relations with all countries being as cordial as those with Burma.

Recent international developments have again aroused the almost dead hope that differences between the two mighty blocs may after all be settled without resorting to war.[2] It seems to be the tragic paradox of our times that while I am sure an overwhelming majority of people all over the world greatly dislike and dread war, we seem to be inexorably drifting towards it as if impelled by some malignant fate. I sincerely hope that these recent developments will mark the first faint heralds of the dawn of international peace and goodwill. It is a great comfort to know that your tremendous influence will always be thrown in favour of peace.

With respectful regards,

Yours sincerely,
Karan Singh

---

1. U Nu originally Thakin Nu (1907-1995); leading member of Anti-Fascist Peoples' Freedom League; foreign minister of Burma under Ba Maw, 1943-45; president, Burmese Constituent Assembly, 1947; prime minister, July 1947-57, 1958 and 1960-62; overthrown and imprisoned following a coup by the military in 1962 but released in 1966.

2. In the international sphere several developments took place that changed the whole aspect of the existing situation. The initiative came from the Soviet Union and China. In March 1953, the Soviet Union agreed to open the Berlin canal, sought release of British civilians in North Korea and resumed armistice talks in Korea. Chou En-lai, on 30 March, requested the UN to break the Korean truce deadlock by making a neutral nation responsible for prisoners refusing repatriation. The US on 4 April 1953 described these developments as 'most dangerous' and a part of the design to stave off defeat in Korea and create differences between the US and its European allies.

——— 81 ———

New Delhi
19 April 1953

My dear Tiger,
I referred the question of your going abroad to our Law Ministry here. The Law Minister[1] has given me his opinion, which is to the effect that you can go abroad while still holding the office of Sadar-i-Riyasat. I am sending a copy of this opinion to Sheikh Abdullah and I enclose it for your information.[2]

This gets over any Constitutional difficulty. Nevertheless, it would be desirable for you to inform the President formally when you intend to go. I have already informed him of your intention to do so.

Yours sincerely,
Jawaharlal Nehru

——— 82 ———
Notes for Talks with Jawaharlal Nehru[3]

A)   Political

1. The situation continues to be far from happy. The agitation though it has been suppressed, is still simmering and resentment has sunk deep. There is tremendous bitterness and the gulf has widened.

2. A particularly unhappy feature is the shocking behaviour of the police, particularly the Punjab police. They have indulged in all sorts of excesses, rape, loot, arson etc.

3. My position has become particularly difficult. When I accepted as you know a large number of people were much hurt. Now, all

---

1. C.C. Biswas (1888-1960); barrister from Calcutta, member, Central Legislative Assembly, 1930-37; judge, Calcutta High Court, 1937-48; vice-chancellor, Calcutta University, 1949-50; member, Rajya Sabha, 1952-60; Union minister of state for external affairs, 1950-52; Union minister for law and minority affairs, 1952-57.

2. In his letter of 19 April to Nehru, C.C. Biswas opined that, 'I have examined the questions of the proposed visit of Sadar-i-Riyasat of Jammu and Kashmir to Europe for a period of about six weeks. I see no objection from a legal or constitutional point of view to Yuvaraj Karan Singh going abroad, while still holding his office of Sadar-i-Riyasat during this period....'

3. The talk was held in New Delhi on 21 April 1953. See the succeeding item.

turn to me and say that why as Sadar do you not do something to stop these barbarities? What is the use of your being Sadar? I am being blamed and my position has become very difficult.

4. I would therefore strongly urge you that you should do something very soon about these excesses. An enquiry into the firings and the other actions will have a good effect (previous practice).

5. As regards implementation, I fear that there is much difference between your interpretation and that of Sheikh. For example the Board of Judicial Advisers is desired to be kept on,[1] although it is completely superfluous with the Supreme Court. You must be firm and get them to implement correctly and without delay.

6. Regarding the movement, I would beg that this be disassociated from Indian politics. Whatever the position may or may not be here we are being ruined and we must not stand on dignity. Can no way be found for the agitation to be called off? I am sure with your statesmanship this should not be impossible.

B)   State Forces

1. You must have received the Government's letter and Bakshi talked to you. I would most strongly urge that the decision of merging the state forces with the Indian Army be implemented very soon and without screening. Talk on lines of the note.

2. Guards for self and Her Highness.

C)   Trip Abroad

1. Arrangements in my absence—no resignation but only someone to perform my duties.

2. Countries—England, France, Switzerland, Luxembourg, Italy, Egypt, Russia? Any other.

3. Exchange etc. have approached States Ministry.

4. Letter to Rashtrapati for leave—draft.

---

1. The Board of Judicial Advisers was constituted by Maharaja Hari Singh in 1939. It exercised appellate jurisdiction in the state cases in appeals on criminal and civil matters.

——— 83 ———

Record of Talks with Jawaharlal Nehru[1]

Met him twice, once in the morning at Parliament House and then at dinner.

Talked to him along the lines of my notes, except that I forgot the song.

He made the following points:

1. He said he had already written a strong letter to Bakshi about the police excesses. He seemed to quite agree that this was all wrong and I got the feeling that he would do something about it.

2. Regarding the political deadlock, it does not seem that he will do any thing at all about bringing about a settlement. He stressed that the whole international case rested upon Sheikh Abdullah. Then I asked him 'what happens after Sheikh Sahib is dead' that shook him. I said that if our relationship is based upon an individual he is not immortal and hence must one day die. Then what will happen. I said that, that was why we were so keen on other ties. He said as usual that constitutional ties were not all important, but he had no answer to my query.

3. I told him my fears about implementation, specially Board. He agreed, that was quite superfluous.

4. He also seemed to be sympathetic to the State Forces.

5. Regarding the guards and the plot, I talked to him but he remained silent.

6. He was interested in my foreign trip and suggested that I also go to Vienna. He said I should write and inform the Rashtrapati.

7. He said that the Jana Sangh movement had got no response in Delhi and was petering out. But he was silent when I told him of the depth of feelings in Jammu.

8. I also urged an enquiry, but he remained silent.

He did not flare up into this usual indignation, but I confess I failed to find any considerable keenness or sense of urgency in bringing this to a close. He seemed to be leaving all to Sheikh Abdullah.

---

1. New Delhi, 21 April 1953.

——— 84 ———

Camp Alhilal, Kangra
1 May 1953

My dear Panditji,

I came here with my mother on our return from Delhi and am spending a few days with her in Kangra. I shall return to Jammu within a few days and expect to go up to Srinagar on the 11th of May. We look forward to seeing you there[1] also before you go to England.[2]

I am enclosing a copy of a letter I have written to Rashtrapati Dr Rajendra Prasad in connection with my proposed trip abroad. Now that I am going, I feel that I might as well spent some time there and I, therefore, expect to be away for about three months. Naturally, if required I can always be back in Kashmir within a few days.

It was a great pleasure seeing you in Delhi. My mother joins me in sending you our very kind regards.

With respects,

Yours sincerely,
Karan Singh

——— 85 ———
Political Situation in Kashmir[3]

1. The political situation here in the Valley continues to be extremely fluid. The division within the party is causing considerable tension. The pro-Indian faction continues to be determined, and claims to be strong and to have a majority both in the Working Committee and in the Assembly. Frequent meetings of the Working Committee continue.

2. I was shocked and astounded to gather from a private meeting with Sheikh Abdullah last week that he seems to have decided to go back upon the solemn agreements which he has concluded

---

1. Nehru visited Srinagar from 23 to 25 May 1953.
2. Nehru visited England from 29 May to 16 June 1953.
3. Message to Jawaharlal Nehru, Srinagar, 10 June 1953. This message was sent through K.N. Katju, the Union home minister, who was on an official tour to Srinagar.

with India and upon his clear commitments.[1] This cannot be allowed, as it will make our position absolutely impossible and be a grave blow to our national interests and naturally to our international position also. I need not mention the grave and widespread repercussions that will result from such a development. The problem will claim your immediate attention upon your return for a final and decisive solution.

3. Uptil now there have been no serious developments here, though the possibility of such developments before your return cannot be ruled out. I have requested Dr Katju to arrange for the Government of India Intelligence Service here to keep in close touch with me, as that will greatly help me in correctly appraising this unstable and most unpredictable situation.

4. The minority community in the Valley, including even those who have been intimately connected with Sheikh Abdullah, is feeling most apprehensive and distressed at the way things are moving here, and there is great panic and despair among them.

5. Your talks[2] with Mr Mohammad Ali[3] have naturally aroused great interest and much speculation here.

6. In the Valley a new party called the Awami Conference[4] has been started by Khwaja Umar Butt, and its membership is reported to be in full swing. This party is reported to have sympathy for the Jammu movement.

Yours sincerely,
Karan Singh

---

1. He also expressed the same view in public meetings. For instance, on 12 April and 15 April 1953 at Jammu and on 18 April at Srinagar, Sheikh Abdullah hinted that he was being forced to reassess the Delhi Agreement due to the growing incidents of communal activities in Jammu and India. He openly criticized the central government for not being able to quell the spread of communal activities and insisted that the state had acceded on only three subjects and had complete autonomy in all other matters.

2. Nehru met Mohammad Ali the prime minister of Pakistan on 5 and 6 June 1953 in London during the Commonwealth Prime Ministers' Conference and discussed several outstanding Indo-Pakistan problems such as sharing of canal waters, evacuee property, East and West Bengal and Kashmir.

3. Mohammad Ali Bogra (1909-1963); member of the Muslim League in Bengal, 1937-47; ambassador of Pakistan to various countries, 1948-53; prime minister of Pakistan, 1953-55.

4. It did not have a large following and soon disappeared.

——— 86 ———

Srinagar
26 June 1953

My dear Panditji,
I am sending this letter by hand of a special messenger.

I intended to be in Delhi upon your arrival, but I felt that you will be overwhelmingly busy immediately upon your return.[1] I shall come to Delhi as soon as you wish me to be there.

I hope you received the message dated 10 June which I sent through Dr Katju. Since then the situation here has become still worse, and it is now very grave. There are clear indications that unless firm and speedy action is taken very soon, the situation may well become irretrievable.

The passing away of Dr Shyama Prasad Mookerjee[2] while under detention[3] here was very sad and unfortunate indeed. Apart from its grave political repercussions[4] it came as a great shock, particularly as we were completely unaware that he had not been keeping good health for some time. I was not informed of his illness or his removal to hospital, and, most amazing of all, I only learnt of his demise several hours after the body had been flown from Srinagar, and that too from unofficial sources. There is a widespread feeling and indeed there are strong reasons which indicate that in this whole unfortunate matter, the State Government, to say the least, acted in a most questionable and incompetent manner. I shall explain further when we meet.

———————————————

1. Nehru was on tour from 29 May to 25 June 1953 to London, Paris, Rome, Switzerland and Cairo. He returned to Bombay on 26 June.
2. Mookerjee was kept in detention in a house near the Nishat Bagh in Srinagar where he died on 23 June 1953.
3. Mookerjee and seven other people were arrested at Lakhanpur on 11 May 1953 under Section 3(i) of the Jammu and Kashmir Public Security Act. They had refused to comply with the warning not to remain in the state, where they had gone to support the Praja Parishad agitation.
4. On 27 June 1953, V.M. Trivedi, S.P. Mookerjee's counsel and Guru Dutt Vaid, a co-detenue alleged that proper medical care had not been provided to Mookerjee and this negligence of the state had hastened his death. The Jana Sangh called for a bandh on 15 July 1953 to be observed as Shyama Prasad Day and demanded a high level impartial enquiry into the circumstances leading to Mookerjee's death. This demand was supported by various other leaders such as Purushottamdas Tandon and Jayaprakash Narayan.

Regarding my proposed trip abroad, many friends feel and I am inclined to agree with them that under the present circumstances it would not be at all desirable for me to be away. I am therefore thinking of postponing my trip for the time being. If conditions permit, the Yuvarani and I might go on a holiday for a couple of months later on in the year. I have, however, not thought it desirable yet to give out here that I am postponing my trip. I will do finally in this matter as you advise.

I hope this finds you in very good health.

With deep regards and respects,

Yours very sincerely,
Karan Singh

——— 87 ———

New Delhi
29 June 1953

My dear Tiger,

I have just received your letter of the 26th June. I returned on the 27th afternoon as my plane was held up in Bombay because of bad weather in Delhi.

Since my return I have tried to gather as much information as I could about the position in Kashmir. Dr Mookerjee's death was indeed sad, more especially, because he was under detention.

The situation in Kashmir is a bad one and has to be taken in hand. But this requires a good deal of care. I have written a long letter to Sheikh Abdullah which is quite frank.[1] I have asked him to come here with some of his colleagues on or about the 3rd July.[2]

My talks with Mohammad Ali, Prime Minister of Pakistan, were

---

1. In his letter of 28 June 1953 Nehru wrote that, 'the question of Kashmir has had not only a logical appeal for me but also an emotional one.... Thus far I have proceeded on a basis of friendship and confidence in you and have been vain enough to expect the same approach from you. Whether that is justified now or not, it is for you to say. Individual relations should not count in national affairs and yet they do count and make a difference.' For full text of the letter see *Selected Works of Jawaharlal Nehru* (second series), Vol. 22, pp. 193–197.

2. Abdullah did not come to Delhi for the 3rd July meeting but sent Bakshi Ghulam Mohammad and Mirza Afzal Beg. He replied on 4 July that, 'I would have certainly come down myself to Delhi but Bakshi and Beg will explain to you why it is not desirable for me to leave Srinagar at present.'

very vague and general. I am likely to meet him about the end of July.

I think, you are right in postponing, for the present, your visit abroad.

Yours sincerely,
Jawaharlal Nehru

———— 88 ————

Srinagar
9 August 1953

My dear Panditji,

For several months the situation in the State has been dangerously confused, primarily as the result of a deep rift among the members of the Government. I have been watching the situation with growing concern and have been extremely distressed to see that instead of regaining harmony, the split within the Cabinet has continued to increase until it assumed critical proportions.[1]

Within the Cabinet three Ministers including the Deputy Prime Minister were strongly opposed to the policies and actions of Sheikh Abdullah and one of his colleagues—Mirza Afzal Beg. For some reason best known to himself, Sheikh Abdullah began to publicly repudiate the policies to which he, his colleagues and the whole National Conference Party were solemnly committed. This naturally caused a great deal of confusion and distress in the minds of the people.

Yesterday matters came to a head when three out of Sheikh Abdullah's four Cabinet colleagues sent him a memorandum[2] a copy

---

1. By the beginning of August 1953, the rift in Sheikh Abdullah's cabinet became more intense. In the cabinet meeting of 6 August, Sheikh Abdullah insisted that Sham Lal Saraf resign but he refused to oblige which precipitated the crisis.

2. In the memorandum of 7 August Bakshi Ghulam Mohammad, G.L. Dogra and Sham Lal Saraf charged Sheikh Abdullah with not only delaying the implementation of the Delhi Agreement but also denouncing it 'purposefully and openly'. They raised that, 'Mr Beg and you in utter disregard of opinions of your colleagues and without their consultation, make public pronouncements which flout the principles of joint responsibility… you have frequently adopted certain arbitrary measures in complete denial of the right of expression of opinion of even your own colleagues in the handling both of external and internal affairs of the State.' They also criticized his economic policies and his support to M.A. Beg who 'has persistently been following policies of narrow sectarianism and communalism which have seriously undermined the oneness of the State.' They added: 'that the Cabinet constituted as it is at present and lacking as it does the unity of purpose and action, has lost the confidence of the people in its ability to give them a clean, efficient and healthy administration.'

of which they sent to me, in which they openly denounced his policies and repudiated his leadership. They expressed that the policies which he was pursuing were proving disastrous to the country and that the Cabinet, lacking as it did unity of policy and action, had forfeited the confidence of the people. This represented a complete breakdown of the Cabinet system and the principle of joint responsibility which is so vital in a Parliamentary Democracy. I met Sheikh Abdullah but he could not satisfy me regarding bringing the situation to a stable and speedy solution.[1] Naturally, this state of affairs could not be allowed to continue as thereby the unity and stability of the State were gravely jeopardized. The continuance of such a Council of Ministers in office would have been a complete denial of constitutional and democratic principles. I had no alternative but to dissolve the Ministry forthwith. I am enclosing for your information a copy of the memorandum which Bakshi Ghulam Mohammad, Deputy Prime Minister, Pt. G.L. Dogra, Finance Minister and Pt. S.L. Saraf,[2] Health Minister, sent to Sheikh Abdullah and also a copy of my letter to Sheikh Abdullah[3] and the order regarding dismissal of his Cabinet.[4]

It was immediately necessary, however, that a new Government be formed so as to avoid a political and administrative vacuum. Taking cognizance of the prestige and regard enjoyed by Bakshi Ghulam Mohammad among the people of the State and his position as the Deputy Leader of the majority party in the Assembly, I called upon

1. On 8 August around noon Sheikh Abdullah met Karan Singh at the latter's residence. Karan Singh pointed out to him that 'it would be useful if he and his Cabinet colleagues were to come to my residence that evening so that the whole matter could be discussed in depth'. But Sheikh Abdullah sidetracked this suggestion by launching into an angry tirade against the Indian press.
2. (1904–1982); businessmen and politician from Kashmir; was associated with the National Conference for many years, member, State Assembly, Jammu and Kashmir, 1951-62; minister in the Jammu and Kashmir government, 1948-62; nominated to the Lok Sabha, 1962.
3. In his letter of 8 August 1953, Karan Singh conveyed to Sheikh Abdullah that the 'conflict within the Cabinet has for a considerable time been causing great confusion and apprehension in the minds of the people of the State. The situation has reached to an unprecedented crisis ... under these conditions I, as Head of the State, have been forced to the conclusion that the present Cabinet cannot continue in office any longer and hence I regret to inform you that I have dissolved the Council of Ministers headed by you.'
4. The order was issued on the same date.

him to aid and advice me in the task of forming a new Ministry. I enclose copies of letters that passed between us regarding the formation of the new Government and my order in this connection. The Council of Ministers was sworn in, as soon as possible, early this morning, as I desired to minimize the period in which the State was without a Government.[1] At present there is only one other Minister, Pt. Girdharilal Dogra, but the Cabinet will, of course, be expanded within a day or two.

The new Government will now tackle the grave issues that are before it. I am convinced that this step which we have been forced to take, grave as it is, is in the abiding interests of the people of the State. I sincerely hope that stability, unity and prosperity will soon return to our people.

As soon as conditions here permit, I propose to come over to Delhi to apprise you personally of the situation here.

With respectful regards,

Yours sincerely,
Yuvaraj,
Sadar-i-Riyasat

——— 89 ———

Srinagar
9 August 1953

My dear Panditji,
Herewith is a semi-formal letter containing all details and documents regarding the events that have taken place here. I have sent an identical letter to the President, Dr Rajendra Prasad. I am sending these letters by hand of a special messenger, my ADC, Captain Kohar Singh.

I tried to talk to you on the telephone several times during this morning but the telephone line was not at all clear and I could not

---

1. Bakshi Ghulam Mohammad became the prime minister of Jammu and Kashmir on 9 August 1953 after Sheikh Abdullah was removed by the Sadar-i-Riyasat on 8 August. His cabinet colleagues included, G.M. Sadiq, minister for education, health, publicity, information and jails; G.L. Dogra, finance minister; Shamlal Saraf, minister for development, industry and local self government; Mir Qasim, minister for agriculture, revenue, rural development and relief and rehabilitation.

get through. I was able, however, to say a few words to Shri Tyagi.

We are all actually aware of the gravity of the step that we have been forced to take and also of the extent of its possible repercussions, both within and without the State. In this whole matter I have attempted to act in a democratic and constitutional manner, keeping especially in mind what you said when we met last. On the whole I feel that we have done the best that was possible under the circumstances.

Regarding what was to be done with Sheikh Abdullah after his dismissal, this was, of course a decision for the new Government to take. On my part I strongly urged them to desist from arresting him soon after the dismissal, but they were most apprehensive that with his presence in the Valley at this juncture reactions would have been greatly intensified and there was a grave danger of the situation getting completely out of hand and even resulting in violence and bloodshed. Consequently, he has been arrested this morning at Gulmarg and is being taken to Udhampur where he will be lodged in the State Guest House. I have stressed that he and his family be accorded all courtesy and consideration.

Naturally, some rather severe reactions in the Valley are expected, but I trust that they will not be of such a nature as to get out of the hands of the Government. If unfortunately they do, then adequate arrangements have been made to restore law and order.

The last forty-eight hours have been a great strain, both mental and physical—and none of us have had a wink of sleep the whole of last night. I am keeping in close touch with the situation and will keep you informed of developments. I feel confident that with your blessings and guidance everything will turn out alright.

Conditions permitting I hope to be able to meet you in Delhi shortly.

With deepest regards,

Yours very sincerely,
Karan Singh

———— 90 ————

New Delhi
10 August 1953

My dear Tiger,

I have received tonight your letter of the 9th August together with the papers which accompanied it.

I quite realize the great strain which you must have undergone during these few days. I think, you have acted with wisdom and dignity.

I made a statement in Parliament[1] today which may have reached you already. I enclose a copy of it.

The recent developments in Kashmir have naturally far reaching consequences. The new Government has to deal with the local situation. It will receive such help as we can give. We shall try to encourage tourist traffic and the sale of Kashmir handicrafts. There are many other matters that we are enquiring into so that some economic help might reach the people of Kashmir.

It is obvious that a new chapter of problems has opened out before us. It would be foolish to imagine that we are out of the wood. Reactions in Pakistan have been strong,[2] as was to be expected. I

---

1. In his statement in the Lok Sabha, Nehru said that, 'certain events have occurred in the State of Jammu and Kashmir with dramatic suddenness during the last two days' which created a serious situation and 'there was progressive tendency towards disruption.' He added: 'The Government of India were naturally gravely concerned at these developments, but they did not wish to interfere except with advice, in the internal structure and administration of the State. Advice was frequently given, but unfortunately it did not succeed in bringing about that unity which had been shaken in course of the past few months.' For Nehru's full speech see *Selected Works of Jawaharlal Nehru* (second series) Vol. 23, pp. 312-16.

2. The dismissal of Sheikh Abdullah and installation of Bakshi Ghulam Mohammad as the prime minister evoked a hysterical reaction in Pakistan. Its press and radio termed it a 'pro-Indian' coup. The *Dawn* described it as 'a challenge to Pakistan' and stated on 10 August that Nehru had shown that anyone who questioned the finality of Kashmir's accession to India was criminal. Similarly, the *Pakistan Times* said that 'any attempt at the consolidation of India's over lordship in Kashmir must gravely prejudice the case for a free and unfettered plebiscite in the State.' The radio, specially the 'Azad Kashmir Radio' also broadcasted extremely provocative anti-India programmes aimed at exploiting religious fanaticism and inciting the people of the Valley to revolt against the new government. Besides, several leaders of Pakistan spoke of the grave consequences of Sheikh Abdullah's dismissal.

have just learnt that the Pakistan Cabinet met this morning and decided to ask their Prime Minister to ask for an immediate meeting with me to discuss the Kashmir question. I have not received a formal request to this effect yet. Probably, it will reach me by tomorrow morning. We shall consider it then and decide what we should do about it. As far as I can see, we can hardly refuse such a meeting and I shall have to give him some time in the near future to come to Delhi.

My general line with him, if he comes here, will naturally be that this is an internal matter for Kashmir and has nothing to do with any major questions which have been discussed or might be discussed between India and Pakistan. It is true, however, that it has an intimate bearing on those questions.

I shall keep you and Bakshi Ghulam Mohammad informed.

With all good wishes,

Yours ever,
Jawaharlal Nehru

––––––– 91 –––––––

Srinagar
16 August 1953

My dear Panditji,
Thank you very much for your letter dated the 10th August and the kind sentiments expressed therein. Your assurance of full help to the new Government here gives added strength and courage to tackle the grave tasks that lie before the country. Indeed such help is invaluable.

Yesterday two more Ministers, Shri Sham Lal Saraf and Khwaja Mir Kasim, were sworn in by me thereby raising the Cabinet strength to four. It will probably be further expanded in due course. I gather that a crystallization of Maulana Masoodi's[1] attitude is being awaited,

––––––––––––––––––––

1. Maulana Mohammad Saeed Masoodi (1905–1999); joined the Muslim Conference of Jammu and Kashmir 1932, moved resolutions for committing the Muslim Conference into the All Jammu and Kashmir National Conference, 1938; general secretary, National Conference, 1939-49; taught Arabic at Prince of Wales College, Jammu, 1928-32; took active part in the freedom struggle in the Kashmir state and was imprisoned, 1932-34, 1938, 1942 and 1946; member, Constituent Assembly and Provisional Parliament, 1945-51, Lok Sabha, 1952-57.

as if it turns out favourable he will probably be welcomed into the Cabinet. Two Deputy Ministers, D. P. Dhar and Ghulam Rasool Renzu[1] were also sworn in yesterday by the Prime Minister.

Independence Day passed off peacefully. In the morning after the swearing in ceremonies, at which senior Government officials and Members of the High Court were present, I hoisted the National Flag over my residence. In the city several pro-Government processions were taken out which were addressed by Bakshi Sahib and Sadiq. I broadcast a short message[2] of greetings to the people, a copy of which I enclose. Last Friday, upon which some trouble was apprehended, also passed off peacefully. Strong internal security measures had been taken.

Since the dramatic events of a week ago there has been trouble at various places in the Valley, reports of which must have been reaching you regularly. In self-defence police had to open fire in some places, on violent and incited crowds, resulting most unfortunately in some deaths.[3] At the time of writing, however, the situation is showing growing signs of improvement and consolidation. Already pro-Government political activity has begun, which will gather momentum when the recently introduced economic and administrative benefits begin to reach the masses. However, we cannot at all afford to be complacent and the utmost vigilance must be maintained. It is very necessary that the present strict internal security arrangements be continued. Recalcitrant and disruptive elements here were taken completely by surprise by the sudden turn of events and are now gathering their wits. They will very likely do all they can to sabotage and wreck the new regime, and it is even possible that they might try and resort to individual violence. It is feared that some disloyal

---

1. He also served for some time as the speaker of the Jammu and Kashmir Legislative Assembly.
2. On the 6th anniversary of India's independence, Karan Singh as the Sadar-i-Riyasat in a broadcast, sent greetings and good wishes to the people. He also said: 'We are particularly in this State at a very crucial period of our history. The forces of disruption and disintegration have to be fought by every man, woman and child, if we are to progress towards peace and prosperity hand in hand with our countrymen in rest of the nation. We must face the crisis before us with calm confidence and courage and not allow ourselves to get carried away by false slogans and rumours put out by those who would distrust our unity and indeed see an end to our peaceful and honourable existence.'
3. About forty-six persons were killed and 148 injured in police firing at various places.

elements within the administrative machinery itself may try and create trouble and difficulties. A very encouraging feature, however, is that a large number of the National Conference workers have rallied round Bakshi Sahib and are actively working to support and strengthen the new administration. The majority of Government officials also seem to have adjusted themselves to the change. There was a move on the part of hostile elements to try and get all Muslim officials to resign, but that seems to have fallen through. There have been a few odd resignations but the administrative machinery has not been seriously affected.

It is possible that pro-Pakistan elements may try and stage something on Eid next Friday. All precautions, however, will be taken. Bakshi Sahib is confident, and I share his view, that unless unforeseen factors intervene normalcy will soon be restored, and a speedy and effective implementation of the new economic and administrative policies will create real enthusiasm in the Valley for the new regime. This implementation has important financial as well as administrative implications, in both of which I am sure the Government of India will help us to its fullest.

As I see it, in addition to the primary function of maintaining law and order, the new regime has four main tasks before it. The first and foremost is to bring swift and substantial economic relief to the hard pressed people of the State, particularly of the Valley. The second, closely linked with this, is to give the people an honest and efficient administration and remove the gross misuses of power and authority which hitherto existed. In this matter, especially appropriate guidance and discreet help from the Central Government is an urgent necessity. Thirdly, the new regime must be able to gain the confidence and active co-operation of the people of Jammu and Ladakh whom the previous regime had succeeded in completely and thoroughly alienating. Unless the component parts of the State, particularly Jammu and Kashmir, work together in close harmony and cooperation the State can never forge ahead towards stability and prosperity. Finally, at the earliest opportunity, the Government has to go ahead with cementing the State's relationship with the mother country by implementing the Delhi Agreement. Bakshi and his colleagues are well aware of these grave tasks and I am glad to say that they have got down to them in right earnest, although naturally they are having to work under disabilities generated by their predecessors.

Pakistan seemed to completely lose its nerve over events here, and they exposed themselves badly by their hysterical speeches and statements.[1] Subsequently, it seems, better sense prevailed and it looks as if they have climbed down. After all, there have been to date four changes in the 'Azad' Kashmir Government[2] each accompanied by upheaval and bloodshed, yet India never as much as mentioned them. I am sure that Mohammad Ali's meeting with you will make him and his colleagues realize the futility of getting desperate and trying to coerce India into abandoning Kashmir.

With kindest regards and respects,

Yours very sincerely,
Karan Singh

---

1. Several prominent people including ministers and governors made very strong speeches at public meetings, and slogans were raised demanding 'Kashmir at all costs'. Shuaib Qureshi, the minister for Kashmir affairs, in Pakistan, in a speech at Rawalpindi on 11 August, assured all possible assistance to the people of Kashmir to ensure an unfettered expression of their will in the matter of the state's accession. On 14 August at a public meeting at Dhaka, Khaliq-uz-Zaman, the governor of East Bengal, exhorted the people to 'keep their swords shining and horses ready' to meet any future calamity. In a radio broadcast on 16 August he said that the objective of carving out an independent country in order to serve Islam had bestirred the Muslims in undivided India and claimed that Pakistan had become 'light house in the ocean of Muslim world affairs defying…the canons of "secularism, tribalism and provincialism".' Feroze Khan Noon, the chief minister of West Punjab, said on 16 August at a public meeting in Lahore: 'The peace loving Indian dove…has again taken to bayonets in mowing down an innocent and peace loving people.' Similarly, at a public meeting in Karachi on 16 August which was also addressed by Abdul Qayum Khan, the minister for food and industries, a resolution was passed calling upon the people of Pakistan to 'join their Kashmiri brethren in their righteous cause and fight for freedom.'
2. The first government of Azad Kashmir was formed on 3 October 1947 headed by Ghulam Nabi Gilkar. On 24 October 1947 he was removed and arrested and Sardar Mohammad Ibrahim formed a new government. On 2 March 1949 Ibrahim had to resign due to differences in the Muslim Conference. Within a few days he was re-appointed. Again on 13 May 1950, Ibrahim was dropped and Syed Ali Ahmad Shah was appointed president. But the Muslim Conference asked him to resign just after three days. After chaos and confusion for several months on 2 December 1951, Mirwaiz Yusuf Shah was appointed administrator for three months. On 18 May 1952, the Muslim Conference nominated Raja Mohammad Hyder Khan as president of the government. But the government of Pakistan refused to accept this nomination and on 21 June 1952, they nominated a new government headed by Colonel Sher Ahmad Khan.

——————— 92 ———————

Srinagar
19 August 1953

My dear Panditji,
Shri A.P. Jain[1] and D.P. Dhar are proceeding to Delhi in order to personally explain to you the circumstances and the situation here. I am taking this opportunity to convey to you a few salient points for your consideration.

Since the changes here last week the political situation has begun to show definite signs of improvement. Public opinion is steadily veering round towards an understanding of the purpose and policies which animate the activities of the new regime. Several ameliorative measures here already been proclaimed which have favourably impressed public opinion. A considerable number of National Conference workers have been impressed by this courageous and dynamic stand and actively support and help the present administration.

Bakshi Sahib in particular, and his colleagues, have been carrying a great burden and working under conditions of great physical and mental strain. I am sure you will appreciate that at this critical juncture we must do all we can to strengthen their hands and support them. In this connection the assurances contained in your letters gave great encouragement to all of us to work courageously and steadfastly for the welfare of the people.

While the Government was engaged in restoring peace and normalcy in the State and rallying the people round it we were extremely perturbed to hear what Shri Jain and Vishnu Sahay[2] told us

---

1. Ajit Prasad Jain (1902-1977); member, UP Legislative Assembly, 1937-39 and 1946-47; parliamentary secretary to Rafi Ahmad Kidwai, 1937-39; member, Constituent Assembly, 1946-50; member, Provisional Parliament and Lok Sabha, 1952-65. Union minister for relief and rehabilitations, 1950-54. Union minister for food and agriculture, 1954-59; president, UPPCC, 1961-64; governor, Kerala, 1965-66; member, Rajya Sabha, 1968-72; publications include *UP Agrarian Law* and *Rafi Ahmad Kidwai: Memoirs of His Life and Times.*
2. (1901-1989); joined ICS, 1925; held various posts in UP upto 1941 and thereafter in the central government; secretary, ministry of food, 1947-48; Kashmir affairs, February 1949-March 1951; ministry of food and agriculture, 1951-52, Kashmir affairs and labour, 1953-57, and of the cabinet, 1958-62; governor of Assam, 1962-67.

regarding your talks with Mr Mohammad Ali.[1] They informed us of the various features of the intended agreement between India and Pakistan over Kashmir, including the fixing of a date for the induction of the plebiscite administrator. This came as a great shock to all, and Bakshi Sahib and his colleagues were stunned and bewildered. They are particularly upset that a decision so vital to the very existence of the people of the State is being taken without ascertaining the viewpoint of those who at this critical juncture accepted the responsibility of Government. We all feel that before coming to any decision on this momentous matter vitally affecting our country, our views must in all fairness be taken into account.

The details of the proposed agreement came to Bakshi Sahib particularly as a grave blow. He has been under great strain and to him this represented a complete reversal of the ideals, and position which, at considerable personal risk and sacrifice, he had fought for all these years. He was very agitated and expressed to me in writing his inability to carry on the Government in these circumstances as he feels that his position among the people will become completely untenable. Thus, it seems as if I will be faced with the unenviable task of having to find a third Prime Minister within a fortnight.

We all firmly hope and believe that the final agreement will not be adverse to our interests and that the interests of the people of the State, which you have all along defended, will not be sacrificed at the alter of Pakistani communal claims. Firmness alone can save the people of Kashmir from falling a prey to the frenzied and communal propaganda which will be unleashed upon them as soon as a date for the plebiscite administrator is announced. As soon as this happens hostile elements will come into open defiance and the administration is likely to collapse and the law and order position become seriously

---

1. Nehru had a two-hour talk with Mohammad Ali, the prime minister of Pakistan, on 17 August 1953 in Delhi on various issues arising from the dismissal of Sheikh Abdullah. In fact, the Pakistan government had reacted strongly over Sheikh Abdullah's dismissal and Mohammad Ali had sent a message to Nehru suggesting an immediate meeting and despite the latter's marked lack of enthusiasm, he finally agreed to bring forward the talks. Mohammad Ali arrived in Delhi on 16 August for talks which concluded on 20 August with a joint communiqué. For full text of the talks, see *Selected Works of Jawaharlal Nehru* (second series), Vol. 23, pp. 331–36.

jeopardised. To maintain the peace and safeguard the minorities it may be necessary to resort to much more severe measures than have yet been used.

In view of these factors and others that will be explained to you personally by D. P. Dhar, I would most strongly urge that the decision may in some manner be kept pending so that all its aspects concerning the situation within the State may be carefully and thoroughly examined. I would also urge that the announcement from Delhi regarding the talks be one that will strengthen and stabilize the secular and progressive forces here. I am sure you will stand by Bakshi and his colleagues who have at this critical juncture accepted the responsibility of running the Government and have never wavered in their convictions or in their faith in you.

With kindest regards,

Yours sincerely,
Karan Singh

———— 93 ————

New Delhi
21 August 1953

My dear Tiger,
Thank you for your letter of August 19th.

D. P. Dhar has been here and has discussed these matters with us fully. He has gone back and will, no doubt, explain the position to you and to Bakshi and others.

We are all fully aware of the great burden that Bakshi Ghulam Mohammad is carrying and we are anxious to help him. But it is no help to him if we do something which turns out to his great disadvantage. While it is perfectly true that Bakshi and others in Srinagar are in a better position to judge of the situation there, there is always the danger of a limited and rather narrow viewpoint being taken and of other major facts being ignored. It is this balanced picture that is necessary; otherwise we shall get into hopeless trouble later.

The immediate objective is some toning down and a quieter atmosphere. Recent events in Kashmir have had a very powerful reaction in other countries.[1] This is against us completely. I am not referring to Pakistan which has grown madly hysterical. If this hysteria continued, it would inevitably produce reactions in Kashmir among the pro-Pakistan elements and their sympathizers. The result would be no period of quiet at all and constant trouble.

But for some kind of an agreement between us and Pakistan, the matter would inevitably have been raised in the UN immediately and they might well have sent down their representative to Kashmir. All this again would have kept the agitation alive and made it grow.

The matter is much too serious to be looked upon from a local or a merely law and order point of view. It is all these considerations that made us agree to the statement that has been issued.[2] I think that, in the circumstances, this is a good statement and helps us in trying to get a quieter atmosphere[1].

I hope Bakshi will come here as soon as he can do so.

Yours ever,
Jawaharlal Nehru

---

1. In several countries, newspapers highlighted this issue in a sarcastic manner. The *Daily Telegraph* expressed on 11 August 1953 that the developments in Kashmir had undone all the good wishes which might have been done by the Karachi talks; the *New York Times* stated on 14 August that no equitable solution of the Kashmir problem was possible without a free plebiscite; the *Daily Mirror* described Nehru's attitude as 'that of an imperialistic conqueror not subject to the UN'; the *Bakhtar-e-Imrooz* (Iran) of 13 August questioned the justification of Sheikh Abdullah's imprisonment; the British edited *Egyptian Gazette* (Cairo) commented on 16 August: 'Nehru is proclaimed as a champion of democracy, but… he has a special brand reserved for Kashmir…labelled "incorporation in India",' and suggested that an early and properly supervised plebiscite should form the basis of conversation between Nehru and Mohammad Ali.
2. The statement was issued by Jawaharlal Nehru and Mohammad Ali on 20 August 1953 in New Delhi. It stated: 'Both the Prime Ministers were actuated by a firm resolve to settle these problems as early as possible peacefully and cooperatively to the mutual advantage of both countries. The Kashmir dispute was especially discussed at some length. It was their firm opinion that this should be settled in accordance with the wishes of the people of that State, with a view to promoting their well-being and causing the least disturbance to the life of the people of the State. The most feasible method of ascertaining the wishes of the people was by a fair and impartial plebiscite…it was decided that the Plebiscite Administrator should be appointed by the end of April 1954.'
3. The statement evoked a sharp reaction from Bakshi who sent his resignation on the evening of 20 August. Karan Singh wrote in his autobiography that after knowing this 'Nehru lost his temper and spoke angrily of this "ridiculous nonsense". I handed the phone to Ajit Prasad who listened for a while until Jawaharlal banged down the phone.' Eventually, Karan Singh and A.P. Jain, the Union rehabilitation minister whom Nehru had sent to discuss matters with Bakshi, persuaded Bakshi to withdraw his resignation.

——— 94 ———

Srinagar
25 August 1953

My dear Panditji,

Many thanks for your letter dated August 21st. You must have received my earlier letter dated August 16th which I sent by hand of Shri Vishnu Sahay.

D. P. Dhar explained the whole position to us on his return from Delhi, and we have also studied the joint statement which you and Mr Mohammad Ali issued at the conclusion of your talks. The position you have adopted and the reasons for it are now very clear and, as you must have seen, Bakshi has issued a statement[1] giving the joint communiqué his complete and unqualified support. We never had any doubt that whatever you did would be in the highest interests of the people of the State and, in the broader context, of the people of the whole nation. Unfortunately, there seems to have been some initial misunderstanding as a result of incomplete information, which caused some flutter here.

On the whole the repercussions of the agreement here do not seem to be unsatisfactory. It is not yet possible to say whether Pakistan and 'Azad' Kashmir will now desist from their vicious and disruptive radio and press campaign against the new regime. Pro-Pakistan elements here, however, seem to have mixed reactions. Many are dejected as they were expecting an immediate settlement. Others say that now that a date for the appointment and induction into office of the Plebiscite Administrator has been fixed it is only a matter of time before the plebiscite is held and the State goes to Pakistan.

Bakshi and his co-workers, as is evident from their statements, are satisfied with the communiqué as it gives them some time to consolidate their position and also clearly recognizes the legal and constitutional position of the Jammu and Kashmir Government. Also, of course, such basic preliminary problems as demilitarization, the quantum and character of the 'Azad' Kashmir forces, the position of the 'Azad' Kashmir Government, refugees, regions and so on will have to be settled before the Plebiscite Administrator can be appointed, and we are confident that in these vital matters India will not

---

1. On 21 August 1953, Bakshi stated that the communiqué was finalized 'with our concurrence and has our unqualified support'.

compromise upon the principles she has firmly held for the last six years.

Eid day passed off peacefully in the Valley, and after the first few days there have been no more serious breaches of the peace and clashes with the police or militia. Of course, the new regime is facing an uphill task but it has got down to work and is actively engaged in translating its new policies into action. I must admit, however, that I am not very satisfied with the present administrative mechanism which the new regime has inherited from its predecessor. In addition to its not being up to the mark in efficiency it is also full of men whose loyalty to Bakshi is far from assured. And now the time factor has assumed great importance as we have only about three months in which to bring concrete benefits to the people before winter sets in and the Valley is cut off from the outside world. Hence the urgency and necessity of Bakshi tightening up and vitalizing the administration cannot be over-stressed, and in this task help and guidance from the Central Government will be invaluable.

Bakshi has gone to Jammu where he received a great ovation from the people, who have a fund of goodwill for him. I feel that at this stage a goodwill gesture to the people of Ladakh, who are bitter and resentful as a result of the treatment they received from the previous regime, will be of considerable value. I have discussed with Bakshi the idea of taking a Ladakhi as Deputy Minister for Ladakh Affairs, a gesture which will not only be much appreciated by the Ladakhis but will also make the task of the administration vis-a-vis Ladakh much easier and smoother.

Before I end, I might mention another factor which deserves notice. This is that in the new set up there is a large and influential group of men whose views are reputed to lean towards the extreme left. Their support in the present context is of great value, but it is possible that problems may crop up later which we will have to face.

I understand that Bakshi has proceeded to Delhi from Jammu. I propose to visit Delhi for a few days along with my wife in the first week of September. She requires some medical treatment and there are so many aspects of the situation here upon which I would like to seek your guidance and advice.

I hope this finds you very well.

With respects and regards,

Yours sincerely,
Karan Singh

Top Secret

14.9.53

My dear Tiger,

I spoke to you about a letter which I sent to some Princes. As this might interest you, I am sending you a copy.

I am also sending you extracts from the London *Daily Telegraph* ~~Times~~ editorial on Kashmir.

Ever yours

Jawaharlal Nehru

Facsimile of a letter from Jawaharlal Nehru to Karan Singh dated
14 September 1953

——— 95 ———

New Delhi
14 September 1953

My dear Tiger,
I spoke to you about a letter which I sent to some Princes.[1] As this might interest you, I am sending you a copy.

I am also sending you extracts from the London *Daily Telegraph* editorial on Kashmir.

Yours as ever,
Jawaharlal Nehru

——— 96 ———

New Delhi
17 September 1953

My dear Panditji,
Thank you very much for your letter enclosing a copy of the letter you have sent to some Princes and also an extract from the London *Daily Telegraph*, both of which I read with great interest.

I am returning to Kashmir by air on the morning of Saturday the 19th. Today I expect you will be very busy the whole day with the foreign affairs debate in the House of the People,[2] of which I shall be an interested spectator. It will be very kind if you would give me a few minutes any time tomorrow, as there are one or two matters I would like to mention to you before I go.

With respects,

Yours very sincerely,
Karan Singh

———————

1. Nehru had written a letter on 10 September 1953 to 102 princes who received a privy purse of rupees one lakh and above. This was not sent to Karan Singh who was Sadar-i-Riyasat of Jammu and Kashmir. Nehru had drawn attention of the princes towards the social and economic changes that had taken place in the country and appealed to them to reduce voluntarily a portion of their privy purses. Most of the replies by the princes were in the nature of provisional replies, stating that this matter was being considered more fully.
2. On 17 September, a debate on the international situation and India's foreign policy took place. For Nehru's reply to various questions see *Selected Works of Jawaharlal Nehru* (second series) Vol. 23, pp. 407-421.

——— 97 ———

Srinagar
4 October 1953

My dear Panditji,

This is in connection with the Convocation of our University which is due to be held around the middle of this month. You may remember that I spoke to you about this when I was in Delhi last month, and you said that Dr Zakir Hussain[1] would be a very suitable person to address the Convocation. We wrote to him, but unfortunately he is suffering from a heart ailment and regretted his inability to come up. Then we contacted Rajkumari Amrit Kaur[2] but she was booked and could not come. After that we got in touch with the Chief Justice of India[3] but he too said that he was very busy and could not come. So in despair I am now writing to you to very kindly suggest somebody to come up here. I had asked Rafi Sahib[4] to come and address us. He said he would come up but would not like to address the Convocation. I wonder if he could be persuaded to change his mind. If not would Dr Katju or Shri Chintamani Deshmukh[5] be free to come and address us?

The tentative date of the Convocation is the 17th of this month

---

1. (1897-1969); vice-chancellor, Jamia Millia Islamia, Delhi, 1925-48; associated with basic education, 1938-48; vice-chancellor, Aligarh Muslim University, 1948-56; governor of Bihar, 1957-62; vice-president of India, 1962-67; president of India, 1967-69.
2. (1889-1964); secretary to Mahatama Gandhi for a number of years; Union minister for health, 1947-57; member, Rajya Sabha, 1957-64.
3. M. Patanjali Shastri.
4. Rafi Ahmad Kidwai (1894-1954); eminent Congressman from Barabanki and a close associate of Nehru; imprisoned several times during the freedom movement, chief whip of the Swaraj Party in the Central Legislative Assembly after 1926 elections; worked among the farmers of Oudh and organized a no-rent campaign in 1931-32; president, UP Provincial Congress Committee, 1935; minister in UP, 1937-39 and 1946-47 and held the portfolio of revenue, home and jails intermittently; Union minister for communications, 1947-51 and for food and agriculture, 1952-54.
5. Chintamani Dwarkanath Deshmukh (1896-1982); joined the ICS in 1918; governor of Reserve Bank of India, 1943-49; president, Indian Statistical Institute, Calcutta, 1945-64; member, Planning Commission, 1950; Union minister for finance, 1950-56; chairman, University Grants Commission, 1956-60; vice-chancellor, University of Delhi, 1962-67.

but it can be modified to suit the convenience of whoever comes to address us.[1] However, we would like to have it before the 20th because the Assembly members will all be here till then and secondly, being an outdoor function it will get very cold later on.

I am sorry to bother you about this, but we all thought that you could guide us best.

Yours very sincerely,
Karan Singh

———— 98 ————

Srinagar
5 October 1953

My dear Panditji,
I have just despatched to you a copy of my fortnightly letter to the President in which I have dealt at some length with the political developments here during last month.[2] These have been very satisfactory and, though there are many knotty and delicate problems ahead, the prospect looks much brighter. Bakshi and his colleagues certainly deserve credit for the energy and ability with which they are tackling the problems before them. Frankly, their achievements within less than two months have exceeded my expectations.

There are, however, certain aspects of the situation here which deserve very close consideration. Sukthankar[3] was here the other

---

1. Finally, the convocation was not held.
2. In his letter of 3 October 1953 to Rajendra Prasad, Karan Singh wrote:'The month under review witnessed far-reaching political and economic developments. In the first week of the month there were some violent demonstrations in Srinagar and Shopian which had to be dispersed by the police. Apparently these demonstrations marked the end of the first phase of violent opposition to the new regime which had been incited by communal and disruptive forces.' He further wrote that the National Conference had organized a big convention in the middle of September in Srinagar which 'included a large majority of members of the Assembly as well as the General Council of the National Conference, who pledged their support to the new regime.' He also pointed out that the 'economic reforms which have been announced recently have now begun to be put into operation. The mass reaction to them has been, as expected, very favourable. Particularly, the bold and progressive step of abolishing the *Mujawaza* (compulsory procurement) system has an electrifying effect upon the agricultural population in the Valley.'
3. Y.N. Sukthankar, cabinet secretary.

day and I had a long talk with him about them. I expect he will convey to you the points that we discussed.

The administrative side has still to be improved. Some administrative reorganization and reshuffling is being planned, but the great problem is the lack of efficient, reliable and honest personnel. I have been trying to persuade Bakshi to get at least half a dozen first rate officers on loan from the Government of India, if necessary by sending some of our officers out to India for training and getting others in return. Only then will our administration have a chance of getting up to the required standard. Particularly, for some key posts such as Chief Secretary, I.G.P., Director of Education etc., I feel it would be most desirable to get good officers from India. Unfortunately, Bakshi is rather obsessed with idea that importing officers will cause heart burning among the local officials. Although there may be something in this contention, in my view the imperative necessity of having an efficient and honest administration far outweighs any such considerations.

I might add here that I feel an experienced political officer for Ladakh, who would be able to advice the local authorities as well as keep the Central Government fully informed of the problems and trends of that strategic area, is a crying necessity. The State Government has neither the personnel nor the resources to adequately deal with the problems and needs of this backward and undeveloped area. And as Ladakh is of such great strategic and political importance to the whole nation I feel that the Central Government should seriously consider taking a more direct hand in its administration.

As it is, the Head Lama of Ladakh[1] was here recently and has returned to Leh very happy and satisfied. Some Praja Parishad leaders were also here recently and met Bakshi and D.P.[2] Although the alleged communist factor may cause friction, I do hope that we shall now see a new chapter of active and constructive cooperation between the various sections and parties in the State so that we can face united the common problems that confront us.

In passing I may mention that a rather distressing feature of the communal activities that are still being carried on in the Valley is

---

1. Kushak Bakula, deputy minister, frontier affairs at this time.
2. D.P. Dhar, deputy home minister.

that the fact that Sheikh Abdullah's family; his Begum,[1] his two daughters[2] and his eldest son Farooq[3] are playing a prominent role in these openly pro-Pakistan activities. Up till now the Government has done its best to avoid having to arrest any of them, but if they continue to act in this way the hands of the Government might be forced and they may all have to be sent to join Sheikh Abdullah at Udhampur.[4]

Before I end this letter there is a personal matter upon which I would like to seek your advice. As you know I have a large palace here in Srinagar called Gulab Mahal, which is at present lying unused. It is a very valuable and beautifully located property, but as I am not using it I feel it would be a good thing if it could be put to some national use. Considering that the Government of India have so many responsibilities to discharge in the State I feel that this property might be of real utility to the Central Government for use as a National Laboratory, a first rate Government-run hotel, Government of India offices or some such purpose. If so I would be very happy to place the use of this property at the disposal of the Government of India.

I have also for some time been considering donating it to the University of Jammu and Kashmir, but have not done so yet for several reasons. Firstly, the University has already had laid the foundation stone of a building of its own, although not another brick has been added since Dr Radhakrishnan[5] laid the stone last year. Secondly, it would cost the University a very considerable sum of money to put in

1. Akbar Jahan (1917–2000); chairman, state level committee, International Year for Women, 1975; vice-chairman State Social Welfare Board, 1975; president, All India Women's Conference, state branch, 1977; member, Lok Sabha, 1977-79 and 1984-89.
2. Khalida and Suraiya.
3. Farooq Abdullah (b.1937); MBBS from S.M.S. Medical College Jaipur; member, Lok Sabha; 1979-82; member, Jammu and Kashmir Legislative Council, 1982-83; member, Jammu and Kashmir Legislative Assembly, 1983-87, 1987-90 and 1996-2002; chief minister, Jammu and Kashmir, September 1982-June 1984; 1986-90 and 1996-2002; elected to Rajya Sabha, November 2002.
4. Sheikh Abdullah was kept in the Tara Niwas guest house in Udhampur.
5. Sarvepalli Radhakrishnan (1888-1975); eminent educationist and statesman; professor of Philosophy, Calcutta University, 1921-41 and of Eastern Religions, Oxford, 1936-52; vice-chancellor, Banaras Hindu University, 1939-48; ambassador to Soviet Union, 1949-52; vice-president of India, 1952-62 and president, 1962-67, works include *Indian Philosophy* (2 vols. 1923 and 1927), *East and West in Religion* (1933) and *Religion and Society* (1944).

order and equip Gulab Mahal, and also to maintain it. And money is the one thing that our University lacks in the first place. Finally, I was a little hesitant because Gulab Mahal lies right in the middle of my private residential property, and a university being an expanding institution it is likely to lead to some friction and unpleasantness in the future to both the donor and the donee, which would be most unfortunate. Your advice in this matter would be of great value.

I was very happy to have met you in Delhi and to have been able to discuss affairs here. I also greatly enjoyed seeing the wonderful cricket match.

I am sure this will find you very well,

With respects and deep regards,

Yours sincerely,
Karan Singh

---------- 99 ----------

New Delhi
30 October 1953

My dear Tiger,

I am sorry for not having written to you for so long and not acknowledged your letter of the 5th October. I have been rather overwhelmed with work.

We are closely following events in the Jammu and Kashmir State and are naturally gratified at the great improvement in the general situation and, more especially, the economic position.[1] We are trying to help to the best of our ability, but we must not delude ourselves into thinking that the basic political problem is much easier of solution

---

1. The Bakshi government had announced certain ameliorative measures: (i) The compulsory procurement of rice was given up and large quantities were brought from India to meet the food problem, (ii) custom duty on salt and medicines manufactured in India was lifted, (iii) education was made free, (iv) the Wazir Committee report on economic reforms which Sheikh Abdullah had pigeonholed was published and steps were taken to implement some of its recommendations. The businessmen had been assured that their capital was sacrosanct, and that the custom duty and other trade restrictions would be removed, (v) the construction of a 1.5 mile long tunnel at an altitude of 7,200 feet under the Banihal Pass started to provide a crucial road communication between Jammu and Srinagar throughout the year.

now. I am not referring to Pakistan or the UN but rather to the minds of men and women in Kashmir. I have no doubt at all that ultimately it is those people who will decide. If we win them over, well and good. Otherwise, well, we just do not succeed.

Therefore, we can never forget the political approach. Bakshi and some of his colleagues are making that political approach, in the rural areas especially, and that is good. Still we have to look ahead and not take any step now which may come in the way of a future step.

You refer to making the administration more efficient and honest. I agree and, to the extent possible, we shall help, of course. There is, however, something in what Bakshi feels. If we put Indian officers in important positions, this may be utilized by our opponents against us. We have, thus, to strike some balance between the two. But, about the necessity for an honest and efficient administration, I have not the shadow of a doubt.

In regard to Ladakh, I think, it will be a good thing for a competent officer from the Centre to be there, though, perhaps, he should go there in the capacity of an adviser rather than as the political officer in charge.

You refer to Gulab Mahal. I think, it is a great pity that this huge house should not be utilized. How it can be utilized, is not clear to me. The various suggestions that you put forward, or some of them, do not seem feasible. We cannot have a Government of India office in Srinagar, at least a major one. It is difficult enough to take them out of Delhi to a nearby place, as they have to remain in constant touch with the Capital. Nor can we have a National Laboratory there. We are not having any National Laboratories in the near future.

It might be worth considering how far it could be made into a State hotel. I think, this certainly is a proposal which might work out. It will have to be a State hotel or, perhaps, while the State owns it, it may give a lease of it to some competent hotel firm. I doubt if there are any in India who are likely to take it up. There are only two such big concerns: Tatas of the Taj Mahal Hotel and Oberois. If we go to a foreign country, I would avoid the USA. Probably, a Swiss concern might consider it. We have been long thinking of a big modern hotel in Delhi situated in the Diplomatic Enclave. At long last, some decision has been more or less arrived at. This shows how long these things take.

I think, you might discuss this matter with Bakshi Saheb and find out what his reactions are.

So far as the University is concerned, you yourself point out the difficulty of having it there.

Vishnu Sahay has left today for Srinagar. You might perhaps consult him about some of these matters.

About Gulab Mahal, it might be worth considering to use it as a first class nursing home or clinic. There is no such place in the whole of India.

Ever yours,
Jawaharlal Nehru

———— 100 ————

Srinagar
5 November 1953

My dear Panditji,

Thank you very much for your letter dated the 30th October which Mr Kaul[1] brought to Srinagar. I am sending this letter by his hand, as he is returning to Delhi today.

The general situation here is indeed improving and the continuing series of conventions that Bakshi is holding in various parts of the Valley are having an excellent effect. He has to a large extent succeeded in creating a new feeling and atmosphere among the people. There is, of course, no question at all of becoming complacent, because as you say the basic political problem remains. This has its root in the dark cloud of uncertainty that has for the last six years been hanging over our State. This has to be dispelled, as then only will all that is being done here assume real and lasting significance. If the uncertainty continues it may in due course succeed in destroying all that has been achieved in the past three months.

Thanks to the very generous aid given by the Central Government,[2] the economic condition in the Valley has considerably improved,

1. Lieutenant-General Brij Mohan Kaul (1912-1972); military attaché, Indian embassy, Washington, 1947; military advisor, Indian delegation in Kashmir, 1948; director of organization, army headquarters, 1952-53; served as a liaison between Srinagar and Delhi during the political crisis of 1953 in Kashmir: chief of staff to the Neutral Nations Repatriation Commission in Korea, 1953-54; chief of general staff, army headquarters, 1961.
2. The government of India had given aid to the Kashmir government for subsidizing foodgrains.

particularly with respect to food and food prices. There does not yet, however, seem to have been a corresponding improvement in the administration. This is largely due to the fact that there is a considerable communal-minded section within the administration which has a very definite bias against India and against Bakshi. Another factor is that there are officers who are known for their corruption. I feel it is a pity that there has yet been no full enquiry into charges of corruption. True some people have been shifted to less key posts, but that is not enough. A stern and determined campaign to root out corruption in Government is required to fulfil the widespread public demand for an honest and efficient administration. Conventions and other political activities have their own undoubted value, but recent experience has shown that the integrity or otherwise of the administration is in the final analysis a decisive factor.

It is likely that the Cabinet will be further expended.[1] Bakshi Sahib told me yesterday that he had decided to take Sadiq into the Cabinet as Minister for Health and Education, and also to appoint three more Deputy Ministers—Kushak Bakula, Major Piar Singh and Ahsanullah Mir.

The Government will move down to Jammu soon, and offices will open there on the 23rd of this month. The political and economic situation there remains to be faced. Uptil now Bakshi has been so busy with work in the Valley that he has not had time to look into the very real problems of Jammu. Now, when he gets down there he will turn his attention to those problems.

A feature of the situation in Jammu seems to be a widespread lack of confidence in those who represent Jammu in the Government and the Assembly. This aspect will require tactful and sympathetic handling.

The people of Jammu have offered their support to Bakshi and they are expecting swift and substantial relief of their genuine grievances and difficulties which had been neglected by the previous regime. I have every hope that Bakshi will do all he can to solve their problems, although several factors, including the alleged communist

---

1. To make the cabinet broad based Bakshi Ghulam Mohammad included G.M. Sadiq, the leader of the National Conference 'Left-Wing' as minister for health and education. Kushak Bakula, Major Piar Singh and Ahsanullah Mir were made deputy ministers and given the frontier affairs, revenue and development portfolios respectively.

influences, may confuse and complicate the issues.

One of the important problems in Jammu is that of the refugees, many of whom are still awaiting rehabilitation. Shri Jain was here a few days ago and the matter was fully discussed with him. I hope that with the assistance that the Central Government has all along been giving us we shall be able to tackle this problem satisfactorily.

I expect to visit Delhi for a few days towards the end of this month. I shall have to come again in the beginning of February as I have received information that the Governors' and Rajpramukhs' Conference is being held on the 1st and 2nd.

I have long standing invitations from the Governors of Bengal[1] and Madras,[2] and the Rajpramukhs of Mysore[3] and Travancore[4] to visit their States. I am keen to avail of these invitations, and shall try and fix up short visits to these places this winter. I shall also have to go to Bombay to see my father, whom I have not visited now for over a year and a half.

I have been deeply distressed at recent events at Lucknow,[5] more so as a student myself. It is our generation that will inherit the future, and such events do not augur well.

I hope this finds you very well. Srinagar, though rather cold, is delightful now-a-days. From my house I view a panorama of gold, as the leaves of the *chinars* have taken on their autumn colours.

With respectful regards,

Yours very sincerely,
Karan Singh

---

1. H. C. Mookerjee.
2. Sri Prakasa.
3. H.H. Maharaja Jayachamaraja Wadiyar.
4. H.H. Maharaja Bahadur Shamser Jung.
5. Students of Lucknow University had started an agitation on 21 August 1953 protesting against an amendment made in the constitution of the university student union by the executive committee of the Lucknow University by which the students' union was made a federation of all the recognized student associations of the university and all the presidents of such associations were made members of the General Council of the University Students Union. They considered this amendment as an infringement of the autonomy of the union. A group of four students observed hunger-strike from 28 August to 4 September and again from 30 October to 2 November. On 2 November the students became more restive and there was complete lawlessness in the city when telephone wires were cut, streets lights were smashed and a number of post offices and buses were set on fire. The police lathi charged the students and also opened fire as a result of which three students died and many were injured.

———— 101 ————

New Delhi
21 November 1953

My dear Tiger,

I have just seen the copy of your letter to the President, dated 19th November.[1] I need not tell you that I am closely following the developments in Kashmir.[2] I had a talk with D.P. Dhar the other day.

What you have written about the Praja Parishad troubles me. I am all for the removal of genuine grievances and I have no doubt that Bakshi Sahib will do his utmost to this end. But, if the Praja Parishad thinks of giving trouble, I have also no doubt that it should be crushed absolutely and whatever the consequences. I think this should be made quite clear to them. They have already done enormous injury to Kashmir and India and, if they persist in this utter folly, India will certainly not tolerate them, whatever the Kashmir Government might do. It is fantastic nonsense for them at this stage to go on talking in the way they are doing. They are ruining their own cause and that of the State. They cannot have a better opportunity of the removal of legitimate grievances. If they want to miss this by their folly, then they are not likely to have another.

I do not think they are really after any real grievances. To talk of one flag, one President and one constitution,[3] is not a grievance of

---

1. In this letter Karan Singh informed Rajendra Prasad that, 'Recent reports in the Press of the negotiations regarding a Military Agreement between Pakistan and the United State of America has caused considerable misgivings and resentment in the minds of the people of the State… Reports that air strips in Gilgit have been leased by Pakistan to the United States of America have greatly distressed the people, the Government as well as the people strongly feel that, despite its being under the forcible and illegal occupation of Pakistan, Gilgit is still part and parcel of the State.' He also informed the president that, 'The Praja Parishad, which continue to be dominant political party among the masses, is continuing its political activity on the basis of the slogan one Flag, one President, one Constitution and this has a very strong appeal to the Jammu Masses.'

2. Various steps were taken to bring the Jammu and Kashmir state closer to the centre. Bakshi's cabinet decided to proceed with the implementation of the remaining clauses of the Delhi Agreement. The telegraph and telephone department was taken over by the government of India. The rules for the recruitment of Kashmiri Muslims to all the three wings of the Indian defence services with the aim to incorporate the State Militia in the Indian army were liberalized.

3. For complete integration of the state with India, the Praja Parishad had raised the cry '*ek vidhan, ek nishan, ek pradhan*'.

the masses. It may be a sentiment of some people and one may even respect it to some extent. But, in the circumstances, to raise this cry is just to invite trouble.

I am convinced that the Praja Parishad is in the hands of the most reactionary people in India who are exploiting it for their own ends, because they can get no adequate footing in the rest of India. With such people we can have no truck wherever they might be.

I am equally convinced that this movement, or whatever it is, is not a movement of the common people, but rather of certain elements who naturally have suffered because of various changes. In every part of India, including my own province, Uttar Pradesh, big social changes and land reforms have affected small groups of people adversely, though they have been for the public good from a larger point of view. Every social reform results in this. We cannot give up such reforms, because unfortunately some people suffer from that. The result would be ultimately far greater suffering for them when an upheaval comes.

I really am greatly surprised at the complete lack of intelligence of these Praja Parishad people.

Ever yours,
Jawaharlal Nehru

——— 102 ———

Jammu
2 December 1953

My dear Panditji,
Thank you very much for your letter dated the 21st November. I am fully conscious of your deep anxiety regarding matters effecting the State and your concern about Jammu. I assure you that I will do all I can do to help and facilitate the handling of problems here by Bakshi. It is a pity that he has been delayed so long in Srinagar. He is now expected here on the 5th December.

I certainly deprecate any action by the people of Jammu which may adversely affect our position in Kashmir. One does sometimes tend to lose patience with people who lack foresight and political maturity. The misfortune is that there seems to be no one here from Jammu who is in a position to guide the people along the right lines. Unfortunately, those belonging to the National Conference who represent Jammu in the Assembly and in the party grievously lack public support and confidence, and attempts to foist them upon the people only result in further ill will and disharmony. This is a very real and very knotty problem.

Whether or not the Praja Parishad will be able to retain the mass leadership which it was able to build up during the agitation will depend largely upon the manner in which the Government tackles the real problems facing the Jammu people. I have always held that the Praja Parishad, ironically enough, owes its following in Jammu more to the calculated policies and attitude of the previous regime than to any inherent strength. If, as I fully trust, the new Government approaches the problems here with complete honesty of purpose coupled with sympathy and understanding, then the ground will be cut away from under the feet of the Parishad and it will find it more and more difficult to mobilize mass support. This, I feel, will be the most thorough and permanent way of counter-acting the Parishad.

I am glad that Bakshi accepted my suggestion of flying the Union Flag upon the Jammu Secretariat above the State Flag. This was long overdue and has had a very healthy effect upon public opinion here.

I would have liked to visit Delhi earlier but I am waiting for Bakshi to come down here as there are several matters I want to discuss with him. I expect to be able to visit Delhi by the middle of this month.

I had written a letter to Dr Rajendra Prasad suggesting that he might consider a visit to Jammu some time this winter. He has replied saying that we might discuss the matter when I get to Delhi.

A couple of days ago I sent a copy of a book[1] by Panikkar[2]—*The Founding of the Kashmir State* which you may find of interest. Being an eminent historian yourself, you are, of course, aware of the manner in which this State was built up. This book gives a good account of the way in which Maharaja Gulab Singh[3] and his Dogras founded this

---

1. The book was first published in 1930 (Martin Hopkinson Ltd, London) under the title *Gulab Singh 1792-1858 Founder of Kashmir*. In 1953, it was published under the title *The Founding of the Kashmir State A Biography of Maharajah Gulab Singh 1792-1858* (George Allen & Unwin Ltd., London).
2. K.M. Panikkar (1895-1963); historian and diplomat, member of the Indian National Congress for some time; served in the Princely States before Independence, ambassador to China, the United Arab Republic and France, member, States Reorganization Commission, 1953-55.
3. (1792-1858); attained eminence in the court of Ranjit Singh as a general, conquered Ladakh, Baltistan and westen Tibet between 1840-42; founded the Jammu and Kashmir State by the Treaty of Amritsar between the British government and Maharaja Gulab Singh concluded on 16 March 1846.

State and added vast territory to the boundaries of India.

The passing away of Sir B.N. Rau[1] was indeed very sad, and a great loss to the nation. To us in Kashmir whom he served for a while as Prime Minister, his memory will remain particularly dear.

With respects and kindest regards,

Yours very sincerely,
Karan Singh

───────── 103 ─────────
Situation in Jammu & Kashmir[2]

1. Internal situation satisfactory—Valley/Jammu/Ladakh—perhaps better than ever since 1947.
2. However recent Pak moves have greatly disturbed us all. We feel that the main, if not the sole, motive of Pakistan in all this is to grab Kashmir.
3. This development has caused great apprehension in all pro-elements. The pro-Pak elements, however, who were quite crushes, are jubilant at the move and go about saying that now it is only a matter of time before Pak shows India where it gets off and that planes will come etc.
4. In view of the fact that Pakistan has enlisted the support of a foreign imperialist power for the sole purpose of imposing its will upon India and Kashmir and coercing us. We all strongly feel that the very basis upon which the Government of India has based its policy since 1947 has changed, and that hence the Government of India should consider a reconsideration of its whole policy vis-a- vis Kashmir in the light of the new developments.
5. The voluntary offer of a plebiscite by India was made under entirely different circumstances and now we feel that India need not remain bound to it.
6. You have always said that the people of Kashmir will decide their

──────────────

1. (1887-1953); member of the Indian Civil Service; judge, Calcutta High Court, 1935, chairman, Hindu Law Committee, 1941; prime minister, Jammu and Kashmir, 1945, constitutional adviser to the Constituent Assembly, 1946-49; India's representative and later leader of India's delegation to the UN, 1949-52; judge, International Court of Justice at the Hague, 1952-53.
2. Note to Jawaharlal Nehru, Srinagar, 18 December 1953.

own future. Well, you have the Assembly which you have recognized as sovereign and which is engaged in framing the Constitution for the State (you recognized its competence regarding the dynasty etc. and also to frame the Constitution).

7. Before the Constitution can be framed naturally the first step is to decide which country we are with. Now, the Assembly will meet in February and will pass a resolution finally and irrevocably reaffirming the accession of the State to India and also condemning a plebiscite. At that time we would submit that the Government of India must back us up and accept that accession. If that is not done then the whole Assembly, the Delhi Agreement and so on become a complete farce.

8. (Only if necessary : there will of course be a risk of conflict, but we feel, with our very limited knowledge of international affairs that this risk will day by day increase, as Pakistan will get stronger while we will grow weaker. And if Pakistan feels strong enough it will start trouble itself.)

9. This is the only way in which the cloud of crushing uncertainty which has plagued us for the last seven years can be removed. Of course, the negotiation with Pakistan can be delayed, but that will not be a solution. That will be condemning the people of Kashmir to a perpetual uncertainty, and if something is not done to finalize the matter soon all the wonderful work done in these four months by Bakshi and Co. will be in danger of being washed away. Again internal dissentions will develop, pro-Pakistan intrigues will start again (many officers unreliable) and the whole internal position might once again deteriorate. Thus, we will drift from one internal crisis to another. Only a bold stand at this very opportune time can, we submit, save the situation.

——— 104 ———

New Delhi
19 December 1953

My dear Panditji,

Thank you so much for your card of good wishes which was redirected to me here from Jammu. I heartily reciprocate the greetings, and hope that the coming year—despite the unpropitious circumstances that exist at present—will bring peace to our distracted world.

My wife and I leave for Calcutta tomorrow, where we shall stay for a few days. On our return we will stay in Delhi for a couple of days, and if you have the time I look forward to being able to see you then again.

With respectful regards,

Yours sincerely,
Karan Singh

——— 105 ———

Jammu
26 January 1954

My dear Panditji,

I have not written for some time firstly, because I knew that with the Congress Session[1] you would be even busier than ever and secondly, because there was really not very much to write about.

Conditions here continue to be fairly satisfactory. Bakshi's tours of some parts of the Jammu Province have been well received, and though a great deal remains to be done, the atmosphere in Jammu is completely transformed as compared to last year. Reports from the Valley show that there also things are quiet, and although some anti-Government activity continues—mostly confined to the city of Srinagar—the countryside seems to be peaceful and fairly contented. The Ladakhis are also reported to be very much happier than they were before.

While all the Ministers are working very hard, there is a feeling that the Secretariat is not doing as well as it should. A section of the Muslim officials continue to be hostile to Bakshi and his regime and indeed carry on propaganda against it. For example, an attempt was made by some of them to again influence the minds of some of the Constituent Assembly members on the wrong lines and to get them to press for a postponement of implementation of the Delhi Agreement.[2] Happily Bakshi, as also Sadiq, took an iron stand

---

1. The 59th session of the Indian National Congress was held on 23-24 January 1954 at Kalyani, West Bengal under the presidentship of Jawaharlal Nehru.
2. Under the influence of a section of Muslim offcials, fifteen members of the Constituent Assembly did not attend its meeting of 6 February 1954, which approved the implementation of the Delhi Agreement of 1952.

against this mischievous move which has been thwarted. The fact remains that a, by no means negligible, section of the official class is unreliable and thus a potential threat in the event of some crisis or emergency.

Regarding constitutional developments, Bakshi and others must have told you in detail about what they intend doing. The Basic Principles Committee of the Constituent Assembly has made out a Report,[1] which will probably be discussed with you by Bakshi and his colleagues while they are at Delhi. There are certain important points in that report which I feel deserve your careful attention, and I am enclosing a brief note embodying my views on those points for your consideration. As all these are matters with far reaching importance, it would be very desirable that any flaw or defect is removed at this stage, when conditions are favourable, so that the possibility of any difficulty arising in the future is minimized.

The full and final implementation of the Delhi Agreement—with all the political and economic implications that will flow there from will go a very long way in further stabilizing the situation in the State. I may again venture to repeat, however, what I submitted when we met last. That is that we all feel that this important step, if it is to have its full and maximum benefit, should be followed by some move whereby—as far as we are concerned—the crushing uncertainty that has been hanging over our heads for the last seven years is once and for all removed. Then alone have we a chance to attain lasting and permanent stability and not continue to drift, as we have been doing, from one crisis to another. What is more, once a final and firm decision is taken and the uncertainty of a plebiscite removed, many uncertain and wavering elements in the Valley and some other parts of the State which are at present sitting on the fence or tending against us will be forced by circumstances to throw in their lot with us and reconcile

---

1. In its report submitted to the Constituent Assembly in January 1954, the Basic Principles Committee recommended that the state would comprise such territories as formed part of the state on 15 August 1947; while retaining the autonomous character, the state would remain acceded to India; an elected head of the state was to remain operative; the drafting committee should put forward proposals defining the sphere of the Union government's jurisdiction in the state; sovereignty vested in people to be exercised by the agents of the state except in regard to matters added to the Union government. Other recommendations were related to the legislature, the high court, the public service commission and amendment of the state constitution.

themselves to that position.

We have all been greatly enthused by the forthright stand you have taken vis-a-vis the proposed Pakistan-USA military pact,[1] particularly by your declaration that this development completely changes the basis upon which the Kashmir issue was being discussed with Pakistan. The people of the State feel that they should now, through the Constituent Assembly, be allowed to exercise their inherent right to finally decide their own future and that the decision thus taken should be recognized and accepted as final, once and for all, by the people and the Government of India.

Of course, it has to be conceded that in the present context this one resolution alone will not be enough to solve the problem. That will have to be followed up by its logical corollaries of closing the issue with the UNO and with Pakistan. Unless these two steps follow soon, there is a real danger that the whole affair may appear unreal and that our trump card may be wasted. The people of the State, as always, have implicit faith in your statesmanship to safeguard their interests at this crucial juncture.

The Congress session at Kalyani must have been stimulating though at the same time exhausting. I followed the proceedings in the paper, and read your inspiring addresses with great interest. May I, as a citizen of India, express my great admiration and appreciation of the manner in which you are guiding the destiny of our nation through this crucial and critical phase of her long and chequered history?

With respects and deep regards,

Yours very sincerely,
Karan Singh

---

1. Since November 1953 various newspapers had been reporting the possibility of a military alliance between Pakistan and the USA in the near future. Pakistan denied any such negotiations. However, on 19 May 1954 the Defence Assistance Agreement between Pakistan and the USA was signed in Karachi.

——— 106 ———

Jammu
27 January 1954

My dear Panditji,

I have unofficially come across a copy of the Report of the sub-committee appointed by the Constituent Assembly Basic Principles Committee. I understand that this is being discussed with you by Bakshi and his colleagues. There are certain important points regarding that Report to which I would like to draw your attention. I feel that these points are of great importance, and that it would be most desirable that they are secured at this stage so that the possibility of difficulty or misunderstanding arising in the future is minimized:

1. Independence of the Judiciary — Whereas the necessity for the Judiciary being independent is recognized in the Report, it suggests that the appointment of the State Chief Justice and High Court Judges be made by the Sadar-i-Riyasat. As in the normal course the Sadar-i-Riyasat is expected to act on the advice of the Ministry, this will virtually mean that the appointments are made by the political party that happens to be in power at the time. It is clear that this sort of procedure will not at all ensure the true independence of the Judiciary from the Executive which is so important if a democracy is really to function as such. Hence I would urge that Article 217 of the Indian Constitution, whereby the appointment of the State Chief Justice and High Court Judges is made by the President, be applied to our State, also, with the modification that the word 'Sadar-i-Riyasat' be substituted instead of 'Governor' for the purpose of consultation. This will ensure the independence of the Judiciary in the State and the true interests of the people will be safeguarded.

2. National Language — The report says that the official language of the State will be Urdu, but that English may be used for official purposes. Thus, there is no mention at all of the National Language, Hindi. It is of great importance that Hindi be given its due place in the State at least equal to, if not superior than, the State Language. This will be an important unifying and binding factor between the State and other parts of the Union. Also, if this is not done, the people of the State, and in particular the minorities in the State, will suffer a very crushing handicap in the matter of entering Government service, the Armed Forces

and indeed any other employment in India. This is particularly so now that Hindi is fast replacing English as the medium of instruction and examinations.

3. It may be argued that there is no ban on the study of Hindi and that anyone who wants to, is at liberty to do so. This is emphatically not enough. It must be made a compulsory subject along with the Regional Language if necessary. In the long run this step will prove to be of the greatest value to the people of the State, particularly to those in the Valley who have no knowledge of Hindi.

4. I may add that the choice of Urdu itself as the regional language is far from uncontroversial and is open to serious objections. However, that is a matter which I need not dilate upon here.

5. Delimitation of Constituencies — There is considerable dissatisfaction at the manner in which the previous regime carved out constituencies. It is alleged that they did so in such a manner as to keep one community in a majority wherever possible regardless of such factors as geographical, cultural and ethnic affinities. To avoid all such controversies and to be sure that the electoral constituencies are made in an equitable manner I would suggest that the task of delimiting our State should be entrusted to the Delimitation Commission which has been appointed to do this job in the rest of India. The Commission consists of men of integrity and competence, and no one can question the desirability of their handling this job in the State. This will put the whole matter above controversy and criticism.

6. Sadar-i-Riyasat – Before I comment on this point I would like to make it clear that I am not at all allowing personal considerations to affect my view. It is clear that I will not and cannot continue to be Sadar-i-Riyasat indefinitely, and any provisions made should be such that with anyone here things should go smoothly and India's interests should always be safeguarded.

7. In this connection I feel that it should be made very clear that the Sadar-i-Riyasat is responsible to the President of India, is very much the same manner as is a Governor or Rajpramukh. The difference in the manner of his choice which has been allowed as a special case to Kashmir should, in no way, affect this basic responsibility which is so important if the state is to be really in fact as well as in theory an integral part of India.

8. Emergency Powers of the President — It is of the utmost importance that the President's powers to declare an emergency in the State

and follow that by such action as the circumstances may warrant should on no account be limited. This is very important keeping in view the fact that we are a border State with peculiar internal and external conditions. While the special provision made in the Delhi Agreement may, if necessary, be allowed care should be taken that this in no way binds the President down or fetters his authority.

9. Secular Character of the State – While the Report says that 'the governing features of the State Constitution would be based on democracy, equality and social and economic justice', there should be further clarification emphasizing the secular character of the State and saying that there will be equal opportunities for all regardless of their race, religion, or area of habitation. This is important to instil a sense of security in the minority communities in Jammu and Ladakh and even in the Valley.

10. Residuary Powers – Although the State has been granted a special position in the Indian Constitution, I strongly feel that the Residuary Powers must vest in the Centre. If this is not done there is always the danger of some undefined power being misinterpreted or misused by the State Government at some future date. The State has already been granted enough autonomy and there is no justification in my mind for insisting upon the retention of the Residuary Powers by the State.

11. Framing of the Constitution – Finally, when the Constitution is being actually framed many matters will come up in addition to these which are at present being discussed with you. In all such matters, it is very important that any action the Constituent Assembly may take should be taken in close consultation at all stages with the Government of India. This will minimize the possibility of any incorrect or undesirable steps being taken.

12. I would add that these points assume special urgency and importance in the light of local conditions and possible future developments. Today things are stable and Bakshi is firmly in the saddle. But we cannot assume that this satisfactory situation will always continue, nor can we rule out the possibility at some future date of other less desirable elements coming into power. Hence any constitutional steps which are taken must be decided upon only after keeping such possibilities clearly in view.

With respectful regards,

Yours sincerely,
Karan Singh

P.S.
I am sending these letters by hand of a special messenger, my ADC
Captain Kohar Singh, in order to ensure prompt and safe delivery.

K.S.

——— 107 ———

Jammu
12 February 1954

My dear Panditji,
I hope you received the two letters[1] I sent through a special messenger
last month.

Tomorrow my wife and I are leaving for Bombay where we shall
spend a few days with my father. I shall reach Delhi in time for the
conference of Governors and Rajpramukhs which begins on the 1st
of March. I look forward to meeting you then.

With kindest regards,

Yours very sincerely,
Karan Singh

——— 108 ———

Jammu
24 March 1954

My dear Panditji,
Thank you for getting a copy of your letter to Mr Mohammad Ali
sent to me.[2] I read it with great interest.

I am indeed sorry that I have not been able to write for so long,
but I have been rather worried with some personal affairs. First my
mother began keeping very indifferent health and so I prevailed upon

---

1. See the preceding two items.
2. In his letter of 5 March 1954 to Mohammad Ali, Nehru wrote that the US decision
    to give military aid to Pakistan 'has changed the whole context of Kashmir issue, and
    the long talks we have had about this matter have little relation to the new facts
    which flow from this aid'. He further added: 'It is not merely the Kashmir question
    that has become much more difficult, but a serious threat has arisen to India's
    security.' For full text of the letter, see *Selected Works of Jawaharlal Nehru* (Second
    Series), Vol. 25, pp. 319-322.

her to come to Delhi where she was admitted into the Willingdon Nursing Home. Then on my return to Bombay after attending the Governors' Conference.[1] I found that my wife had to undergo an operation for both gall bladder and appendix from which she is now convalescing in a nursing home there. To add to this, my father was also unwell for a few days. However, by God's grace everyone is now progressing well.

I was distressed to learn that you also have not been keeping very good health and that you were indisposed for a few days. If I may take the liberty of saying so, I do feel that you should try not to overwork so much as the country needs your inspired leadership for many years more.

I returned to Jammu only yesterday so as to be able to address the Legislative Assembly this afternoon. I enclose a copy of the speech which I delivered for your persual.[2] Incidentally, tomorrow I celebrate my twenty third birthday.

Just as a matter of record, I sent two letters dated the 26th and 27th January by hand of my ADC, Captain Kohar Singh. As I received no acknowledgement, I would like to make sure whether those letters were placed before you or not.

I was very glad to have had the opportunity of meeting and talking with you in Delhi recently.

I hope this finds you now very well.

With respects and kindest regards,

Yours very sincerely,
Karan Singh

1. Held on 1 March 1954.
2. In his inaugural address to the winter session of the Assembly, Karan Singh said: 'The uncertainty hanging over the State for the last seven years has had an extremely undesirable and unhealthy effect upon our political and economic development. Now, with the recent measures enacted by our Constituent Assembly that phase has ended once for all as far as we are concerned. We could no longer afford to be indefinitely in the back waters of uncertainty.' He also spoke on the steps taken by the government for removing the economic distress of the people, rehabilitation of refugees and reorganization of administration.

——— 109 ———

New Delhi
12 April 1954

My dear Tiger,
I have received a letter from Punya Dev Sharma[1] who has gone to
Jammu and Kashmir State at my instance. He writes to me that you
have suggested to him to take charge of some kind of an Ashram
which you intend establishing. I do not have any particulars of this,
but if he can do good work in Jammu or Kashmir, I shall have no
objection. Punya Dev is a simple honest worker and he can do good
work in his own line.

Yours sincerely,
Jawaharlal Nehru

——— 110 ———

Alhilal, Kangra
18 April 1954

My dear Panditji,
Thank you for you letter regarding Shri Punya Dev Sharma. He meets
me off and on both in Jammu and in Srinagar and tells me about the
social work which he is doing in the State. The need for real dedicated
social service in our State is very great, but unfortunately we lack
people who can work effectively in this respect. I, therefore, suggested
to Shri Punya Dev that he start a small Ashram near Jammu on
Gandhian lines which could become a centre for his activities and a
place where he could train social workers within the State which
would enlarge the scope and area of his activities to cover ultimately
the whole State. He welcomed the idea and said that he would need
about 25 acres of agricultural land so that the Ashram could be self
supporting. I have offered to give him the land at a place about eight
miles from Jammu which he has visited and liked. I am so glad you
approve of the idea. I shall now give him the land, as he is willing to
start the work immediately.
    The President's visit to Jammu went off very smoothly and was

---

1. Punya Dev Sharma (1901-1972); prominent Congress leader from Bihar; attended
    Amritsar Congress session in 1919 while a student at BHU; gave up studies at

very successful indeed.[1] All the people of Jammu, regardless of political, religious or any other sectional affiliations, joined hands to accord him an enthusiastic and sincere welcome. The abolition of customs duties with effect from Baisakhi day has also been greatly welcomed by all sections of the people. On the whole the situation within the State continues to be satisfactory. We are expecting an even better tourist season than last year.

I am at present here in Kangra on a short visit to my mother who has not been keeping very well. I shall return to Jammu within a few days. The Government is moving up to Srinagar by the end of the month and I expect to follow by the 10th of May. I do hope you will be able to spare time to come to Srinagar in May or June. You have not visited the State for almost a year now.

We have all been following with keen interest and admiration your efforts to mobilize public opinion in the country and indeed the world over against the untold horrors of the atomic and hydrogen bomb,[2] and to turn the present disastrous trend in world affairs in favour of an atmosphere of peace and realistic sobriety. May I wish you all strength and success in this noble endeavour.

I hope this finds you in perfect health. My mother sends you her kindest regards.

With respects,

Yours very sincerely,
Karan Singh

Gandhi's call; took active part in the Non-Cooperation movement; founded Gandhi Ashram at Bikram in 1921, which became a centre of nationalist activities; delegate to the Gaya Congress, 1922 where the Congress broke into Pro-Changers and No-Changers; joined the Nagpur Flag Satyagraha, 1923; participated in all Congress-led anti-colonial movements; imprisoned several times and altogether spent seven-and-a-half years in jail; elected to the Bihar Legislative Assembly in 1937, 1946 and 1952; undertook social work in Jammu and Kashmir at the instance of Nehru between 1953 and 1964.

1. Rajendra Prasad visited Jammu from 10th to 13 April 1954.
2. In his various public speeches, Nehru appealed to the nations of the world to stop 'threatening each other with atom or hydrogen bombs' and to only think over the burning issues of the day and try to solve them. He made a statement on 2 April 1954 in the Lok Sabha calling for a Standstill Agreement on hydrogen bomb tests. The USA declared on 10 April 1954 in the UN Disarmament Commission that the statement made by Nehru was 'clearly entitled to respectful attention'. For full text of Nehru's statement see Selected Works of Jawaharlal Nehru (Second Series) Vol. 25, pp. 445–48.

With Jawaharlal Nehru and Yasho Rajya Lakshmi, New Delhi, 1 March 1954

———— III ————

Jammu
3 May 1954

My dear Panditji,
In a few days I am moving up to Srinagar for the season. The Secretariat has already moved and opened there today.

There is a matter about which I have been wanting to write to you for some time. Since the new administration took over eight months ago there has been improvement in many spheres, particularly in the economic sphere. But much remains to be done to bring the administrative machinery up to a commensurate level. I feel that this is an aspect which deserves closer attention then it has hitherto received. In this connection there are some points I wish to submit.

Now that the State has come politically and financially much closer to the Centre then before, I feel that the prospect of the Centre taking a more direct hand in the administration of those matters over which it has jurisdiction should be seriously considered. This will not only lead to more intimate all round contact but also increase the efficiency of the State administration.

Secondly, I believe there was talk a while ago of exchanging some officers between our State and the Centre or other States on a reciprocal basis. I feel this will be an excellent idea as it will lead to valuable contacts between our officers and those outside and broaden their experience, outlook and efficiency.

Finally, I understand that our present Chief Secretary, Mr M. K. Kidwai[1] will shortly apply for leave preparatory to his transfer away from here, thus leaving the post vacant. There are some local candidates, but without belittling the ability of our own men to fill the job I feel it my duty to convey to you my view that it would be most desirable if the post is filled by a really capable officer from the Government of India with ICS or similar qualifications. I say this because as you know the Chief Secretary is the pivot around which the administration revolves, and it is imperative that the person should not only be a very

---

1. M.K. Kidwai (1908–2000); served in the UP judicial service, 1934–46; attached to the ministry of law, government of India, 1947–48; deputy secretary and deputy legal remembrancer, UP government, 1950–51; chief secretary, government of Jammu and Kashmir for sometime in 1954; charge d' affairs, Indian Legation, Jeddah, 1954–55; India's ambassador to Saudi Arabia, 1957–60.

capable administrator but also have intimate knowledge of the affairs of Jammu and Kashmir. The conditions are still fluid and delicate and there are numerous groups and factions to be adjusted and dealt with in the day-to-day administration. I would therefore strongly suggest that a trusted and experienced person be sent here as Chief Secretary. A view that might be advanced is that importing someone will cause resentment and heart burning among local officials, but in this case this argument does not carry weight as the job is already in the hands of a person from outside.

I may add that these are my personal views. I have talked to Bakshi about this but he appeared to be non-committal. I feel that if the suggestion comes from you he will have no objection in accepting.

I shall write next from Srinagar.

With respects and warm regards,

Yours sincerely,
Karan Singh

——— 112 ———

New Delhi
5 May 1954

My dear Tiger,
I have you letter of the 3rd May.

Regarding the new Chief Secretary, this must necessarily depend upon Bakshi Ghulam Mohammad. We cannot obviously push a person there against the wishes of his Government.

I am sending your letter to Dr Katju[1] who will, no doubt, give it every consideration.

Yours affectionately,
Jawaharlal Nehru

———

1. Union home minister, K.N. Katju.

─────── 113 ───────

Srinagar
18 June 1954

My dear Panditji,

I have not bothered you with our State Forces problems for some time now as I know that you are so very busy, and I have therefore been corresponding[1] with Tyagiji.[2] As a result of this correspondence the Government of India have passed some orders revising the pension rates payable to our State Forces. It is most gratifying that the special position of the Forces has been recognized and we are indeed grateful to the Government of India for this consideration. There are, however, a few matters regarding the order about which I have written in some detail to Tyagiji. I am enclosing a copy of that letter. I am sure the Government of India will give sympathetic consideration to these points.

With respectful regards,

Yours very sincerely,
Karan Singh

─────── 114 ───────

New Delhi
22 June 1954

My dear Tiger,

Thank you for your letter of June 18, together with a copy of your letter which you have sent to Shri Mahavir Tyagi. Tyagi is giving every consideration to this matter in consultation with our Defence Ministry.

As regards the integration of the Jammu and Kashmir Forces, we

─────────────

1. In his letter of 18 June 1954 to Mahavir Tyagi, the minister for defence organization, Karan Singh urged that the revised rates of pension to the Jammu and Kashmir state forces 'should be made applicable with retrospective effect from 1st November 1947'.
2. Mahavir Tyagi (1899-1980); Congressman from UP; member, AICC, 1923-65, of Constituent Assembly, 1946-49, of Lok Sabha, 1952-67 and of Rajya Sabha 1970-76; Union minister of revenue and expenditure, 1952-53, of defence organization, 1953-57 and of rehabilitation, 1964-66; chairman, Fifth Finance Commission, 1968-69.

had practically decided to do this sometime ago, but then other considerations came before us and we decided to postpone the matter. It can be considered afresh. It would be desirable for Bakshi Ghulam Mohammad's views also to be obtained.

Ever yours,
Jawaharlal Nehru

———— 115 ————

Srinagar
3 July 1954

My dear Panditji,
Thank you very much for your letter dated the 22nd June. Regarding the integration of our State Forces, I am discussing this matter with Bakshi Sahib and will write to you again in about a fortnight.

We are having an excellent tourist season. Indeed, the crowds on the Boulevard and at the gardens have been thicker than I can ever remember; probably thicker than they have been since the War years. The political and economic effect of this is, of course, excellent and this has been augmented by the large number of important All India Conferences that have been held here.

One thing Srinagar needs very badly is a first rate hotel. As a matter of fact it needs two or three. You may have noticed the mention in my last fortnightly letter to the President regarding my having leased Gulab Mahal for a hotel. As you know there had been various suggestions for the use of this building and I have finally leased it out to India's leading Hotel Company, Oberoi Hotels Ltd. It is beautifully situated and ideally suited for a hotel. Mr M.S. Oberoi,[1] who has travelled in most of the countries of the world, thinks that this will be one of the world's most beautiful hotels.

It might interest you to know that the Ramakrishna Mission[2]

1. Mohan Singh Oberoi (1900–2002); leading businessman in the hotel industry, member, various national and international business organizations; president of honour, Federation of Hotel and Restaurant Association of India, member, Rajya Sabha, 1962-68 and 1972-78; member, Lok Sabha, April 1968-70.
2. The Ramakrishna Mission was founded in 1897 by Swami Vivekananda, the chief disciple of Ramakrishna Paramhamsa to propagate the gospel of the master. It advocated service of humanity as divinity and was opposed to the materialist influences of western civilization.

opened a centre in Srinagar about two months ago. This organization as you know does selfless and devoted work, and it has started here with a charitable dispensary and a small library and reading room.

I hope this finds you very well.

With respects,

Yours very sincerely,
Karan Singh

——— 116 ———

New Delhi
7 July 1954

My dear Tiger,

Thank you for your letter of July 3rd.

I entirely agree with you that there should be a first class hotel at Srinagar, and Gulab Mahal should be a very suitable place for it. I am glad to know that you have made arrangements for this with Oberoi Hotels.

I am also glad to learn that the Ramakrishna Mission has opened a centre at Srinagar.

Yours ever,
Jawaharlal Nehru

——— 117 ———

Srinagar
20 July 1954

My dear Panditji,

Thank you very much for your letter of July 7th. I venture to write to you about a matter which I consider to be very important and which affects not only our State but in the broader context, the security of the whole nation. I refer to Ladakh

As you know there is at present no road link with Leh. The Army has constructed a road up to a few miles beyond Kargil, but that still leaves a gap of about a hundred very difficult miles to Leh, which have to be traversed on foot or by pony. The route being slow and laborious, it is not suited to carry goods and supplies in any large quantity to and from Leh. Neverthless, it is at present the only route available.

Probably, it would be possible for the Army to complete this road from Kargil to Leh but, apart from the considerable expense that will be involved, that road will be most unsafe and precarious, passing as it will right under the enemy positions which overlook it from the mountain tops. In the event of a renewal of hostilities that road could be cut in half an hour by the enemy and rendered completely useless to us.

It is clear that from the political, economic and strategic points of view, it is essential that there should be a safe road linking Leh to the rest of the country. There is, of course, the Air Force, but a plane flight, apart from costing a lot of money, is also wholly dependent upon the exigencies of the weather.

Keeping these facts in view, and also keeping in mind the considerations that I shall outline below, I feel that a direct road between India and Leh deserves to be taken in hand as soon as possible. The route that immediately suggests itself is from Manali, from where a footpath to Leh already exists. As a matter of fact it was along this path that in 1947 a gallant band of officers and men of the Indian Army pushed on to Leh by foot and reached there just in time to prevent it falling into the hands of the Pakistani invaders. Roughly, as the crow flies, the distance that will have to be covered will be only 150 miles, which will probably mean about four to five hundred miles of road. I believe that this road has actually been surveyed a few years ago, and that the approximate estimate came to between ten and twelve crores. However, keeping in view the great importance of the road, the money that is spent on it will certainly not be wasted.

I will now briefly outline the reasons why I consider this road so very important, grouping them broadly into three heads: strategic, economic, and political:-

1. Strategic – In the event of renewed hostilities with Pakistan, or aggression from any other quarter, it will be very difficult to maintain an adequate garrison at Leh unless it can be supplied with arms, ammunition, rations etc. by road. Air supplies can at best be limited, and bad weather can prevent planes from landing there for days together.

What is more it is at present impossible to get even a jeep to Leh, far less trucks or weapon-carriers, unless they are taken in pieces and flown there which is a tedious and impractical undertaking. If the

Kargil route is cut—which is very likely—then our one means of supply will be cut off.

A road linking Leh with Manali, and thus with Delhi, will therefore be of great military value in the contingency of serious trouble on our Northern frontiers which I do not think we can rule out.

2. Economic – As you know, the economic condition of the people of Ladakh is very poor indeed. This can only really be improved if the flow of goods to and from Ladakh is greatly increased, which is not possible unless there is a road link. At present Ladakh depends for its salt, butter, cloth and many other things upon trade coming in from Tibet. This is a precarious and unsatisfactory position, as we never know when for some reason that trade might abruptly cease. The only way we can at present supply Leh is through Kargil or by air, both of which are most uneconomical. Under our Five Year Plan we have some schemes and projects planned for Leh but many of them are held up because it is just not possible to get machinery or other articles to Leh except by air.

Particularly, in view of recent developments in Tibet, it is imperative that the economic condition of the Ladakhis be improved and to see that they feel clearly the advantages of their association with India. A direct road connection with the rest of India would completely change the present unsatisfactory position and the benefits that would accrue to the economy of Ladakh would be immense.

I may also mention that Ladakh offers a vast and still unexplored field for the exploitation of mineral wealth. It is possible that those vast and inhospitable wind swept plateaus may conceal under their forbidding exterior immense treasures in the form of oil or even uranium, which one day may more than repay the debt that Ladakh owes to India.

3. Political – Addressing as I am a renowned historian, I need not dwell upon the past history of Ladakh. Suffice it is to say that until 1834 (the year of its conquest by Maharaja Gulab Singh's Dogra troops) it was an integral part of Tibet. To this day it retains its ethnic, linguistic, religious, economic and social ties with that country.

However, for over a century, Ladakh has been part of the Jammu and Kashmir State, and for about seven years part of India. I feel that its people have loyalty and affection for India, and left to themselves they will remain loyal. But in view of recent developments on the 'Roof of the World', it is most important that these ties with India must be strengthened so that they become virtually unbreakable. Uptil now, the authorities in Tibet have not shown too much interest in Ladakh, but there is no guarantee that this attitude will continue indefinitely, and after consolidation in Tibet it will be too optimistic to believe that Ladakh will escape an undue share of attention.

Our information, meagre as it is, shows that the Chinese are fast completing the road linking Lhasa with Peking, thousands of miles away, and are also engaged in constructing a network of roads within Tibet.

I can think of no one factor that will be more important in cementing the political feelings of the Ladakhis for India (and in the process turning their eyes away from Tibet) than the construction of a road directly linking Leh with India. They will then feel very much closer to India than to Tibet, as it takes about four months to get from Leh to Lhasa. And after all, it must be remembered that Lord Buddha was born, lived and preached in India not in Tibet. There is, therefore, no reason why the Ladakh Buddhists should not feel culturally and religiously as close, if not closer, to India than they do to Tibet. Indeed, I feel that instead of going to Lhasa (where reports show that they are beginning to find conditions very difficult and uninviting) lamas and monks from Leh should be encouraged to go for their higher studies to places such as Sarnath and Bodh Gaya. But all this will only be practicable if the Ladakhis can get to India directly and easily.

The road will be a lifeline linking distant Leh with the mainstream of the mother country. I may also add that if some day conditions arise in which the Government of India decides to take over directly the administration of Ladakh, the road will prove to be invaluable.

Before I close I would like to mention that if the construction of the road is taken up, either by the Army or by the civil authorities, it can hardly be completed in less than three or four years. Time, therefore, is of the essence.

I hope you will forgive me for having inflicted such a long letter upon you, but this matter had been revolving in my mind for a long time and I felt it my duty to convey my thoughts to you for what they are worth.

Yours respectfully,
Karan Singh

———— 118 ————

New Delhi
28 July 1954

My dear Tiger,
Thank you for your letter of the 20 July.
    You have advanced powerful arguments in favour of a road from Manali to Leh. The proposal attracts me greatly and I wish we could take it up. The difficulties, however, are formidable. Nevertheless, I am having this matter looked into again and, so far as I am concerned, I should like to have this road if at all possible.

Yours ever,
Jawaharlal Nehru

———— 119 ————

Srinagar
11 October 1954

My dear Panditji,
I had thought of coming down to Delhi last month for a few days, but due to the severe floods[1] here I had to give up the idea. Bakshi Sahib and Sadiq are in Delhi and will convey to you in detail the situation here. On the whole this season has been a successful one from several points of view. The floods, however, have hit us hard. The State Government will soon start a relief fund to help alleviate the suffering of the flood victims.
    I have been distressed to read in your fortnightly letter to Chief Ministers and also in some press reports[2] that you were feeling somewhat fatigued by the onerous duties that the nation has entrusted in your hands. It is but natural that with the tremendous mental and physical strain to which you have been subjected for the last so many years, particularly since the death or departure of your closest colleagues,

---

1. There was a devastating flood in Jammu and Kashmir during August and September 1954 because of heavy rainfall.
2. In the beginning of October 1954 some newspapers reported that Nehru wanted to relinquish the prime ministership. Nehru also wrote about this in his letter of 10 October to the chief ministers. On 11 October, he wrote a similar letter to the Pradesh Congress committees.

you should have begun to feel rather weary. The role that you have played in the service of the nation, particularly after it emerged into freedom from centuries of servitude, has been a unique and magnificent one. We of the younger generation, the heirs to the future, particularly value the inspiration and the right lead you give us in facing the tremendous problems ahead, as there is something remarkably youthful and vital in your approach which appeals to us greatly. We need your noble and inspired leadership for many years more, and I pray that you will for long continue to serve the nation and the cause of world peace.

In the end of December I am planning to visit South India for a few weeks, along with my wife and mother. We are likely to pass through Delhi and look forward to the pleasure of paying our respects to you at the time.

This letter will reach you just before you leave for China,[1] and I send with it my best wishes for a very successful trip. You carry with you the hopes and aspirations of a nation.

With respectful regards,

Yours very sincerely,
Karan Singh

——— 120 ———

Jammu
23 December 1954

My dear Panditji,
Thank you so much for your card of New Year greetings, which I warmly reciprocate. I hope and pray that in the coming year, under your dynamic and enlightened leadership, our nation will continue to make substantial progress on all fronts.

I was very happy after so long to have had the opportunity of meeting and talking with you recently in Delhi. There are some other aspects of the situation in our State which I hope to put before you when I am in Delhi at the end of February for the Governors and Rajpramukhs Conference.

Next week my mother, my wife and I leave for a month's trip to

---

1. Nehru undertook a twelve day tour of the Peoples' Republic of China from 18 to 29 October 1954.

south India – Madras, Travancore and Mysore. I will have to be back in Jammu for the Republic Day celebrations, though my mother and wife are thinking of staying on in Delhi to see the giant parade and pageants there.

I hope you have a very pleasant and successful trip to Indonesia.[1] With respects and deep regards,

Yours very sincerely,
Karan Singh

——— 121 ———

Jammu
19 March 1955

My dear Panditji,

I was very happy to have met you during the Conference[2] and, despite your heavy engagements, to have been able to have a talk with you.

I have a small personal request to make though I am rather reluctant to do so as I do not ever want you to feel that I am presuming upon the great kindness and consideration you have always shown me. However, I am sure you will not misunderstand.

As you know, I am very keen to travel abroad and have always wanted particularly to visit our next door neighbour, the USSR about which I have read and heard so much. My desire is prompted not merely out of love for 'sight-seeing' but also because Russia being a country that has had to tackle so many of the problems that face us today, it would be highly educative and revealing to see for oneself how they have done and what they are doing at present.

Now, that you are going on a visit to the USSR[3] I wonder whether it would be possible to include me in your party. That would give a youngster like me a unique opportunity, and an invaluable one, to see Russia from the closest quarters. And to do so along with you would be too wonderful for words.

I may add that I would not at all want to be a burden upon the

---

1. Nehru visited Indonesia from 27 to 30 December 1954.
2. The Conference of Governors and Rajpramukhs was held at Rashtrapati Bhavan in New Delhi on 25 February 1955.
3. Jawaharlal Nehru visited the USSR from 6 to 22 June 1955.

Government and would be quite prepared if necessary to meet all the expenses of my trip privately.

I do hope you will give this your consideration. If for some reason it is not possible for you to include me in the party I shall understand perfectly. The last thing I would want to do is to embarrass or worry you in any way.

With deep regards and respects,

Yours very sincerely,
Karan Singh

——— 122 ———

New Delhi
21 March 1955

My dear Tiger,

Your letter of the 19th March.

I quite understand your desire to go to the USSR but I do not think it will be feasible or desirable for you to go with me. I am going in response to a special invitation. I take a small staff with me to do my work. Otherwise, it will not be proper for me to add any important person to my party. Also, your going would have a certain political significance which might not be good for Kashmir at present.

I hope, however, that you will have a chance of going there later. There is no particular difficulty about it.

Yours ever,
Jawaharlal Nehru

——— 123 ———

Jammu
29 April 1955

My dear Panditji,

I would like to congratulate you upon you return from the historic Bandung Conference[1], to the success of which your inspiration and

1. The Asian-African Conference or the Bandung Conference, sponsored by the five Colombo Powers—India, Burma, Ceylon, Pakistan and Indonesia—was held from 18 to 24 April 1955 at Bandung, Indonesia. Delegates from twenty-nine countries participated in this conference.

personality contributed so much. The event marks the beginning of a new phase in world history, of a mighty resurgence of the peoples of Asia and Africa after an eclipse lasting many centuries. It is my hope that one day it will be possible to hold such a conference in Kashmir, the most beautiful spot not only of Asia but perhaps of the whole world. I am sure some day this shall come to pass.

I have just returned after spending a few days with my mother in Kangra. I am deeply worried about her health as she has not been keeping at all well for the last few years. For three years, I have been trying unsuccessfully to persuade her to come to Srinagar for a few months. I am sure that would do her a world of good, and I shall try again this year.

I do hope we shall see you in Kashmir this season. It is almost two whole years now since you have paid us a visit, and we are all looking forward eagerly to having you amongst us soon. I am moving up to Srinagar on the 9 May.

I hope this finds you very well. My wife joins me in sending you and Indiraji our very best wishes. Mummy asked me to convey her kindest regards.

With respects,

Yours very sincerely,
Karan Singh

———— 124 ————

Srinagar
12 July 1955

My dear Panditji,

My warmest felicitations upon your return home after your historic trip which we have all been following with great pride.[1] Last night we saw a newsreel which covered the first phase of your visit to the USSR. It was most interesting.

Shri Kaul[2] is returning to Delhi this afternoon and I am taking this opportunity to send you some green almonds and fruits from my garden.

---

1. Nehru was on a visit to the Soviet Union and other countries from 6 June to 11 July 1955.
2. B. M. Kaul.

My wife joins me in sending you and Indiraji our very best wishes. With deep regard and respects.

Yours sincerely,
Karan Singh

——— 125 ———

Srinagar
5 September 1955

My dear Panditji,
It was very nice of you to have had us over to dinner during our recent visit to Delhi. I do hope we shall have the pleasure of seeing you here before the close of the season. Despite your multifarious preoccupations, it would be very nice if you could spare a few days for us. I am sure you would find the change and rest helpful.

Bakshi Sahib is on a visit to Delhi, and must have conveyed to you the latest situation here in full detail.

My mother, who has been very ill for some time, arrived here a week ago and already her health has begun to show gradual improvement.

With respects and deep regards,

Yours sincerely,
Karan Singh

——— 126 ———

New Delhi
21 November 1955

My dear Tiger,
You spoke[1] to me about Bulganin[2] and Khrushchev[3] going to Kashmir.

---

1. In the course of a conversation with Khrushchev and Bulganin at the prime minister's house on 21 November 1955, Karan Singh had suggested that the Soviet leaders should pay a visit to Kashmir.
2. Nikolai Alexandrovich Bulganin (1895-1975); joined the Soviet secret police, Cheka in 1918; helped organize Moscow's defence in World War II; marshal of USSR in 1947; minister of defence, 1947-49 and 1953-55; prime minister of the Soviet Union, 1955-58.
3. Nikita Sergeyevich Khrushchev (1894-1971); elected to Central Committee of the Communist Party of the Soviet Union in 1934; member, Presidium, 1949; secretary general of CPSU, 1953-64; premier, 1958-64; first to denounce Stalin in a speech in February 1956; ousted from power by Leonid Brezhev and Alexei Kosygin in 1964.

Later this evening they told me that they had decided to go there and left it to me to fix a suitable day. This is not an easy matter, but, of course, we shall have to find some day. We cannot change their programme before they go to Burma. They are leaving for Burma on the 1st December and returning on the 6th. In the normal course they would have reached Delhi on the 9th December[1] and gone to Kashmir the next day. I would, however, like them to go there a little earlier, but the earliest can only be two or possibly three days earlier. We shall try to work this out. I have written to Bakshi Ghulam Mohammad also.

They want to spend one clear day in Srinagar. That will mean really two nights and a good part of two days. I shall keep you informed.

Ever yours,
Jawaharlal Nehru

——— 127 ———

Jammu
23 November 1955

My dear Panditji,
Thank you very much for your letter. We are all delighted that Mr Bulganin and Mr Khrushchev have decided to come to Kashmir[2] despite their very crowded schedule. It is very kind of you to have taken a personal interest in this, and I am sure their visit will be a great success. Bakshi will be sending you a draft programme for your approval and directions.

It was, as always, a great pleasure to have met you while we were in Delhi and to have partaken of your hospitality a number of times. I do hope you will be able to visit Jammu sometime during this winter or early spring. We know how incredibly busy you are, but we still hope that you will be able to spare a few days.

I shall be in Delhi next for the Governors' Conference which I expect will be held as usual towards the end of February.

With respects and deep regards,

Yours very sincerely,
Karan Singh

———————

1. In fact, they arrived in New Delhi on 18 November 1955.
2. They were in Kashmir on 9 and 10 December 1955.

——— 128 ———

New Delhi
23 November 1955

My dear Tiger,
It is almost settled now, though not quite, that the Soviet Leaders will go to Srinagar on the 9th December. They will be flying direct from Jaipur reaching Srinagar airport at about 12:30. They expect to return to Delhi on the 11th morning at 9:30. Thus they will have nearly two days and two nights there. I am waiting for confirmation of this programme from them. As soon as I know positively, we shall inform you by telegram.

I think, you should go to Srinagar for this occasion. In fact, it was largely due to your insistence that they agreed to go there.

I have spoken to Bakshi Ghulam Mohammad on the telephone. He thinks of arranging a party in the Shalimar Gardens. That is all right. He also suggests a banquet. I am rather nervous of Kashmiri banquets. I fear that the food they will get there might upset them. I have told Bakshi of this.

I think, it would be desirable for you to give a lunch to them in your house.

Ever yours,
Jawaharlal Nehru

——— 129 ———

New Delhi
24 November 1955

My dear Tiger,
Your letter of the 23rd November. I have now heard from Mr Bulganin and Mr Khrushchev accepting the programme I had sent them for a brief visit to Kashmir. I have informed Bakshi.

The broad programme is as follows:
December 9
Arrive Srinagar airport about 12:30 hours.
Spend that day and the next day and night in Srinagar.
December 11
Leave Srinagar airport 9:30 am. Reaching Delhi about 12 noon.

I have tried to impress upon Bakshi that he should not have too heavy a programme and more particularly, that food given to them should be light. I fear he will not accept my advice in this matter.

In a previous letter, I have suggested to you that you might give a lunch to them in your house.

It is possible that Indira might also go with the Russian leaders, but I am not sure.

Very special security precautions are taken for the Soviet people. It is desirable not to make a public announcement of their visit too early.

Yours sincerely,
Jawaharlal Nehru

––––––– 130 –––––––

Jammu
25 November 1955

My dear Panditji,

Many thanks for your letter of the 23rd, just received. Your telegram to Bakshi Ghulam Mohammad was also repeated to me this afternoon, and I have been in touch with him and Sadiq on the telephone.

My wife and I will both be in Srinagar to receive and welcome the distinguished guests. I well understand your apprehension about Kashmiri banquets, which are often formidable, but this one will be from me and I shall make quite sure that nothing is overdone. We will also arrange for them to have lunch in my little house one of the two days they are here. I wonder whether I should personally write and invite them or whether it will be enough to include it in their programme.

There was some discussion as to which would be the most suitable place for them to stay. My view is that Gulab Bhavan (now known as the Oberoi Palace Hotel) would serve the purpose admirably. Besides being beautifully situated and well-furnished, it is large enough comfortably to accommodate the whole party, which, of course, neither Chashmashahi nor the Guest Houses along are big enough to do. I do not think it will be a good idea to split the party up into several different houses situated miles apart. What is more, Gulab Bhavan has lovely lawns and also a tasteful banquet hall and other reception rooms.

Bakshi is away from Srinagar on a tour of the interior, and is expected back there tomorrow. I hope he will send the draft programme to you within a couple of days.

With respects,

Yours as ever,
Karan Singh

———— 131 ————

Jammu
26 November 1955

My dear Panditji,

I despatched a letter written yesterday early this morning, and this afternoon I received yours of the 24th.

It would be wonderful if Indiraji also came up with the Russian leaders. I do hope she does, and if so my wife and I would be very happy if she stayed with us in Karan Mahal. We would be delighted to have her with us, and it may be nicer than staying in the hotel or the Guest House.

I shall try and see that the programme and the food are not made too heavy. As for the public announcement, I do not think one has yet been made, but somehow everyone seems to know of the programme. It was in all the papers yesterday, though no dates were mentioned.

We are glad that they will be able to spend a clear day and a half in Srinagar. It is not very long, but it is much better than just a single day. I do not think it will be worthwhile taking them to Gulmarg or Pahalgam at this time of year. As it is we shall be pressed for time, and either of these visits will involve a fairly long and tiring drive.

Bakshi has just arrived back in Srinagar from his tour. I spoke to him a few minutes ago on the telephone, and he said that we would get down to finalizing the draft programme immediately.

With respects,

Yours as ever,
Karan Singh

——— 132 ———

New Delhi
26 November 1955

My dear Tiger,

Thank you for your letter of the 25 November.

Information reaches me that both Bulganin and Khrushchev are on the point of collapsing because of the strain of the heavy programme. They have asked me to cut out many items from their future programmes, and I am doing that. This means that, in Srinagar, their programme must be very light indeed. Bakshi had suggested taking them to Pahalgam, but I did not agree. Let them spend a day and a half in Srinagar itself, with plenty of time to rest. Also, they would have time to do some official work. They are getting papers from Moscow almost daily.

I agree with you that Gulab Bhavan is the best place for them to stay from every point of view. The party should be kept together. That place will also be proper from the security point of view, and this is important.

Yours sincerely,
Jawaharlal Nehru

——— 133 ———

New Delhi
2 December 1955

My dear Tiger,

I have spoken to Bakshi Ghulam Mohammad on the telephone about the programme of Bulganin and Khrushchev. We now hope that they will reach Srinagar airport at about 11:30 a.m. on the 9th December. Bakshi wanted to give them lunch at the airport but this is neither desirable nor necessary now. They will thereupon go straight to the weir and participate in the boat procession, after which they will proceed to the Palace Hotel and have lunch.

The rest of the afternoon should have no formal function, but it will be a good thing if they can go for a drive to Nishat Bagh, Harvan[1]

_____

1. A reservoir in Srinagar from which drinking water is supplied in the city.

and Dachigam.[1] But this should depend entirely on their wishes in the matter. Quiet dinner.

The next morning, 10th December, they should have an easy time. The only engagement before lunch should be to go to the Emporium. If they feel like it and there is time they can be taken on a *Shikara*[2] on the Dal Lake. Then lunch.

I gather that there is a big reception at the Shalimar in the afternoon and, later, there is the banquet and, possibly, some music or dancing. This is all right subject to two considerations. One is this that they do not understand Indian music, and it is no good having this kind of high class music. What they would like are folk songs or folk dancing. Secondly, they must go to bed early. I want them to rest there. They have not been well. If possible, you should release them by 10 o'clock or at the latest by 10:15 or so.

I have already told you that food should be light. For safety's sake, have a little boiled chicken prepared apart from your regular menu, in case Khrushchev or one of them is not well and wants it.

Bakshi wanted some other functions at the Nedou's Hotel and some children's show. I have told him to cancel these. These are not necessary at all.

Indira is thinking of going to Srinagar at this time. She cannot accompany the Soviet people because they will go direct from Jaipur. Therefore, Indira will go a day before, on the 8th December, by the normal service plane. She will return with them on the 11th. I think, it will be better if she also stayed at the Palace Hotel with these people.

Ever yours,
Jawaharlal Nehru

---

1. A game resort during the time of Maharaja Hari Singh, it is now a wildlife sanctuary, specially for the highly endangered Kashmir stag known as the 'Hangul'.
2. A long narrow Kashmiri boat similar to a gondola.

———— 134 ————

Srinagar
6 December 1955

My dear Panditji,

Thank you very much for your letters of the 26th November and the 2nd December.

I flew up here from Jammu yesterday. The programme has been finalized in accordance with your instructions, and preparations are in full swing. The only uncertain factor is the weather. Today it was fairly clear, but the radio forecast for tomorrow is not very encouraging. If the weather lets us down, it will be a tragedy.

We are hoping for the best. At the same time it may be wise to provide for the worst. If we find that on the 8th the weather has so deteriorated that there is hardly any possibility of their being able to get over, then, instead of cancelling the programme, we may consider shifting the venue to Jammu. Jammu is also a capital of the State, and indeed at present it is the seat of Government. The weather there at this time is perfect, and it should be possible to give them a pleasant day and a half there. Of course, the change in venue will involve tremendous administrative difficulties and we will all have to hurtle down by road during the night, but I think it will be worth it. After all, they have extended their stay in India, just for Kashmir, and we cannot let them go without visiting the State.

The accommodation problem in Jammu would not be insuperable, because I can put up the principal guests in my own houses, and the rest can go into the guest houses. This alternative requires your consideration and approval. I have mooted the possibility here also. However, I fervently hope that the problem will not arise, and that the weather will remain fine until they come and go.

It is cold here at night, and in the mornings and evenings, though the days are quite pleasant if it is clear. I am afraid Kashmir is looking far from its best at this time of year. However, the mountains and lakes are as lovely as ever.

With respects,

Yours very sincerely,
Karan Singh

With N.S. Khrushchev and N.A. Bulganin, Srinagar,
10 December 1955

——— 135 ———

My dear Panditji,
Once again the weather prophets have, happily, been proved wrong. This morning it is beautifully clear, and if it remains like this, everything will go through excellently. All arrangements here are virtually complete, including elaborate decorations, arches, gates and illuminations.

I learnt from Bakshi yesterday that there had been some controversy about whether or not as Head of State I should accompany the Russian leaders in the procession. It appears that he insisted that I should do so, and that this was ultimately agreed. I knew nothing of the matter and am sorry if any embarrassment was caused. As far as I am concerned I have absolutely no desire to do anything which may be contrary to protocol.

Indiraji will be arriving this afternoon. After lunch we would like her to look through and give us her opinion on the articles which have been selected for presentation to the distinguished guests.

With respects,

Yours as ever,
Karan Singh

——— 136 ———

My dear Panditji,
By God's grace and your blessings, the visit of the Russian leaders has been a resounding success. Indiraji will be able to give you a first hand report. Everything went off excellently and even the weather, which gave us some anxious moments, cooperated in the end despite the dire predictions of the meteorologists.

I think, they have returned well impressed. Their statements[1] here, particularly Mr Khrushchev's long and somewhat outspoken speech

---

1. Speaking in Srinagar on 9 December 1955, Bulganin, the Soviet prime minister referred to Kashmir as the 'Northern part of India'.

yesterday,[1] are of great political value. The Russians are the first great power to have definitely and clearly gone on record as accepting the accession of Kashmir to India as final.

It was very nice that Indiraji was here during the visit. We are sorry she could not stay on for a few days.

My wife and I are returning to Jammu tomorrow.

With respectful regards,

Yours as ever,
Karan Singh

———— 137 ————

Jammu
26 December 1955

My dear Panditji,

Thank you very much for your card of New Year greetings, which I warmly reciprocate.

I am sure that under your dynamic and inspiring leadership the year that is about to dawn will see further progress within the country as well as towards the larger objective of world peace and brotherhood to which you have contributed so much.

Incidentally, the Mathura Buddha which is pictured on the card is to my mind one of the most beautiful pieces of sculpture in India. Until recently it was used to be displayed in the Central Hall of the National Museum at Rashtrapati Bhavan, and every time I visited Delhi I would go there in order to gaze upon that remarkable work of art. The master-artist of a bygone age, to whom we owe an immense debt of gratitude, has beautifully expressed in stone the spiritual glory that is Buddha. The last time I was in Delhi I was distressed to learn that this statue was being removed to a museum in some other city. It seems a pity that the capital should be deprived of this master-piece.

You must have received the letter which Indiraji kindly took with her from Srinagar.[2]

With deep regards and respects,

Yours as ever,
Karan Singh

---

1. In a speech in Srinagar on 10 December 1955, Khrushchev observed that 'Kashmir is a part of India and the people of Kashmir have themselves decided to be so'.
2. Dated 11 December 1955.

——— 138 ———

Jammu
11 January 1956

My dear Panditji,
Bakshi Sahib has seen me after his return from Delhi. Among other things he mentioned that on the advice of the Government of India it has been decided to release Sheikh Abdullah towards the end of this month. No doubt this decision has been arrived at after careful consideration by all concerned, but as this is a matter of considerable importance I thought I should put my views before you.

Since the new regime took over on 9th August 1953 there has, as you know, been marked improvement and consolidation in many spheres, specially the economic and the constitutional. It is unnecessary to recount these achievements, and it is in no spirit of belittlement that I add that they have to be viewed in their proper perspective. Despite all that has been done we cannot say that the political problem in the Valley has been solved. The reasons for this are primarily communal, but an important factor is that the Kashmir question still continues to be a live dispute with Pakistan and the subject of negotiations with that country. Nevertheless, the communal elements in the Valley are at the moment considerably demoralized, specially as a result of the recent statements[1] of King Saud[2] and the Russian Leaders.[3] What is more they do not have any outstanding leader around whom they can rally their forces.

In the light of the position now obtaining, the probable repercussions of the release of Sheikh Abdullah require careful consideration. Of course, it is not possible to make precise predictions,

---

1. King Saud Ibn Abdul Aziz in a statement on 10 December 1955 in Bombay said: 'the fate of Indians Muslims is in safe hands as Mr Nehru is bravely determinedly executing a wide policy of affection and neighbourliness to all Indians irrespective of creed'. He also advised the Indian Muslims to preserve the unity of the country and 'to be true to your country and good to your neighbours, your national duties must be executed with sincerity and straightforwardness.' The King had declined an invitation from the Kashmir government to include Kashmir in his tour.

2. Saud Ibn Abdul Aziz (1902-1969); second son of Ibn Saud, the founder of Saudi Arabia and its first king; became king on 9 November 1953; visited India from 27 November to 13 December 1955; deposed in November 1964.

3. See *ante,* p. 175.

but I feel it would not be justified to minimize the potentialities of the situation.

There is little doubt that upon his emergence from detention, he will immediately become the rallying point for all the disruptionist forces and disgruntled factions. There emerges the distinct possibility of widespread lawlessness and violent clashes between the various parties, to cope with, which it may well become necessary to use forcible means. I am not suggesting that with the resources at its disposal the Government will be unable to face the situation. What I do submit is that the trouble may assume considerable proportions necessitating measures which may expose us to severe criticism and distorted allegations in the sphere not only of local but of wider public opinion. There is no lack of those who are only too eager to exploit anything that might discredit the Government of India and the State Government, and this would be for them a heaven-sent opportunity.

It is said that if any such trouble takes place it can easily be faced, and if necessary Sheikh Abdullah himself can again be detained. But would not that be widely interpreted in a manner which cannot but seriously undermine the prestige and position of the present regime both within and outside the State? In such an event we will very probably have to face a situation even more difficult than the one which confronted us in 1953.[1]

Apart from the grave danger to law and order, there are three other distinct possibilities which cannot easily be ruled out. First, there is the danger that Sheikh Abdullah might be able to browbeat enough MLAs to gain a majority in the Assembly, of which he continues to be a member. This body is still functioning both in a legislative as well as a constituent capacity, and the potentialities of such an eventuality are too obvious to require any elucidation. Though Bakshi Sahib denies the possibility of any considerable defection from his ranks, I find myself, in the event of the stress of those peculiar circumstances, unable to share his optimism. Secondly, there is a section among members of the administrative services whose political bias may, in an atmosphere of communal excitement, cause large-scale desertion or even sabotage which can render any administration virtually powerless. Thirdly, there is a real danger of serious differences emerging within the ruling party itself as a result of the severe strain

---

1. When S.M. Abdullah was removed and arrested.

to which it will be subjected, and in the present context this would have obviously undesirable results.

One thing at least is almost certain. The atmosphere of permanence and stability which has been steadily built up will suffer a severe shock, and the whole issue will, in the minds of the people of the State, be thrown once again into the melting pot. This may lead many who support the present situation to reconsider their position. Fresh life will be infused into the communal movement, the immediate and cumulative impact of which can hardly fail to have serious repercussions.

It has, of course, to be considered how long he can be kept in detention. I support the widely-held view that the proper time to release him, keeping in view the security of the State which is our primary responsibility, would be only after it is found possible to declare that the Kashmir dispute is finally closed, or at the very least until the State Constitution has been completely enacted and the Constituent Assembly dissolved, after which the situation can be reviewed. Until that time, I venture to submit, releasing him would be taking a formidable risk. Even from the wider aspect the detention of one man is likely to be the lesser evil than having on our hands a widespread law and order problem and acute political disturbance in an area where above all stability and peace is required. Large-scale trouble may shake the faith and support even of staunch friends.

Finally, I may submit that we cannot ignore the existence of powerful forces who would be eager to support financially and otherwise any disruptive movement within the State which would shatter its present stable and progressive association as an integral part of India. Specially, at a time when we are on the threshold of a new phase of substantial economic and social progress as envisaged in the Second Five Year Plan, an essential pre-requisite for the success of which is peace and stability, we need to avoid any step which would play into the hands of such forces.

Knowing how very busy you are, I seek your indulgence for having written at such length, but in view of the consideration you have always shown me, and of the duties which you have entrusted to me, I felt that I should lay before you in as clear and objective a manner as possible my views on this important matter.

With respectful regards,

Yours very sincerely,
Karan Singh

P.S.
Because of the highly confidential nature of the communication, I am
sending the letter by hand of a special messenger, my ADC Captain
Goverdhan Singh.

K.S.

──────── 139 ────────

New Delhi
11 January 1956

My dear Tiger,
Your letter of the 11th January has just reached me.

During the last year or more, the question of Sheikh Abdullah's
release has often been discussed. Obviously, it is a difficult question
and one has to balance various factors. So far as I am concerned, my
whole mind rebels against the long detention of any person without
trial. I have objected to this so often in the past that naturally I do not
like it. But I realize that sometimes circumstances compel one to take
action which is normally undesirable. In the balance, therefore, I left
it to the judgement of the Jammu and Kashmir Government to decide
what they should do in the matter.

In every such case the advantage that one gains by the action taken
gradually diminishes and the disadvantage increases. It has seemed to
me that this stage was passed some time ago. It may thus become
progressively more risky to release Sheikh Abdullah. Sometime or
other that risk has to be taken and it is impossible to keep him or any
other person indefinitely in detention. That very detention will become
an increasing factor for instability and for reactions against us in India
and abroad, apart from its effect in Kashmir itself.

You say that it would be desirable to keep him in detention till it
is found possible to declare that the Kashmir dispute is finally closed.
That, I think, is not feasible. In fact, so long as Sheikh Abdullah is in
prison, the dispute will not be finally closed. It is only when he has
been released and we have faced the consequences of that release and
survived them, that it will be possible for the situation to develop
towards a final end.

There are the risks which you have mentioned. The question is
whether the risks grow less or more by delay. The question also is as
to whether internal stability in people's minds and administration

will become more favourable later. These are factors which it is difficult for me to judge. But I am inclined to think that there will be no marked change for the better within some months or so and the change might well be the other way. People in Jammu and Kashmir State are at present conscious of the considerable improvements, economic and other, in the State. They will forget them a little later.

This is my broad line of thinking. But as I have said above, I have avoided imposing my wishes on Bakshi Ghulam Mohammad or his government. If he has come to the conclusion that this is a suitable time to face the risk, I would abide by his decision and certainly not come in his way. I have no doubt that internationally speaking, the release would have powerful effect in our favour. Internally I cannot judge. But I have a very uncomfortable feeling that our position is constantly undermined by Sheikh Abdullah's detention, both internally and abroad.

I realize fully the risks involved. But one does not solve a problem or really avoid risks by running away from them. Therefore, after giving a great deal of thought to this matter, I have felt that Bakshi Ghulam Mohammad should take the action he has decided upon. This is as favourable an opportunity as is likely to occur. Of course, we should be fully prepared. Having got over this difficulty, the future of the Kashmir problem will be very much simpler.

I would add that the visit of the Soviet leaders to Kashmir and its effect on the internal and external situation, which has been all to the good and has influenced many people in the right direction, is a factor to be considered. The conditions in Pakistan and in 'Azad Kashmir' are bad. Sheikh Abdullah may behave very foolishly but the effect of his behaviour is likely to be less now and can be dealt with more easily.

All these are speculations and appraisal of a difficult situation which has to be faced now or later. The question is what the most suitable time will be. It is bad to live in apprehension all the time. It is better to take the ghost out of our minds and deal with it.

Ever yours,
Jawaharlal Nehru

I realise fully the risks involved. But one does not solve a problem or really avoid risks by running away from them. Therefore, after giving a great deal of thought to this matter, I have felt that Bakhshi Ghulam Mohammad should take the action he has decided upon. This is as favourable an opportunity as is likely to occur. Of course we should be fully prepared. Having got over this difficulty, the future of the Kashmir problem will be very much simpler.

I would add that the visit of the Soviet leaders to Kashmir and its effect on the internal & external situation, which has been all to the good and has influenced many people in the right direction, is a factor to be considered. The conditions in Pakistan & in 'Azad' Kashmir are also bad. Shaikh Abdullah may behave very foolishly but the effect of his behaviour is likely to be less now and can be dealt with more easily.

All these are speculations and appraisals of a difficult situation which has to be faced now or later. The question is what the most suitable time will be. It is bad to live in apprehension all the time. It is better to take the short relief on minds and deal with it.

Ever yours
Jawaharlal Nehru

Last paragraphs of Jawaharlal Nehru's letter of 11 January 1956 to Karan Singh

——— 140 ———

Jammu
19 January 1956

My dear Panditji,

Thank you for your letter of the 11th in reply to mine of the same date. It was very kind of you to have written so promptly.

I am writing this letter after studying the communiqué issued by the Government of India on 16th January in connection with the States Reorganization Commission's report.[1] Your wise and statesman-like approach to this complex problem will, I am sure, bring about the best possible solution under the circumstances.

It appears that Jammu and Kashmir was considered by the Commission to be outside their terms of reference, for they have made no recommendations for this State. Although at present any change in the existing territorial position here is out of the question, yet there are some important points which do have a direct bearing upon our State and which I feel deserve serious consideration. Among these I would at this time like to mention the following:

1. For some reason this State has been omitted from the list of States mentioned in the communiqué as comprising the Northern Zone. The Zonal Councils as at present envisaged are to be advisory and deliberative bodies, and it is difficult to see why Kashmir should be left out of them. Its exclusion will deprive the State of the benefits of co-ordination with adjoining States forming the Northern zone, with which we have many matters of common concern. What is more, the omission will be exploited and misinterpreted by interested parties, while inclusion will act as a stabilizing and beneficial factor.

2. The recommendations concerning safeguards for linguistic minorities to which the Government of India attaches great

---

1. In a communiqué issued by the home ministry on 16 January 1956, the government announced its acceptance of most of the recommendations of the States Reorganization Commission. But it was decided to divide the Bombay region into Maharashtra including Vidarbha, Gujarat including Saurashtra and Kutch, and a centrally administered Bombay city including some surrounding villages. Decisions on the future of the Punjab and the Telengana area of Hyderabad were still under consideration.

importance, is sharply relevant in our case. As you know there are two important linguistic minorities in this State, the Dogras and the Ladakhis, and I am sure that no one will want them to be deprived of the safeguards that are to be provided for other linguistic minorities in the rest of India. Of course, as the communiqué says, this is a matter for consultation with the State Governments, but my point is that it should not be overlooked in our case on the ground that the States Reorganization Commission's recommendations do not directly pertain to us.

3. Then there is the fundamental matter of the abolition of the existing constitutional disparity between different States of the Union and equation of Part B with Part A States. Jammu and Kashmir is mentioned in the Constitution as a Part B State, though it is still governed by the Temporary Provision of Article 370. Although it may not be possible for us immediately to assume exactly the same position as other States, yet I feel that the question of the Headship of this State is of great importance and merits careful consideration at this stage, specially in view of the decision to abolish the institution of Rajpramukhs[1] and to bring all states under the same system of Governorship.

I may immediately submit that I am not considering this question from a personal point of view at all. It does not matter who is the Head of State here so long as we can be sure that it will always be someone who will keep the larger national interests paramount and enjoy the complete confidence of the Centre. I think, you will agree that the present arrangement does not ensure this. Although the Sadar-i-Riyasat is to be recognized by the President, this recognition is to be on the recommendation of the State Legislative Assembly which, in turn, is through election by Assembly Members. Theoretically, it may be possible for the President to refuse recognition to a person in case he is considered undesirable, but in practice, keeping in view political and constitutional conventions, this will be very difficult. And even if it could be done, the initiative will always remain with the State Assembly.

In view of the peculiar internal, international and geographical factors that operate in this State, I feel that the importance of vesting

---

1. Abolished in November 1956.

in the President of the Republic the authority to nominate the Head
of State (whatever the name of that office in Kashmir may be) can
hardly be overestimated. I appreciate that this change will probably
require constitutional action from our side, but this should not prove
an insuperable obstacle. The importance of the matter, and the
potentialities of the present situation, will amply justify any difficulty
which may have to be encountered in solving it. What is more, the
present phase in which there will be far reaching constitutional changes
affecting the whole country appears to me to be the ideal time to get
over this problem also. Later, when the changes in other States have
all taken place and the position in respect to the Headship here has
crystallized as a result of continued usage, it will be much more
difficult.

I have not discussed these points with Bakshi Sahib yet, but I trust
that he will not fail to appreciate their validity and importance.

With respectful regards,

Yours very sincerely,
Karan Singh

———— 141 ————

New Delhi
20 January 1956

My dear Tiger,

Thank you for your letter of the 19th January. The question of including
Jammu and Kashmir in our decisions regarding states reorganization
did not arise. It is, of course, possible to include that State in the
Northern Zone. But that will have to be subject to the approval of
the Jammu and Kashmir Government.

It would certainly be a good thing for safeguards to be given for
linguistic minorities in Jammu and Kashmir. How exactly this could
be done will have to be thought.

Jammu and Kashmir State may have been mentioned in the
Constitution as a Part B State, but it has obviously been treated
differently. In fact, it has been treated as something slightly more than
a Part A State. In future, there are going to be no Part B or Part C
States. There will be only one category of states. In view, however, of
our special agreements with the Jammu and Kashmir State, these

agreements will necessarily stand unless they are varied. They cannot be carried unilaterally.

I am sending a copy of your letter to Pantji.[1]

Ever yours,
Jawaharlal Nehru

———— 142 ————

New Delhi
26 January 1956

My dear Tiger,

I am deeply grateful to you for your message for Republic Day. This day is a day of rejoicing for all of us but, at the same time, it is a day for a searching of hearts. Recent events in some parts of India have pointed out the dangers we have to face.[2] These come much more from our internal weaknesses than from any external source. We have, therefore, to face and overcome our own failings.

All good wishes to you,

Yours sincerely,
Jawaharlal Nehru

———— 143 ————

Jammu
1 February 1956

My dear Panditji,

For the last few years my wife and I have been wanting to go abroad, but for various reasons we have not been able to do so. We were all

1. G.B. Pant (1887-1961); eminent Congressman from UP; member, Kashipur Municipal Board; leader of the Swaraj Party, UP Legislative Council, 1923-30; president, UPPCC, 1927-30; took part in the Congress movements, 1930, 1940 and 1942 and was imprisoned several times; member, Central Legislative Assembly, 1934-36; leader of Congress party, UP Legislative Assembly, and premier, 1937-39; chief minister, UP, 1946-55; member, Rajya Sabha, 1955-61; Union minister of home affairs, 1955-61; awarded Bharat Ratna, 1957.
2. Following the announcement on 16 January 1956 of the decision of the government of India for acceptance of most of the recommendations of the States Reorganization Commission, there occurred disturbances and violence in various parts of the country, mainly in Maharashtra and Gujarat.

set to go in 1953, but had to cancel the programme at the last minute due to political development. This year, after completing my M.A. (previous) examination of the Delhi University in April, we are thinking of going abroad on a private trip for a month or six weeks some time in May. I mentioned this to Bakshi Sahib and he has no objection. Naturally, my going will depend upon the absence of any unusual development here.

I am writing this to get your approval before I formally make a request to the President. Last time, in the absence of any constitutional provision, the question arose as to who would carry on the functions of Head of State during my absence. After much discussion it was held on the advice of the Union Law Ministry that there was no necessity for anyone to officiate and that important papers could continue to come to me wherever I was.

We are planning to visit England, France, Switzerland and perhaps Italy. In England we have many friends, and in France I want among other places to see my birthplace at Cannes which I left when I was five weeks old and have not visited since. I am particularly keen to visit Switzerland because it has so much in common with Kashmir and I am sure we can learn a great deal from it as regards tourism as well as small-scale industries. The trip would thus be a change, holiday as well as a great education for us.

As you know, I am also most keen to visit the Soviet Union, and Mr Bulganin and Mr Khrushchev also repeatedly invited my wife and me to come there. I am not sure whether it would be proper for us to go or not. If it is, then we would love to include Russia also, if necessary dropping some of the other countries.

As soon as I receive your approval I will set about drawing up a detailed programme, and then write to the Government of India for the necessary passports, visas etc.

With respects and kindest regards for you and Indiraji from us both,

Yours very sincerely
Karan Singh

───────── 144 ─────────

New Delhi
5 February 1956

My dear Tiger,
I have your letter of the 1st February. I think it would be a good thing if you went abroad for a while, though your absence should not be for too long. For the present, however, I think, it is a little difficult to decide about this matter. You might wait a little and see what developments take place in Kashmir and elsewhere.

I am consulting Pantji also on this subject.

Yours ever,
Jawaharlal Nehru

───────── 145 ─────────

Delhi
14 April 1956

My dear Panditji,
I have been reading with much interest newspaper reports of your speech yesterday.[1] Your recent pronouncements on Kashmir[2] have had a profound effect in the State, and have been enthusiastically welcomed by large sections of the people. The last traces of uncertainty

───────────────────

1. On 13 April at a public meeting in Delhi on the occasion of the celebration of the National Week, Nehru spoke at length on the Kashmir issue. He said that until Pakistan withdrew its forces from Kashmir in accordance with the UNCIP resolution there could be no talk of a plebiscite. He further said: 'I have not a shadow of doubt that India has followed the right policy in regard to Kashmir, a policy of decency and restraint and a policy that will do justice to the people of Kashmir, to the people of India and to the People of Pakistan. We shall not accept any step which seeks to create in the slightest manner any upheaval in Kashmir'. He also condemned the activities of the Praja Parishad in Jammu and declared that the tone adopted by the Parishad only succeeded in fostering the Muslim League's two-nation theory.
2. On 29 March 1956, Nehru stated in the Lok Sabha that the talk of plebiscite in Kashmir was 'entirely besides the point' and there could be no question of holding it until Pakistan had withdrawn all her armed forces from the state. He also said that the Kashmir problem had to be viewed afresh because of the American military aid to Pakistan and added that Pakistan's joining the Baghdad Pact and SEATO had invalidated the old arguments relating to the question. Again on 2 April 1956, at a press conference on Delhi, he spoke on the same lines on the Kashmir issue.

regarding the State's future have been dispelled, and the results of this will naturally be further normalization, consolidation and progress. Of course, Pakistan's bellicose and aggressive attitude, combined with her growing military strength as a result of American military aid, naturally causes some concern and anxiety. But under your able guidance the nation has nothing to fear, and I am sure that we shall progress from strength to strength on all fronts.

I have been here since the beginning of the month. Several times we have tried to fix up an interview through your Secretariat, but you must have been very busy. I hope I shall be able to see you for a few minutes whenever you are free.

I am here in connection with the M. A. examination of the Delhi University which commences on the 24th and ends on the 30th of this month.[1]

With respects and deep regards,

Yours very sincerely,
Karan Singh

——— 146 ———

Delhi
22 April 1956

My dear Panditji,

I enclose a copy of the letter I have written to the President in connection with our trip abroad.

Many thanks for autographing the *Autobiography*.[2] It is a great book which I never tire of dipping into whenever possible, and once I take it up it becomes difficult to put it down.

I am returning to Jammu on the 30th, which is the day my papers end. I do hope you will be able to come to Srinagar this season. Please do try.

With deep regards and respects,

Yours very sincerely,
Karan Singh

1. Karan Singh passed his M.A. in Political Science with a first class first creating a still unbroken university record.
2. The reference was to Nehru's *Autobiography*, which was first published in 1936 by John Day & Company.

——— 147 ———

New Delhi
25 July 1956

My dear Panditji,

I enclose the note which I mentioned last night, containing my immediate reaction and observations on the Draft.[1] I have sent a copy to Vishnu Sahay.[2] I have not dealt in great detail with the rather cumbersome document, but have confined myself to points of cardinal importance. I do feel that careful and thorough consideration at this stage from all angles will be of immense value in clearing the path for the future and obviating unnecessary difficulties and complications.

It has been a great pleasure and privilege seeing you so often in England and here. I do hope you will be able to visit Srinagar before the close of the season.

With respects and deep regards from us both,

Yours very sincerely,
Karan Singh

——— 148 ———

Observations on the Draft Constitution for Jammu and Kashmir[3]

Preamble

1. The preamble is much too long, pompous and repetitious, which makes it faintly ludicrous. Also, there are several unnecessary and undesirable phrases in it, such as in para 4 'conversations', in 5 'desired by us', in 6 'peoples' and in the end 'our country' etc. It would be much better to shorten and simplify the Preamble.

Part 1 (Form of State)

1. It may be considered whether it would not be more realistic to take cognisance of the de facto occupation, albeit illegal, of part of our State by Pakistan. Indeed, we might derive some political advantage

---

1. For note on the draft constitution of Jammu and Kashmir, see the next item.
2. Secretary, Kashmir affairs, ministry of home affairs.
3. Note to Jawaharlal Nehru, Jammu, 25 July 1956.

by making provision for that part of the State also to enjoy the advantages of this Constitution when it is freed from occupation.

Part 2 (Permanent residents)

No comment at present.

Part 3 (Directive Principles)

1. Here again the principles appear to be inordinately long, complex and repetitive, full of sweeping generalizations and favourite cliches. It would really be much better if they are reduced to a few general principles, as after all they do not have any legal or constitutional validity per se.

2. Article 3 lists the Capitalist Sector as part of the economic order, but Article 8 is heavily and even viciously biased against it. Such an approach, which savours strongly of dogmatism, appears to be quite unnecessary and even harmful. It will not only discourage local capital and initiative, but will completely frighten away all outside capital which is so necessary for our swift economic development. Clearly, Government Agencies alone cannot do everything; there must be adequate scope for the private sector. And while the private sector must necessarily be made to function in the framework of the larger national interest, there is no need to phrase the matter as it has been done in this article. After all we need not assume that the transformation of all private enterprise into public ownership is inevitable or even necessary.

Part 4 (The Executive)

1. Article 10, which provides for the impeachment of the Sadar-i-Riyasat, is an extraordinary provision. It will have the effect of placing the SR entirely at the mercy of the party in power and make it almost impossible for him, if the necessity arises, to act in the broader national interest. After all, as Head of one of the State of the Union, the SR must necessarily be to some extent responsible to the President, particularly as like Governors he will very likely be acting as an Agent of the President for many Union matters. The proposed article would make it possible for the Assembly to initiate impeachment proceedings even on frivolous grounds just to browbeat the SR, and make it almost impossible for any self-respecting person to undertake the job. At the

most there may be a provision that in very exceptional circumstances the Assembly may by a ¾ majority request the President to investigate a certain matter in connection with the actions of the SR. Then it would be for the President at his discretion to institute the necessary judicial proceedings at the end of which, if he is satisfied that there has been some gross misbehaviour, he may withdraw recognition from the SR. Even otherwise, of course, the President is competent at any time to withdraw his recognition. But such a procedure should be quite sufficient to save the State from the depredations of an irresponsible SR.

2. Article 15 should be recast on the lines of Article 164 of the Indian Constitution. The convention, of course is there, but it will not be wise to make it a constitutional provision, as under some circumstances it may well be that the appointment may precede a confidence vote in the Assembly.

3. Read in the context of Article 14.3, Article 14.2 appears to be superfluous.

4. Article 21-24 provide only for the event of resignation by the Prime Minister. But there must be some general provisions regarding the breakdown of the constitutional machinery, of which such a resignation need not necessarily be part. In regard to other states the power vests with the President under Article 356, but this Article does not apply to our State. Therefore either this article must be made applicable or the power must specifically be vested in the SR. Otherwise, in the event of a constitutional crisis it may become impossible to prevent chaos. In view of the peculiar political conditions attaching to the State, this question assumes still greater significance.

5. Article 27 should be recast on the lines of Article 167 of the Indian Constitution. As it is it has been so watered down as to make it virtually meaningless. As an elected person it is even more important for the SR to be in the closest touch with affairs of State, and this must be ensured in the Constitution.

Part 5 (The Legislature)

1. The question of having a second chamber for a tiny State like ours should be ruled out at once as unnecessarily cumbersome and expensive.

2. It would be probably better and simpler to fix the number of reserved seats for five years at this stage, rather than leave the matter open. Such reservation should kept down to it irreducible minimum.

3. In Article 32.1, the national language, Hindi, should also be mentioned along with English.

Part 6 (The Judiciary)

1. It is hardly necessary to stress the paramount importance of having a really free and independent judiciary, if our State is to enjoy the substance of democracy and not only the name. In this connection the proposal that our High Court judges should be appointed not by the President but by the SR is open to serious criticism. It would be much more conducive to be dignity and independence of the Court if its judges were to be appointed by the President, if necessary in consultation with the SR.

2. Article 6.2 regarding removal of High Court judges, is a still more drastic and disastrous inroad into judicial freedom. It has the effect of putting the judiciary entirely at the mercy of the party which happens to be in power in the State at a certain time, and would make it almost impossible for the judges to function without fear or favour. They would constantly have the threat of an adverse Assembly vote hanging over their heads, and the prestige and effectiveness of our court would be seriously minimized. The procedure laid down in the Indian Constitution (Article 217.1.0) is infinitely preferable.

3. This is a good time to consider the advisability of extending Article 136 of the Indian Constitution (empowering the Supreme Court of grant special leave of appeal from any court or tribunal) to our State also, as it will be all to the good.

4. In Article 23 the reference to the High Court should properly be made by the Sadar-i-Riyasat rather than the Council of Ministers, on the analogy of Article 143 of the Indian Constitution.

Part 7 (Finance, Property and Contracts)

I do not feel competent to offer any comment. I hope it has been thoroughly vetted by a financial expert.

Part 8 (Services)

No comment at present.

Part 9 (Elections)

1. The broad question of the necessity of having a separate Election Commission for the State should be carefully reconsidered. The Indian Commission would naturally be more efficient and evoke more respect both within and without the State.

2. The present practice of our Members of Parliament being elected by the State Assembly and then nominated by the President should cease, and with the advent of the new Constitution our MPs should be elected by open franchise the same way as they are in the rest of India. There is no good reason why our people should be indefinitely deprived of the privilege of directly electing their representatives to Parliament.

3. Similarly, at least for the Parliamentary constituencies, if not for the State Assembly constituencies also, the work should be entrusted to the Indian Delimitation Commission, as its competence and impartiality is established and recognized by all. This important task should not be left to some minor official of the State.

4. Article 2 reduces the voting age from 21 in the rest of India to 18. There do not appear to be reasons sufficiently strong to justify the departure.

Part 10 (Cultural and Regional development)

1. The idea of following the Punjab Formula seems to be an excellent one, as the very geographical and historical facts of the State make this necessary. But the provision in Article 3 for nomination of persons to these Regional Committees by the SR is completely out of place, as it will alter the whole point and purpose of the Committees and render their value nugatory. The Regional Committees are Committees of the Assembly, and this they should remain. Any provision for nominating others will be highly suspect.

2. The frontier district of Ladakh poses special problem, and if necessary there may be a special provision authorizing the SR to nominate up to a maximum of three members on that Regional Committee only.

Part 11 (Miscellaneous)

1. The mention of impeachment of the SR in the proviso to Article 1 should be reconsidered in the light of the comment on this matter earlier.

Part 12 (Amendment)

No comment at present

General points not specifically mentioned in the Draft Constitution

1. The safeguards for Linguistic Minorities which, on the basis of the S.R.C. report, are proposed to be given to such minorities in the rest of India should be extended to our State also, there being two distinct minorities speaking Dogri and Ladakhi.

2. These two language, along with Kashmiri, should be recognized in the Constitution as Regional and Official languages of the State to respect of such matters as primary and secondary education, Assembly proceedings, petitions etc.

3. The integration of our services with the All India services should be finalized and completed without further delay.

4. The jurisdiction of the Comptroller and Auditor General of India should be extended to our State also. The benefits of this, particularly for the State, are too obvious to require repetition.

––––––––––– 149 –––––––––––

Srinagar
19 August 1956

My dear Panditji,
We were all greatly distressed to hear on the radio this morning about your jeep mishap[1]. Thank God it resulted only in minor injuries, which I hope you will completely get over very soon. My mother and wife join me in our anxious inquiries.

I wonder whether you have had occasion to glance through the Draft Constitution. I believe it is still under consideration at Delhi, and I sincerely hope that from this process it will emerge free from any defects which may plague us in the future.

––––––––––––––––

1. In Kutch on 18 August.

Independence Day celebrations here went off very well. Next month we will celebrate the festival of Kashmir.[1]

The Suez tangle appears to have very grave potentialities.[2] I only hope better sense prevails and that the sane and wise position adopted by you in Parliament[3] emerges victorious over rasher counsels of despair.

Please do not bother to reply. I know how extremely busy you are and would not have imposed upon your time, were it not my desire to convey to you our distress of your accident and heartfelt thanksgiving that you are safe and well.

With respect and deep regards,

Yours as ever,
Karan Singh

---

1. Jashn-i-Kashmir, a cultural festival.
2. The Suez Canal crisis originated when Gamal Abdel Nasser, the president of Egypt, announced at a rally in Alexandria on 26 July 1956 the nationalization of the Suez Canal and termed the Suez Canal Company as an 'exploiting' agency and a 'State within a State'. This action created very strong reactions, more specially, in the UK and France. Anthony Eden, the prime minister of the UK, stated on 27 July that Nasser's unilateral decision to 'expropriate' the Company affected the rights and interests of many nations. On 2 August he said that his government had conceded 'it necessary to take certain precautionary measures of a military nature.' Similarly, the French premier, Guy Mollet denounced Nasser as a 'would be dictator' and an imitator of Adolf Hitler. He warned that France and her allies were determined to launch 'an energetic and severe riposte' to Nasser's ambitions. The UK, USA and France convened a conference in London from 16 to 23 August to consider the situation arising after the nationalization of the Suez Canal. It presented proposals to Nasser which sought that the operation and development of the Suez Canal should be the responsibility of an international Suez Canal Board. Egypt refused to agree to it.
3. In his speech of 8 August 1956 in the Lok Sabha, Nehru stated that, 'I have no desire to add to the passion aroused, but I would fail in my duty to this House and to the country and even to all the parties involved in this crisis, and not least of all to Britain and France, if I do not say that threats to settle this dispute or to enforce their views in this matter by display or use of force is the wrong way.' He further added: 'it would be unrealistic and imprudent not to express our deep concern at these developments and point to their ominous implications. We deeply regret these reactions and the measures reported to be taken in consequence, and we express the hope that they will cease and the parties will enter into negotiations and seek peaceful settlements.'

——— 150 ———

Jammu
13 November 1956

My dear Panditji,
My mother and wife join me in sending you our warmest congratulations upon your birthday and in wishing you many happy returns of the day. May you be spared for many years to guide us and lead us onwards as our historic destiny unfolds.

I expect to be in Delhi for a week towards the end of this month, and look forward to the pleasure of seeing you then.

With deep regards and respect,

Yours very sincerely,
Karan Singh

——— 151 ———

New Delhi
6 December 1956

My dear Panditji,
This is just a note to inform you that I got into touch with Dr Radhakrishnan this morning and he has kindly agreed to perform the opening ceremony of the tunnel.[1] He will fly to Jammu on the 14th and proceed to Banihal by car for the ceremony on the 15th. He will be back in Delhi by the 16th.

It would have been wonderful if you could have managed to come for this historic function, but in your unavoidable absence I can think of no one in India better suited than our distinguished Vice-President.

With respects and deep regards,

Yours very sincerely,
Tiger

PS
Many thanks for autographing all those photographs. They will remain with us as treasured possessions.

T.

——————————

1. Banihal, one of the longest tunnels in the world, provides an all-weather link between the Valley and the rest of the country. It crosses the Pir Panjal range six miles south-west of Varinag, in the Shahabad Valley.

———— 152 ————

Jammu
26 December 1956

My dear Panditji,

May I wish you a very hearty welcome home after your trip abroad.[1]
We have all been following with the greatest interest your activities
since you left India, and it is a matter of deep gratification that the visit
has been so successful and that you are safely home.

You will be pleased to know that the opening of the new Banihal
tunnel by Dr Radhakrishnan on the 22nd was a great success.[2] We
are all very grateful to him for having at considerable personal
inconvenience agreed to perform the ceremony. It was rather strenuous
because of two successive days we had to drive long distances in the
cold weather and, in places, through snow. But the occasion was indeed
historic and it was fitting that a person of the stature of Dr
Radhakrishnan was associated with it. Involving as it does the piercing
of a geographical barrier, the event will have a profound impact—
political and economic—upon our State.

Many thanks for your card of New Year greetings, which I most
warmly reciprocate. I have a feeling that the year ahead will not be an
easy one for our country, but under your leadership and guidance I
am sure we will be able to weather all storms and progress along the
road that destiny has placed before us.

It was a great pleasure seeing you in Delhi recently, and also meeting
Mr Chou En-lai[3] and the Lamas.[4] I do not know when the Governors'
Conference will be held this year. At any rate, I expect to be in Delhi
for a couple of days in the middle of February at which time I look
forward to paying my respects to you, unless of course, I am required
there earlier.

With respects and deep regards,

Yours as ever,
Karan Singh

———————————————

1. Nehru was on a tour of the USA from 16 to 21 December, of Canada on 22 and 23
   December and of England from 24 to 27 December 1956.
2. After the inaugural ceremony Radhakrishnan took aside Karan Singh and quipped:
   'you invite me to open the tunnel and then name it after Jawaharlal Nehru'.
3. Chou En-lai was on a visit to India from 28 November to 10 December 1956.
4. The Dalai Lama and the Panchen Lama were in India at this time as guests for the
   Buddha Jayanti celebrations.

With Jawaharlal Nehru, the Dalai Lama, the Panchen Lama and Govind Ballabh Pant, New Delhi, 24 November 1956

——————— 153 ———————

Delhi
18 April 1957

My dear Panditji,

May I congratulate you upon the formation of your Ministry.[1] The country is indeed fortunate to have you at its helm at this crucial juncture of our history, and I pray that you may be spared for many years to lead and guide us towards the glorious future that lies ahead.

My mother and wife join me to sending you our warmest congratulations and wishes for a most successful tenure of office.

With respects,

Yours very sincerely,
Karan Singh

——————— 154 ———————
Efficient Administration[2]

1. Cabinet: Bakshi Sahib may be given a free hand in the formation of the new Cabinet, but the supreme importance of removing the abuses in his administration and party must be impressed upon him. In this context the active intervention of Panditji and Pantji will be invaluable.

2. Chief Secretary: He is the pivot around which the administration revolves, and the post must be filled by a really first-rate man from the Centre. The present incumbent can be appointed to the new Public Service Commission.

3. Services Integration: This has been agreed to a long time ago, but has been unnecessarily delayed. It should be implemented forthwith.

4. Secretary for Kashmir Affairs: The need of a full-time man who has experience, ability and energy is being keenly felt. The present incumbent,[3] who has been at the job for almost a decade,

---

1. The new Congress ministry was sworn in on 17 April 1957 at the centre following the party's victory in the second general elections, held from 25 February to 12 March 1957.
2. Note to Jawaharlal Nehru, sent through Indira Gandhi, 13 July 1957.
3. Vishnu Sahay.

has a full time job elsewhere and can hardly devote enough attention to Kashmir affairs. There must be someone who can keep a constant watch on developments here, so that the Government of India can react to any situation in good time. As it is the Government of India's liaison here appears to be sporadic, fitful and inadequate. Indeed, many feel that this has resulted in a deterioration of the situation here.

———— 155 ————

Srinagar
May 1957

My dear Panditji,
When I had the pleasure of seeing you at the end of April, I promised that I would write after coming up to Srinagar. I reached here on the ninth and since then have had occasion to talk individually with members of the Cabinet and others. Elections to the State Legislative Assembly are now over,[1] though a fair number of election petitions are pending for which a tribunal is to be appointed. After the formation of the Legislative Council[2] in June, it will be time for the new Cabinet[3] to be sworn in. Bakshi Sahib is proceeding to Delhi shortly, and I thought that I should place my views before you in case you may find them of some value. I am sending this letter by special messenger, my ADC, Major Madan Lal Vaid.

Regarding Cabinet formation, Bakshi Sahib is naturally entitled to choose a team upon whom he has confidence and trust. This will make him feel more secure and remove any uneasiness or misgivings that he may have. However, the following points deserve to be kept in mind by him:-

1. It is desirable to avoid the impression of a 'purge', as that will have unhappy political repercussions.

2. If changes are to be made in the present team, the newcomers

---

1. The elections to the Jammu and Kashmir Legislative Assembly were held in March 1957 under the new constitution. In Jammu these were held on 25 March and in Kashmir on 30 March.
2. In fact, the Jammu and Kashmir Legislative Council was formed in July 1957 when the new state assembly elected 18 members to the council.
3. The new cabinet headed by Bakshi Ghulam Mohammad was sworn in on 27 July 1957.

should be selected with an eye to their integrity, reputation and ability. Mere loyalty to the leader should not be the only criterion.

3. For the last ten years Jammu had admittedly been under-represented in the Cabinet. Bakshi Sahib agrees that now is a good opportunity to remedy this.

Apart from the Cabinet, however, there are some other important matters concerning the administration of the State which require immediate attention:-

1. It is almost universally admitted here that the administrative machinery of the State is not functioning to the desired efficiency. The integration of services, details of which have recently been finalized, will be a welcome development, but other effective steps are also needed. Perhaps, the most important concerns the post of Chief Secretary which is the pivot of the administration. The present man has had some experience of the job, but almost everyone here is agreed that unless he is replaced by a really top-class administrative officer from outside the State, preferably an ICS man, the administration will not improve. The present incumbent can conveniently be appointed to the Public Service Commission which is to be set-up soon.

2. The appointment of the Public Service Commission should not be delayed any longer. The members can be the present Chief Secretary and the present Chairman of the Recruitment Board, and the Chairman should be a man of proved integrity from outside the State. This will considerably improve the administrative set-up.

3. There are widespread allegations with regard to the role being played by the party bosses. Apart from undue interference in the administration, they are alleged to use unwarranted strong-arm method with the help of various official and non-official agencies that they control, thus unnecessarily alienating public opinion. Bakshi Sahib must be persuaded to use his undoubted influence to stop these excesses. The same applies to certain individuals who have lately dominated the business community and who are alleged to be grossly misusing their privileged position. This is bringing a very bad name and should be strongly discouraged.

I am sure that Bakshi Sahib, if he realizes the extent of the damage that is being done to him and to the cause by these elements, will agree to curb them effectively. If effective steps are not taken soon to remove both these abuses, severe consequence may well follow.

I am sure that with the personal interest that you take in us we will be able to tide over all difficulties successfully.

With respectful regards,

Yours very sincerely,
Karan Singh

————— 156 —————

New Delhi
October 1957

My dear Panditji,

I am leaving for Jammu this evening by train, and after spending a couple of days there will return to Srinagar. Before I leave I would like to express my gratitude to you for your personal advice and guidance. In the last eight years it is through your blessings that I have been able to be of some little service to the country, and in the future also it is upon this that I rely.

In the papers today I saw the names of our new MPs.[1] By and large I cannot say that I am much impressed.

The Ram Lila that day was very enjoyable, and yesterday I went again and saw it through to the end. It is a fresh, colourful and rhythmic attempt at a 'popular' portrayal of the great epic, and a welcome change from the stereotyped Ram Lilas which one sees so often.

I expect to be in Delhi again in November. By that time my little house, which is only a couple of furlongs from here, should also be ready. Incidentally, I have been well impressed by the Ashoka Hotel, and am now more optimistic than before that it will soon become a paying proposition.

With respects and deepest regards,

Yours very sincerely,
Tiger

---

1. The president had nominated six members of the National Conference as members of the Lok Sabha. These were: Abdul Rashid, Thakur Das Malhotra, Srimati Krishna Mehta, Abdur Rahman, Mohammad Akbar and A.M. Tariq. From 1967 members of the Lok Sabha began to be elected by the people.

——— 157 ———

Jammu
22 December 1957

My dear Panditji,
Just a line to thank you for your card of New Year greetings, and warmly to reciprocate them. By present indications it does not seem as if 1958 will be any less tense than the year which now draws to a close. But in this desert of strife and turmoil every heart in which dwells harmony and love and charity is an oasis of peace. Knowing as I do the staggering burden that you are carrying, my sincerest prayer is that such inner peace be granted to you, along with the strength to lead us onwards for many years more.

It was a great pleasure seeing you again in Delhi, and I would thank you for your hospitality and your unfailing kindness to me.

Bakshi Sahib met me yesterday. He is going up to Srinagar in a day or two, for obvious reasons.

With respects and deep regards,

Yours as ever,
Tiger

——— 158 ———

Srinagar
2 June 1958

My dear Panditji,
This is just a line to say how very much Asha and I have enjoyed seeing Vijaya Lakshmiji[1], Gautam[2], Tara[3] and the children here.

---

1. Vijaya Lakshmi Pandit (1900-1990); Jawaharlal Nehru's sister, married to R.S. Pandit in 1921, imprisoned several times during the freedom movement; minister in the UP government, 1937-39 and 1946; ambassador to the USSR, 1947-49 and to USA, 1949-52; president, UN General Assembly, 1953-54; high commissioner to UK, 1956-61; governor of Maharashtra, 1962-64.
2. Gautam Sahgal (1923-2005); a business executive, married to Nayantara in 1949, divorced in 1967.
3. Nayantara Sahgal (b.1927); eminent author; second daughter of Vijaya Lakshmi Pandit, publications include, *Indira Gandhi: Her Road to Power*, (1978), *Mistaken Identity*, (1988), *Lesser Breeds*, (2003).

I am sure you enjoyed your short holiday in the lovely Kullu Valley. We are sending a case of cherries from our garden and some fresh trout which I hope will reach you in good condition.

My mother and Asha join me in sending you and Indiraji our kindest regards. Love from baby Jyoti.[1]

With respects,

Yours as ever,
Tiger

-------- 159 --------

Camp Dachigam
29 June 1958

My dear Panditji,

I am writing this from Dachigam where Asha and I have come to spend a quiet week. As a matter of fact I am convalescing after a painful attack of herpes and wanted to be away from official work and engagements for a few days. I am sure your holiday in the lovely Kulu Valley has refreshed you greatly, both physically and mentally.

You may remember that when I had the pleasure of seeing you in Delhi in April I mentioned that we were keen to go abroad, if possible to the Soviet Union. At that time, the Kashmir issue was due to come up before the Security Council and you thought it would be better to wait a while. I wonder whether it would meet your approval if we went either later this year in September-October or in April-May next year, whichever you prefer. We do not in any way want to be a nuisance to the Soviet Government, but as Mr Khrushchev has suggested that we come, it might be necessary to refer the matter to them as you think fit.

The reasons we are so keen to travel are twofold. On the one hand there is so much happening in the world today that travel is more of an adventure and education than ever. On the other, as you know, I have a horror of getting stagnated and into a rut at my age and despite all its beauty and charm Kashmir is not the most vital place in the world. I am therefore keen, local and international conditions

---

1. Jyotsna Singh, Karan Singh's daughter; potter and social activist; holds a Ph.D from the University of Delhi; taught philosophy at the Lady Sri Ram College and also at the University of Delhi.

permitting, to be able to go on a trip outside the country at least once every other year. Perhaps Vijaya Lakshmiji, to whom in the course of a general conversation I mentioned this, also conveyed this to you.

Knowing how busy you are, I always feel guilty in bothering you about a personal matter, but your unfailing kindness prompts me to take this liberty.

With respectful regards,

Yours as ever,
Tiger

———— 160 ————

New Delhi
2 July 1958

My dear Tiger,

Thank you for your letter of the 29th June. I am sorry to learn that you have been suffering from an attack of herpes. That is a very painful affair. I hope that you have got over it now.

As for a visit to the Soviet Union, I should like you to go there. But, somehow, events happen or are anticipated which rather come in the way. At the present moment, there is a good deal of feeling in many countries about the execution of Imre Nagy[1] and his colleagues[2] in Budapest, and the Soviet Union is somehow tacked on to this affair. I think therefore, it would be better for us not to raise the question of your visit to Moscow just yet. That means that it will not be possible for you to go there in September-October. You might provisionally think of paying a visit to the Soviet Union in April next.

It would, of course, be necessary to mention this matter to Mr Khrushchev before you go there. But it would be rather premature for us to tell him this now, if you intend going there in April next. Remind me of this somewhat later.

1. Imre Nagy (1896–1958); Hungarian political leader, minister of agriculture, December 1944–November 1945; minister of the interior, November 1945–1946; prime minister, 1953–55; and 23 October–4 November 1956; led resistance against the Russians in a 1956 uprising and was executed on 16 June 1958.
2. General Pal Maleter, military leader of the Hungarian uprising and former defence minister, Miklos, a journalist and Joseph Szilagyi, were executed with Imre Nagy for their role in the uprising.

I hope that in another month's time or so, our direct service from Delhi to Moscow will be established. That will make travel much easier and swifter.

Yours affectionately,
Jawaharlal Nehru

——— 161 ———

Srinagar
10 July 1958

My dear Panditji,
Thank you very much for your letter of the 2nd July. We have, as you suggest, tentatively planned our visit to the Soviet Union in April next and I will take up the matter again when I come to Delhi in November. The New Delhi–Moscow air service will indeed be very convenient.

I am now quite well again. I hope this finds you in the best of health.

With respectful regards,

Yours as ever,
Karan Singh

——— 162 ———

Srinagar
8 August 1958

My dear Panditji,
Copies of your fortnightly letters to Chief Ministers go to Heads of States also, and as such I have the privilege of going through those vastly interesting documents. Alongwith your letter dated 13th July you attached a note[1] in which you indulged in some 'loud thinking' upon the problems that face us. The result was most thought-provoking. Belonging as I do to a much younger generation I thought you might be interested in some random reflections that your letter

---

1. For the note in full see G. Parthasarathi (ed.), *Jawaharlal Nehru: Letters to Chief Ministers 1947–1964*, Vol. 5 (New Delhi, 1989), pp. 80–90. It was also published as 'The Basic Approach' in AICC *Economic Review* (August 1958).

induced in me, which I have set down in the enclosed note.[1]

With respectful regards,

Yours as ever,
Karan Singh

─────── 163 ───────
Issues and Idealism[2]

1. At the outset it may be repeated, because it is not always realized by older people, that ours is what may be termed the post-Independence generation in the sense that our active political thinking and activity began after India had become free. Thus, even the great freedom struggle, in which you were privileged to play so distinguished a role, has not really got a deep personal significance for us and we judge men and ideas by their post rather than pre-Independence performances. This is not to say that we were indifferent to the freedom movement. On the contrary even as teenagers we were thrilled to the core by the great nationalist upsurge that swept the British out of the country. I still remember the feverish excitement when I first (and last) met Gandhiji here in 1947,[3] and again when for the first time you came into my sick-room at Jammu later the same year.[4] I recall how avidly I used to read your books in my school-days, but surreptitiously for fear that my father would see me and discover that I was fast becoming a youthful revolutionary, as indeed I was. But my point is that by the time we reached maturity, the British had already departed, and the freedom struggle is thus not an integral part of our emotional make-up as it must be of older generations. Even Gandhiji is for us a somewhat shadowy figure, very great, of course, but nevertheless belonging to the past rather than to the present or future.

2. After centuries of servitude we became free and Mother India,

---

1. See the succeeding item.
2. Reflections on Nehru's 'The Basic Approach', Srinagar, 8 August 1958.
3. Karan Singh met Gandhiji on 1 August 1947 under a chinar tree in the front lawns of Gulab Bhavan in Srinagar.
4. Karan Singh met Nehru in December 1947 when he was sick and his father brought Nehru to his room and introduced by saying 'Tiger is your great admirer'. Karan Singh had been thrilled to see his hero and asked Nehru to autograph the *Autobiography* (Nehru's) which he was going through with great interest.

though grievously amputated and bleeding, awoke to a new-found strength and vigour. India's freedom was an event of historic significance, symbolising and heralding as it did the re-awakening of Asia after a torpor of ages. A thrill of pride shot through us as we took our rightful place among the great nations of the world and, under your inspiring leadership, began the Herculean task of national reconstruction. In the sphere of foreign policy we have made a creditable contribution towards the maintenance of world peace and lessening of international tensions, and your advocacy of Panchsheel has given the world a new philosophy of peaceful co-existence which will have to be accepted if mankind is to survive in this nuclear age.

3. Internally also, we embarked upon an attempt at planned economic development, and in this first decade of Independence, we have made much progress on many fronts. But at the same time there is much that is unsatisfactory and indeed alarming in our present situation. The idealism that inspired public life in the half century preceding Independence appears to have largely evaporated, leaving behind a noxious residue of self-seeking opportunism. As you have so often pointed out in your speeches and writings, fissiparous tendencies seem to be growing and caste and communalism, though outlawed by our Constitution, appear to be getting more firmly entrenched. Several observers have pointed out that these forces played a much more important role in the second[1] than in the first general election.[2] Corruption has established itself at almost all levels of public life, and it is this above all that corrodes the idealism of youth. Indeed our generation, which is always the mainstay of idealism, seems to have become largely frustrated and cynical. As you point out, this is to some extent a world phenomena. But it is yet surprising that this should be so in India where vast fields of constructive work have opened out before us since Independence and fresh vistas of progress lie ahead.

4. The older generation of national leaders, no doubt retain their idealism, but they are necessarily fast diminishing, leaving gaps in public life which it is being found difficult to fill. The recent demise

---

1. The second general elections were held in February–March 1957.
2. The first general elections were held between October 1951 and May 1952.

of the Maulana[1] is a case in point. As Sri Aurobindo wrote in 1909 on the passing away of Romesh Chandra Dutt[2], 'The landmarks of the past fall one by one and none rise in their place.' I am more than forty years younger than you, and between our generation lies a vast gap only occasionally lighted by outstanding inspiration and idealism. You stand as a titanic figure, forward-looking, young in mind and spirit, full of noble ideals allied with the constant endeavour to actualise them. But, with a handful of exceptions, you stand alone, though we pray that you may be spared for many more years to guide us.

5. What is the cause of this lack of idealism in our country, even among the younger generation as is so often reflected in our universities? I for one do not feel myself competent to offer an analysis of the complex economic, social and psychological factors that operate to shape the consciousness of our youth. But I think, a fair share of responsibility must be borne by our political parties whose task it is in a democracy to infuse a spirit of hope and dedication among the people, specially the younger generation. They appear to have failed in this vital duty, and almost without exception have proved incapable of evoking in our generation genuine idealism on any substantial scale.

6. In your note you mention the views of a colleague that 'In our attempts to ensure the material prosperity of the country we have not paid any attention to the spiritual element in human nature. Therefore, in order to give the individual and the nation a sense of purpose, something to live for and, if necessary, to die for, we have to revive some philosophy of life to give, in the wider sense of the word, a spiritual background to our thinking.' I feel that this is a crucial point, because it is widely admitted that the general level of national character—discipline, honesty, integrity—has seriously declined and continues to do so. This is a very serious matter because without a high level of national character the new India of our dreams will remain a mirage. It is our educational institutions and, perhaps, the

---

1. Maulana Abul Kalam Azad passed away on 22 February 1958.
2. (1848-1909) ; historian and civil servant ; joined the Indian Civil Service in 1869 and served in different capacities in the Orissa division of Bengal; revenue minister, Baroda state, 1904-07, president, Indian National Congress, 1899, publications include, *Peasantry in Bengal* (1875); *England and India* (1897), *History of Civilization in Ancient India* (1899), *Famine in India* (1900).

Community Development organization, that must spearhead this 'spiritual renaissance', if I may use the term in its broadest sense. But mere words are not enough, concrete steps are called for before it is too late. The spiritual motive has always been an important element in our past—greatness as witness the Buddha, Ashoka, Gandhiji— and if our country is to achieve the pinnacles of greatness in the future she must adhere to this ideal.

7. Finally, a word about our economic problems. Whether or not a spiritual motive permeates us, there is no doubt that we will be judged, and indeed our democracy itself will be judged, by the extent to which we can solve our economic problems and ensure to the people of India a reasonable minimum standard of material goods and services. We have of course achieved a good deal since Independence, but the expectations of our people always expand faster than our capacity to meet them with the result that the gap remains and even grows. I am not an economist and so I will not venture to say anything with regard to the method or content of our economic planning, but there is one matter which I feel bound to mention and that is the question of population. In almost all your letters you lay great stress upon the supreme importance of raising agricultural production and the need for a vigorous, sustained and coordinated drive in this direction. This is, of course, extremely important and must be done. But, however much we may increase our food output per acre, however much we may extend our irrigation and improve our methods of production, our huge and rapidly increasing population will inexorably swallow up all that we produce and millions will remain in economic distress. It appears that the disastrous consequences of our terrifying population growth are not really being brought home to the people. Our public leaders talk constantly on a large variety of subjects but are conspicuously silent with regard to the supreme necessity of limiting our population. It may be argued that mere words will achieve nothing unless we have the concrete means of mass birth control. This is, of course true, but before any such campaign can be launched we must create the necessary climate of opinion in the nation, particularly in the rural areas. Are we making full use of all the modern means of publicity at our control to educate the nation with regard to this basic problem? We are spending hundreds of crores upon numerous development works, but are we spending enough upon family planning and birth control on a mass scale? Even China, which at one time impatiently brushed aside the population problem as a 'capitalist

myth' which would automatically disappear in a communist society has now, I understand, adopted stern and active measures to limit its population growth. Unless we do the same all our plans and schemes will be gravely jeopardized and we will never succeed in lifting the mass of our people out of the morass of poverty in which they have been sunk for so many centuries. Population control is the most fundamental and important national problem facing us today, not excepting even food production. Have we a proper awareness of this, and if so, are we doing all we can to meet it?

———— 164 ————

New Delhi
31 August 1958

My dear Tiger,
Some time ago, I received your letter of August 8th. I read your note with great interest and, I think, profit. What appealed to me especially was a young man of your generation looking at the world as it is. I wish I could enter a little more into the mind of your generation.

Yours as ever,
Jawaharlal Nehru

———— 165 ————

Srinagar
3 September 1958

My dear Panditji,
I am sending by hand of Vishnu Sahay some green *pista* from our garden.

   I look forward to paying my respect, to you when I come to Delhi at the end of October for the Governors Conference.

   With affectionate regards,

Yours as ever,
Tiger

PS
I wonder if you received my letter and note dated the 8th August?

T.

SADAR-I-RIYASAT.

Karan Mahal
Srinagar.
3rd September 1958.

My dear Panditji,

I am sending by hand of Vishnu
Sahay some green pista from our
garden.

I look forward to paying my
respects to you when I come to
Delhi at the end of October for
the Governors' Conference.

With affectionate regards,

Yours as ever

Tiger

P.S. I wonder if you received my
letter & note dated the 8th August?

T.

——— 166 ———

New Delhi
14 November 1958

My dear Tiger,
Thank you for your message of greetings. Every new birthday is a bit of a burden and not always one of rejoicing. But the affection and good wishes of friends lighten that burden.

Yours affectionately,
Jawaharlal Nehru

——— 167 ———

Jammu Tawi
19 November 1958

My dear Panditji,
I have just received a copy of *Nuclear Explosions and Their Effects*[1] so kindly sent by you. I remember your mentioning this book in the course of our last conference in Delhi[2] and I shall go through it with keen interest.

It was as always a great pleasure to have seen you again and I must thank you for your courtesy and hospitality. My mother, wife and I are coming to Delhi again at the end of this month and we look forward to seeing you at that time. If it is at all possible we would be very happy if you and Indiraji could have a meal or even a cup of tea with us at our new house in Chanakyapuri.[3]

In the light of your remarks when we last met I am looking forward to being able to visit the Soviet Union next year,[4] perhaps in April-May.

With respects and kindest regards,

Yours very sincerely,
Karan Singh

———————————

1. On Nehru's suggestion, the Defence Services Organization of the government of India had made an objective study of the consequences of the use of nuclear, thermonuclear and other weapons of mass destruction. It was published by the publications division, ministry of information and broadcasting in book form in June 1956 under this title. The foreword of this book was written by Jawaharlal Nehru.
2. Perhaps the Governors' Conference.
3. 3, Nyaya Marg, Chanakyapuri, New Delhi - 110021.
4. Karan Singh visited the Soviet Union from 24 April to 15 May 1959.

——— 168 ———

My dear Panditji,
As mentioned in my latest fortnightly letter dated the 1st July I enclose a note[1] containing some impressions of my visit to the Soviet Union.
　With kind regards,

Yours sincerely,
Karan Singh

——— 169 ———
Reflections on Soviet Union[2]

The fabric of our lives is woven of many memories, some pleasant and others not so. My visit to the Soviet Union provided me with some very pleasant and interesting memories, and in the pages that follow I have sought to give a brief account of this vast visit. Of course, three weeks in a country as vast and varied as the Soviet Union does not make one an expert, and indeed I have made no attempt to be dogmatic or to draw final and profound conclusion from what I saw. All I have tried to do is to lay down what I saw and left as clearly as I can recall, and to let the reader draw from my words whatever strikes him as important or significant. Not many Indians have had the opportunity of visiting the Soviet Union so far, and of those who have done so, not many have been able to travel as extensively as we did, and so I thought I should share my impressions with a wider circle. My essay is thus essentially a travelogue, but I have not hesitated to put down the ideas that occurred to me from time to time.

　On 23 April 1959 our Air India International Super Constellation 'The Rani of Ayodhya' took off from Palam airport for Moscow. It

---

1.　See the next item.
2.　Note for Jawaharlal Nehru on a visit to the Soviet Union from 23 April to 15 May 1959. The note was written after Karan Singh came back to India. Karan Singh also sent the note to Dr Rajendra Prasad on 1 July 1959 and in his letter of 11 July to Karan Singh, Rajendra Prasad wrote: 'Thank you very much for sending me your impression of your visit to the Soviet Union which I have found informative and interesting.'

was with a thrill of excitement and anticipation that I settled down in my seat. It is indeed curious how, in spite of the fact that one prepares for a visit months ahead in great detail, one never really believes that it will come off until the plane actually takes to the air. However, we were off at last, and within a couple of hours we were flying over Lahore, a city I had last visited in 1946. The next landmark we passed was Ghazni in Afghanistan after which the country begins to get mountainous and then we were flying over Kabul. From the air Kabul looked a modern, well planned city and I was sorry the plane did not land there to enable me to get a closer view of this historic place. After Kabul the mountains suddenly assumed heroic dimensions and the higher ranges of the mighty Hindukush soon lay beneath us. This was the border between Afghanistan and the Soviet Republic of Uzbekistan. Upon crossing the border the patchwork of fields with which we are familiar in India was replaced by huge units of land covering hundreds of acres which were, of course, State and Collective Farms. After flying for five hours we began to descend and the pilot announced that we were landing at Tashkent. As we descended I recalled the occasion at the end of 1955 when I had met Mr Bulganin and Mr Khrushchev in Delhi and invited them to visit Srinagar. Although it had not been in their original schedule they agreed to come and spent three days with us there in December. At the time of their departure they had invited my wife and me to visit the Soviet Union, and subsequently this invitation had been renewed through diplomatic channels. It had finally been decided that we would visit the Soviet Union as guests of the Soviet Government for just over three weeks from 23 April to 15 May.

The plane landed smoothly at the modern Tashkent airport and we emerged from it into a fresh and clear afternoon. We were greeted by the Deputy Premier[1] and Foreign Minister,[2] the Minister for Trade[3] and other ladies and gentlemen, who presented us with bouquets of lovely flowers. I noticed that the air had a pleasant tang in it very much like Srinagar in spring, and that tulips, iris and small chinar trees, were also abundant. We were taken to the handsome new airport building where in a well appointed room a sumptuous

1. A.I. Mikoyan.
2. A.A. Gromyko.
3. N.S. Patolichev.

repast had been laid for us. The food was delicious and included several dishes with which we are familiar in India such as *naan* and *kabab*. In the course of the meal there were toasts and speeches, a practice which we were to discover was universal in the Soviet Union. The Uzbek men look very much like North Indians with a slight trace of Mongolian features. The women seem to be more Mongolian and they were delighted when my wife told them that they looked Nepalese.

We took off again after an hour and a half and our plane flew for seven hours over seemingly endless plains. At one point we crossed the Volga River, which we could see clearly. The flight would have been boring except for the pleasant feeling of anticipation which we had and also the fact that one of our travelling companions happened to be an eminent professor who regaled me at length with his views on a large number of topics ranging from economics and politics to religion. At 8.40 p.m. (Moscow time) we touched down at Moscow airport. As we emerged from the plane we were greeted by a flood of light and a battery of photographers. The Secretary[1] of the Presidium of the Supreme Soviet, the Minister for Higher Education of the USSR and other Soviet dignitaries received us at the airport and we drove eighteen miles to the city. It was a full moon night and as we drove off from the airport a huge yellow moon rose above a bank of dark clouds, forming a memorable first impression of Moscow. We finally reached our residence, a delightful wood panelled bungalow on 13, Alexei Tolstoi Street.

The next morning we woke early and after two formal calls on Soviet Government leaders decided to look around Moscow. Moscow is an impressive city. Huge new blocks of apartments for workers are coming up rapidly in order to meet the acute housing shortage. Perhaps the most impressive parts of Moscow are the new University area and Red Square. We visited the colossal department store called GUM which we found packed with people as well as goods. Our first lunch in Moscow was at the Kremlin and our host was Mr Kozlov,[2] Deputy Chairman of the Council of Ministers. After lunch we walked through a part of the Kremlin and saw some beautiful halls and galleries including the huge hall which seats three thousand people, where

---

1. M.P. Georgadze.
2. F.R. Kozlov.

both the Houses of the Supreme Soviet meet. Later we also visited the rooms where Lenin lived and worked after the Revolution and which are still preserved with his books and personal effects. It was interesting to see a place so closely associated with one of the most remarkable men of this century. We also visited a museum in the Kremlin which contains a superb collection of coaches, costumes, gold and china services and numerous other exquisite curios from all over the world. Before leaving we went into the church where the Czars used to be crowned. The church is very ornate and covered with paintings but does not compare with the churches of Rome for architectural and artistic beauty.

In the evening we visited one of the famous underground Metros. We descended on a very steep and fast escalator to the station. Electric trains rushed in and out every few seconds, and we travelled on one for quite a distance before emerging in Komsomol Square. The subways are beautifully decorated and indeed the stations and waiting rooms look like palatial ante-chambers. After this we visited some newly built apartment houses for workers. Evidently, the occupants were comparatively low paid but they looked healthy and happy. I noticed that the blocks of apartment houses seven or eight storeys high were soberly designed and had no outstanding architectural feature. Several were still under construction and it seemed to me that much less cement was used than in buildings of comparable size in India.

When we arrived in Moscow winter had just ended and spring was about to begin. The trees were still very bare, giving the city rather a desolate look, but the buds were almost ready to break into bloom and indeed, before we left the country, spring had arrived and the whole city was covered with greenery.

Dinner at our Embassy was again a diplomatic affair with toasts and speeches, but the atmosphere was friendly and informal, and I conversed freely with Soviet leaders. Our host was our Ambassador, Shri K.P. S. Menon[1] who has been in Moscow for over six years and is one of our senior most diplomats. After dinner an Azerbaijan girl sang Indian songs very well and a Russian girl performed Bharat Natyam with commendable skill. We broke up past midnight after a

---

1. (1898-1982); joined the ICS, 1921; agent of the government of India in Sri Lanka, 1929-32; agent-general in China 1943-47; ambassador to China, 1947-48; foreign secretary, 1948-52; ambassador to the USSR, Hungary and Poland, 1952-61.

long and tiring, but extremely interesting, first day in the Soviet Union.

In the morning we visited the Lenin Stalin Mausoleum in Red Square. This is a low structure built of a red material known as porphyry. My wife and I laid a wreath outside the Mausoleum where the bodies of Lenin and Stalin have been carefully embalmed and preserved. Outside a flame burns constantly in a marble receptacle. Inside the chamber it is almost completely dark except for the bodies which are illuminated giving the place a rather mysterious atmosphere. The chamber is hushed and the two bodies appear to exude light. Both men are every pale and look rather small lying with their arms folded over their chests. It seemed like the sanctum sanctorum of some ancient religion, and indeed the thousands of visitors who flock to the Mausoleum every day, visit it with as much reverence as worshippers at their shrine.

In the afternoon we flew to Leningrad by the excellent new TU-104-B jet service, covering the distance of 400 miles in exactly fifty-five minutes. It was my first flight in a jet plane and I enjoyed it a great deal. Leningrad, which was the capital of Russia for about two hundred years and has played an extremely important role in her history, is the most beautiful city I saw in the Soviet Union and one of the finest in Europe. It is criss-crossed by numerous canals and waterways and the gracious architecture of the pre-revolution days has been retained. Among the many sights in Leningrad are the Winter Palace with its superb Square; the fine equestrian statue of Peter the Great[1] in which the horse, trampling underfoot a serpent symbolizing the enemies of the Czar, appears about to fly off into space like a sputnik; the magnificent Hermitage which is among the finest collections of art in the world and possesses superb treasures of European art; and a fine Sports Stadium on the sea coast which can seat eighty thousand spectators. We also visited the blue domed mosque which is used by the Muslim Tatars numbering about thirty thousand who live in the city. We met the Imam of the mosque, a Russian with a short beard who has done the 'Haj' pilgrimage. He told us that regular prayers were held on Fridays and Sundays and also on Muslim festival days. The most impressive feature inside the mosque was a gigantic wrought iron and plate glass chandelier with Quranic inscriptions. From there

---

1. Peter the Great (1672-1725); originally Peter I, czar of Russia, 1682-1721; emperor, 1921-25; introduced a series of military, domestic and ecclesiastical reforms.

we visited the great Leningrad Cathedral, one of the largest in Europe. This is now no longer used for worship but is maintained as a national monument. The Government spends millions of roubles on its upkeep and repairs, and indeed repair work was in progress when we visited it. The bronze door to the Cathedral is a magnificent piece of work, and I was particularly struck by a beautiful sculpture of Joseph, Mary and the child Jesus on one of its panels. Inside, the Cathedral is superb, with numerous mosaics and paintings depicting various scenes relating to the life of Jesus. As usual I was deeply moved by scenes of the crucifixion and of Jesus being taken down from the cross. From the centre of the dome a small metal pendulum is suspended which demonstrates the movement of the earth by moving perceptibly during its swing.

During our stay in Leningrad we visited several other institutions including the Institute of Ethnology which has an Indian section of which they are very proud to which I presented a Kashmiri shawl, and the Institute of Pediatrics which is the highest institute for training medical child specialists in the Soviet Union. We saw some lovely Russian babies who were pictures of health. Orphans and abandoned children are brought up with special care, and indeed a great boon of Soviet society is its social security and the fact that every child is assured of the utmost care even if its parents are unable to provide it. Our first contact with the Soviet educational system also took place in Leningrad when we visited an 'English School', that is, a school, where English is taught in all classes. It was very interesting to the healthy and vivacious Russian children speaking fluent English. The school was housed in a new building four storeys high, which cost two million roubles. The approach road was still unmetalled, but the institution itself was clean and healthy. At the end of our visit some of the students gathered in the Music Room and sang for us. In addition to Russian songs they insisted on singing a couple of English ones which they did excellently. It was indeed surprising to hear Polly Wolly Doodle sung in flawless English in the heart of Leningrad! I wondered how many school children there were in England or the USA who could sing Russian songs with equal fluency.

Next, we visited a Palace of Pioneers. The movement known as the 'Young Pioneers', of which a large section of Soviet school children are members, is an essential adjunct to the Soviet educational system and is one of its most attractive features. The children spend part of their spare time everyday in magnificent palaces of pioneers, some of which are indeed old palaces of the Czarist times. Here, amidst delightful surroundings, the children engage in multifarious activities including music, painting sculpture, dancing astronomy, science, cooking, toy making, drama, geography, history and games of all kinds. We visited several of these palaces and each time we were impressed by the atmosphere of joy and healthy pleasure which pervades them. Indeed, it is clear that Soviet society pays special attention to the care and education of its youth, and I think this is one of its great sources of strength.

In Leningrad also we had our first introduction to Soviet ballet. We saw a performance of Spartak, based on the story of Spartacus,[1] leader of the famous Slave Revolt in Rome. This is a modern ballet and the music was pleasant though not outstanding. The scenes and sets were very impressive and colourful and the atmosphere of debauchery and decadent grandeur of the Roman Court was skilfully recreated. I noticed that the spacious hall was packed and that the audience was not dressed in formal clothes but consisted of people wearing ordinary everyday clothing.

During our three day stay in Leningrad we were guests of the City Soviet whose chairman Mr Smirnov entertained us to a banquet one night. At such functions the warmth, friendship and hospitality of the Russian people, becomes very evident, and I shall long remember that dinner in Leningrad for this reason. On the fourth day we left Leningrad in the two engine Ilyushin plane which was at out disposal throughout the tour and flew to Stalingrad in the heart of Russia.

During the Second World War the name Stalingrad became synonymous with the courage and indomitable spirit of the Russian people to resist and defeat aggression. The epic battle that was fought there which ultimately resulted in a defeat for the invading forces was one of the important turning points of the war. In the process, the city was completely destroyed and there was literally not one single building standing by the time the battle ended. Stalingrad is one of the four Soviet 'hero cities', the others being Leningrad, Odessa and Sevastopol. It is now in the process of being completely rebuilt and a good deal of construction work has been completed. The population now is six

---

1. Thracian born slave and gladiator at Capua, who led the most serious slave uprising in the history of Rome (73-71 BC); inflicted numerous defeats on the Roman armies sent against him until defeated and killed by Crassus.

lakhs as against four and a half lakhs before the War. A graceful embankment has been built along the famous Volga and many streets including the impressive Mir Prospect (avenue of peace) have been constructed. Thousands of people, however, still live in tiny wooden shacks on the outskirts of the city waiting to move in as the apartment houses are completed. On our drive from the airport to the city we passed hundred of such tiny decrepit hutments.

In the evening we visited the Planetarium, a present to Stalingrad from the Democratic German People's Republic (East Germany). Here we saw a film showing actual scenes of street to street, house to house, floor to floor fighting and the incredible destruction of the city during the War. The film showed one scene of Stalin speaking during the War, one glimpse each of several Russian Generals including Marshal Zhukhov and several scenes of Mr Khrushchev. After the film, the planetarium gave us a view of the sky over Kashmir!

At night we were entertained to a banquet by the Chairman of the City Soviet, who gave us interesting information regarding the city administration. The City Soviets are much more important and powerful than our Municipalities. They control the entire economic life of the city and are important agents of Government. We were told that the annual budget of the Stalingrad City Soviet was sixty crore roubles, and that the bulk of its income (eighty-seven per cent) was derived from profits on factories, shops, hotels and cinemas etc. Taxes made up only five to seven per cent of the budget. Taxes on income were very low, ranging from two to eight per cent, and there was a special tax on childless couples. This led me to remark that in India we were faced with the reverse problem and should institute a tax on every family having more than two children!

The next morning we laid a wreath at the simple but impressive memorial to the war dead and then, after driving around the city, visited the large Stalingrad Tractor Factory which employs fifteen thousand workers and produces thirty thousand tractors a year. After visiting the factory we were taken to the Palace of Culture for the workers, which is another interesting and praiseworthy feature of Soviet society. Each important factory and collective farm in the country has one or more such Palaces of Culture where workers relax during their spare time. These are impressive buildings with spacious halls, cinema theatres, indoor and outdoor games, libraries and so on, and they give a welcome opportunity to workers to engage in pleasant cultural activities. This feature confirms that the Soviet Union pays special attention to its workers. Another such feature is the system of Rest Homes which I shall mention later.

From the factory we drove several miles out to the huge Stalingrad Hydro-Electric Project where a dam is being constructed on the mighty Volga which when complete will generate two and a half million kilowatts of electricity. The projects has reached an advanced stage and is scheduled for completion in 1961. The dam is not very high but is very long and we walked across it to the other bank of the river. It was a long tiring walk but fascinating to see the Volga coming down from the reservoir in giant crystal cascades and swirling in turbulent agony as it fell and flowed on. On the far bank we had to wait for about an hour for our boat and while we were sitting on the pier a curious incident occurred. A young man dressed in working clothes came up to our interpreter and asked her whether we were foreigners. I immediately said that we were Indians, and he began talking to me. He said that he used to study in Leningrad but that he had been rusticated for a year and was now a concrete worker in this project. He spoke good though halting English, and said that he was very interested in Yoga. When I asked him what he had read on the subject he said that he had read Romain Rolland's[1] Life of Ramakrishna. He evidently wanted to talk more but a young friend who had been with him all the time caught him by the arm and dragged him off. Our boat ultimately arrived stocked with caviar, biscuits and other delicacies and we had a delightful cruise on the Volga.

In Stalingrad, as in every other place we went to, we were impressed by the warm friendship shown to us and for our country. Indeed, Indians are extremely popular in the Soviet Union. After my return, I have often been asked by people the reason for this popularity. I think, it is compounded of several factors. To begin with, neighbouring India is known and respected as an ancient nation with a great civilization, the very word carries with it a certain respect and reverence. Secondly, the fact that we were until recently a colonial possession under foreign rule and have just attained our independence causes the Soviet people to have friendly and sympathetic feeling towards us. Thirdly, our policy since independence of non-alignment and

---

1. (1866-1944); French writer who wrote several books on Indian leaders and was a close friend of Gandhi; received the Nobel Prize for Literature in 1915; publications include, *Mahatma Gandhi, Life of Ramakrishna, Life of Vivekananda* and *The Universal Gospel*.

positive neutrality is greatly appreciated, and *Panchsheel* as a policy of peaceful coexistence is warmly welcomed in the Soviet Union. Indeed, in almost every speech made by our hosts during visit, there was an inevitable approving mention of *Panchsheel*. Finally, the stature and popularity of our Prime Minister, Pandit Nehru, is also an important contributory factor. The Soviet people realize that he is working for world peace, and having seen incredible destruction in the past two Wars they have an obsession with peace themselves.

On 30 April we returned from Stalingrad to Moscow, as I had an interview with Mr Khrushchev scheduled for that afternoon. I had met Mr Khrushchev in Delhi and Srinagar, and he received us warmly. As we entered the room he advanced to greet us amidst a battery of lights and photographers. Our Ambassador Shri Menon and his wife were also present and we all sat down at a long table along with interpreters and talked for about minutes. Among other things Mr Khrushchev talked with great enthusiasm about Siberia. He said that many people, including Indians, had the impression that it was a vast uninhabited iceberg, but in fact it was a land rich with all types of mineral wealth and also excellent for agricultural purposes. He said that at present great emphasis was being laid upon Siberia, which was developing with astonishing rapidity.

We had been invited by Mr Khrushchev to lunch also and at the end of the interview he accompanied us to another part of the Kremlin for the meal. We walked from his office to banquet hall, about 300 yards through the Kremlin compound. The Kremlin is now open to visitors, and there were a fair number of sightseers strolling around the compound. A few of them greeted Mr Khrushchev informally and he returned their greetings, walking briskly on tiny feet. We had a drink in what Mr Khrushchev told us was the ante-chamber of Catherine the Great, and lunched in the next room off a round table. It was a small intimate party consisting of not more than a dozen people including Mr Khrushchev, the Menons, Mr[1] and Mrs Andrei Gromyko, Mr Mukhitdinov.[2] the

---

1. Andrei Andreyevich Gromyko (1909-1989); Soviet ambassador to the USA, 1943-46; participated in Tehran, Yalta and Potsdam conferences; Soviet representative at the UN, 1946-1948; first deputy minister, foreign affairs, 1949-52; foreign minister, 1957-85; president, 1985-88.

2. Nurutdin Akramovich Mukhitdinov (b. 1917); member, CPSU since 1942; member, Central Committee, Uzbek Communist Party, 1949-58; member, Presidium and secretary, Central Committee, CPSU, 1957-61; Soviet ambassador to Syria, 1968-77.

Uzbek Member of the Party Presidium, two interpreters and us. Conversation was free and informal, in which we all participated. Earlier, Mr Khrushchev had remarked that he was glad to see both of us looking so well and that he thought my wife's eyes had grown darker since he last met us! In turn I observed him closely. He appeared to be a little less exuberant than during his visit to India, but he spoke with added assurance and power. Towards the end of the lunch he delivered a speech which was extempore but was reported in some detail the next day in *Pravda*. Our interpreter produced an English translation of the report, which is reproduced below:

We are glad to greet you, our dear guests, in the Soviet Union. It is a pleasant to us to note that you have kept your word and by coming to our country have accepted our invitation made during our stay in Kashmir. You have the opportunity to get acquainted with everything that you find of interest in the Soviet Union, as well as with the life and work of the Soviet people. I think, you will find out many interesting things for yourselves while getting to know the economical, cultural, artistic, scientific and State institutions of our country. We belong to States with different social structures, but these differences should not be stressed. One should proceed from the common features that exist between out countries and our governments. These are the desire to raise the living standard of the people, to give people everything they need to meet their material and spiritual requirements and to ensure peace and security.

Now, the Soviet people have set about the large-scale construction of communism. Some people abroad do not approve of the ideas of socialism and communism. But no one can ignore the great achievements of the Soviet people. It is known under what conditions the Russian people and other peoples of the USSR lived before the October Revolution and to what unprecedented heights they have risen now. It gives me satisfaction to see that the foreign press admits the fact that the Soviet people will realize their great historic task, determined by the XXI Congress of the

CPSU.[1] Now, nobody doubts that we will be able to catch up and surpass the USA in the economical field and the production of goods. Now, they have started arguing as to the time when we will realize this task. We say in 1965-70; some people abroad assert that it will happen later.

The results of the fulfilment of the People's Economy Plan in the first quarter of this year, a plan that, as is known, was fulfilled and exceeded by 5 per cent show that if we have the same achievements in the future as well, we will accomplish our task much earlier than the time we have set. That reminds me, what does the 5 per cent overfulfilment of the plan in the Soviet Union mean? Now, one per cent overfulfilment means an increase in production of 11 billion roubles per year, and at the end of the Seven Year Plan a one per cent increase will equal 19 billion roubles. This as you see is a considerable figure.

We are sure the time is not far when this argument—when we will catch up with the USA—will be finally settled in our favour.

Some people abroad dread the word communism. Communism is a great idea and it's not abstract. Its essence is material good; food for the people, high level of the economy of the country, plants, factories, a wide network of high and secondary schools and cultural institutions.

Communism provides an uninterrupted growth of the material and cultural levels of the life of the people, the shortest working day in the world and the shortest working week. We are finally confident that the Soviet people will reach their cherished goal and will build communism.

It's pleasant for me to note that good relations have been established between the people and the governments of the Soviet Union and India.

We hope that friendship and cooperation between the

---

1. The 21st Congress of the Communist Party of the Soviet Union was held in Moscow from 27 January to 5 February 1959. Its main purpose was to approve the Seven-Year Plan for 1959-65. The object of the Seven-Year Plan was 'to establish the material and technical basis of communism, to strengthen further the economic and defensive power of the Soviet Union, and to provide for the fuller satisfaction of the growing material and spiritual requirements of the people.'

peoples and the governments of our two countries will gain strength and further develop. We are very glad to receive guests from India. The only thing we can wish is that more guests come to us from friendly India, and more often. It's with pleasure that we often recall our visit to India and the hospitality accorded to us by the great Indian people, their government and in particular by the people of Kashmir and personally by you.

It is our pleasure to accord hospitality to you, and we would like you to stay with us longer and to come once again. I propose a toast to the health of our dear guests and wish them happiness and success. To the friendship between the Soviet and Indian peoples!

In reply, I conveyed to Mr Khrushchev the warm greetings and good wishes of the people of India and thanked him and his Government for their hospitality.

In the afternoon we did some shopping. The shops in the Soviet Union are all State owned, and we were interested to see the display of goods. By and large few luxuries are available, and there is not nearly as attractive a variety of consumer goods as there is in leading department stores in Western Europe. Prices also appeared to us to be rather high. However, the shops were packed with goods and with customers. I gathered that the position with regard to consumer goods has eased considerably in the past few years and is getting steadily better.

In the evening we visited the Stanislavsky Theatre where we witnessed a superb performance of Tchaikovsky's,[1] 'Swan Lake'. The music of course was excellent, and the dancing was also exquisite, featuring a young ballerina named Vinogradova. The whole performance was a delight. I noticed that it was pure beauty divorced from any social realism. Of course, the contemplation of beauty is itself one of the greatest joys of life and collectively a very valuable feature in any society. But some people still hold the rigid theory that every work of art or music should, irrespective of its intrinsic beauty,

---

1. Tchaikovsky or Tschaikaovsky Piotr Iltyich (1840–1893); Russian composer; his greatest works are the ballets *Swan Lake* (1876–77), *The Sleeping Beauty* (1890) and *The Nutcracker* (1892).

contain some sort of social message. The glorious Russian ballet seems to me to be a refutation of this view.

The next day was the first of May, celebrated as 'May Day' in several parts of the world. We were at the Red Square to witness the famous May Day parade. The whole Square was decorated with huge portraits of Marx and Lenin and smaller portraits of the twelve Members of the Party Presidium led by Mr Khrushchev. Incidentally, these fourteen portraits are very much in evidence throughout the Soviet Union, although a fifteenth, that of Stalin, was also occasionally in evidence. The spectators were on one side of the Square adjoining the Lenin Stalin Mausoleum and we had got an excellent vantage point from the diplomatic gallery. We reached Red Square at nine forty, and just before ten the Soviet leaders led by Mr Khrushchev mounted the rostrum on the Mausoleum. The parade was drawn up in front, and at ten sharp a car bearing the Parade Commander drove up from the left and another bearing the Soviet Defence Minister, Marshal Malinovsky[1] drove up from the right. They met in front of the Mausoleum and the Marshal them began his inspection of the parade, stopping at intervals to greet the troops who shouted in unison the Russian equivalent of 'It is an honour to serve the Soviet Union.' After the inspection the Marshal also mounted the rostrum, from where he addressed the gathering. The address was in Russian but in the papers the next day we saw that he spoke about the virtues of the communist system and party, and sent his greetings to the communist countries, China being mentioned first and the rest in alphabetical order. After the address the parade began, first foot-soldiers with rifles and light automatic weapons, sailors and boy cadets, marched past smartly with stiff steps. Then came the vehicles, armoured cars, small, medium and large tanks and artillery. There were no planes or rockets, and we were told that this time the emphasis was less militaristic than in previous years. After the armed parade came the civilian 'demonstration' in which members of each of the twenty three districts of Moscow and important sports bodies such as Spartak and Dynamo walked informally past waving banners, flags and balloons. They included a large number of women and also many children, several of whom were carried on the shoulders of their parents.

---

1. Rodion Yakovlevich Malinovsky (1898–1967); Soviet soldier and statesman, born in Odessa, Ukraine; led the Russian advance on Budapest and into Austria, 1944–45; took leading part in the Machurian campaign; minister of defence 1957–67.

The May Day parade lasts for the greater part of the day, but at half past eleven most of the diplomatic corps left and we followed. In the evening we attended a colourful and entertaining performance of Russian folk songs and dances at the Tchaikovsky Hall. The Russian people are full of song and dance and the women's dresses are gay and colourful. They excel at ensemble shows including group dancing and singing. After the show we drove out to the promenade in front of the new University and from there looked down upon Moscow city illuminated for May Day. The University itself looked very lovely with its dappled illumination.

The next day turned out to be almost wholly occupied with the Church. The day had been kept free, but as all the shops were closed following May Day we decided to spend some time out in the country. Several places were suggested and we ultimately chose to visit Zagorsk, a small town about 40 miles from Moscow which is an important centre of the Russian Orthodox Church. We drove through a part of Moscow we had not seen before and passed the premises of the permanent Agricultural Exhibition with the huge figures of a man and a woman dramatically poised outside the entrance. Soon after leaving the city small wooden shacks began to appear on either side of the road with tin roofs and small gardens in which vegetables were grown. Some of these houses looked quite smart, but most of them were somewhat derelict. I was told that these people were also waiting to be moved into the huge new apartment blocks that are going up in Moscow. I asked our Russian friends whether some workers might not prefer to stay in these small private country houses even though they did not have all the amenities available in the flats. They replied in the negative saying that the water, heating and other amenities in the flats were a great attraction and everyone wanted to move in as soon as possible. On the road we noticed a few picnickers and also a fair number of cars. Cars in Russia appeared to be neither very numerous nor very attractive.

After a drive of about an hour and a half we reached the town of Zagorsk and went straight to the great complex of buildings belonging to the monastery which dominates the area. Our visit was entirely unscheduled and it took a few minutes to contact the local monks. A young monk, short, with a beard and a beautiful face came to greet us and showed us around the premises. He spoke English haltingly but fairly well, with a charming accent. He took us first to the great church, and as it happened to be the Eve of Easter there was a large gathering.

The morning service was just drawing to a close and the church was full of worshippers, mostly elderly women, who in turn kissed the image of Jesus lying in a small sarcophagus. The church was profusely decorated inside and there was an atmosphere of devotion. Next, we visited the shrine where the relics of St. Sergei, the Founder of the monastery were buried. We lined up along with the worshippers and went past the relics in single file bowing to them. After this we were taken to meet the Vice-Patriarch, a tall, youngish man, who received us cordially in his office and presented us with picture albums of the monastery. He was glad to hear from me regarding the ancient and numerous Christian community in India.

We were next taken into the building of the Theological Institute. On the way we asked our young escort whether the number of religious believers was on the decrease. He replied with a certain enigmatic irony that no one could be dragged forcibly into the kingdom of heaven, and that although its doors were open to everyone who wished to come, there could be no compulsion. Inside the Theological Institute we were received by the Inspector, Father Leonid. He was clearly a gifted man and spoke to us at length with self-confidence and an absolute lack of fear or hesitation. He gave us a wealth of information about the functioning of the Church in the Soviet Union, and the members of our entourage, who had probably visited a church for the first time in their lives, also listened with great interest. He told us that there was complete freedom of religious belief and practice in the Soviet Union but that all religious institutions had to be financed by private offerings and did not receive any aid from the State. The Church had, of course, been deprived of the large estates that it owned in the pre-Revolution days, and was now allowed only the space occupied by the Church building and the compounds, plus a small area for growing vegetables for private consumption. Education and the church had also been completely separated after the Revolution, and the Church was no longer allowed to run its own schools. Nevertheless, the Russian Orthodox Church had a large number of monasteries and theological seminaries where its monks were trained. The institution which we were visiting in Zagorsk itself had a seminary, theological college, library, a museum, a hospital, hostels for the monks and so on The expenditure on all this was about five million roubles a year, and the fact that this amount of money was forthcoming for this one institution every year seemed to show that there were still a large number of believers in the Soviet Union. I asked Father Leonid also whether the number of believers was on the decrease. He replied that they had no statistics on that point, but that if the amount of offerings was any indication, they were increasing. After a very interesting conversion the Father took us round the museum, which was small but contained a fine collection of religious art including a Tibetan banner, and then we went to the Teachers Retiring Room where we had bread and a delicious strawberry jam. We learnt that there were twenty two chairs in the Theological College with one Professor and one or more other teachers for each. The students have to study an extraordinarily wide range of subjects including no less than five foreign languages, Latin, Greek, Hebrew, Old Slavonic and either German, French or English. We returned to Moscow in the evening after a really interesting and educative outing. Before we left Father Leonid had suggested that we attend the Service on the Eve of Easter in Moscow which would be presided over by the Grand Patriarch, Alexi Nikolai.

In the evening we attended a ballet performance of *Don Quixote*[1] at the famous Bolshoi theatre, starting a leading ballerina, Grupshinka, who danced superbly. The Bolshoi, 'big' in Russian, is an impressive theatre, though for size and magnificence it cannot rival the Scala in Milan which we visited in 1956. The Russian ballerinas are wonderful, their movements are perfect and they seem to fly into the air like birds. They also have fine stage personalities and love applause. With glowing eyes they acknowledge the cheers of the audience after each Act, and are bombarded with flowers from all parts of the theatre. While witnessing the performance I was mentally comparing the Russian ballet with our finest from of classical dancing, Bharat Natyam. I noticed that some movements were very similar but the styles were entirely different. Our *tala* adds to the aesthetic appeal of the dance, and for an individual virtuoso performance a top flight Bharat Natyam dancer is hard to beat. In the Russian ballet the chief performers dance a scene for a few minutes and then go off the stage, and continue to do this throughout the performance, whereas in Bharat Natyam the dancer has to be on the stage for a long period without any break. Of course our dance, like our music, its much more individualistic whereas the Europeans excel in group dancing.

---

1. A novel by Miguel de Cervantes; one of the most widely read classics of western literature.

After the performance we went to the great Yelohovsky Cathedral where we witnessed a most impressive Easter Eve Service presided over by the Grand Patriarch of the Russian Orthodox Church. The Cathedral was packed to capacity with devotees, many of whom were constantly crossing themselves in a state of devotional ecstasy with tears streaming down their faces. The congregation included a fair number of young people. The chanting of the ritual was in Old Slavonic which sounded strangely like Sanskrit, and the waving of the lighted candles and burning of incense to the accompaniment of choral singing was very similar to the Hindu practice. Priests with flowing beards wearing red brocade vestments performed the solemn ritual. At a quarter to twelve the Patriarch asked for a fifteen minute silence and entered the sanctum sanctorum, from which he emerged at the stroke of midnight carrying three lighted candles in a stand and swinging an incense burner. 'Christ has risen, Christ has risen', he announced in a fine resonant voice which belied his great age. The devotees responded with the words 'Verily He is Resurrected'. Then the procession led by the Patriarch carrying the candles and brazier went thrice around the Cathedral where a milling crowd of thousands had gathered to catch a glimpse of the ceremony. It was indeed a moving and memorable experience.

My visit to Zagorsk and to this Cathedral indicated that at least nowadays religious believers in the Soviet Union are at liberty to pursue their worship freely and without fear of persecution. It need hardly be added, of course, that atheism is one of the cardinal tenets of the communist creed, and that the provision in the Soviet constitution guaranteeing freedom of religious belief is accompanied by the specific freedom to carry on anti religious propaganda. At one of the banquets I asked a top ranking communist leader whether it was possible for a person to be both a communist as well as a religious believer. He said that this had never happened and was not possible, but added that the communists respected the religious belief of others and that many believers played important roles in Soviet society in the sphere of science, art and so on.

The following day we flew to the Black Sea coast. After a flight of five hours the plane landed at a place called Adler where we were received by the Chairman of the Sochi City Council. From there we drove in an open car twenty miles to Sochi through beautiful countryside. On one side lay the Black Sea and on the other the

Caucasian Mountains began to rise. The buildings of Sochi had looked like a string of pearls along the sea coast from the plane. The air was fresh and crisp. Sochi is one of the 360 resort towns in the Soviet Union where workers spend a month every year holidaying amidst beautiful surroundings. In Sochi, itself there are forty seven Rest Homes for workers, known as Sanatoria, and over five lakh workers come there every year.

We were housed in a dacha overlooking the sea, and soon after our arrival we were taken round the town. The permanent population is only about 87,000, but the huge Sanatoria dominate the town. We visited two such buildings. They were indeed palatial, built in the neo-classical style with huge columns and several storeys. These Sanatoria are equipped with their own cinema halls, recreation rooms, libraries and restaurants in addition to residential accommodation for the workers. It costs sixteen hundred roubles a month to stay in Sochi, but we were told that the bulk of this expenditure is met by the trade unions and only about twenty five per cent is borne by the workers themselves. The workers get five meals a day and spend most of their time swimming on the delightful beach. Several of the bigger Sanatoria have their own funicular ropeways which take them directly to the beach. We travelled down one of these tunnels.

The Sanatoria 'Metallurg' is a most imposing building situated on a height overlooking the Black Sea. It has a lovely central fountain which gushed spectacularly against the panoramic background. The residential rooms were pleasant and airy. Workers usually come here alone but they can bring their wives also, though children are usually left at home so that they can get a real holiday. The dining halls, libraries and auditoria were very impressive, and it must be a great attraction to workers to get the opportunity to holiday in such lovely surroundings. I may add that we saw a large number of women workers holidaying in Sochi. Almost all women in the Soviet Union work, including the wives of important Government leaders and officials. Soviet women on the whole dress soberly and not very many cosmetics are used.

The next day we visited the modern Railway Station and Port Building that had recently been constructed in Sochi, which were among the few really modern pieces of architecture that I saw throughout the Soviet Union. In the afternoon, we had a cruise in the Black Sea in a motorboat. It was an exhilarating experience with the

Spray flying in all directions. Incidentally, the Black Sea is really not black at all but blue, and looks very much like the ocean except that there are hardly any waves. I tried to find out why it was so named, and the only answer I could get was that due to certain properties in the water if a coin is thrown into the sea it turns black. As we cruised in the sea I realized that we were at an interesting geographical point. Turkey was only 160 miles away. The moving landscape with the impressive buildings in the foreground and the mountains behind made a memorable scene.

Our dacha in Sochi was beautifully situated, and it was so pleasant and restful that we decided to stay on there an extra day. I may add that ever since we had arrived in the Soviet Union we had an extremely busy schedule, and it was only in Sochi that we were able to relax and have some rest. On the third day we decided to do some shopping. As far as presents are concerned we discovered that the best buys in the Soviet Union were caviar, lacquer boxes and vodka. Being teetotallers the vodka did not appeal to us but we bought quite a lot of boxes and caviar which were greatly appreciated by our friends in India. I visited a bank for the first time in Sochi in order to cash some rupee travellers cheques for which I got the special tourist rate of 2.1 roubles to a rupee. At the bank, while waiting for my money, I conversed with the Manager and learnt that there was no limit on individual holdings and that the interest on fixed deposits was 3 per cent.

In the evening the energetic young Chairman of the City Council and his colleagues had dinner with us, after which we played a game of chess. I am very fond of the game but was extremely nervous to even mention the fact in the Soviet Union, knowing how high their standard is. The City Chairman, however, though a fairly strong player was by no means a grand master, and after a terrific duel I ultimately prevailed. The next day he good humouredly presented me with a chess set as a memento of the game!

On the evening before our departure from Sochi my wife cooked us some delicious curry, the first Indian food we have had since leaving Delhi. Food in the Soviet Union is plentiful but I must admit that I missed Indian food a great deal. The normal Soviet meal lasts for at least two hours. One enters the dining room to find the table loaded with numerous plates containing a variety of salads, cold fish, raw cucumber, caviar and so on. After pecking at this for about fifteen minutes soup arrives in huge bowls which, if one were to finish, would constitute a meal in itself. Then there is generally a long break of about half an hour before the next dish arrives which is usually fish, and then another long break before the chicken or mutton is served. The helpings are enormous and throughout the meal there is a constant stream of conversation, toasts, speeches and drinking. Being teetotallers we were in a bit of a fix but were lucky that there was always a lot of lemonade available. Russian lemonade is the best I have ever tasted. Indeed, it appears to be a national drink, because it was in evidence wherever we went in the Soviet Union, particularly at conferences and interviews. It has a delightful flavour completely different from the lemonade in India, and looks very much like champagne. The farther south we got, the better the food became, until by the time we were in Central Asia there were many delicious dishes in common with us.

After three very restful and enjoyable days in Sochi we continued our journey and flew to Tbilsi, the capital of the neighbouring Republic of Georgia. This is an ancient and historic city and it had recently celebrated its fifteen hundredth anniversary. Tbilsi is built on the river Kura—which flows through the city—and on a series of low hills. As we drove in from the airport the first thing we noticed was a huge statue of a woman holding a sword dominating one of the hills. Later we learnt that this was a wood model for a permanent memorial to mark the fifteen hundredth anniversary of the city. It portrays a woman holding a sword in one hand and a cup in the other, symbolizing the determination to resist enemies—Georgia has had a turbulent history with many invasions—while welcoming friends. On entering the city I noticed that in places the cliff rises sheer from the river and several houses are built on its very edge. It almost appears as if the front doors of these houses open into space, which brought back to my mind memories of Chaplin's[1] classic comedy, *The Gold Rush*. It was perceptibly warmer in Tbilsi and the people also had distinctive features. The men have sharp aquiline noses and small moustaches, and are considered to be among the best looking people in the Soviet Union.

---

1. Charlie Chaplin (1889–1977); film actor, director and comedian; born in London, went to Hollywood in 1914; in his early silent comedies he adopted the bowler hat, out-turned feet, moustache and walking-cane which became his hallmark; films include *The Kid, The Gold Rush, The Great Dictator, Limelight*.

Our dacha here overlooked pleasant scenery, very reminiscent of the Suket Valley in Himachal Pradesh. After lunch we called on the Chairman of the Council of Ministers of the Georgian Republic. His office is on the famous Rustaveli Prospect, the main street of Tbilsi, named after the great twelfth century Georgian poet. At the head of the street is a huge statue of Lenin in his familiar pose of addressing the people. Incidentally, statues of Lenin are very much in evidence all over the Soviet Union, and he is indeed looked upon with almost religious reverence. Also, prominently displayed are the photographs of the twelve members of the Presidium of the Communist Party starting with Mr Khrushchev. In Georgia, however, which was Stalin's home State I noticed that statues and portraits of Stalin were also prominent and this was also true to a certain degree in Sochi which I was told was one of Stalin's favourite resorts. Stalin was born in Gori about eighty miles from Tbilsi, and the Georgians mention him with a good deal of obvious pride. In the north, however, even in Stalingrad, there was no reference to Stalin and hardly any evidence of his portraits or statues.

Our interview with the Chairman of the Council of Ministers and his colleagues was most interesting. The Deputy Chairman and Foreign Minister had recently visited India along with the Soviet delegation[1] and had lunch with me in Jammu. After the interview we went sight-seeing. We first drove to a park which overlooks a huge sunken botanical garden with neat flower beds, rows of cypress trees and one of the most attractive foundations I have seen. From here we drove to the Palace of Pioneers where we were introduced to some charming Georgian children and witnessed their joyful activities.

After dinner we went to the Opera House to witness a performance of the ballet 'Othello'. It was excellent and dramatically by far the most impressive work we saw in the Soviet Union. The dancers portraying Othello and Iago were superb, and I was amazed at the manner in which the play came alive without a single word being spoken. I realized for the first time that ballet was not only a rhythmic dance form, but a powerful medium which can portray the whole gamut of human emotions. The music for the ballet was modern, and was composed by a young contemporary Georgian composer. One

---

1. The Soviet goodwill delegation led by A. A. Anreyev visited India from 24 February to 6 March 1959.

scene of this ballet was particularly memorable. At the end of the Third Act, Othello, torn by the conflicting emotions of love and jealousy aroused by Iago's base intrigues, dances in agony and finally collapses flat on his back. Iago enters, crawling like a serpent, the very personification of evil. With sharp wicked darts he makes his way towards the prostrate Othello. Then he rises, places one foot on Othello's chest and stands over him with outstretched arms and head crouched like some horrible and malevolent vulture. The curtain falls. This was perhaps the most compelling scene I have ever witnessed on stage or screen.

The following morning we paid a visit to the new town Rustavi which has a population of sixty thousand and was built to house workers of the great Steel Plant nearby. This Plant, which was constructed fifteen years ago and has an annual capacity of a million tons, served as the prototype for our Bhilai Steel Plant at which a number of Georgian technicians are also working. We visited the Plant and saw the huge furnaces in which iron ore and coal ore are converted into steel ingots. The workers here are particularly well paid and, I was told, the average salary was twelve hundred roubles a month. They have nice living quarters and there are several Palaces of Culture attached to the Plant.

We returned for lunch, after which we visited the museum on Rustaveli street with its famous collection of icons. From there we proceeded to the Academy of Science where we met some academicians and had an illuminating discussion with them. In the Soviet Union each Republic has an Academy of Science which is the highest educational body controlling all post-graduate research. Each of the Republic Academies is represented on the Union Academy of Science which is the supreme body of its kind in the whole nation. The Soviet educational system lays immense stress upon highest research in almost all fields, and a great deal of money is spent on the Academies. In the Georgian Academy I was told that there were forty research institutes with four thousand full-time paid research workers. Special emphasis is laid on Georgian art, history and literature. After this we visited the Institute of Marxism-Leninism where we did not learn much except that the Institute had ninety full-time workers, conducted research into the history of the Georgian Communist Party and published works on its history, biographies of Georgian communist leaders and documents connected with the Revolution. There was a huge statue of Stalin in the main hall.

In the evening after a short rest we visited the gigantic wooden statue which I have mentioned earlier. It appeared to be about sixty to seventy feet high and must be one of the biggest wooden statues in the world. From there we drove to delightful part on the top of the hill where a fine, unusual type of pavillion has been constructed. It was here that the Chairman of the Council of Ministers had arranged the banquet in our honour, and mentioned that Panditji had also visited this spot a few years ago.[1] The pavilion commands a fine view of Tbilsi and the Kura Valley. By the time dinner had finished it was quite dark and as we stepped out onto the veranda, the lights of Tbilsi twinkled below us like an inverted sky. We descended by means of a funicular ropeway, almost the same height and distance as the Shankaracharya Hill in Srinagar. Our cars awaited us at the foot of the hill and we drove together with our hosts to a concert hall where we saw a performance of Georgian songs and vigorous Georgian dances. As often happened during our visit the whole audience rose and applauded when we entered the room and we clapped back rather sheepishly in the Soviet fashion.

The next morning I paid a visit to the University where we met the Pro-Rector, the Head of the Sanskrit Department, a Hindi teacher and a lay expert in English literature. The budget of the University is five crore roubles a year. It is housed in a fairly old building with wooden floors and pleasant academic atmosphere. We were presented with some Georgian literature, and during our conversation I discovered that there must have been considerable contact between Georgia and India in ancient times. I was told that tombs of Georgian merchants have been found in Calcutta and that the hero of Rustaveli's famous poem 'The Man in the Tiger Skin' was from India. The scholars there suggested that Georgia was probably known in ancient India as Gurjistan.

After a hurried lunch we took off for Taskhkent by a jet plane. Like an arrow it shot into the air and soon we were flying over endless wastes with hardly any sign of human habitation. One the way we get glimpses through the clouds of the Caspian Sea sprawling beneath us. Shortly we descended to Tashkent. Once again we were received by representatives of the Council of Ministers and the City Council, and drove several miles to our residence. Tashkent, with a population

---

1. In June 1955.

of 9,11,000 is the most important city of Central Asia. It is a modern
city with a lot of new buildings, but I found Stalinabad, the capital of
Tajikistan, more attractive. Soon after our arrival we changed dined
then went to the Opera House for a performance of the opera
'Dinaram' based on a famous poem by the ancient Tashkent poet Ali
Sher Navai. Both the hero and the heroine of this opera are Kashmiri,
and the first scene is set in Kashmir. I noticed that the set was very
interesting in that it combined in the same building the architectural
features of the Shah Humdan mosque in Srinagar and the Raghunath
temple in Jammu. The costumes also were Kashmiri and the music
resembled the Kashmiri *Sufiana Kalam*. The whole performance was
an index of the close cultural affinity that exists between the Central
Asian Republics of the Soviet Union and the Northern States of India,
specially Kashmir.

After a disturbed night—beds in the Soviet Union are generally
small and rather uncomfortable—we were ready at ten and called on
the Chairman of the Council of Ministers of the Uzbek Republic.
After an interesting conversation with him during which we dwelt
upon the remarkable similarities between Uzbekistan and India, we
visited a huge modern textile factory with over two thousand automatic
looms and employing eleven thousand workers. The finished cotton
fabrics had attractive colours and designs. In the afternoon we visited
the Institute of Oriental Studies where we had a meeting with
representatives of the Uzbek Academy of Sciences. This Academy
also employs over four thousand full-time research workers. We were
presented with several bulky volumes of academy publications and
also a microfilm copy of *Dewan-i-Ghani*, the work of an eminent
Kashmiri poet. Next we visited the University where we met a young
Indian in the Department of Hindi and Urdu as well as two Uzbek
teachers of these subjects. Hindi and Urdu are taught in the University
and also in some schools in Uzbekistan. They are also contemplating
opening departments of other modern Indian languages.

We learnt later that Hindi was also taught in some selected schools
in Moscow and other cities of the Soviet Union. Comparatively, we
have greatly neglected the study of Russian in our country. As a result
of our long association with Great Britain our whole educational
structure is oriented towards the English system. While I do not for a
moment suggest that the study of English should be discontinued—
indeed I have often felt alarmed at the declining standard of English
and feel strongly that this great language must continue to be taught

in India—I do feel that it is not wise for us to neglect the study of Russian. In view of the facts of geography, and of international politics today, it is of the utmost importance that the study of Russian should be started in India on a seriously planned basis. Even from the narrow utilitarian point of view our lack of knowledge of Russian makes us incapable of taking advantage of the great body of technical literature that is being published in that country which would be most useful to us in our industrial and technical progress. It needs to be added that in order to be effective such a study must begin from the secondary school stage. It is, of course, not necessary for Russian to be introduced as a subject in all schools, but in some selected schools and colleges the language can be introduced.

In the evening we attended as usual a banquet given by the Chairman of the Council of Ministers. This particular banquet, however, was distinguished from the others by a rather amusing incident. During the meal there were numerous speeches and toasts, and Uzbek artists danced and sang. Their repertoire included two Indian film songs, both of which I discovered were very popular in Central Asia *Bachpan ki mohabbat ko* and *Chanda mama dur ke*. The latter is a favourite lullaby of my little baby whom we had left behind in Kashmir and I was rather moved on hearing it. Immediately the song ended, however, I moved in an entirely unexpected manner. The chair upon which I was sitting suddenly collapsed and I crashed dramatically to the ground. Consternation! Luckily, I was quite unhurt and was able to pass the incident off amidst laughter and camaraderie. On resuming my seat I remarked that Soviet hospitality was so good and I had eaten so much since I had been in the country that it was becoming difficult for the chair to support me any longer. The Deputy Chairman of the Council of Ministers replied that they had a saying in Uzbekistan that a person who falls while sitting will live to be a hundred, and invited me to come back to Tashkent on my hundredth birthday to celebrate the event!

After dinner we were shown a documentary film: *Come to Uzbekistan* which contained some lovely scenes of the Republic, many of them closely resembling Kashmir. We were presented with Uzbek costumes which are colourful and attractive, and which we have now turned into lovely dressing gowns.

The next morning we boarded our Illyushin plane and flew to the ancient and historic city of Samarkand which we reached in just under one hour. This city, one of the most ancient in Asia, is now a modern provincial town with a population of two hundred thousand. However, it still has some impressive ancient monuments which we visited with great interest. These included the 'Shah Zinda', a monument built by Timur and his ancestors to house the bodies of his teacher and several of his relatives. It also contains what is claimed to be the tomb of a cousin of the Prophet Muhammad, the legendary Qusum-Ibn-Abbas, whose tomb is considered to be almost as holy a place as Mecca itself. Next we went to 'Jama Masjid' or 'Bibi Khanum' built by Timur and named after his eldest wife. This consists of two gigantic arched gates, one the entrance and the other the mosque, facing each other. It must have been a most imposing building when in use, and in ruin is still very impressive. The domes of these monument are of blue glazed tiles which look as fresh as if they had been recently made. We then visited the famous Square known as the 'Registan' three sides of which consist of huge Madrasa buildings including the famous Ulug Beg and Sher-dar Madrasa. Finally, we went to the tomb of Timur, an exquisite little mosque. This building was in the best state of repair, and as we entered the courtyard the clean blue dome with two slender, beautifully proportioned minarets, rose against the pale blue sky. In a corner of the courtyard is a large block of what is known as 'green' marble but which looks whitish. On this the formidable Timur used to sit and hold audience. He is buried inside the mosque. There is a tombstone immediately inside the entrance, but as in the Taj Mahal the real tombs are underground. We walked down a flight of winding steps into an underground chamber containing the tomb of Timur, his religious teacher and several other relations including his astronomer grandson Ulug Beg. Timur's tomb is made of green nephrite and is covered with inscriptions. In 1940 his bones were exhumed for scientific investigation and then replaced. It was discovered that he was indeed lame, one leg being five centimetres shorter than the other, that one arm was withered and that he had probably died of tuberculosis.

It was indeed interesting to visit this historic city connected with the life of a man who had such a malevolent impact on Indian history. Timur's hordes must have set out from here on their expeditions of loot and rapine to India. But time is a great healer and today the people of this land have the friendliest feelings towards us.

After visiting the monuments we went to the local museum whose exhibits covered the history of Samarkand from prehistoric times down to the present day. I noticed that the ceilings of the museum were decorated with colourful and attractive designs very similar to the Durbar Hall in Srinagar, and that the wood work was also very much like ours.

In the afternoon we continued our flight and proceeded to Stalinabad, the capital of Tajikistan. This flight took us over an impressive mountain range very much like the approaches to the Banihal Pass, with many other ranges in the distance. On nearing Stalinabad the high mountains are fringed by green curiously dappled foothills. The leader of the Soviet party attached to us, Mr Imamov, was Minister of Culture of the Tajik Republic and was greatly excited as we neared his tome town.

Stalinabad is a lovely city, with a population of about two and a half lakhs. It is situated in a valley, on one side of which are snow-covered mountains, and on the other low hills. The cultural and geographic affinities between Kashmir and Tajikistan are quite remarkable. Indeed, of the five Central Asian Republics, Tajikistan is the closest to us both geographically and culturally. It is the only one whose language is based upon Persian (the others are more akin to Turkish) and hence with my working knowledge of Urdu I was able to converse quite freely with the people without the help of an interpreter. The trees of this area are very much like those of Kashmir and include the chinar, which grows as tall as it does in Kashmir, almond, pistachio, walnut, apricot, peach and plum. Stalinabad is a new city, constructed in 1929, and is situated on the river Dushambe. On the evening we arrived we were entertained to a delightful concert of Tajiki dances and music in the impressive Opera House which is decorated inside with purely local motifs including the chandeliers and the curtains. The performance was a memorable one, and consisted of some excellent Tajiki songs and colourful dances. There were two Indian dances and a song *Bachpan ki mohabbat ko* again! The master of ceremonies, who made announcements in flawless Persian, was a brilliant performer himself. In Stalinabad the food was also very similar to North Indian food, and included several of our favourite dishes such as *pulao, kabab, naan, sheermal* and trout. The scenery is also somewhat similar to Kashmir and indeed we felt entirely at home in this Republic.

The next morning we called as usual on the Chairman of the Council of Ministers who is a law expert and who reeled off detailed statistics about Tajiki industry and agriculture without any reference to notes. Then we proceeded on a sightseeing trip around the lovely city. We visited the newly constructed stadium which seats twenty-five thousand spectators, an artificial lake, the public library, and a delightful 'Chae-khana' or tea house which is built in Tajiki motifs with a coloured glass roof. The tea house was full of people who looked very much like Kashmiri foremen and also like our nomadic *Bakarwals*. This is a popular gathering place in the city and is a very attractive feature. We then proceeded to the one and only 'Kolkhoz' or collective farm included in our programme. This was a few miles outside the city, and the drive took us through scenery exactly like that in Kashmir, including mud hut villages. At the Kolkhoz we were met by the Director, a local Tajiki who is a Hero of Socialist Labour. He took us round the farm and showed us the inevitable Palace of Culture, the general store and a workers home. We then went to his office where we asked him a large number of questions with regard to the functioning of the Kolkhoz. Apparently, the population of the farm is divided into several 'Brigades' each under a 'Brigadier'. This farm produces cotton, wheat, corn, maize and several other minor products. The total production is delivered to the management, and out of this eleven per cent is paid to the State as income tax, twenty-nine per cent is set aside for capital development and the balance of sixty per cent is distributed as wages. The average wage amounts to between thirteen and seventeen roubles a day. In addition to this education, medical facilities, water, fruits and vegetables are free. The farmers pay for their house and electricity.

The entire land in the Soviet Union is divided into two categories, State Farms and Collective Farms. The former are run entirely as Government institutions, and the labour is engaged on a wage basis. In the latter, however, the Collective Farm has a distinct corporate entity. Of course, targets of production are laid down by the State which also appropriates a sizeable portion of the profit as income tax. However, we were told that recently of good deal of decentralization had been effected and that more power had been given to the farm authorities. The tractors and service station were also being transferred from State to Kolkhoz ownership.

We were entertained to lunch by the Director of the farm and his colleagues, and the meal lasted as usual for well over two hours. In the afternoon we visited the State Academy of Sciences where we met several eminent academicians including the poet Mirza Tarsunzada. It is clear that in the Soviet Union men of science and learning are held in high regard, and it is considered a great distinction to be a member of the Academy. Financially also, scholars and intellectuals are specially favoured.

Stalinabad's was the first Academy where we found that the emphasis was more on humanities than on the physical sciences. At the time of our visit they were celebrating the eleven hundredth birth anniversary of the great Tajiki poet Rudaki. It is obvious that local tradition and culture in each of the constituent Republics are given special encouragement, and it seems clear that the people of Central Asia have made remarkable progress in the past three or four decades. I was told that illiteracy had been completely eradicated and that there was full employment. Before the revolution there was no institute of higher learning in Tajikistan. Now, with a population of twenty lakhs, there were seven institutes of higher learning with eighteen thousand students. After the Academy we visited the University of Stalinabad, where I was presented with a welcome address on behalf of the students to which I replied. Finally, we paid a lightning visit to a textile factory which seemed even more modern than the one in Taskhkent. After a very hurried dinner we attended a performance of the ballet 'Laila Majnu'. In which again the emphasis was on local tradition and culture. We returned home almost at midnight after a long and exhausting but extremely interesting day.

In the morning we drove to a pleasant spot a few miles from Stalinabad where a stream flows down the hillsides and a new Guest House has been built commanding a fine view of the snowy mountains. On the way back we visited a 120 bed children's hospital. It was clean and I was struck by the high ratio of doctors and nurses to the number of patients. After some shopping we were entertained to lunch by the Chairman of the Council of Ministers, at the end of which we were presented with attractive Tajiki dresses. In the afternoon we flew back to Tashkent and the next morning we returned to Moscow in the jet service. The flight was extraordinarily smooth and it took us just over four hours to cover the immense distance between Tashkent and Moscow.

We drove from the Moscow airport to our dacha. The trees in Moscow were now in full bloom and the city was looking much prettier than before. After a quick lunch we visited the magnificent new University building where we were received by the Rector, Mr Petrovsky, a distinguished mathematician and a charming person. For three quarters of an hour we sat with him and a few of his colleagues around a table, and I asked him many questions with regard to the

University. Then for over an hour we chatted with a group of young English speaking Humanities students who had been specially invited to meet us by the University authorities. It was our first opportunity to get into personal contact with Soviet youth, and I was impressed by their demeanour and their evident seriousness. The students numbered about fifteen, including several girls, and were studying a variety of subjects such as Law, Economics, Hindi, Japanese and Indonesian. One young law student was making a special study of the Indian Constitution and we had an interesting discussion regarding Indian and Soviet Federalism. I found that he was fairly well informed and was familiar with most of the important books on the Indian Constitution.

We gathered that Rabindranath Tagore is held in high esteem in the Soviet Union and preparations were afoot to celebrate his birth centenary throughout the country. Inter alia one of the students said that almost the entire student community in Moscow University were atheists with the exception of a few foreign students. I remarked that Rabindranath Tagore was a deeply religious person and that his poems were imbued with devotion to God, and I wondered how in view of this fact he was so greatly appreciated in the Soviet Union. The students replied that they did not agree with his religion but liked him as a poet nevertheless.

After our discussion we were taken around parts of the huge new building. The thirty-six storey skyscraper is built on an eight hundred acre campus, and the top seven floors contain a magnificent geological and geographical museum. There are six thousand compact two bed cubicles for students, and twelve thousand students live in the building out of a total strength of over twenty-two thousand students. Indeed, it is almost a self contained town with a two thousand seat auditorium, a students club, gymnasiums, swimming pools, restaurants, shops and so on. The annual budget of the University is 260 million roubles. The students' cubicles are tiny and compact and each has a separate bath and toilet. We met a few Indian and Nepalese students who were studying in the University.

Both in the University and at my meeting the next day with the Union Minister for Higher Education, I was keen to learn something about the educational system in the Soviet Union. From what I could gather it appeared that Primary and Secondary Education is free and compulsory, and is under the jurisdiction of the constituent Republic

Governments. Higher Education is, however, a Union subject and Minister for Higher Education controls and coordinates Junior Ministers and Departments throughout the country. Education in the Soviet Union seems to be planned and purposeful, and there is no aimless drift from school to college with which we are so familiar in our own country, indeed it is not easy to gain admission to an institution of higher learning, and there is a stiff examination at the end of high school for admission to such institutions. Admission is regulated on the basis of carefully planned future requirements. I was told that the Ministry for Higher Education works out the number of trained personnel required in the various professions at the end of a certain period and admission is given accordingly to technical colleges of various kinds. Thus only about one third of the total number of the students who get through High School are allowed to go on to college and the rest are absorbed in various technical school and professions. The students who continue their studies are of course assured of employment at the end of their courses. Three months before the end of their studies, experts from industrial and other enterprises visit the institutions and select students for various lines. The Director of the college sees that a student gets a fair deal vis-à-vis conditions of work, pay, etc. after which a three year agreement is signed. After that period the students is free to go anywhere else if he so chooses.

Even students who do not immediately get admission into higher institutions can take advantage of correspondence courses. A new development is that admission to arts courses is now allowed only after the student has had two years experience of practical life in some farm or industry. I enquired whether this did not cause a break in the continuity of studies and thus adversely affect the interests of the students. I was told that to some extent this was true, but that it was felt necessary for the students to have some experience of practical life before they undertook studies in the fields of such subjects as law, economics, journalism and philosophy, as they would thus be better able to assimilate the courses. This does not apply to technical faculties where the students carry on their studies without a break.

After high school there is a five year Graduation course (six years for medicine) after which the students get a diploma. There is then a further three years course for the Master's degree, and of course Doctoral studies take several years after that to complete. Thus, the Soviet student has to study for eight years in college before he gets his Master's degree as against five years in the revised course in our country.

Attendance at all lectures is compulsory, although the Director can exempt students in some rare extraordinary circumstances.

Eighty per cent of the college students get stipends, ranging from 300 roubles per month in the first year up to 600 roubles per month in the fifth. Students who come in the upper ten per cent of their class get an additional twenty five per cent bonus. There is a special Commission in each college, which includes the management as well as representatives of the students, whose task is to recommend stipends based on applications. The more well to do students generally do not apply. I was told that there are no serious problems of mass student indiscipline, and that individual problems are dealt with by social organizations which include representatives of the students.

The examination system is interesting and is very different from the one with which we are familiar. There are a number of home assignments, laboratory works, projects, papers etc. during the term, and only if the student has done his term work satisfactorily can he appear in the end of term examination. These examinations, strangely enough, are oral. Students choose questions by lottery tickets, and have to answer immediately all the questions on the tickets they have chosen. If a student fails in two subjects he can appear the next month, but he is expelled after three failures. For technical subjects, of course, a student has in addition to prepare a written thesis of a hundred pages plus twelve drawings, and to defend it against an outside expert.

I made enquiries regarding the medium of instruction, and I was told that in the Russian S.E.S.R. the medium is Russian while in the other Republics there are two alternatives. Russian and the Republic language, according to the student's choice. In secondary schools also there is this choice, which is exercised by the parents. I was told that on purpose Russian was not made compulsory, but in view of the obvious advantage of learning Russian and the love which people all over the nation had for that language it was unlikely that any student would not want to learn it. I also gather that there was no special training for the administrative or foreign services and that personnel for these were chosen from any of the professions.

As I have mentioned earlier, in the Soviet Union, universities are not the highest academic bodies. This honour is reserved for the Academies of Science, which spend enormous sums of money on research. The whole Soviet educational system has a marked technological bias and its efficacy has been amply demonstrated by the remarkable advances made by Soviet science in the past few years. Indeed planning progress and hard work, seem to be key concepts in Soviet education.

There is no such thing as university autonomy in our sense of the term. Of course, in their internal affairs the university authorities obviously have a good deal of discretion but all the funds are provided, and appointments made, by the Union Education Ministry. The Academies of Science are likewise under the respective Republic Governments.

It is clear that Soviet education at all levels is imbued with the official ideology of Marxism and Leninism. Although the number of the students belonging to the Communist Party is not large, eighty to ninety per cent belong to the Komsomol or Young Communist Organization. Every institute has three compulsory subjects which form eight per cent of the entire curriculum. These are:

1. History of the Communist Party of the Soviet Union.
2. Political economy based on Marx.
3. Philosophy based on Marx.

All branches of philosophy are studied, including idealism, but obviously all other systems are studied critically in the light of the Marxist-Leninist ideology. Indeed, the role of the Communist Party in the Soviet Union is central to the whole system. I was told that a considerable proportion of the members of the various legislative organs from the Supreme Soviet down to City Councils are not Communist, but there is little doubt that such people can be elected only with the approval of the Communist Party. Everywhere I went I was told that the City Councils and other organs were elected, but invariably I also learnt that there was only one candidate for each electoral seat. It appears that although theoretically the organs of Government in the Soviet Union are formed in very much the same way as in India, in practice the whole system is dominated by the Communist Party.

To revert to academic matters, although the ideological bias is not likely to have any adverse effect upon the technical sciences, in the study of the humanities it certainly leads to a one-sided and somewhat restricted approach. On the other hand the unitary ideology gives the nation valuable homogeneity in tackling national problems.

After our visit to the University we went to the Institute of Oriental Studies of the Union Academy of Sciences where we met a distinguished group of Indologists, many of whom spoke fluent Hindi. These included Mr George Roerich,[1] son of the famous Russian painter Nicholas Roerich,[2] who said he had been to India in 1925. I was once again impressed by the great interest taken in the study of Indology and Indian languages in the Soviet Union.

In the evening we were hosts at a dinner party in the Sovietskaya Hotel which was attended by several important Soviet leaders including Mr Kozlov, Mr Mukhitdinov, Mr Andreyev, Marshal Malinowsky, Mr Pushkin and others. After the party we waited for all the guests to leave and then stepped out of the hotel to get into our car. It seems that the car had been parked elsewhere and we decided to stroll on the street outside the hotel until it came. What happened, however, was that our chauffeur drove to the entrance of hotel and seeing that we were not standing on the steps returned to our dacha thinking that we had gone in another car. We were stranded outside the hotel without any transport and after strolling up and down for about half an hour we took a taxi. The taxi driver was a pleasant and voluble young man. When we said we were from India he put up his hand and counted off on his fingers. 'Nehru, Krishna Menon, Rajendra Prasad, Indira Gandhi, Raj Kapoor[3]— kharoshow (good)'. When we reached home we found everyone in a state of great consternation as they thought that we had been lost.

The fourteenth of May was our penultimate day in the Soviet Union. In the morning my wife visited a Hindi School in Moscow where she was greeted by children speaking Hindi and singing Hindi songs. I paid a visit to a leading Machine Tools Factory named 'Krasny Proletary'. We drove up to what looked like a block of flats but

---

1. (1874-1947); Russian artist and a renowned landscape painter; spent five years exploring the Himalayas; settled down in Kangara valley in 1935.
2. George Nicholas Roerich (1902-1960); Russian scholar well-known for his profound knowledge of Buddhism; took part in his father's archaeological expeditions (1926-29) to Tibet, China, Mongolia which revealed information on Indian influences there; lived many years in Darjeeling and Kulu valley; returned to the USSR in 1956; author of *Travels to Inmost Asia* (1935) and *Blue Annals* (1949).
3. (1924-1988); doyen of Indian cinema; worked as actor, director and producer; received the Filmfare Award, 1959, 1961 and 1964 and the Dada Saheb Phalke Award, 1988; films include, *Awara, Shree 420, Jagte Raho, Boot Polish*.

turned out to be the factory, and were met at the entrance by the Chief Engineer, Mr Victor Romanoff—'Like the Czars' as he smilingly remarked—a handsome, greying, well-built man who exuded ability and self confidence. He took us round the factory and showed us the various processes whereby they produced a thousand lathes a month plus a smaller number of specialized machines. Romanoff, who spoke fairly good English, told us that he had worked for thirty-six years in that very plant, starting as a boy apprentice. With pride he pointed out improved machinery that the factory had evolved to cut down production time and increase productivity. One process for making a part of the gear box which used to take ten hours was now completed in ten minutes by the new machinery. He also showed us what he claimed was the only machine in the world which produced gears of various sizes absolutely automatically, combining nine different operations. He mentioned that many of the machines manufactured in the factory were exported to foreign countries including India.

I might mention here that on almost all levels, right up to the topmost rung of the ladder, leadership in the Soviet Union is almost exclusively made of technicians, usually construction or other engineers. Almost all the Ministers and Chairmen of City Soviets we met were engineers by profession, and their main interest appeared to be to increase the productivity of the nation. Few of these people appeared to be theoreticians. Indeed, the Soviet Union can well be described as a technocratic society.

We lunched at the Indian Embassy and then visited the Tretsikov Gallery of Russian Art where we were escorted through the halls by a charming old lady who spoke excellent English. This collection consists of purely Russian art, and there were some outstanding paintings including two portraits of Tolstoy,[1] a picture of a girl with the most living eyes I have ever seen in a painting and a superb, gigantic canvas portraying Christ appearing before the multitude which took the artist twenty-six years to paint.

From the Art Gallery we visited the Institute of Philosophy of the Union Academy of Sciences where we met the Director of a number

---

1. Count Leo Nikolayevich Tolstoy (1808-1910); Russian short story writer, moralist and mystic, known for his epic *War and Peace* (1865-69) and *Anna Karenina* (1875-77).

of his distinguished colleagues. We had a most lively and interesting discussion ranging over Sri Aurobindo,[1] Bertrand Russell,[2] Lysenko,[3] Dialectical Materialism and so on. They said that their system was Historical Materialism but that they also studied other schools of thought including the idealists. I gathered that Russell, Dewey[4] and Radhakrishan were well known, but none of them seemed to have heard of Albert Schweitzer.[5] The Institute is at present undertaking the translation of our Sanskrit classics into Russian, and are also publishing a five volume *History of World Philosophy*, the first two of which were presented to me.

In the evening we attended a reception in our honour by the Union of Societies for Cultural Relations with foreign countries. There was a distinguished gathering including the inventor Mr Tupolev,[6] creator of the wonderful TU (A & B) jet planes. The Chairman of the Union as well as of the Indian Friendship Society spoke at the function, and I replied—stressing India's policy of peace and the close and friendly relations between our two countries. This was followed by a small concert including some singers and Indian dancers, an excellent conjuring couple and a famous puppeteer who had recently returned from India. From this reception we went to the

---

1. Aurobindo Ghosh (1872-1950); poet and a leader of the national movement; learnt Greek, Latin, French, German, Spanish and Italian during his stay in England (1879–93); principal, National College (later, Jadavpur University), Calcutta, 1906-07; edited *Jugantar*, a Bengali daily and an English daily, *Bande Mataram*; left Calcutta and reached Pondicherry, 4 April 1910 and spent the rest of his life in spiritual pursuits founding an ashram there; author of: *Savitri, The Life Divine, Secret of the Vedas, Synthesis of Yoga* and *Essays on the Gita*.
2. (1872-1970); British philosopher, mathematician and essayist; after the Second World War he became a champion of nuclear disarmament; awarded the Nobel Prize for literature in 1950.
3. Trofim Deniovich Lysenko (1898-1976); geneticist and agronomist from Ukraine; director, Institute of Genetics, Soviet Academy of Sciences, 1940-65.
4. John Dewey (1859-1952); philosopher and educator; leading exponent of pragmatism; developed the philosophy of education which laid stress on development of the person, understanding of the environment, and learning through experience.
5. (1875-1965); German medical missionary, theologian, musician and philosopher; set up a hospital to fight leprosy and sleeping sickness at Lambarene, French Equatorial Africa; awarded the Nobel Peace Prize in 1952.
6. Andrey Nikoloyevich Tupolev (1888-1972); aircraft designer from the USSR; produced over 100 types of aircraft, including the first Soviet civil jet, the TU-104 (1955) and in 1968 completed the first test flight of the supersonic passenger aircraft, the TU-144.

television studio where we appeared on a television programme. Our interpreter, the lady announcer, my wife and myself sat at a table facing the cameras, and I gave a brief account of my impressions of the Soviet Union which was translated into Russian, sentence by sentence.

The next morning, 15 May, I had a meeting with the Union Minister for Higher Education to which I have previously referred and also with the Deputy Minister for Social Welfare of the Russian S.F.S.R. He gave me interesting information with regard to the functioning of Social Welfare Ministers, which exist only in the Republics and not at the Centre and which deal with many subjects including pensions. They are specially concerned with the training and rehabilitation of disabled labour, and run over seventy factories which produce special apparatus for these people. He told me that all citizens working in industrial establishments get pensions, women at fifty-five or after twenty years service, and men at sixty or after twenty-five years service. Agriculturists also get pensions which are paid through the collective farms, but this payment is also organized and controlled by the Ministry. Pensions range from three hundred to twelve hundred roubles a month in the cities and two hundred and fifty to a thousand roubles a month in the villages.

In the afternoon we drove for the last time to the airport. We had become really fond of the Russian people and of Moscow, and it was with a good deal of emotion that we prepared to take leave. At the airport several dignitaries and officials had assembled to see us off and we chatted for about an hour in a light drizzle. As we took leave of the men and women who had been with us throughout the trip and who had done such a lot to make our visit pleasant and memorable, we were quite moved and indeed my wife and our charming lady interpreter were on the verge of tears. As our plane took off in the direction of Stockholm we waved farewell to a great country and a great people, carrying with us warm and happy memories of our visit.

——————— 170 ———————

Mashobra
12 July 1959

My dear Tiger,
I have received your letter of July 7 here at Mashobra near Simla, and
I have read the report of your impressions of the Soviet Union with
interest. I am circulating it to members of our Cabinet for their
information.

As you know, I decided to go to Kashmir for a few days, but the
floods[1] intervened, and now I am here at Mashobra. This is a pleasant
enough place, and I am having full rest. We shall be returning to
Delhi on the 19th July.

Yours ever,
Jawaharlal Nehru

——————— 171 ———————

Srinagar
16 July 1959

My dear Panditji,
Thank you very much for your letter of July 12 from Mashobra. I am
happy that you found my note on the Soviet Union of some interest.

We had all eagerly been looking forward to your visit but the
floods disastrously intervened. I do hope you will be able to come
here for a few days later in the season. Indiraji and the children also
have not come up yet.

It was very kind of you to have telephoned from Mashobra. After
our conversation I contacted Bakshi Sahib and also sent a telegram
to the President. I received his reply yesterday in which he conveyed
his approval and wholehearted support for the proposed Sadar-i-
Riyasat's Flood Relief Fund. Today I have opened the Fund and
have also set up a broad-based Committee under my Chairmanship
including representatives of the main political parties in the State, to

———————————

1. During the second week of July 1959 devastating floods ravaged the Kashmir valley
   crippling all communication.

administer it. I enclose a Press Note which gives the names of the Committee members and also the Appeal which I have issued. We will now get down seriously to the task of collections and at the same time work out how best these can be distributed to the flood victims. I look forward to your guidance, support and blessings in this work.

I hope this finds you in excellent health and refreshed after your holiday in the mountains.

With deepest regards,

Yours as ever,
Karan Singh

———— 172 ————

New Delhi
20 July 1959

My dear Tiger,

I returned from Mashobra yesterday rather the worse for my visit there. I have much to my regret given up the idea of going to Kashmir tomorrow. Perhaps, later I might come for a day or so.

I have just seen your letter of July 16th. I am glad you have started a Sadar-i-Riyasat's Flood Relief Fund. I am sending you herewith a cheque for Rs 1,00,000/- from the Prime Minister's National Relief Fund for this Fund of yours. Also a personal contribution of Rs 1,000/-.

Yours ever,
Jawaharlal Nehru

———— 173 ————

Srinagar
20 July 1959

My dear Panditji,

Last evening I received your telegram informing me of your generous contributions to the Sadar-i-Riyasat's Flood Relief Fund. Thank you very much indeed. Your contribution will act as a great encouragement to us all.

We have been much distressed to learn of your indisposition. I do hope you have completely got over it and are now quite well again.

With respects and deep regards,

Yours as ever,
Karan Singh

——— 174 ———

Srinagar
24 July 1959

My dear Panditji,
I write to acknowledge with thanks receipt of your two cheques for Rs 1,00,000/- and Rs 1,000/-.

The first grant from the Fund I have sent some money to the Chief of the Army Staff, General Thimayya for distribution as immediate relief to the families of twenty-one army personnel who lost their lives in the recent floods here.

With respects and deep regards,

Yours as ever,
Karan Singh

——— 175 ———

New Delhi
30 July 1959

My dear Tiger,
I have received intimation from the Soviet Red Cross that they are sending me a sum of money for flood relief in Kashmir. I think, the sum is Rs 60,000/- or perhaps a little more. When I receive this, I shall send it to you.

As I mentioned to you in Srinagar, I think, you should send a substantial amount from your fund to Bakshi Sahib for relief work. Most of this relief must necessarily be done through governmental agencies. I think, you should send about Rs 50,000/-, to begin with.

Yours affectionately,
Jawaharlal Nehru

——— 176 ———

Srinagar
9 August 1959

My dear Panditji,

Thank you very much for your letter of July 30. It is a generous gesture on the part of the Soviet Red Cross to send money flood relief in Kashmir.

I shall be happy to send a sum of money to Bakshi Sahib from my Fund, but in the absence of any specific suggestions as to how it is to be used he will probably only credit it to the Government Relief Fund. This would amount to a mere transfer of money from one fund to the other which may cause confusion in the public mind. If you approve, I will suggest in the next meeting of my Fund Committee that we should send a sum of Rs 50,000/- to the State Prime Minister for some specific purpose which we will decide upon.

I may take this opportunity to write to you about two important matters. The first is with regard to the flood control plans that are now being drawn up and are likely to involve an expenditure of several crores of rupees over the next few years. It is clear that the limited technical and administrative resources of the state are already strained to the utmost in meeting ordinary plan expenditure. As such it will not be possible for the normal administrative and executive channels adequately to cope with the enormous extra work that will be involved in the implementation of the vast flood control schemes, which in view of their vital importance deserve to be tackled on a top priority basis. In view of this I suggest that a special high-powered authority should be set up to deal with the preparation and execution of flood control schemes in the State. This should be presided over by the State Prime Minister and may consist of :-

The Chairman and a Member of the Central Water and Power Commission;

The two State Chief Irrigation Engineers;

The Secretary for Kashmir Affairs;

A financial expert each from the Centre and the State.

This will ensure on the one hand full co-ordination between the Centre and the State in the implementation of these vital measures, and on the other top priority for the works. It will also raise the whole matter above the plane of routine administration and will therefore be welcomed by public opinion. If you agree, I think, this suggestion should come from the Government of India. It needs to be pointed out to the State Government that this step is designed solely to help in the successful execution of a project vital to the State's economy, the bulk of expenditure on which is going to be borne by the Centre.

The second matter is with regard to our Ladakh–Tibet border. Recently a patrol party of CRP was kidnapped by the Chinese[1] while they were on our side of the border, and I learn that the Chinese have built roads, check-posts, bunkers and other fortifications well inside Indian territory. As you know, the border with Tibet is still undemarcated, but that does not mean that gradual encroachment and occupation of our territory can be countenanced. I submit that this is a matter of grave concern and deserves to be looked into carefully and expeditiously. I understand that the Chushul[2] airport, upon which you will recall we landed in 1952, is now out of commission. This is close to the border and hence strategically very important. Psychologically also, both vis-à-vis the Chinese and the local population, it would be a good move for us to use this airport at least occasionally. It is most important that the Ladakh–Tibet border should be strengthened, for unless adequate measures are taken at this stage we may have to face a very serious problem in a few years when the Chinese have consolidated their positions in our territory. The situation appears to be developing into something more than mere 'cartographical aggression'.

With respectful regards,

Yours as ever,
Karan Singh

——— 177 ———

New Delhi
15 August 1959

My dear Tiger,
Thank you for you letter of the 9th August.
As regards the relief funds, I take it that these are chiefly meant for

1. On 21 September 1959, the Chinese opened fire on an Indian patrol near the Kongka Pass, killing five policemen, wounding four and capturing ten.
2. Chushul airport in Ladakh is India's highest airport.

urgent cases of relief and not for any major schemes for the future. The schemes and projects are on a much bigger scale and have necessarily to be undertaken by Governments. But Government rules and regulations are normally such that quick relief cannot be given as sanctions have to be obtained and all that. Therefore, whenever an emergency like this occurs, the money for relief is meant to be utilized with speed to remove suffering. In most parts of India the practice is for this relief to be given by District Magistrates. If I send money, it goes to the Governor or Chief Minister and part of it he sends to the District Magistrates for such relief. Part of it is sent to recognized organizations which can be entrusted with this relief work there.

I do not know what your agency for such urgent relief is or can be. It would be a pity if money is not used when most needed and is kept for some scheme or other in the future. I realize that perhaps the district apparatus in Jammu and Kashmir may not be very adequate for this purpose, but for the moment I can think of no other. It may be that in a district the District Magistrate forms a small committee including some non-officials. How Bakshi Sahib uses the money in his Fund, I do not know. But if the money is to go to the local authorities, it should go through Bakshi Sahib and not directly through your Fund. I see no harm in the money you give him being for the moment credited to his Fund. In fact, there is an advantage in that because people will realize that the two are cooperating and not rival Funds. There has been some propaganda both in India and Pakistan to indicate that there is rivalry in this matter. I do not understand what specific purpose you can mention to Bakshi Sahib for the expenditure of these Relief Funds. You may discuss with him the manner of spending it, that is, the agencies through which relief is given to the persons actually suffering. Any specific purpose must be in the nature perhaps of rehabilitation. That is good if it can be clearly stated that the money has to be used quickly to give relief.

I am anxious to put an end to this propaganda about rivalry between the two Funds.

I agree with you that it will be desirable to have some kind of formal authority or informal committees to deal with flood control schemes. Bakshi Sahib mentioned to me that insofar as the big scheme is concerned for increasing the outlet of the Jhelum from the Valley, he would like the Government of India to take charge of it completely. It is a very big scheme totally beyond the capacity of the State Government. I shall discuss this matter with Bakshi Sahib when he comes here, which, I understand, is going to be soon.

We are much concerned at the development near the Ladakh-Tibet border. We are going into this matter fully. I think we should use the Chushul airstrip and keep up our check-post there.

Yours affectionately,
Jawaharlal Nehru

——— 178 ———

Srinagar
18 August 1959

My dear Panditji,

I have received a further cheque for Rupees one lakh from your National Relief Fund for flood relief in this State, which includes the Rs 80,000/- contributed by the Soviet Red Cross and Red Crescent Societies. I write to thank you for your generous support which is a source of encouragement to us all. Our appreciation for their donation may very kindly be conveyed to the Soviet societies also.

Thank you very much for your letter of the 15th August in reply to mine. It is indeed unfortunate that some interested people have sought to misinterpret the existence of two Funds, but a recent statement issued by the State Government (copy enclosed) should clarify the matter once and for all.[1]

I am sending a cheque for Rs 50,000/- to Bakshi Sahib from my Fund. I understand he is leaving for Delhi tomorrow. I am also likely to pass through Delhi on the 4th September and look forward to paying my respects to you there if convenient to you.

I do hope you are now perfectly well again.

With deepest regards,

Yours as ever,
Karan Singh

---

1. Issued on 7 August 1959, the statement clarified that, 'the Jammu and Kashmir Flood Relief Fund under the Chairmanship of the Prime Minister had been in existence for a number of years and was constituted at the Cabinet level . In view of the magnitude of suffering caused by recent floods the Sadar-i-Riyasat had also constituted a Flood Relief Committee on the pattern of Governor's Relief Fund in Assam and some other States.'

——— 179 ———

Jammu
25 December 1959

My dear Panditji,
Many thanks for your New Year Greetings which I very warmly reciprocate. In the present crucial phase of our history every year that comes brings new challenges and fresh opportunities. We can only pray for strength, under your leadership, to meet the former and take advantage of the latter so that our ancient nation may move forward towards a happy future as part of an harmonious world order.

It was a great pleasure seeing you in Delhi, and Asha and I were very happy that Indiraji, Tara and the kids were able to drop in at our new house.

With respects and deep regards,

Yours as ever,
Karan Singh

——— 180 ———

Jammu
2 February 1960

My dear Panditji,
You may recall that a couple of months ago I mentioned to you that Asha and I were thinking of going to Nepal this year, as she had not been back there since she was married ten years ago and I had never been at all. You approved of the idea, as did the President to whom I also mentioned the matter. We are now planning to fly from Delhi to Kathmandu, via Patna, on the 25th of March and to be there for about ten days to a fortnight. I will, of course, get the formal permission of the President to be away from the country for that period.

In Kathmandu we will stay with Asha's parents[1] at Lakshmi Nivas. I think, it will be proper for me to call on His Majesty[2] and the Prime Minister[3] while I am there. Perhaps, we should inform our Ambassador,

1. Rani Sajjan Kunwar and General Sarada Shumsher.
2. King Mahendra.
3. B.P. Koirala.

in Kathmandu of our proposed visit. I will as usual send a copy of
my programme to the Foreign Secretary[1] for any action that he may
deem fit.

I hope this finds you in excellent health.

With respects and deepest regards,

Yours as ever,
Karan Singh

———— 181 ————

New Delhi
3 February 1960

My dear Tiger,
I have just received your letter of the 2nd February. I am glad you are
going to Nepal. It will be certainly desirable for you to call on the
King there as well as the Prime Minister. We are informing our
Ambassador, Harishwar Dayal,[2] and he will I am sure give you all
possible help.

Yours sincerely,
Jawaharlal Nehru

———— 182 ————

Jammu Tawi
18 April 1960

My dear Panditji,
You will recall that I had the pleasure of meeting you for a few
minutes on my return from Nepal. I am now taking the liberty of
sending a confidential note containing some general observations
on the situation there, which you might find of some interest. I
need hardly add that my visit was purely private and the views

---

1. Subimal Dutt.
2. (1915-1964); joined ICS, 1937; served in various capacities in Bihar and Orissa,
   1937-42; and in the external affairs department, 1944-48; political officer in Sikkim,
   1948-52; joint secretary, ministry of external affairs, 1952-56; minister in the embassy
   of India in the USA, 1956-59; ambassador to Nepal, 1960-64.

contained in this note are also personal and are forwarded entirely in good faith.

I am also sending a copy of this note to the President.

With respectful regards,

Yours very sincerely,
Karan Singh

——— 183 ———
Situation in Nepal[1]

1. My wife and I visited Nepal from the 25th March to 7th April 1960. The visit was a private one, but the Nepal Government extended certain courtesies to us such as placing at our disposal a State car, an official from their Foreign Ministry and a police guard at our residence in Lakshmi Nivas.

2. A good deal of our time in Nepal was taken up by visits to various temples and shrines in and around Kathmandu. We also paid a flying visit to Pokhra in Western Nepal which is a beautiful lake district overlooked by mighty Himalayan ranges. In addition to this, however, we had the opportunity of meeting a number of important Nepalese leaders including His Majesty King Mahendra,[2] the Prime Minister, Shri B.P. Koirala,[3] the Deputy Prime Minister, General Suvarna Shumsher,[4] Shri Bharat

---

1. Note for Jawaharlal Nehru, 18 April 1960.
2. Mahendra Bir Bikram Shah (1920-1972); king of Nepal, 1955-72; introduced social and legal reforms; abolished the parliamentary system in 1960.
3. Bishweshwar Prasad Koirala (1914-1982); member, Communist Party of India, 1931-32; took part in the civil disobedience movement, 1931-32; member, Congress Socialist Party, 1935; imprisoned for participating in the Quit India movement, 1942-44; founder-member and acting president, Nepali National Congress, 1946; led an armed struggle which led to the overthrow of the Rana regime in Nepal in 1950; founded Nepali Congress Party, 1950; prime minister of Nepal, 1959-60; imprisoned, 1960-68; in exile in India, 1968-76.
4. Suvarna Shumsher Rana (1909-1979); major general, Royal Nepalese Army, 1929; deported from the country by the Rana regime, 1933; returned to Nepal, 1947; one of the founders of the Nepal Democratic Congress, 1947, and later the Nepali Congress, 1949; commander-in-chief, Mukti Sena which was involved in the revolution of 1950; minister for finance, 1951; chairman, Council of Ministers, 1957; deputy prime minister, 1959-60; self-exiled in India, 1960; president of the banned Nepali Congress Party, 1960-68.

Shumsher,[1] leader of the Gorkha Parishad[2] which is the main opposition party in the Nepal Assembly, and several other high ranking political and military dignitaries. With all of these persons I had friendly and informal conversations, as also with our Ambassador in Nepal, Shri Harishwar Dayal and senior officials of our Aid Mission and Military Mission.

3. The growing economic and military power of China, and that country's increasing tendency to push southwards, forms as it were a back-drop against which political events in Nepal may at present be evaluated. By and large, I was struck by the immense fund of goodwill that exists for India in Nepal. But it is clear that the Chinese advent involves a deep and fundamental challenge to our position there, and if we are successfully to meet this challenge we shall have to galvanize and revitalize our functioning in that country. I shall have something more specific to say about this later in the note. There can be little doubt that Nepal is at present playing what may be termed 'balancing' politics, trying to keep in with both of its powerful neighbours on the North and the South. For a small country which seeks to maintain its independence this is an understandable attitude, though not without grave dangers which the Nepalese seem increasingly to be realizing.

4. I had an audience with His Majesty King Mahendra, and also met him at a couple of social functions in Kathmandu. He is a quiet and reticent person, and did not say very much. On one occasion he expressed the desire to visit Kashmir on the conclusion of his foreign tour in July, and Shri Harishwar Dayal told me that he was likely to visit Delhi for a couple of days after this before returning to Nepal. The King is a very important political force in the country and it will obviously be valuable to cultivate his friendship. His close family ties and relationships with India make this task somewhat easier.

---

1. Rana Bharat Shumsher (b.1925); founder-president, Rashtravadi Gorkha Parishad, 1950; elected to the parliament in the first general elections in Nepal, 1958; leader of the opposition in the parliament, 1959; merged with Nepali Congress Party in India after abolition of the parliamentary system in Nepal, 1960; organized armed resistance against the panchayat system, December 1960; self-exiled in India since 1960.

2. Gorkha Parishad was originally a Rana revivalist party which formed the main opposition to the Nepali Congress in the 1959 elections. Its leader Bharat Shumsher and many of his followers joined the Congress after King Mahendra abolished parliamentary democracy.

5. I had several occasions of meeting and conversing with the Nepal Prime Minister, Shri B. P. Koirala. He had just returned from his visit to China,[1] and clearly the experience had impressed him deeply. He appeared to be rather awed by the immense mobilization of manpower and resources that he witnessed in China. He repeatedly stressed that in China the whole nation was mobilized to work at an intensive rate, and that unless Nepal and India also devised rapidly some means of securing mass mobilization they would be left far behind in the race for progress which was also a race between the two political systems of communism and democracy. He said that the foremost task in Nepal was to keep the people happy by raising their economic standards, and that this was, in fact, the only real way of combating Chinese pressure.

6. He was also rather overwhelmed by the extremely lavish hospitality and welcome that was accorded to him by the Chinese Government, though he hastened to add that it was an official welcome devoid of the warmth and emotion which he had experienced during his recent visit to India.[2] Both he and the Deputy Prime Minister, General Suvarna Shumsher appeared to have genuine feelings of friendship and goodwill towards India, but it was obvious that they were apprehensive of the growing might of the Chinese leviathan. Turning to the question of foreign aid, Mr Koirala seemed to attach considerable significance to the clause in his recent Agreement with China[3] regarding their technicians living while in Nepal at the Nepalese standards.[4] He felt that if there was too great a difference in the living standards of those connected with giving foreign aid and the recipients it was likely to create resentment and ill will and thus defeat the very purpose for which the aid was given.

7. I asked Shri Koirala whether the Chinese had mentioned anything regarding their dispute with us over our Northern borders.

---

1. B.P. Koirala visited the Peoples' Republic of China from 11 to 23 March 1960.
2. From 17 to 31 January 1960.
3. On 21 March 1960, B.P. Koirala negotiated an agreement with the Chinese leaders agreeing that the two countries would respect the existing boundary lines and live in amity. They also signed an agreement on economic aid by which China agreed to give aid to Nepal to the extent of Rs 10 crores in addition to the aid given in 1956.
4. According to the Article 4 of the agreement the Chinese experts and technicians during their period of work in Nepal would be paid according to the standard of living of the personnel of the same level in the kingdom of Nepal.

He said that they had told him that they had enough spare land for a hundred years of economic expansion and population growth and would not trespass an inch into foreign territory. But, they added, India was being terribly unreasonable as the land in question had never belonged to it at all but had always been Chinese. Shri Koirala felt that the Chinese would take a stiff attitude in their forthcoming negotiations in Delhi.[1]

8. During his visit to China Shri Koirala was given demonstrations of Chinese military power including an impressive and extremely accurate mass parachute landing display. Shri Koirala felt, however, that Chinese pressure was likely to be more political than military, and hence it would have to be combated on both fronts. He mentioned that the Communist Party in Nepal,[2] though small, was very active.

9. With regard to Nepal's economic development Shri Koirala said that they had started work on a planned basis but things were still progressing slowly and had not achieved the necessary momentum. He remarked that they should try and plan labour-intensive schemes as against capital-intensive ones so as to more fully utilize their manpower resources. Incidentally, many of the economic problems of Nepal are very similar to those we face in Kashmir, particularly such matters as road communications, tourism, handicrafts and fruit-growing. I suggested that he might visit Kashmir during his next trip to India so that he could see for himself what we are trying to do in these spheres.

10. The leader of the main opposition party in the Nepalese Parliament is Shri Bharat Shumsher who heads the Gorkha Parishad's 19 members. He happens to be a close relative of my wife, and I had occasion to have several free and informal talks with him. I also met a number of other Ranas in Kathmandu. Even after the end of Rana rule[3] a large member of Ranas continue in important positions, specially in the Army, and in fact they provide a significant section

---

1. After a series of talks between Nehru and Chou En-lai from 19 to 25 April 1960 on the Sino-Indian border issue, in a joint communiqué on 25 April they said:'The talks did not result in resolving the differences that had arisen'.
2. The Communist Party of Nepal was formed in Calcutta in 1949 by Pushpa Lal Shrestha and others. It broke into several factions after King Mahendra abolished the parliamentary system in 1960.
3. Rana rule or the system of hereditary prime ministership ended in 1951 after 104 years.

of the country's administrative machinery. With their education and wealth they are an important factor, and despite their initial phase of anti-Indian feelings soon after the events of 1950[1] they now appear to be staunchly pro-Indian. In fact, they are too closely connected by ties of history, culture, family relationships and economic interest really to be otherwise. Bharat told me that since the advent of the Chinese threat his party, which incidentally is predominantly non-Rana, had taken a clear and unequivocal attitude regarding Nepalese foreign policy. When I was there the Everest incident[2] occurred which created a wave of resentment in Nepal against the Chinese.[3] You must have followed in the papers, Bharat's speeches[4] and questions in Parliament in which he called for an outright condemnation of the Chinese claim, and also for a clear enunciation by the Nepal Government of the fact that China had committed aggression against India in Ladakh.

11. It is fairly certain that the Everest incident has gravely embarrassed Shri Koirala. In fact, after an initial period of jubilation, many Nepalese have begun having second thoughts with regard to the recently negotiated agreement with China. In particular, I noticed that there was a good deal of trepidation and resentment regarding

---

1. During the second half of 1950 there had been a good deal of political trouble in Nepal. The Nepali Congress launched an agitation in September 1950 for the establishment of democratic government in Nepal. Mohan Shumsher, the prime minister dubbed the Nepali Congress an anti-national party. He accused it of trying to subvert Nepal's independence with India's help. Nehru advised him to keep pace with the rapidly changing world. Mohan Shumsher resented it and accused India of trying to influence and interfere in the affairs of Nepal.

2. On 25 May 1960, three Chinese mountaineers reached the summit of Mount Everest, planted the Chinese flag there and proclaimed it the highest peak of their fatherland. Nepal asserted that the southern face and summit of the peak lie within Nepalese territory.

3. B.P. Koirala reiterated Nepal's stand on Mount Everest that, 'it belonged to Nepal and Nepal alone'. A Nepalese newspaper from Kathmandu, *Kalpana* said that the Chinese attempt on the Everest was a 'bad sign of arrogance'. Similarly the *Commoner*, another newspaper from Kathmandu questioned the propriety of the Chinese sending an expedition to Mount Everest without Nepal's permission.

4. Bharat Shumsher, the leader of Gorkha Parishad, stated on 17 January 1960 that there had been Chinese incursions 'amounting to aggression' into Nepal and also into India and urged the prime minister B.P. Koirala, then on a visit to India, to initiate a move with Indian prime minister for 'joint defence talks' with south east Asian countries.

the clause whereby Nepal has agreed not to militarise a 20 kilometre strip of its territory adjoining Tibet. There is a feeling that this will gravely weaken Nepalese military preparedness, as in some places to strip covers vitally strategic areas.

12. I may come finally to our functioning in Nepal in the light of the new political conditions created there by the Chinese advent. It is accepted on all hands that with the opening of the Chinese Embassy in Kathmandu and the stepping up of their economic aid there will be a marked increase of Chinese activity in this part of the world. Most of this activity, directly or indirectly, is likely to be aimed at undermining and weakening the Indian position there. In the light of this known fact it is clearly essential that we also should mobilize and galvanize our efforts in Nepal so that this aim is defeated and we are able to further strengthen and consolidate our position. I do not for a moment suggest that Government is not fully aware of the situation, but from what I could study during my short visit to Nepal I have felt that the following points deserve special consideration:-

a) Our procedures for implementing aid programmes might be looked into so that they may, if possible, be further streamlined and any unnecessary red tape and delays obviated;

b) So far our emphasis has been mainly upon economic aid upon projects which have definite economic value. In the new context it will be valuable if we considerably broaden our concept of aid to cover certain essential extra-economic factors also. In particular, it is important that we should step up greatly our cultural activities in Nepal. In fact, this is one of our trump cards vis-à-vis China, because they do not have nearly as close or deep a cultural contact with the Nepali people as we have. On the basis of history, religion and culture the people of Nepal are emotionally very close to India and this aspect needs to be fully emphasized in our aid programmes. More specifically, it might be a good idea for us to set up a permanent cultural centre in Kathmandu with a permanent theatre, exhibition and instruction in Indian classical dances, Indian music performances, both classical and light, and folk dance troupes. Also, we could arrange translations into Nepali of our classical works such as the Upanishads and the *Gita*, and of our modern classics including the writings of Mahatma Gandhi, Rabindranath Tagore, Panditji, Dr Rajendra Prasad and Dr Radhakrishnan. Works of important Nepali writers, such as their greatest poet, Shri

Lakshmi Prasad Devkota[1] who passed away recently, could be translated into Hindi and other modern Indian languages. In addition to this, we could open an institute of Sanskrit studies in Kathmandu and Janakpur, and of Buddhist Studies in Kathmandu and Lumbini. A system of giving scholarships to promising Nepal students for pursuing higher studies in various Indian universities could be instituted and given wide publicity. In the present context in Nepal, the importance of such cultural activities cannot be over-stressed. A few such activities have been undertaken over the last few years, but not—as far as I could gather—on a really sustained basis or on a nationwide scale. In fact, the Prime Minister Shri Koirala also felt that such activities on a regular and permanent basis would be very helpful in promoting closer Indo-Nepalese relations and strengthening the deep cultural links which already exist between our two countries;

c) With regard to the Nepali Army, I understand that it is being organized and trained very much on the lines of our Indian Army. This is an excellent thing, but in a mountainous country like Nepal such a force needs to be supplemented by lighter and more mobile guerrilla units. There are in Nepal lakhs of ex-servicemen, all of whom are capable of wielding arms. If they could be organized into some form of territorial army or militia with light weapons and highly mobile units their value in the event of an emergency would be very great. Of course, this is not a matter within our jurisdiction, but perhaps we might consider it and, if we think desirable, pass on the suggestion along with the offer to supply the necessary arms for the scheme;

d) The large number of Indian Army ex-servicemen residing in Nepal and drawing their pensions from us constitute a valuable asset. We might consider stepping up our welfare activities for these people, most of whom lived outside the Kathmandu valley scattered in the trans-Himalayan hilly tracts. I visited an ex-servicemen's hospital in Pokhra, run I think, by our Central Soldiers Board, which is doing excellent work. An expansion of such welfare activities would not only fill a real need but would strengthen the affection and goodwill for India which these people

---

1. Celebrated poet of Nepal; served for some time as minister for education and culture.

already possess. Representatives of ex-servicemen could be invited regularly to attend functions at our Gorkha Training Centre, thus keeping up valuable army contacts with them. Some of them could also perhaps participate in our Republic Day parades and other similar occasions.

――――― 184 ―――――

New Delhi
13 June 1960

My dear Tiger,
I am thinking of coming over to Srinagar, chiefly with a view to paying a brief visit to Ladakh. Probably, I shall reach Srinagar on the 2nd July forenoon. If the weather is good I shall go on the 3rd early morning to Leh and come back to Srinagar by lunch time. The next day I want to go from Srinagar early morning to Chushul and the border, also coming back the same day. Another day might be spent at Srinagar, and on the 6th I would like to return.

I have been thinking that it might be better for me to return by road and thus see the new tunnel. This would also enable me to go from Batote[1] to Kishtwar[2] where I have not been previously. From there I would go by road to Jammu and by air to Delhi.

This is a tentative programme which I have suggested to Bakshi Sahib. I have particularly requested him not to have formal receptions or other functions as I want to have a quiet time.

Yours affectionately,
Jawaharlal Nehru

――――― 185 ―――――

Srinagar
16 June 1960

My dear Panditji,
Thank you very much for your letter of the 13th June. We are delighted to know that we will have you in our midst again, and the programme

――――――――――

1. A small town in Doda district.
2. A small town in Jammu district.

will, of course, be arranged in accordance with your wishes.

I think it is a good idea to return from Srinagar to Jammu by road through the new tunnel. With regard to Kishtwar, however, it is just possible that the monsoon will have broken in the Jammu province by the first week of July, and in that event the roads leading to Kishtwar will be extremely unsafe and uncertain. In any case it should be possible for you to motor down to Jammu and perhaps spend a day there before flying back to Delhi.

My first book,[1] a collection of essays and poems, was brought out earlier this month by Asia Publishing House. I had intended to send a copy to you, but now that you are coming here I shall have the pleasure of presenting it personally.

With respects and deep regards,

Yours as ever,
Karan Singh

——— 186 ———

Srinagar
21 June 1960

My dear Panditji,

Bakshi Sahib has just informed me that he has written to you suggesting that you stay in Dachigam. Of course, Dachigam is a beautiful place, and in fact I myself have just returned after spending a most restful weekend there. If, however, you would prefer to stay a little closer to Srinagar then may I suggest that you stay at Chashmashahi. Mummy is there at present but she insists on moving into our Lake Pavilion[2] for a few days so that we can place the Chashmashahi house at your disposal. I can assure you it will give us the greatest pleasure if you would like to stay there. I have spoken to Bakshi Sahib about this and he also agrees that we should leave the choice between Dachigam and Chashmashahi entirely up to you.

Looking forward to seeing you soon, and with deepest regards,

Yours as ever,
Tiger

———

1. *Varied Rhythms* (Essays and Poems), Bombay, 1961.
2. A small picnic cottage on the Dal lake.

─────── 187 ───────

New Delhi
23 June 1960

My dear Tiger,

Thank you for your letter of June 21. I shall be happy to stay at the Chashmashahi Rest House. But I do not at all like the idea of your mother to have to move to some other place.

Dachigam does not suit me. It is too far out, and I shall be repeatedly going to the airport in the early morning for my visits to Chushul and Leh.

I hope to reach Srinagar on the 2nd July morning at about 8.30 by the Viscount. As at present arranged, I want to go to Chushul at 6 a.m. on the 3rd.

Yours affectionately,
Jawaharlal Nehru

─────── 188 ───────

New Delhi
9 November 1960

My dear Panditji,

As I mentioned to you at lunch yesterday, Asha's younger sister[1] is getting married on the 28th of this month to the Yuvaraj of Nawanagar.[2] The wedding will take place from our house here on Nyaya Marg, Chanakyapuri, and on the 29th we are giving a lunch party at 1.00 p.m. in honour of the bride and bridegroom. It would give both of us great pleasure if you were to grace the occasion.

With respects and deep regards,

Yours as ever,
Tiger

(Note: At our meeting at PM's residence on the 9th November, Panditji made a note of the engagement and said he would come. The C.P. of Japan is reaching Palam the same day at 3.00 p.m.)

───────────

1. Chaitanya Rajya Lakshmi.
2. Shatrushalya Singh Jadeja.

——— 189 ———

New Delhi
30 November 1960

My dear Panditji,
I write to say how deeply Asha and I appreciated your attending our lunch party[1] yesterday, and giving your blessing to the bride and bridegroom.
With kindest regards,

Yours as ever,
Karan Singh

——— 190 ———

Jammu
26 December 1960

My dear Panditji,
I write to thank you for your beautiful card of New Year greetings. We enter the new decade amidst an encircling gloom in international relations,[2] but one must continue to hope and work for the best. I can well imagine what tremendous strain you must be bearing. I shall be thirty next year, and even for a young man like me there is much within and without the country that can lead to pessimism and discouragement. May I send you my very warmest greetings for strength to face the problems of the New Year with vigour and success.
The swearing in ceremony of our new Ministers[3] will take place on the first day of the New Year.
With deepest regards and respects,

Yours as ever,
Karan Singh

---

1. Hosted in the honour of newly married Chaitanya Rajya Lakshmi.
2. The growing rift between India and China and the Belgian armed intervention in Congo were the main issues at this time.
3. The Democratic National Conference which came into existence in 1957 after a split in the National Conference, decided in December 1960 to reunite with the National Conference. With the merger came an offer to join the cabinet of the state. On 1 January 1961, the four leaders of the now dissolved Democratic National Conference were taken in as cabinet ministers. G.M. Sadiq was given education, G.L. Dogra became finance minister, Syed Mir Qasim was given judiciary and D.P. Dhar took over planning.

——————— 191 ———————

Jammu Tawi
6 February 1961

My dear Panditji,
You may recall my mentioning to you in Bombay that Asha and I
were planning to go on a private visit to Japan, Indonesia and some
other countries of South East Asia later this year. After that I saw the
President in Delhi, and also got his approval. On my return to Jammu
I discussed the matter with Bakshi Sahib, and he also has no objection
to my going. As such we have planned a two-month trip which will
take us to Thailand, Cambodia (Angkor Vat), Japan, the Philippines,
Indonesia, Singapore and Hong Kong. As neither of us has ever done
an ocean voyage, we are planning to come back to Bombay from
Hong Kong by boat.

According to the programme we have drawn up, we shall be
away from India from the 6th April to the 8th June. Upon getting
your approval I will write formally to the President requesting
his permission to be away from the country during that period.
As you know, both Asha and I are very keen on travel, and we
are greatly looking forward to this trip. It will be very interesting
to see how other Asian countries, with backgrounds in many
ways similar to ours, are tackling the problems of economic
development and political organization. In particular, there is a great
deal that this State can learn from Japan in the field of sericulture
and small-scale industries. We already have some contacts with
Japan in this regard, and I can take advantage of my visit there to
develop them further.

We are all greatly looking forward to your visit here later this
month. Along with the rest of North India we are experiencing a
severe cold wave, and all communication with the Valley was disrupted
for over a week. Bakshi Sahib himself was held up there for days. He
met me yesterday, and his unhappy experience seems to have convinced
him of the folly of requesting you to go to Srinagar during the winter.
I really think it would be much better if you came to Jammu for two
days. The people here will be delighted to see you, and if you desire
we can also arrange a short trip somewhere into the interior. When
you come to Jammu, Asha and I would consider it a great pleasure

and honour if you stayed here with us. If Indiraji can also come we would be delighted.

With respects and deepest regards,

Yours as ever,
Karan Singh

———— 192 ————

New Delhi
8 February 1961

My dear Tiger,

I have just received your letter of February 6th. So far as I am concerned, you and Asha can certainly go on your eastern tour. If you let us know your programme abroad, we shall inform our missions there.

Perhaps, you know that I have given up the idea of going to Jammu or Srinagar at the end of this month. This is not because of the cold, but because of a fact I had overlooked. That is just the time when our Budget is presented.

Yours sincerely,
Jawaharlal Nehru

———— 193 ————

Jammu Tawi
11 February 1961

My dear Panditji,

Many thanks for your letter of the 8th February. I will now go ahead with preparations for the eastern tour, and will send a copy of the programme to the Foreign Secretary.[1]

We are very disappointed that you will not be coming here this month. Perhaps, you may be able to spare a couple of days in March.

With respects and deepest regards,

Yours as ever,
Tiger

---

1. Subimal Dutt.

──────── 194 ────────

Jammu Tawi
31 March 1961

My dear Panditji,

As you know, I had planned a visit to South East Asia for two months from the 6th April to 8th June, and had received permission from the President to remain out of the country for that period. Unfortunately, the foreign exchange situation turned to be more difficult than I had expected, and the Finance Ministry did not find it possible to sanction a single rupee of exchange for this trip. As the result, I have had reluctantly to cancel the visit.

I happen to have a few pounds in London, and as Asha and I were all prepared for a trip abroad we have decided to go on a short holiday to England instead.[1] We are therefore planning to leave India on the 7th April, and will return on the 10th May. These dates fall within the period of absence previously authorised by the President.

We will be returning to Delhi on the 10th May, and spending a few days there before proceeding to Srinagar on the 15th. In case you are in the capital at that time I look forward to being able to pay my respects.

With deepest regards,

Yours as ever,
Tiger

──────── 195 ────────

Srinagar
30 August 1961

My dear Panditji,

I have just come to learn that the incident of my having given a dinner party here last month has been conveyed to you in a manner which may have caused you a certain amount of disquiet. In view of the great kindness that you have always shown to me I feel compelled, even at the risk of encroaching upon your time, to write this letter in order to place the matter before you in its correct perspective and to

───────────────

1. They visited England and Italy at this time.

dispel any doubts that may have sought to have been created.

Upon my return from Delhi to Srinagar after the issue of the Presidential Order, a large number of citizens from all walks of life and faith spontaneously called upon me to offer their congratulations upon my succession.[1] Consequently, in order to fulfil my social obligations, I decided to give a dinner party for about four hundred guests, and the list was drawn up carefully to see that no section of the citizens of Srinagar was left unrepresented. As the party was in connection with my own succession, it was felt that it would be indelicate for the invitations to issue on my own behalf. After some consideration they were issued on behalf of my Staff Officer. From what followed it appears that it might have been better for me to have issued the invitations in my own name, but for interested persons to attempt to impute motives and to create a furore over an innocuous social function is grossly unfair.

Bakshi Sahib met me about three days before the party was due to be held, and expressed the view that the invitations should have issued not from my Staff Officer but from myself. The next day I wrote him a letter extending to him and his Cabinet colleagues my personal invitation to the party. I am glad to say that he as well as most of his colleagues did attend the function.

In closing, I must remark that certain interested political sections, for motives into which it is not necessary for me to enter here, do not appear happy at my continuing in the office of Sadar-i-Riyasat. For a long time they had been waiting in vain for an opportunity to attack me in some way. The matter of my succession, which unexpectedly arose on the death of my father, gave them the opening they were looking for, and long before the Presidential Order was issued they began a mischievous campaign in the press and public on this issue. This dinner party of mine, though given entirely in good faith and at considerable personal expense, was sought to be utilized by them to further their designs.

With respects and deepest regards,

Yours as ever,
Karan Singh

---

1. After the passing away of Maharaja Hari Singh on 26 April 1961, Yuvaraj Karan Singh was recognized by the president on 6 July as the successor to Maharaja Hari Singh.

copy

SADAR-I-RIYASAT.

Jammu
9th January 1962.

My dear Panditji,

Thank you very much for your
beautiful card of New Year greetings.
The Buddha's message of peace and love has
never been so urgently needed in the
world as it is today, when hatred &
strife cast their ominous shadows over
all our hopes and aspirations.

I most warmly reciprocate your
good wishes, and pray that you may be
granted strength to lead our nation
for many years in this crucial juncture
of the history of mankind.

With respects & deep regards,

yours as ever

T.

——— 196 ———

Jammu
14 November 1961

My dear Panditji,

I write to express on behalf of Asha and myself our warm greetings and felicitations upon your birthday. May you be spared for many years to guide the destiny of the nation at this crucial stage of our history.

    With respects and deepest regards,

Yours as ever,
Tiger

——— 197 ———

Jammu
9 January 1962

My dear Panditji,

Thank you very much for your beautiful card of New Year greetings. The Buddha's message of peace and love has never been so urgently needed in the world as it is today, when hatred and strife cast their ominous shadows over all our hopes and aspirations.

    I most warmly reciprocate your good wishes, and pray that you may be granted strength to lead our nation for many years in this crucial juncture of the history of mankind.

    With respects and deep regards,

Yours as ever,
T.

——— 198 ———

Jammu
10 April 1962

My dear Panditji,

This is just to convey our warm congratulations, on behalf of my mother, Asha and myself, upon your assumption of a fresh term of office as Prime Minister.[1] We wish you all success in the historic task of leading the nation forward along the path of national development and progress.

We have all been extremely concerned at reports of your somewhat prolonged indisposition. I do hope you are now much better and that you will soon be restored to normal health.

With respects and deep regards,

Yours as ever,
Tiger

——— 199 ———

Srinagar
24 May 1962

My dear Tiger,

I have read your thesis[2] and have liked it. I am returning it to you.

I enclose a foreword for it as you asked me to do.[3]

If you like it, you can use it. If you want me to change any part of it, you might let me know.

Yours as ever,
Jawaharlal Nehru

I have made one or two minor verbal corrections in your mss. The Indian National Congress was started in 1885 not in 1895.

---

1. The new Union council of ministers headed by Nehru was sworn in on 10 April 1962 after the third general elections in which the Congress party secured 361 seats out of 494 in the Lok Sabha.
2. Karan Singh wrote a thesis 'The Political Thought of Sri Aurobindo Ghosh, 1893-1910' for which he was granted a Ph. D degree by the University of Delhi. However, he received the degree formally at the convocation held on 1 December 1962. Based upon this thesis, the book *Prophet of Indian Nationalism* was published by George Allen & Unwin Ltd, London in May 1963.
3. After going through the typescript, Nehru wrote a foreword on 24 May 1962 which begins thus: 'I have read this little book with much interest and occasionally with some excitement.'

——— 200 ———

Srinagar
25 May 1962

My dear Panditji,
It was extremely kind of you to have taken the trouble of going through my thesis, and to have encouraged me by writing such an inspiring foreword. George Allen and Unwin are planning to bring out the book early next year, and your lines will greatly enhance such value as my work may possess.

Asha, Jyoti and I were delighted that you could drop in for a short while this evening. I am deeply grateful for the unfailing affection and consideration that you have always shown to me.

With respectful regards,

Yours as ever,
Karan Singh

——— 201 ———

Srinagar
26 August 1962

My dear Panditji,
I am taking the liberty of writing this confidential letter to bring to your notice two points of importance in the light of Bakshi Sahib's forthcoming visit to Delhi.

The first point concerns the possibility of his inclusion in the Union Cabinet.[1] In the course of a private conversation with him day before yesterday I gathered the distinct impression that his views had undergone an important modification and that, if the matter is broached by you at this stage, he may now be ready to accept. I may, of course, have been mistaken, but I thought I should pass on my assessment to you for your personal information.

The second matter concerns the appointment of the commission under the provisions of our recently enacted anti-corruption legislation. The measure has aroused widespread public expectations, and can be an important step towards eradicating corruption and

———

1. Bakshi Ghulam Mohammad was not included.

improving the efficiency of our administration. A great deal, however, will depend upon the personnel of the commission. I have been urging strongly that it should consist of men of the highest integrity, and be headed by some prominent person from outside the State. The Cabinet has selected three retired local sessions judges as members, but the chairmanship is still open. Bakshi Sahib said he would seek your advice in the matter, and also remarked that he had in mind Shri Khosla,[1] retired justice of the Punjab. For my part I mentioned the name of Shri K.P.S. Menon and General Jai Singh (retired). In any event, I feel most strongly that we should get someone of stature from outside the State to head the commission, a person with the stature, ability and impartiality necessary to inspire unquestioned public confidence from all sections of the people.

In view of the fact that Bakshi Sahib will discuss the matter with you I thought I should place this background before you and respectfully urge that you be good enough to take a personal interest in the matter so that we get someone really suitable.

I hope you will enjoy your forthcoming visit abroad,[2] and that we shall have the pleasure of seeing you up here again in October.

With respectful regards,

Yours very sincerely,
Tiger

PS
I am sending this letter by a special messenger, Shri Milap Chand.[3] I am also sending some peaches from my garden and hope that they reach you in good condition.

T

---

1. Gopal Das Khosla (1901–1996); ICS, district and sessions judge in 1930; judge, Lahore High Court 1944–47; after Partition migrated to India; chief justice of Punjab High Court, 1959–1961; headed several enquiry commissions; publications include *Stern Reckoning* (1948), *Our Judicial System* (1949), *The Last Mughal* (1969).
2. Nehru visited England from 8 to 17 September, France from 21 to 23 September, Nigeria and Ghana from 23 to 27 September and Egypt from 28 to 30 September 1962.
3. Milap Chand Katoch, private secretary to Yuvaraj Karan Singh.

With Jawaharlal Nehru, Bakshi Ghulam Mohammad and daughter
Jyotsna, Srinagar, 25 May 1962

──────── 202 ────────

Srinagar
27 October 1962

My dear Panditji,
Your announcement regarding the opening of a National Defence Fund[1] is most welcome and timely. I have pleasure in enclosing herewith a cheque for Rs one lakh as my personal donation towards this fund.

　　With deepest regards,

Yours as ever,
Tiger

──────── 203 ────────

Srinagar
29 October 1962

My dear Panditji,
There being no other nominee for the office, I was this morning declared duly elected by the Legislative Assembly for a third term as Sadar-i-Riyasat. The papers have now gone to the President for being pleased to accord his recognition. It was, as you rightly guessed, a rather tame election, and I must see if I cannot come up with something more exciting next time. I would like to take this opportunity to express my deep gratitude for all your kindness and affection to me during the thirteen years that I have functioned as Head of this State. I venture to hope that in the future also I will continue to enjoy this privilege.

　　The Government of India have been good enough to include me as a member of the Indian delegation to the forthcoming General Conference of UNESCO beginning in Paris early next month.[2] I feel, however, and I think you will agree, that in view of the National

---

1. The National Defence Fund was launched on 26 October 1962 by the government of India to provide an opportunity to the people to make voluntary contributions in the form of money, gold and gold ornaments in order to purchase defence equipment to face the Chinese aggression.
2. The annual conference was held on 4 November 1962 in Paris.

Emergency[1] and the serious military situation on our border[2] including Ladakh—it would not be appropriate for me to go abroad at this juncture. I would therefore request to be excused from attending this time. I need hardly add that in normal times I would have been honoured to avail of the opportunity to represent the country at this important Conference, and that in any case my services are always at the disposal of Government to be used in whatever capacity you think fit.

Asha and I look forward to seeing you and Indiraji in Delhi on the 3rd November when we will attend your kind invitation to lunch.

With respects and deep regards,

Yours as ever,
Tiger

———— 204 ————

New Delhi
29 October 1962

My dear Tiger,

Thank you for your letter of 27th and your personal cheque for Rs 1 lakh for the National Defence Fund. This is a generous donation which I appreciate.

I have also received you letter of the 29th October. I think you are right in not going to the UNESCO meeting in Paris.

Yours as ever,
Jawaharlal Nehru

1. On 26 October 1962 the government of India proclaimed a state of emergency in the country in view of the Chinese invasion.
2. On 20 October 1962, China mounted a massive attack on NEFA along a twelve mile sector. Indian posts were overwhelmed by about 20,000 Chinese troops, who attacked them with heavy mortars and machine guns. Khizemane and Dhola posts were captured and Chip Chap in Ladakh came under heavy fire. Indian supply planes were also attacked. Similarly, there were frequent incidents of firing on Indian eastern borders with Pakistan.

———— 205 ————

New Delhi
28 November 1962

My dear Panditji,
On the 1st December I will receive my doctorate at the Delhi University Convocation. That evening we have invited a few friends to a private dinner at our home here at 8.30 p.m. Knowing how extremely preoccupied you are, I hesitate to request you to grace the occasion. If it is at all possible for you to come, however, it would give Asha and myself the deepest pleasure.[1]

We have just arrived from Jammu, and will be here for a few days. I look forward to paying my respects to you at your convenience.

Deepest regards,

Yours as ever,
Tiger

———— 206 ————

New Delhi
29 November 1962

My dear Panditji,
Thank you for your letter and your kind invitation to us to dine with you tomorrow evening. I am particularly looking forward to seeing you, as there are aspects of utmost importance in the present situation[2] about which I would like to place some views before you.

With deepest regards,

Yours as ever,
Karan Singh

————————

1. Nehru replied on the same day (letter not printed) expressing his difficulty in joining the dinner but assured Karan Singh that he would meet him during his stay in Delhi.
2. A grave situation had arisen on India's northern frontiers because of continued and unabated aggression by China.

——— 207 ———

To Jawaharlal Nehru

New Delhi
15 December 1962

My dear Panditji,

I understand that the weather in Ladakh is likely to get more difficult for flying later in the month, and it may be inconvenient for the Air Force to have to fly me there. As I am very keen to visit Leh at the earliest opportunity, I wonder if—provided there is enough room and no one is inconvenienced—it would be possible for me to accompany you tomorrow.

My plane for Varanasi does not leave till 5.15 tomorrow evening, and I expect you will plan to be back from Leh much earlier than that.

Respectful regards,

Yours as ever,
Tiger

——— 208 ———

New Delhi
19 December 1962

My dear Panditji,

I returned from Varanasi this afternoon, and enclose a copy of the convocation address I delivered there on 17th December.[1] On the 18th yesterday, I visited your home town of Allahabad and inaugurated there a convention on National Defence organized by the National

---

1. In his address at the Banaras Hindu University, Dr Karan Singh said among other things that the future would 'be deeply influenced by the recent shocking aggression upon our motherland by a neighbour whose friendship we had consistently sought ever since we attained our Independence in 1947. It is indeed a monumental tragedy that the two most populous nations of the world with great civilizations stretching back unbroken into the very dawn of human history, should be locked together not in the bonds of peace and friendship but in the toils of conflict and strife.' He further said: 'Ours is largest democracy in the world but we must never forget that the roots of democracy in this country are constantly in need of careful nurturing. The last decade has witnessed virtually the wholesale collapse of democracy in Asia and India stands out as almost its sole beacon in this part of the world.'

Council of University Students of India.[1] I also took the opportunity of visiting Anand Bhavan, where your housekeeper very kindly showed me round the historic building.

With respectful regards,

Yours sincerely,
Tiger

——— 209 ———

New Delhi
26 February 1963

My dear Panditji,

I do not know whether the report of Professor Galbraith's[2] visit to Jammu carried in *Link* magazine of 24th February (pages 18-19) has come to your notice.[3] It is indeed unfortunate that interested parties are trying deliberately to give a mischievous distortion to an innocuous social visit.[4] I will submit fuller details when I see you on the 28th evening.

With respectful regards,

Yours as ever,
Tiger

---

1. The three-day All India Students Convention on National Defence was held in the senate hall of Allahabad University from 18 to 20 December 1962. It discussed the historical and political perspective of Chinese aggression and the defence needs of India.
2. John Kenneth Galbraith (1908-2006); economist and diplomat; professor of Economics, Harvad University, 1949-75; United States ambassador to India, 1961-63; publications include, *The Great Crash* (1955), *The Affluent Society* (1958), *The New Industrial State* (1967) and *Ambassador's Journal* (1969).
3. The *Link* reported that, 'Galbraith has been taking an active interest in the current series of Indo-Pak talks and is named as the author of the plan which provides a foothold to Pakistan in Kashmir Valley, lent credence to the view that he was on some "diplomatic" mission'. It further said that, 'even the State Prime Minister lacked knowledge of the visit till newspapers reported on it made the argument suspect that it was mere a private visit.'
4. In fact, this visit was arranged on a private level between the Sadar-i-Riyasat, Dr Karan Singh and Galbraith. Ghulam Mohammad, secretary to the Sadar-i-Riyasat issued a clarification that since Galbraith was an eminent economist, 'Dr Karan Singh arranged at his residence a small function at which the Professor gave a talk on Economic Development in the USA. The invitees were the staff and students of the University Post-graduate departments, staff of other University Post-graduate departments situated in Jammu, Principals and teachers of Economics of the Jammu Degree College and members of the small private book reviewing society known as the Wayfarers.'

With Jawaharlal Nehru and Bakshi Ghulam Mohammad, Srinagar, 25 June 1963

——————— 210 ———————

Kashmir
24 June 1963

My dear Tiger,

Thank you for your letter which I received this afternoon. We shall be happy to come to dinner with you on the 27th evening.

Indira and the children went yesterday to Kolahai. They are expected to come back tomorrow afternoon. I shall probably go tomorrow morning to Aru to meet them on their way back.

Ever yours,
Jawaharlal Nehru

——————— 211 ———————

Srinagar
8 October 1963

My dear Panditji,

I am sending a sealed cover by hand of a special messenger, my P.A. Milap Chand Katoch. In case you wish him to bring back a reply he will be available at my Delhi house (Tel: 35291) and can wait there as long as necessary.

K. N. Bamzai[1] is also flying to Delhi today. He will be able to give you fuller details of various developments here.

I hope this finds you very well.

With respectful regards,

Yours as ever,
Tiger

———————

1. Kashi Nath Bamzai (1915-1988); member, Jammu and Kashmir National Conference; worked for *National Herald, Daily National Standard,* 1944-45, and *Blitz,* between 1939 and 1946; officer on special duty (Kashmir publicity), Union ministry of information and broadcasting, 1949-65; chief press advisor, 1965-66; registrar of newspapers, government of India, 1966-72; director, publications division, government of India, 1972-1974.

SADAR-I-RIYASAT.

Karan Mahal
Srinagar.
8th October 1963

My dear Panditji,

I am sending a sealed cover
by hand of a special messenger, my
P.A. Dilap Chand Katoch In case you
wish him to bring back a reply he
will be available at my Delhi house
(del. 35291) and can wait there as
long as necessary.

K. N. Bamzai is also flying to Delhi
today. He will be able to give you fuller
details of various developments here.

I hope this finds you very well.

With respectful regards

————— 212 —————

Srinagar
8 October 1963

My dear Panditji,

Since Bakshi Sahib and I returned to Srinagar on the 16th September after meeting you in Delhi the political situation here has developed in a very peculiar manner.[1] Our hope that there would be a smooth transition has been belied, and instead an unfortunate situation has developed which has grave potentialities. I am therefore writing to seek your advice and guidance as to how best I should proceed to fulfil my responsibilities at this crucial juncture.

In pursuance of his earlier announcement Bakshi Sahib submitted his resignation to me on the 4th October, while accepting the resignation I requested him to carry on until a new Ministry was formed. There is therefore no question at all of his not giving up office. Any move to retract or to prolong the life of the caretaker Government would obviously be untenable. Not only would it damage the impact of the Kamaraj Plan[2] but it would also have undesirable repercussions on the local political scene. In his talks with me Bakshi Sahib seems to be quite clear on this point, although yesterday he did mention the possibility of his staying on for another few months after appointing Sadiq[3] Deputy Prime Minister and himself remaining mainly out of the State. I think, you will agree that such a step would reduce the whole matter to a virtual farce, increase the political unrest and uncertainty that have been generated and make even more difficult

---

1. Bakshi Ghulam Mohammad had resigned on 4 October 1963 under the Kamaraj Plan. A day before his resignation Bakshi announced before the Legislative Council that the prime minister of Kashmir would in future be designated as chief minister like in other provinces of India. He also hinted at the possibility of the merger of the National Conference of Kashmir with the Indian National Congress for emotional integration at the organizational level. Besides, an anti-Sadiq group became more active in its bid to form the ministry.
2. K. Kamaraj, the chief minister of Madras proposed a plan in August 1963 that leading Congressmen in government should voluntarily relinquish their ministerial posts and offer themselves for full-time organizational work. On 10 August 1963, the Congress Working Committee unanimously adopted a resolution to endorse this proposal. The Kamaraj Plan aimed at revitalizing both the administration and the Congress party.
3. G.M. Sadiq.

a transition at some later stage.

Once it is quite clear that Bakshi Sahib must now relinquish office within a few days, the next question is that of his successor. You have on more than one occasion indicated clearly your view that Sadiq is the only suitable successor at this juncture. Bakshi Sahib has also reiterated this view to me strongly on many occasions. In my personal opinion also Sadiq—one of the most senior leaders of the National Conference and a man with a political stature and reputation for integrity which even his worst opponents are forced to admit—is at present the only suitable man to succeed. In a crucial state like Jammu and Kashmir, with thousands of square miles of its territory under the forcible occupation of two hostile foreign powers and a peculiarly complex set of internal political problems it would be unwise to indulge in experimentation on a trial and error basis with people whose integrity is by no means above suspicion and who are hardly likely to generate public confidence. Bakshi Sahib's decision to resign, although regretted insofar as it will remove from the helm a man of great political dynamism, has also been welcomed as a prelude to certain essential political and administrative improvements in the State. It is, therefore, necessary to ensure that the change over has a beneficial impact upon the general public and takes place without delay.

You will recall that in Delhi Bakshi Sahib had drawn up a list of the proposed new Cabinet headed by Sadiq including Rashid[1] but excluding D. P. This consisted of nine Cabinet Ministers and two Ministers of State. He showed me the list on our flight from Delhi to Srinagar and here he gave it to Sadiq. Sadiq did not reject it but he did not forward for Bakshi Sahib's consideration certain apprehensions regarding its composition. A few days later Bakshi Sahib met me and complained that Sadiq was being very uncooperative and had virtually rejected the formula. He suggested that I should talk to Sadiq about this. I did so immediately, both alone and also in the presence of D. P. and Qasim.[2] I was able to persuade them to accept the list without

---

1. Bakshi Abdul Rashid, a relative of Bakshi Ghulam Mohammad.
2. Syed Mir Qasim (1919-2005); advocate, Kashmir High Court; took part in the 'Quit Kashmir' movement, 1946; member, Constituent Assembly, Jammu and Kashmir, 1951-57; elected to the Jammu and Kashmir Legislative Assembly, 1957, 1962, 1967 and 1972; quit the National Conference in 1957 and formed the Democratic National Conference; rejoined National Conference, 1960; joined Congress in 1967; minister, Jammu and Kashmir government and held various portfolios between January 1961 to 1971; chief minister, Jammu and Kashmir, December 1971 to January 1975; elected to Rajya Sabha, July, 1975; Union minister for civil supplies, 1976-77.

any reservations, specially as Bakshi Sahib had agreed that Sadiq retain the portfolios at present with the Prime Minister which include the Home portfolio. I at once conveyed this acceptance to Bakshi Sahib, and was hopeful that there would be no further hitch. This was on the 29th September.

In the meantime there were disquieting political developments. Reports began to circulate that Rashid had begun a signature campaign among the legislators giving him the authority to select the new leader. Bakshi Sahib made no clear pronouncement about his preference for Sadiq, and Sadiq and his supporters were unable to speak or act for fear that this might be considered as canvassing and be resented by Bakshi Sahib. The city became thick with rumours. The names of the most unlikely and undesirable people were bruited as potential Prime Ministers, and an atmosphere of uncertainty and confusion continues to spread. The National Conference Working Committee held a series of meetings at which speeches were made containing barely veiled attacks on Sadiq. He refused to be provoked. Then Bakshi Sahib began saying that he wanted to make drastic change in the agreed formula. Although Sadiq pointed out that any change in the agreed formula would be incorrect he did not take a rigid stand. On the 6th evening Bakshi Sahib called Sadiq and said that Rashid had refused to join the Cabinet and that he now wanted Sadiq to drop Qasim and Kushak Bakula—both persons of high integrity—and replace them with certain other people who do not enjoy that reputation. This gravely disturbed Sadiq, but finally I was able to persuade him not to make an issue of it. The next morning Sadiq met Bakshi Sahib and gave him a new list in which Rashid, D. P., and Qasim were excluded. This was followed by a meeting of the Working Committee in which Bakshi Sahib asked for authority to nominate his successor. This was not agreed to, Bakshi Sahib reportedly lost his temper and threatened to resign from the National Conference, and the meeting broke up.

This was yesterday. In the evening Bakshi Sahib came and saw me. He seemed to be very upset at the attitude of the Working Committee which, he asserted, meant political disaster for him as it would show that he did not have control over his own party and would gravely weaken his position and utility in the wider political field. He again reiterated that Sadiq was 'not only a hundred per cent but a thousand per cent' the correct choice, but lamented that the party would not agree to elect him. He said that he was thinking of calling the legislators in small batches tomorrow and getting them to sign a paper in which he had proposed Sadiq as Leader of the legislative party. If that failed then he would consider what next to do. He mentioned the possibility regarding appointing Sadiq Deputy Prime Minister, though he admitted that this would make his position highly vulnerable. He also referred to his earlier idea that he could advice me to call upon Sadiq as the Deputy Leader of the party to form the Government. In this case, however, he felt that it would mean that at the next session of legislature the Government would be overthrown. Sadiq, D. P. and Qasim met me later. They feel that if Bakshi Sahib were wholeheartedly and unreservedly to propose Sadiq's name as his successor he would have no difficulty in getting a majority among the legislators. Alternatively, if Sadiq is given an opportunity to form the Government they were certain that in the next session they would be able to get a handsome majority.

It is now almost a month and a half since Bakshi Sahib's intention to resign was first announced on the 24 August. Since then there has been intense political activity here which in the last couple of weeks has resulted in a virtual paralysis of the administrative machinery. Bakshi Sahib himself admitted this to me when he saw me yesterday. This would be undesirable anywhere, much more so in a border State like ours where hostile foreign-sponsored political activity can always burst out into the open. There is an atmosphere of utter confusion in the general public. Pakistan has made no secret of its plans to step up internal subversion. I am of the opinion that continuance of the present impasse would militate against the larger national interests.

Keeping all these factors in view I would like to commend for your approval a suggestion first made to me by Bakshi Sahib himself as one of the possible solutions to the problem. Sadiq is already Deputy Leader of the National Conference party. The Legislature Party has not been able to elect a new leader. Let it therefore disperse for the time being. In these peculiar circumstances I could, in pursuance of my constitutional responsibilities, call upon Sadiq to form the new Ministry. Indeed, if Bakshi Sahib were formally to make this suggestion to me it would be a graceful gesture. The Legislature has just completed its autumn session and is not scheduled to meet again until the Budget Session in Jammu at the end of February. Sadiq and several other political observers are certain that the Government will be able to get a vote of confidence from the Legislature at that time, and that as soon as some clear decision is announced a large number of legislators who are at present sitting on the fence will support the new

Government. In any case the new Ministry will have a fair chance of showing its worth before it faces the legislature, and the present political uncertainty will be set at rest.

Further delay or procrastination will be dangerous, and in fact the whole situation may well drift towards a point, where drastic measures such as those envisaged in Article 92[1] of the State Constitution (copy enclosed) may become inevitable. I would, therefore, request that you be kind enough to give this matter your personal attention and favour me at your very earliest convenience with your advice as to how I should proceed in the matter.

With deepest regards,

Yours very sincerely,
Karan Singh

———— 213 ————

New Delhi
10 October 1963

My dear Tiger,
I received your letter on the 8th evening. I did not reply to it because various developments were taking place and Bakshi was expected here yesterday. I had two fairly long talks with Bakshi. I confess I am not at all happy with these developments and what has happened. I told Bakshi so.

Apart from expressing my opinion about this matter to Bakshi, I could not see what more I could do. I suggested to him that a further effort should be made to get Sadiq as leader. But apparently things

---

1. Article 92 envisaged that, 'If at any time the Sadar-i-Riyasat is satisfied that a situation has arisen in which the Government of the State cannot be carried on in accordance with the provisions of this Constitution the Sadar-i-Riyasat may by proclamation: (a) assume to himself all or any of the functions of the Government of the State and all or any of the powers vested in or exercisable by any body or authority in the State; (b) make such incidental and consequential provisions as appear to the Sadar-i-Riyasat to be necessary or desirable for giving effect to the objects of the proclamation including provision of this Constitution relating to any body or authority in the state. Provided that nothing in this section shall authorize the Sadar-i-Riyasat to assume to himself any of the powers vested in or exercisable by the High Court or to suspend in whole or in part the operation of any provision of this Constitution relating to the High Court.'

had gone too far for this. Bakshi looked upon any arrangement now as a temporary arrangement for a few months. That is not an adequate reason for it, and all kinds of difficulties may arise later. But there it is.

I am quite sure of one thing, and I consulted the President who was also sure of it. We cannot think in terms of the President taking over the administration of the State. This would have no constitutional justification in present circumstances, and would create very serious difficulties in many ways. It would also, to some extent, play into the hands of Pakistan.

I might mention that Bakshi told me that you had mentioned to Sadiq the possibility of some such thing. This was widely talked about in Srinagar, and it was further stated by the opponents of Sadiq that he had partially agreed to this proposal. This had the effect of making many persons even more opposed to Sadiq than they had been previously.

News has come this evening of the election of Shamsuddin as leader.[1] I am not at all happy about this. Bakshi had asked me to press Sadiq to agree to Dogra and Mir Qasim joining the new Cabinet. I mentioned this to D. P. Dhar, who has been here. He did not think that would be possible in the circumstances. On the whole, I am inclined to think it would be desirable for them to join the Cabinet. For them and their whole group to keep out may not have good results.

All I can say now is that we have to watch developments and remain wide awake. I am going tomorrow morning to Dehra Dun for three days, returning on the 14th forenoon.

Yours ever,
Jawaharlal Nehru

---

1. Khwaja Shamsuddin (1922-1999) the revenue minister in the outgoing ministry, was unanimously elected on 10 October 1963 as the leader of the National Conference Legislature Party. On 12 October he became the prime minister. He had to resign on 27 February 1964 because the Sadiq group did not cooperate at the cabinet level to revitalize the administration.

——— 214 ———

Srinagar
15 October 1963

My dear Panditji,

Thank you for your letter of the 10th October. I am flying to Delhi on the 28th and look forward to discussing in detail the new position that has emerged, particularly the 'temporary' nature that Bakshi envisages for it. Here I will only refer to two points mentioned in your letter.

At no time did I make any proposal to Sadiq regarding the President taking over the administration of the State, and therefore the question of Sadiq's having partially agreed to it does not arise. For one thing, I had no authority from the President or yourself to make any such suggestion. Secondly, all my efforts were directed towards trying to smoothen the transfer of power from Bakshi to his successor who, to take him at his word, was to have been Sadiq. During my talks with Sadiq at the stage when he was somewhat reluctant to accept Bakshi's formula for the new cabinet, he stressed the danger of Rashid and his associates in the proposed cabinet creating a situation in which it would be impossible for him to function. He wanted to know what steps could be taken if such a position arose. I told him that in such an eventuality, when all normal processes had been exhausted and a failure of the constitutional machinery was imminent, it was open to him to advice me to use the special powers given to the Sadar-i-Riyasat by the State Constitution (Section 92). Ever then those powers could be used only with the 'concurrence' of the President.

It is possible that this reference may somehow have gone out and been deliberately misinterpreted by the anti-Sadiq faction.[1] I think, I should also add that during this crisis particularly in the later part when the chances of Sadiq being elected began to fade, there was a strong current of public opinion in the Valley which favoured Sadar-i-Riyasat's rule as the best way to ensure a stable and efficient administration. As such a step may well have led to a dissolution of the present Assembly and the holding of fresh elections, however, it is unlikely that the MLAs would look upon it with favour. I mention

---

1. The anti-Sadiq faction included Khwaja Shamsuddin, Pir Gyasuddin and D.N. Mahajan.

At the Governors' Conference, New Delhi, 23 October 1963, Karan Singh who had become the seniormost governor, is seated next to Prime Minister Jawaharlal Nehru

this merely to put this point in its proper perspective.

With regard to Qasim and Dogra joining the new cabinet, I am not aware that any firm offer was made to them by Shamsuddin.

I hope you enjoyed your short holiday in Dehra Dun[1] and have returned to Delhi somewhat refreshed. The situation here, as you have pointed out, requires careful watching and utmost vigilance.

With respectful regards,

Yours as ever,
Tiger

———— 215 ————

Bombay
29 November 1963

My dear Panditji,
I have been in this Nursing Home for a week. On the 21st I underwent an operation to remove the metal plate and six screws from my left leg, as they had been troubling me for some time and their removal had been advised both by doctors here as well as by the experts whom I consulted in London earlier this year. I am glad to say that the operation was very successful, and I am recovering well. The stitches will be out on Sunday and I am leaving for Delhi on Monday evening. I will be there for two days before returning to Jammu on Thursday. I know that you will be extremely busy with Parliament in session, but if you could spare a few minutes to see me any time on Tuesday or Wednesday I would be grateful.

The recent crop of disasters has been really shattering. In particular the assassination of President Kennedy[2] was truly a world tragedy.

With respects and deep regards,

Yours as ever,
Tiger

---

1. Nehru visited Dehra Dun from 11 to 13 October 1963.
2. John F. Kennedy (1917-1963); member, US House of Representatives, 1947-53, and of the senate 1953-60; president of the United States from 1961 till his assassination on 22 November 1963.

———— 216 ————

New Delhi
7 May 1964

My dear Tiger,
Your letter of the 7th May. Please come and see me on the 10th May
at 2.30 p.m.[1]

Yours as ever,
Jawaharlal Nehru

---

1. Dr Karan Singh and his wife met Nehru on 10 May. This was their last meeting.

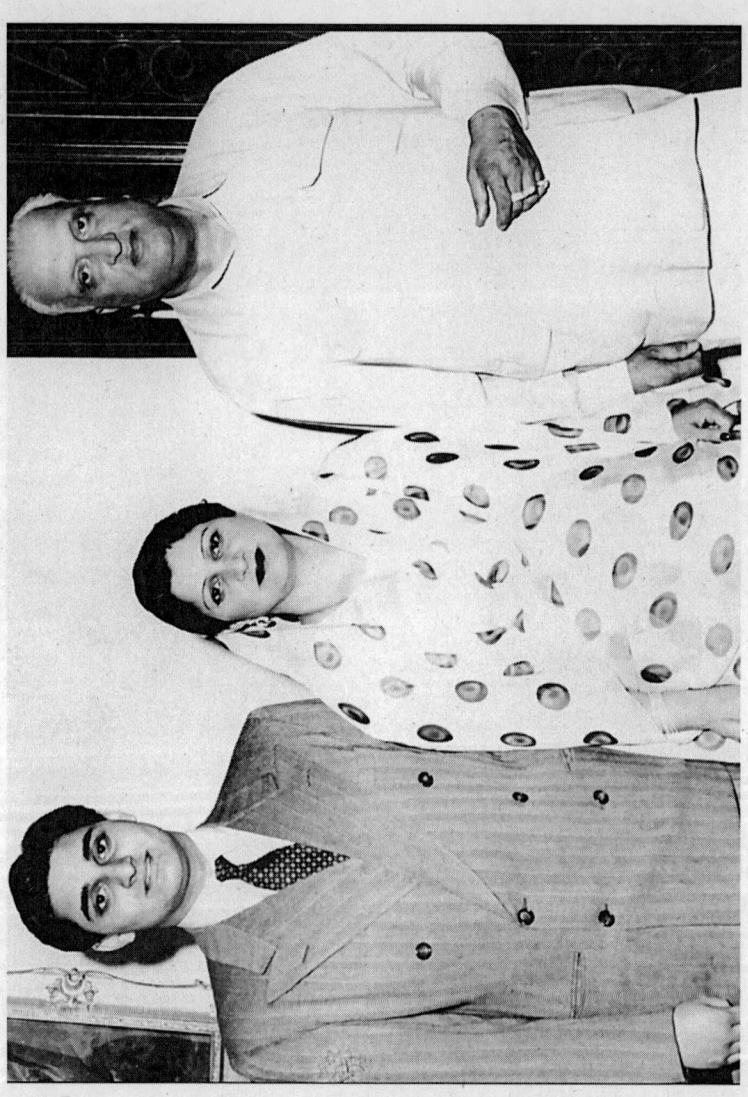

With his parents Maharaji Hari Singh and Maharani Tara Devi, Jammu, February 1949

APPENDIX

MEMORANDUM

August 1952
Poona

Dr Rajendra Prasad
President of India
New Delhi

Sir,
I am making a direct approach to you in the matter of the affairs of the State of Jammu and Kashmir and its Ruler as the situation has become acute owing to the rapid developments that are taking place and the further steps which are being taken in the next few days as these will vitally affect me personally apart from the repercussions they will have on the subjects of the State.

2. It is necessary to set out very briefly the events that have happened so far as the State of Jammu and Kashmir is concerned since my accession to the *Gaddi*.

3. I became the Ruler of the State in 1925. I then found that the British had strengthened their hold on the State by taking advantage of certain circumstances because, it being a border State of great strategic and political importance, they wanted it to be completely in their grip. The British created the myth of paramountcy without any historical or political sanctions and exploited the State as a set off against the fast approaching political awakening and urge for freedom in what was then known as British India.

4. Realizing what was coming. I took it upon myself to shake off the British yoke by insisting that the relations of the State with the British should be governed by the Treaty and all other strings which had been attached to such relationship with a view to gain domination over the State should be removed. I succeeded in my efforts to a large extent but incurred the wrath of the British who thenceforth became openly hostile to me.

5. Simultaneously with this, I started taking measures to ameliorate the condition of my people and to organize my Government on progressively democratic lines. I enacted laws to relieve rural

indebtedness and to improve generally the lot of the agriculturist and the economic and social condition of my people. Some of these enactments were resented by my Hindu subjects who thought that their interests were being sacrificed in the cause of Muslim uplift. I established industries and made provisions for education and medical relief far in advance of any other State. Special provision was made for the educational advancement of Muslims who were then considered backward. I was even more enthusiastic as regards the better organization of my Government. In this, I had the assistance of men of unquestionable integrity and ability from British India as my Prime Ministers and other Ministers and heads of the various Departments. It will not be out of place to name a few of them, such as, Raja Harikrishen Kaul, Mirza Sir Zaffar Ali, Mr V. N. Mehta, Mr Vijahat Husein, Sir Burjor Dalal, Sir Abdus Samad Khan, Sir Lal Gopal Mukerji, Sir K. N. Haksar, Sir N. Gopalaswami Ayyangar, Sir B. N. Rau. As a result, the administration of the State in the matter of efficiency and organization was better than even in some of the Provinces of British India. One further fact to which I wish to draw your attention in this connection is that I invariably acted on the advice of such Ministers and did not interfere or overrule their directions. It therefore, follows that if any fault is now to be found with the administration of the State and/or the policies then pursued, the blame cannot be laid at my door alone. It is significant that for six year (1938 to 1943) Shri N. Gopalaswami Ayyangar was the Prime Minister of the State and he will bear me out that I never interfered with his policies and decisions adopted and taken from time to time. Consequently, with my desire to give to the people of the State complete self government, I discussed in 1945 with my Prime Minister, Sir B. N. Rau, in the presence of Sir Tej Bahadur Sapru and Sir Kailash N. Haksar, the inauguration in the State of Full Responsible Government with Provincial Autonomy and a Central Government comprised of Representatives of the Provinces and a Board of Judicial Advisers with myself as the Constitutional Head. I was prepared to do this even with the knowledge that it would not be relished by the British. Sir B. N. Rau wanted this to be put into execution within the next fortnight. I was of opinion that it should be done in about six months so as to enable us to complete the scheme. The news leaked out, there were intrigues, position became very difficult and Sir B. N. Rau left shortly thereafter.

6. The finances of the State were governed on modern principles.

My expenditure was strictly limited and kept separate and distinct from the State finances and proper and well defined limits were laid down as between my personal and private matters and matters of the State. Thus, I had a well organized and efficient Executive, a democratically elected Legislature, an independent judiciary, definite policies for expansion of education, medical relief and all other essential features of a progressive state. The eminent administrators and judges who worked for the State from time to time will bear testimony to this.

7. All that I did aggravated the hostility of the British towards me as they were not sincerely inclined towards ameliorating the conditions of the people or for the freedom of the country.

8. In those days, the Rulers of Indian States were judged by the condition and feelings of their subjects and I can say, without fear of contradiction, that the people of my State were content and had no cause for grievances against me or the administration of the State.

9. It is not unknown that trouble started in the State in 1931 and what has on occasions been described by so called 'national leaders' of the State as 'the Freedom Movement' was engineered by elements outside the State under the instigation of the British. The movement in the beginning was a religious movement with slogans like 'Down with Hindu Raj' and 'Islam in danger'. The leaders of the movement were men who now figure as Ministers and Administrators in Azad Kashmir under Pakistan such as, Chaudhary Ghulam Abbas and Maulvi Yousuf Shah and some others. To gain sympathy and cooperation from those fighting for freedom from the British yoke in British India, the Muslims who were running this movement gave it the name of 'National Conference'. The name was adopted also to fall into line with the movement carried on in other States in the name of the 'States People Conference' and to take advantage of the declining prestige of the British. The movement thus gained the sympathy of the Indian National Congress. It became known in British India as the National Movement in the Jammu and Kashmir State.

10. These facts clearly showed that my people had no grievance against me, that the movement was started by disgruntled people with the British behind them and that those in charge of the movement gained the confidence and sympathy of the Indian National Congress by adopting the name of the 'National Conference'.

11. I have been accused by the Prime Minister of not listening to the advice of the Congress leaders during the fateful period 1946-47.

I deny that charge. In 1946 when the leaders of the Indian National Congress formed the Viceroy's Cabinet for the Interim Government, I had occasion to meet Mahatma Gandhi and Shri J. B. Kripalani, the then President of the Indian National Congress, when they both visited the State. Mahatma Gandhi suggested that I should have the backing of the people in whatever I did, Shri J. B. Kripalani suggested the immediate release of Sheikh Abdullah because the nominees of the National Conference who were in the Government had resigned. I pointed out to them that I had already set up a Constitutional government which included two nominees of the National Conference and that it was not then possible to entrust the Government entirely in the hands of one group, viz, the National Conference. I said to them that I was willing to make such further changes as might be suggested towards making it a completely popular Government in consonance with the safety of the State and to keep the balance between the divergent views of different parts of the State. The matter rested there for the time being.

12. Then came the development of 1947 and the question of accession. The position of my State was very difficult, situated as it was in contiguity to India and Pakistan as also to Afghanistan, Tibet and Russia. The situation therefore required to be dealt with more tact and foresight than in the case of other states. Mahatma Gandhi and the Prime Minister were anxious that I should not make a declaration of Independence and the Prime Minister was anxious to secure the release from prison of Sheikh Abdullah. Having regard to what my Government had done when the Prime Minister visited the State in 1946, Lord Mountbatten chose to visit the State in June 1947 and we had several talks. Lord Mountbatten then urged me and my Prime Minister, Kak, not to make any declaration of Independence but to find out in one way or another, the will of the people of Kashmir as soon as possible and to announce our intention by the 14 August to send representatives accordingly to one Constituent Assembly or the other. Lord Mountbatten further told us that the newly created States Department was prepared to give an assurance that if Kashmir went to Pakistan, it would not be regarded as an unfriendly act by the Government of India. Lord Mountbatten stressed the dangerous situation in which Kashmir would find itself if it lacked the support of one of the two Dominions by the date of the transfer of power. The impression which I gathered from my talks with Lord Mountbatten who explained the situation with plans and maps was that, in his

opinion, it was advisable for me to accede to Pakistan. I thought that in the circumstances it was advisable to have Standstill Agreements with India and Pakistan and get breathing time to decide which accession would be in the interests of the State. Pakistan very quickly and willingly agreed to a Standstill arrangement, perhaps with mental reservations, as appears from their subsequent conduct. On the other hand, the Government of India did not make up their mind and, if I may be permitted to say so, dealt with the situation in a half-hearted and desultory manner; thus, giving an opportunity to Pakistan to do mischief, as they did. This gave rise to misunderstandings on both sides resulting in dissatisfaction and delay in coming to an understanding. The results have been detrimental to both the State and India. Pakistan became impatient and, having failed to force accession, started with blockading the supplies to the State and ended by invading the State. Lord Mountbatten realizing the uncertain and dangerously unstable position of the State, asked Lord Ismay to approach me and get me to decide on accession without further delay to whichever Dominion I and my people desired. This was at the end of August 1947.

My difficulties were as follows:-

(1) The People of the State were divided in several groups, each group having its own ideas about accession;

(2) The Border Feudatory Territories such as Hunza, Nagar and Chitral and the District of Gilgit, where British influence was supreme were definitely for accession to Pakistan and were pressing me to accede to Pakistan without delay and threatening me with dire consequences if I did not act according to their suggestion;

(3) The Muslim population of the State was also divided into groups with divergent views. Muslims from parts of Jammu such as, Mirpur, Poonch, Muzaffarabad, were for accession to Pakistan because of Pakistan propaganda inside the State. Muslims of Kashmir and some Muslims of Jammu who were led by Sheikh Abdullah and the leaders of the National Conference did not want the question of accession to be decided at that stage but wanted me to part with power in their favour so that they could decide the question independently of me. They made no secret of their views and obstructed me in deciding the question of accession instead of helping me to accede to India;

(4) Hindus of Jammu and all the people of Ladakh were for affiliation with or accession to India;

(5) A portion of the population of Kashmir was also for accession to Pakistan.

Thus, there was a sharp division of opinion. The Partition aggravated the situation and unhinged and unbalanced the minds of the people with the result that the people of the State were not in a position to give any considered opinion if I chose to consult them.

13. In September 1947, it was suggested to me that it would be a wise move on my part to appoint Shri Mehr Chand Mahajan as my Prime Minister as he would be able to handle the affairs of the State in the then critical period firmly and in a statesmanlike manner. Before Shri Mehr Chand Mahajan took up his appointment he discussed with Sardar Patel about immediate requirements of the State and Sardar Patel promised him full support and cooperation on behalf of the Government of India. Sardar Patel also wrote to me stating this and adding, that the Government of India fully realized how difficult the situation in the State was and assured me that the Government of India would do their best to help the State in the critical period. I then wrote to Sardar Patel that a little further elucidation of the points of view regarding the essential requirements of the movement would result in a satisfactory solution. Sardar Patel replied on the 2 October 1947 that he had a further talk with Shri Mahajan and understood that Shri Mahajan was joining my service very shortly. As by that time I had proclaimed a general amnesty, Sardar Patel expressed his pleasure at the step I had taken and stated that this would rally round me the men who might otherwise have been a thorn in my side. He also stated that he was expediting as much as possible the linking up of the State with the Indian Dominion. Shri Mahajan then received Sardar Patel's letter of the 21 October 1947 in which he said that he had further discussion with Sheikh Abdullah, that Sheikh Abdullah seemed to him genuinely anxious to cooperate and sincerely desirous of assisting the State in dealing with the external dangers and the internal troubles with which the State was threatened. He further said that at the same time Sheikh Abdullah, as was natural, felt that unless something was done and done immediately, to strengthen his hands, both in popular eyes and in dealing with the dangers, it would be impossible for him to do anything substantial. He said he felt that the position which Sheikh Abdullah took up was understandable and reasonable,

that in the mounting demands for the introduction of a Responsible Government in the State, such as was witnessed in Travancore and Mysore, it was impossible for me to isolate myself, that the upsurge was bound to affect me sooner or later, that the Government of India on their part had pledged to give me the maximum support and would do so, but without some measure of popular backing, particularly from amongst the community which represented such an overwhelming majority in Kashmir, it would be difficult to make such support go to the farthest limit that was necessary if the disruptive forces which were being raised and organized, were to be crushed. He advised me in the circumstances to make a substantial gesture to win Sheikh Abdullah's support. He said he had no desire to suggest that I should do so in a manner which would be completely revolutionary in character, that such a step might undermine the loyal and willing support which the State had commanded from strong elements of the body politic.

14. Shri Mahajan also received the Prime Minister's letter dated 20 October 1947 in which he referred to the friendliest feelings the Government of India had towards Kashmir and its people and their desire to help to the best of their ability in providing Kashmir with the commodities it needed. He said the Government of India would like to do so for humanitarian reasons as well because of their deep interest in the future of the people of Jammu and Kashmir State. That the self interest of India also demanded that and that Government of India were strongly of the opinion that no coercion should be exercised on Kashmir and its people and that they should be allowed to function in their own way and to make such decision as they thought fit and proper and that in the furtherance of this policy the Government of India would direct their efforts. The Prime Minister in his letter dated 21 October 1947 to Shri Mahajan said that the future of Kashmir was of the most urgent importance to the Government of India and for him, it was both a personal and a public matter, that it would be a tragedy so far as he was concerned, if Kashmir went to Pakistan. The Prime Minister referred to the urgent need of Pakistan to get Kashmir's accession to Pakistan and that they were threatening every now and then to that end and that everything else that they did was an accessory to the same, that the top ranking leaders of Pakistan were continually approaching the Kashmir National Conference leaders, that they assured to them for their best behaviour and promised them something approaching independence if only they would agree to Kashmir

acceding to Pakistan. They were even prepared to give the right of secession. The Prime Minister then suggested the urgency of taking some step like the formation of a Provincial Government and that Sheikh Abdullah, who was obviously the most popular person in Kashmir, might be asked to form such a Government. The Prime Minister further added that in view of all the circumstances he felt that it would probably be undesirable to make any declaration of adhesion to the Indian Union at that stage, that this should come later when a popular Interim Government was functioning.

15. After the amnesty proclaimed by me, Sheikh Abdullah wrote to me on the 26 September 1947 in which, after referring to his incarceration for about a year and a half, he said as follows:-

> In spite of what has happened in the past I assure Your Highness that myself and my Party have never harboured any sentiment of disloyalty towards Your Highness' person, throne or dynasty. The development of this beautiful country and the betterment of its people is our common aim and interest and I assure Your Highness the fullest and loyal support of myself and my organization.

He added:-

> In order to achieve the common aim set forth above, mutual trust and confidence must be the main step. Without this it would not be possible to face successfully the great difficulties that upset our State on all sides at present.

He concluded:-

> Before I close this letter, I beg to assure Your Highness once again of my steadfast loyalty and pray that God may grant me opportunity enough to make this country attain under Your Highness' aegis such an era of peace, prosperity and good Government that it may be second to none and be an ideal for others to copy.

16. I wrote to Lord Mountbatten on the 26th October 1947 informing him of the situation in the State. I received his letter dated 27th October 1947 stating as follows:-

> In the special circumstances mentioned by Your Highness my Government have decided to accept the accession of Kashmir State to the Dominion of India x x x x
> It is my Government's wish that as soon as law and order has

been restored in Kashmir and her soil cleared of the invaders the question of the State's accession should be settled by a reference to the people x x x x
My Government and I note with satisfaction that Your Highness has decided to invite Sheikh Abdullah to form an interim Government to work as your Prime Minister.

The Prime Minister also wrote to me on the 26th October 1947 stating as follows:-

Shri V.P. Menon returned from Jammu this morning and informed me of his talks there. He gave me the Instrument of Accession and the Standstill Agreement which you had signed and I saw also your letter to the Governor General of India. Allow me to congratulate you on the wise decisions that you have taken. I earnestly hope that they will lead not only to the effective protection of Kashmir State in the present but also to the freedom and well-being of Kashmir and India as a whole.'

I then acceded to India.

17. The Prime Minister in his letter dated 13th November 1947 pointed out to me that the only person who could deliver the goods in Kashmir was Sheikh Abdullah, that he was obviously the leading and popular personality in Kashmir, that the way he had risen to grapple with the crisis had shown the nature of the man, that the Prime Minister had a high opinion of his integrity and his general balance of mind and that he was likely to be right in regard to major decisions.

18. Shri Gopalaswami, who was then a Minister without a portfolio, wrote to me on the 9th December 1947 indicating for my consideration his views on the changes which in the critical situation of the State, were immediately called for in the then existing constitutional and administrative set up in the State.

19. A draft of the Proclamation which I was intended to issue, was sent to me by the Government of India. It was seen by Sheikh Abdullah. Sheikh Abdullah also saw the correspondence which had passed between Sardar Patel and myself. Shri Gopalaswami wrote to me on 1st March 1948 as follows:-

1st March 1948

My Dear Maharaja Sahib,

Messrs V.P. Menon and Mahajan are going to Jammu this afternoon to discuss and finalize with you the draft of the Proclamation which Your Highness has to issue for appointing Abdullah as Prime Minister and others on his advice. The draft has been very carefully considered by myself, Panditji and Sardarji, and we are of the opinion that the whole of it should be accepted by you. Anything less would not satisfy the requirements of the present situation.

2. As a friend of yours, I consider it most important that Your Highness must make a very big gesture in order to rally the maximum percentage of the population of the State behind you with the help of Abdullah. Things are moving very fast and we have yet to fight a great battle at Lake Success. I have already stated during the discussions at Lake Success that Your Highness had only been waiting for Sheikh Abdullah to return from America to convert the Emergency Administration into an Interim Council of Ministers with Abdullah as Prime Minister. I am leaving Delhi for Lake Success the day after tomorrow, and it would be a great strength to the cause I have to plead there on behalf of Kashmir if this Proclamation is issued before I leave. I have not the slightest doubt that the issue of this Proclamation at this juncture, is, in the circumstances that confront us at present, in the best interests of yourself and your people.

3. It is further very important that everything that has happened in the past should be forgotten and forgiven and that Your Highness should take Sheikh Abdullah into your fullest confidence. In fact, I was almost going to suggest that you should give up your usual reserve, come out in the open and put yourself at the head of your people, both Muslims and non-Muslims, for the purpose of consolidating and strengthening the large volume of support for preserving the integrity of the State and maintaining its accession to India, which thanks to Sheikh Abdullah and the Indian Army, you have already behind you. With kind regards,

Yours sincerely,
N. Gopalaswami

Sheikh Abdullah in his letter dated 24th March 1948 stated as follows:-

The situation in the Jammu and Kashmir State is, as you are well aware, a difficult one and requires the most careful handling. The emergency continues and has to be dealt with as such till normal conditions are restored. The burden of a Prime Minister in these circumstances will be a heavy one. He cannot function effectively without the fullest cooperation of his colleagues and the people as well as, of course, Your Highness. I have consulted some of my colleagues, who were available and have come to the conclusion that it is my duty in these circumstances to undertake this burden. I trust that in the heavy work ahead I shall have Your Highness' full help and cooperation. I appreciate the spirit in which you have made the offer of the Prime Minister to me and on my part I assure Your Highness that I shall fully reciprocate it.

20. Then came the Proclamation dated 5 March 1948 which was drafted by Shri Gopalaswami and approved by the Government of India and Sheikh Abdullah. It has been referred to in Article 370 of the Constitution of India and the State of Jammu and Kashmir has so far been governed under the constitutional set up for that Proclamation.

21. It is necessary to set out briefly what happened in the State and between the Government of India and Sheikh Abdullah in relation to the State after the Proclamation of 5 March 1948 and my leaving the State at the end of April 1949. Sheikh Abdullah and the men of his party took all power to themselves, ignored my existence and where they felt necessary, they got the consent of the Government of India to do what they liked in the State disregarding me and my wishes. This gradually led to a deterioration and to the outside world, the State and Sheikh Abdullah became convertible terms. The people of Kashmir were utterly ignored and everything that Sheikh Abdullah desired to do was done in the name of the State with the express or tacit consent of the Government of India. At this juncture on a suggestion from Sardar Patel, I and my wife began a tour of the State. This did not suit the books of Sheikh Abdullah. He approached the Government of India with the result that I was asked to stay out of the State for a few months. I accepted the advice of Sardar Patel and agreed to stay out. The Yuvaraj was appointed Regent. It need hardly be pointed out that the Yuvaraj became a figurehead and had to take orders from Sheikh Abdullah. In this connection it may also be pointed

out that although my Proclamation of 5th March 1948 was based on the Mysore Constitution, which stipulated the appointment of a Dewan and reserved subjects yet gradually Sheikh Abdullah succeeded in getting the approval of the Government of India to making changes in the Constitution of the State, so as to make it very different from what it was expressly intended to be. The mischief began with Sheikh Abdullah going direct to the Government of India on certain points over my head and the Government of India countenancing him and giving the desired directions and then informing me of what they had done at the instance of Sheikh Abdullah. The correspondence on the subject and the events following on each change bear testimony to what Sheikh Abdullah was trying to achieve in breach of the solemn promises and assurances given by him and also by the Government of India on his behalf. After my leaving the State things went from bad to worse. Sheikh Abdullah was not satisfied with what he had achieved and aspired to absolute control of the State. He became openly inimical and hostile to me. He even interfered with my private properties and personal belongings, issued order to humiliate me and even interfered with the administration of the Dharmartha Trust, a Trust created by my forefathers of which I am the Trustee and which is being administered from day to day by the President of the Dharmarth Council appointed by me. The charities and institutions maintained from the revenues of Trust are starved. Even the routine expenses of the Trust, such as, for Puja in temples and *Devasthans* cannot be met because it pleases Sheikh Abdullah to prevent the income of the Trust coming to my hands or to the hands of President of the Dharmarth Council. The Jammu branch of the Imperial Bank of India refused to pay even to me the amounts of the fixed deposits of the Trust and also refused to transfer such deposits to the Bombay Office of the Imperial Bank of India with the result that I had to renew the deposits to avoid loss of interest to the Trust. It would be interesting to know under whose order the Jammu branch of the Bank acted in the manner it did. As will be apparent from my correspondence with the States Ministry my complaints as regards both my personal properties and the Dharmarth Trust have been galore and none of them has been remedied either by Sheikh Abdullah or by the States Ministry. Leaving aside for the moment my grievances as regards what is being done with reference to my personal properties in Jammu and Kashmir how can Sheikh Abdullah's attitude towards the administration of the Dharmarth Trust be reconciled with secularism and impartiality?

22. I may now refer to Mr V. P. Menon's letter to Shri Mahajan

dated 30 January 1948 in which he stated as follows:-

As I told you, I have already contradicted the news that the Maharaja fled from Srinagar to Jammu. I propose again to take up this question with the Ministry of Information and have asked Sharma, our Publicity Co-ordination Officer, to get into touch with foreign correspondents and give them the correct picture. I hope, this canard will stop once for all.

This gives a direct lie to the report set afloat both inside and outside the State by Sheikh Abdullah and this party that I had run away from my State in October 1947 leaving the State in chaos and the people at the tender mercies of the invaders. It appears that the Prime Minister was deliberately misinformed as to what I then did and he was also misinformed that my officers had deserted their posts and runaway. In third week of October 1947 Lord Mountbatten was of opinion that it would be dangerous to send any Indian troops to the help of the State unless the State first offered to accede particularly as such accession would be temporary, being prior to a plebiscite. No final decision was, however, taken on these vital questions by 25th October 1947 but Mr V. P. Menon was asked to fly to Srinagar to find out the true position there. He met me at Srinagar and I made him realize the urgency of the situation and that unless India helped immediately, all would be lost. It was then that on the strong advice of Mr V. P. Menon who said it would be foolhardy for me to stay in Srinagar when raiders were as near as Baramulla then, I left Srinagar with my wife and son. I also ignored the Letter of Accession which Mr V. P. Menon took back with him.

None of my officers fled. The families of some of the officers left for Jammu as the Government used to move to Jammu at the end of October and open at Jammu on the first Monday in November.

On the other hand, it was Sheikh Abdullah who fled from Srinagar and did not return till the Indian troops had started coming into Srinagar.

23. Regarding my leaving the State, I may refer to my letter dated 6th May 1949 to Sardar Patel and Sardar Patel's letter to me dated 23rd May 1949. I may also refer to my letter dated 1st June 1949 to Sardar Patel and Sardar Patel's letter dated 9th June 1949 to me. I attach herewith copies of the letters. In June, 1949 I issued a Proclamation appointing the Yuvaraj as my Regent during my stay outside the State.

24. This was in compliance with the wishes of the Government of India.

25. In November 1950 I received from Mr Vishnu Sahay his letter dated 30th November 1950 wherein he drew my attention to the resolution passed by the Council of the National Conference asking that a Constituent Assembly be set up for the State and to my Proclamation of 5th March 1948 wherein the setting up of such an Assembly was foreshadowed and stated that it appeared to the States Ministry that the time had come to reduce the uncertainty in Kashmir by going ahead with this proposal. He sent a copy of the draft Proclamation to set up the Constituent Assembly, for my comments. I took exception to the proposed manner and method of setting up the Constituent Assembly. I summarized my objection to it as follows:-

(1) That the Proclamation with the object and spirit of which I wholeheartedly agree be issued by me as Ruler who is the properly constituted authority in law to promulgate it and not by my Regent;

(2) The powers and functions of the body intended to be constituted should be express, well defined and accurately worded and should exclude from the purview of their enquiry and consideration matters not expressly entrusted to them;

(3) They should report to the authority that constitutes it, i.e., the Ruler who shall seek the advice of the Parliament of India in the matter.

I refer to the correspondence that took place, the interview which Mr Menon had with me in Bombay in February 1951 under the instructions of the Prime Minister and the subsequent negotiations which ended with my giving consent to the Yuvaraj for setting up the Constituent Assembly. I also refer to the assurance given to me by the Minister for States (Shri N. Gopalaswami Ayyangar) in the course of the negotiations as to the position of myself and my dynasty and other important matters. I am constrained to refer to the relevant portions of his letter which, I quote below.

5 April 1951

x x x x x

Developments have, however, since taken place both in the State and at Lake Success which make it imperative that the issue of this proclamation is not delayed any longer. The Government of India are committed to the convening of a Constituent Assembly, the preparations for which are in active progress in the State. That Assembly will be held whether the formal Proclamation issues or not. In the view of the Government of India it must be convened, if both their commitments to the people of Kashmir and their stand at Lake Success are to be implemented in spirit and in the letter. From the beginning they have held that this Constituent Assembly should be called under the provisions of the Constitution of India and that this should be done from both a tactical and constitutional point of view, on the authority of Proclamation issued by the Head of the State. The draft of the Proclamation has been agreed between the Government of India and the Government of Jammu and Kashmir. No purpose will, therefore, be served by any act of Your Highness which holds up the signing and issue of this Proclamation by Shri Yuvaraj.

On neither of the two matters about which I can understand your entertaining apprehensions, namely, the continuance of the accession of the Jammu and Kashmir State or of part thereof to India and the connection of the Headship of the State with your dynasty, no final decision could be taken by the Constituent Assembly to be convened. They are essentially matters which could be decided only as a matter of agreement between the Government of India and the Parliament on the one side and the Government of Jammu and Kashmir and the State Constituent Assembly or Legislature on the other. The Government of India will, no doubt at the proper time take the decision on these matters, which, I need hardly assure you, will be essentially be just from the standpoint both of your dynasty and the people of the State. You have obviously to put your trust in the people of State and the Government of India in respect of this matter. I hope, therefore, you will immediately lift the ban which you have placed on Shri Yuvaraj affixing his signature to the agreed Proclamation and which naturally has placed him in great embarrassment.

26. Apprehending what was coming and in order not to embarrass the Government of India and the Yuvaraj, I have been prepared to abdicate provided that a satisfactory arrangement was to come with me by the States Ministry and provided also that the Yuvaraj's position as the Head of the State was assured. The negotiations in this behalf which were carried on with Shri Gopalaswami as the States Minister were left in an indecisive state because of Shri Gopalaswami having been succeeded as the States Minister by Dr K. N. Katju. Having regard to the trend of events I wrote to Dr Katju on the 29th June 1952. I waited for Dr Katju's reply as foreshadowed in the Prime Minister's letter. I then received Dr Katju's reply dated 30th July 1952. I replied to Dr Katju by my letter dated 8th August 1952. I enclose copies of these letters as they have an important bearing on the situation.

27. These letters speak for themselves Dr Katju's reply is not a reply at all. The legal position, it appears to me, has not been considered and it further appears that it is being taken for granted by the Prime Minister and Dr Katju that the relevant Articles, particularly Article 370, of the Constitution of India can be altered and/or amended to suit the present attitude of Sheikh Abdullah. It would not be out of place to point out that Article 370 refers specifically to my Proclamation of 5th March 1948. That is the law which governs the State of Jammu and Kashmir until a new Constitution is framed, approved and adopted not only by the Constituent Assembly of the State but also approved by me and then by you and yet, I learn that the Prime Minister has asked the Yuvaraj (who is acting only as my Regent and represents me) to agree to be the elected Head of the State forthwith, that is to say, even before the Constitution of the State is framed much less approved and adopted thus throwing over not only me but also the dynasty. I do not know what reply Dr Katju proposes to make to me but it appears that the Prime Minister is dealing with the matter. (vide his letter dated 5th July 1952). I have, therefore to specifically deal with the charges made in the Prime Minister's letter.

28. The Prime Minister in para 4 of his letter refers to the Constitution of India as having been based on and derived from the people of India and says with regard to the Jammu and Kashmir State that the Government of India felt that the people would prefer

accession to India but the matter was delicate and not beyond dispute and, therefore, the Government of India did not press for the accession of Jammu and Kashmir State but suggested that the matter should be considered at a later stage when the people's wishes could be ascertained in some form or the other and the suggestion was that some kind of a Constituent Assembly might be set up in the State to decide the question of accession as well as other questions. I grant all this but how can the Government of India take all these steps over my head on whose authority they entered the State and are continuing there and who was the Chief Author of the Proclamation on which is based the future construction of political set up in the country? In para 5, the Prime Minister says that on the invasion of the State by tribal raiders and others late in October 1947 the crisis arose and at that time I left Srinagar at the dead of night for Jammu and many of my officers followed me and the State was left without leadership or means of defence in so far as official authority was concerned. This is in fact, untrue as pointed out above. I left Srinagar for Jammu on the advice of the Government of India conveyed to me through Mr Menon. The Prime Minister says further that in the basic picture of the crisis of Kashmir I do not come in at all. That statement amounts to *suppresio veri* and *suggestio falsi*. I have acted all throughout from September 1947 under the advice of the Government of India, Lord Mountbatten, the Prime Minister, Sardar Vallabhbhai Patel and Shri Gopalaswami and, as pointed out herein above, Sheikh Abdullah himself made promises and gave assurances, which he is now backing out of. Even in the book called *New Kashmir* published by the Kashmir Information Bureau, New Delhi, in 1950 and which is the political Bible of Sheikh Abdullah, Sheikh Abdullah has based his case for a Responsible Government in the State under the aegis of the Maharaja and even gone to the length of setting out what functions the Maharaja was to perform. The Prime Minister in his letter says that the people of Kashmir must decide their own future. I may well ask whether Sheikh Abdullah is a synonymous term with the people of Kashmir. The people of Kashmir have not been consulted. According to Sheikh Abdullah, the people of Kashmir have changed their mind to such an extent that they are determined to get rid of the idea of a hereditary ruler of the State. The Constituent Assembly has been packed with Sheikh Abdullah's men and even that Assembly has not yet come to a decision nor has it framed any constitution providing for the functions of the Head of the State either hereditary or elected and what one would like to know is where is the reason for this frightful hurry to elect the Head of the State thus doing away with me and my dynasty before the Constitution is framed and before the fate of the State is determined in the fight that is raging before the UNO between India and Pakistan. Are myself and my dynasty to be pawns in the game which Sheikh Abdullah is playing with the Government of India on the representation that he is actively helping India in the case before the UN Security Council. The Prime Minister says that he has seen no evidence of any sympathy on my part for the people of Kashmir who have gone through fire and suffering during the past four and a half years. May I ask who is responsible for this state of affairs? Have the Government of India given any choice of action to me during the last four and a half years? Have they at any time pulled up Sheikh Abdullah knowing as they did, on what promises and assurances Sheikh Abdullah became the Prime Minister? May I again point out that even before I left the State under the advice of Sardar Patel, I and my wife had started on a tour of the State as Sardar Patel had told me that I should see more of my people and they should see more of me. Sheikh Abdullah did not like this tour and approached the Government of India with the result that I was called at Delhi and asked to desist from returning to the State and finally to leave it. The Prime Minister says at the end of this letter that the only assurances he can give to me is that the first place will be given always to the rights of the people and to the wishes of the people and that if I fall in with those rights and wishes, the Government of India will endeavour to help me to the best of their ability. I am prepared to take up the challenge. Let the people of Jammu and Kashmir freely decide between me and Sheikh Abdullah without interference from the Government of India. Let me point out what has been happening. The world has been given to understand that the march of events, the changed political values have brought about rapid and inevitable changes and we must accept them no matter what the obligation of the Government of India, Government of Jammu and Kashmir, the assurance of both the Governments to me and their duties under certain legal and constitutional arrangements may be. With all due deference to this opinion, I must say that I emphatically challenge the contention that whatever has happened is in accordance with the will of the people and that the sovereignty has effectively and really passed to the people as it should and that they are consciously exercising their will and ask for the changes which are being brought about by an oligarchy backed by Government of India. I cannot conscientiously recognize the changes in the Proclamation of 5th March 1948 which governs the relations of the State with India. But if the Government of India and you, Sir, feel that in the present stage of negotiations with Dr Graham it would be inconvenient for the Government of India to allow this matter to be raked up, then at least, the Government of India should not succumb entirely to the wishes of Sheikh Abdullah but hold the balance equally between him and me and at least preserve the status quo as regards the headship of the State until the field is clear for the necessary steps to be taken to determine the will of the people of Kashmir.

29. Copies of the following documents are attached for your ready reference:-

(1) Note given to Prime Minister of Kashmir by Prime Minister of India on 26th October 1947;

(2) Letter dated 26th October 1947 from the Prime Minister of India to the Prime Minister of Kashmir;

(3) Letter dated 27th October 1947 from Prime Minister of India to the Prime Minister of Kashmir;

(4) Letter dated 27th October 1947 from the Prime Minister of India to me;

(5) Letter dated 26th October 1947 from me to Lord Mountbatten;

(6) Letter dated 27th October 1947 from Lord Mountbatten to me;

(7) Letter dated 24th December 1947 from Shri N. Gopalaswami to me.

30. Secure in the knowledge that I was out of the picture and could not reply I was, by a series of false statements and speeches intended to humiliate and malign me, painted black and unpatriotic. The Government of India who had assured me that I would be protected against such onslaughts remained an unconcerned spectator. Not only that, it is most distressing to know and feel that whenever Sheikh Abdullah and his party talked of me in disparaging and spiteful terms, the highest authority in the Government of India immediately endorsed it. If Sheikh Abdullah said I could not return to the State, the Prime Minister with all the authority, prestige and might at his back, endorsed it. If Sheikh Abdullah said I had lost the confidence of the people the Prime Minister referred to my alleged wrong-headed

and mistaken policies, without saying what exactly they were and said the people had suffered on account of these. This no doubt had the effect of suppressing what is said to be the will of the people. Being placed as I was, I was absolutely unable to answer any of these accusations. I feel grievously wronged in that the Government of India whom I looked up to as the ultimate authority I could go to for redress, instead of stopping such malicious and false propaganda, not only went on countenancing it but endorsing it disregarding their solemn assurances.

Having eliminated me in a manner which had neither the sanction of law nor political morality, it was the duty of the Government of India to protect me. But that was not done and the matter did not end there. My properties and privileges etc., were attempted to be interfered with. I protested and asked for redress but never got it.

As I have said above, I was eliminated by a process which was neither fair nor honourable. It was not and it has never been due to the will of the people. It was due entirely to the machinations of Sheikh Abdullah and his party. They got themselves appointed on the definite assurances and later, with the connivance of the Government of India., systematically ignored all their legal and moral obligations and ultimately without rhyme or reason but to suit the books of Sheikh Abdullah successfully got me out of the State. Taking advantage of my absence and helplessness, started a campaign of vilification and harassment and thus created conditions wherein they could tell an unknowing world that they were doing what the people desired. I have taken the responsibility of making these statements and I earnestly request you, Sir, to ascertain the views of your Government about them and then come to an independent opinion as to whether I have not been seriously wronged and to redress the wrong.

31. I may be permitted to summarize the position:-

   (1) The Government of the State of Jammu and Kashmir was more advanced and enlightened than that of my other Indian State in the pre-Partition days;

   (2) I employed men of undoubted ability and standing to be my Ministers from time to time;

   (3) In August 1947 Lord Mountbatten gave me the impression that I should accede to Pakistan, Government of India was undecided about the matter, wanted every step by me endorsed by Sheikh Abdullah, the people of Jammu and Kashmir were divided in their opinion and I decided to

enter into Standstill Agreement with both India and Pakistan in order to have time for things to settle down;

(4) Pakistan did not act up to the Standstill Agreements, blocked supplies to the State and aided and abetted the raiders;

(5) I released Sheikh Abdullah as advised by Sardar Patel and relied on the assurance given by Sheikh Abdullah backed up by assurances given by the Government of India;

(6) I took Sheikh Abdullah in my Government;

(7) I issued the Proclamation of 5 March 1948;

(8) Sheikh Abdullah with the connivance of the Government of India started tinkering with the Constitution of 5 March 1948;

(9) Sheikh Abdullah persuaded the Government of India to drive me out of the State;

(10) I left the State and appointed the Yuvaraj, my Regent;

(11) My rights of personal property and the affairs of the Dharmarth Trust were interfered with by Sheikh Abdullah;

(12) Sheikh Abdullah by maligning me created an impression that the people of Kashmir were against me;

(13) The Constituent Assembly was set up;

(14) The will of the people of Jammu and Kashmir is now judged by the whims and caprices of Sheikh Abdullah;

(15) Sheikh Abdullah having made up his mind to get rid of the Ruler and his dynasty, persuaded the Government of India to see eye to eye with him and to lay down that this could be done even before the new Constitution was framed much less approved by you on behalf of India;

(16) I get no redress and am told that I am in the wrong, the will of the people is all that counts and I must abide by such will;

(17) The Press carries reports from day to day creating feelings against me. False reports are not contradicted;

(18) The Prime Minister got angry as evidenced by his letter dated 5th July 1952 because I stated facts;

(19) The States Minister avoids giving a proper reply to me and yet the Press says I have been asked and have not replied;

(20) The Yuvaraj is being coerced by the Prime Minister and Sheikh Abdullah to accede to their suggestions.

32. Finally, I have to say that I had my range of controversy with

Sheikh Abdullah and the Prime Minister and I am bitter about the fact that the Government of India have been unable to afford me protection and safeguard my rights in spite of the fact that throughout these four and a half years, I have given full cooperation and the fact that my pre-1947 conduct did not compare unfavourably with that of the other Rulers who at present enjoy Government of India's protection and favour. During the last three years of my enforced absence from the State I have given them no cause for grievance and at the most, I have been charged with delay in permitting the Yuvaraj to take action which having regard to the consideration involved and my better experience, was natural and understandable. Even in this matter ultimately I did fall in line with the Government of India. If the result of all this in the final stage has again to be a betrayal by the Government of India of their assurances and promises etc. and is to result not only in my final removal from the State but also of the sacrifice of the Yuvaraj whom I had entrusted to the Government of India's protection. I can only say that it would be an ill return for the faith which I and the Yuvaraj placed in the Government and the help and cooperation to the extent of self effacement that we rendered to it. Only history and posterity will be able to do justice to our respective points of view.

33. In these circumstances, I appeal to you to consider the matter impartially in all its aspects with your sagacity and wisdom and guide me as to what would be in the best interests of the State.

I remain,
Yours faithfully,
Hari Singh

Maharaja Hari Singh to Vallabhbhai Patel

6 May 1949
New Delhi

My dear Sardar Patelji,
With reference to the discussions I had with you on 29th April and 1st May 1949, I have been revolving the matters in my mind and am now in a position to let you have my settled reactions to the proposal in regard to my temporary absence from the State which you put to me.

I should like to say at the outset that I was completely taken aback by this proposal but coming as it did from you, in whom I have since the very beginning placed implicit trust and confidence and whose advice I have throughout followed on the many questions affecting me personally and my State both in the present and in future, I have been able somehow to adjust myself to it. I would not, however, be human if I did not express my sense of keen disappointment and bewilderment at having been called upon to make such a sacrifice of personal prestige, honour and position when all along I have been content to follow, sometimes even against my own judgement and conscience, the advice in regard to the constitutional position in the State which I have been receiving from the Prime Minister of India or yourself, some times even against arrangements which were agreed to only a few months before. Now would it be fair on my part to conceal from you my own feeling that while Sheikh Abdullah has been allowed to depart from time to time as suited his inclination from the pledged and written word, to act consistently in breach of the loyalty which he professed to me prior to his release from jail and the oath of allegiance which he took when he assumed office, and to indulge openly along with his colleagues in a campaign of vilifications and foul calumny against me, both inside the State and outside, I should have had to be driven from position to position each of which I thought I held on the advice of the States Ministry.

The contrast naturally fills me with poignant feelings. However, once again putting my complete trust in your judgement and benevolent intentions towards me, I might be prepared to fall in with your wishes and to absent myself from the State for a period of three or four months in consideration of the fact as emphasized by you namely complications created by the reference to UNO and the plebiscite issue.

There are, however, certain questions arising out of this proposal on which I would venture to make my position clear to you and on which I would be grateful to have your assurance. I hope you will kindly appreciate the necessity of my seeking these assurances. I have to think of the immediate future in the light of my bitter experiences of the last several months and I owe it to myself, my family and my dynasty to procure a clear declaration in respect of these matters:-

1. I should like to be assured that this step is not a prelude to any idea of abdication. I should like to make it clear now that I

cannot entertain the latter idea even for a moment and am fully prepared to take the consequences. I regard such a demand from my Prime Minister and his colleagues as a clear breach of the many understandings on which constitutional arrangements have been based from time to time and a positive act of his disloyalty, treachery and deception.

2. Sheikh Abdullah should be clearly told to stop the campaign of vilification against me and to abandon all activities, both on his part and that of his followers, aimed at securing my abdication. I feel that the sacrifice which I am being called upon to make would be in vain if I continued to be the target of their public or private attacks.

3. There should be a clear assurance of protection of myself and my adherents against any victimization. In this connection, I should like, especially to draw your attention to the facts that have been reported to me about persons having been detained in jail for their failure to sign for my abdication.

4. The question that I should remain out of the State for three or four months for reasons of health, will, I am afraid, not be believed by anybody and is likely to give rise to many misgivings and speculations within and outside the State as:-

  (i) Everybody knows that I am not in such a state of health as would necessitate a long rest outside the State. I have on your advice been recently touring parts of the Jammu Province in the heat of April;

  (ii) For everybody in bad health Kashmir is considered to be the best health resort and it will certainly look strange if I went outside the State giving out that I am doing so for reasons of health.

  (iii) Wherever I take my temporary residence I cannot confine myself to the four walls of the house. I am bound to meet people, who, when they meet me, will never believe that I am staying there for reasons of health;

  (iv) Some other reasons which may be plausible and may also at the same time not compromise my dignity and position, should be given out. The best thing would be that the Government of India should find a suitable position for me in Delhi where my services may be utilized in a fitting manner during the above period of three or four months.

5. It is a matter of paramount necessity that Her Highness should remain with the Yuvaraj in the State during the period of my absence. He is young and impressionable and requires paternal guidance and personal supervision of at least one of his parents. I can see no reason either of political expediency or justice in insisting on the separation of a mother from her only child whom she is seeing after thirteen months of absence abroad. Considerations of humanity alone should suffice to rule out this altogether.

6. My private estates, houses and other property should be protected against the aggressive acts of Sheikh Abdullah's party. They will attempt to take possession of my houses, gardens, lands and other property. The Indian Dominion should guarantee against that act of aggression. While I am there they dare not do these things but in my absence they will attempt this. I have received information that even during the last few days, after I left Jammu for Delhi, encroachments have been made on my lands at Srinagar.

7. No change should be made without my consent in the present arrangements regarding the State Forces or the constitutional position, Prerogatives etc. of the Ruler as now subsisting. Arrangements will continue for me to draw my staff (both State and Private Depts) from amongst Officers of my Forces. Guards mounted by my forces at my Palaces will also continue as at present as per agreement reached vide my letter of 30th August and Mr Menon's reply of 3rd September thereto. I shall also take whatever staff etc. I require with me outside.

8. I should be entitled during my stay in India to suitable strength of military guards wherever I stay.

9. Yuvaraj's safety and protection should be the concern of the Indian Dominion. State and Indian Military should guard his person.

10. Outstanding matters with the States Military, Civil Lists, Hazur Departments etc. should be decided with me immediately.

In conclusion I wish to say that I shall take the final decision on getting assurances from you on the points above mentioned.

With kindest regards,

Yours very sincerely,
Hari Singh

Vallabhbhai Patel to Maharaja Hari Singh

Camp Doon Court
Dehra Dun
23 May 1949

My dear Maharaja Sahib,
Thank you for your letter dated the 6th May 1949.

2. I am very glad to know that Your Highness has reconciled yourself to the proposal which I put forward at my discussion with you. It was with no light heart that I did so. No one can be more cognizant than myself of the attitude which Your Highness has adopted ever since you signed the Instrument of Accession. I am grateful to Your Highness for the spirit of cooperation and understanding which you have always extended to me and also for the kind sentiments which you have expressed. I can assure Your Highness that, before putting forward my proposal, I had, after careful consideration, come to the conclusion that the interests alike of Your Highness, the dynasty and the country demanded the step which you have now agreed to take. I know full well the personal sacrifice involved in it, but, I am sure, along with so many other changes to which Your Highness has accustomed yourself, you will undertake this step also with a sense of duty to your country and in a spirit of calm resignation to the superior dictates of events.

3. Regarding the points which Your Highness has referred to me, I should like to state that the question of Your Highness' abdication does not arise. We have made the position quite plain to Sheikh Mohammad Abdullah, and we hope there will be an end to the public controversies centring round this matter as well as to the derogatory references to Your Highness in the press and on the platform in the State. Your Highness will of course, appreciate that the future constitution of the State would be determined by the duly elected Constituent Assembly. I am afraid, in the absence of any specific instances of victimisation to which Your Highness refers in paragraph 4, it may not be possible for me to give any assurance, but I can tell Your Highness that, if any such instances are brought to our notice, we shall look into them and try to see that justice is done.

4. I appreciate what Your Highness says in regards to the reasons for your remaining outside the State, but I feel that it would be best just to say that Your Highness has decided, after the strain of the last so

many months and continued ill-health, to stay out of the State for a few months. The actual period need not be stated.

5. We have carefully considered the question of Her Highness staying with the Yuvaraj during your absence, but for a variety of reasons, we feel that it would be best, for the present, for her also to stay away for a while. Later, she can certainly visit the Yuvaraj from time to time, and the Yuvaraj can also visit Your Highness and Her Highness occasionally.

6. We would be grateful if Your Highness would let me have a list of the private estates, houses and other property belonging to Your Highness and referred to in para 6 of you letter. On receipt of the list we shall take up the matter with your Ministry. In the mean time, I hope that, with the understanding that has been reached with Sheikh Abdullah on the various controversial issues, he will himself take steps to safeguard Your Highness' property against encroachments. In particular, I hope that the feelings which he entertains for the Yuvaraj will succeed in closing the chapter of the past several months and in introducing a healthy change in the approach of both the Government and the National Conference workers to these and other problems affecting Your Highness and the family personally and the dynasty in general. I hope that no need for a change in the arrangements to which Your Highness has referred in paragraph 7 would arise, but should any such need arise, we would of course consult Your Highness. We would also make necessary arrangements for guarding you during your stay in India, and we take full responsibility for the Yuvaraj's safety and protection.

7. As regards outstanding matters, we have already informed Your Highness separately that your Civil List has been fixed at Rs 15 lakhs, out of which Rs 6 lakhs would be paid by the State and Rs 9 lakhs by the Government of India during the period of the emergency. Out of this sum, Your Highness will have to make allotment to Her Highness and the Yuvaraj. The latter's expenses would, of course, be larger than before on account of his being Regent. I hope Your Highness will agree to make a suitable allowance for him, bearing in mind his needs. I should be glad to know your suggestion in this respect. Similarly, I should welcome Your Highness' proposal regarding Her Highness' allowance. As regards Hazur Departments, Sheikh Sahib has already agreed to our suggestion that an allowance of Rs 5 lakhs should be made to Your Highness for this purpose. A list of items, which will be controlled by Your Highness, and during your absence, by the Yuvaraj

as Regent, has been furnished to Sheikh Sahib, and he has promised
to let us have his comments as soon as possible. After his comments
are received, we shall finalize the whole matter, but in the meantime,
Your Highness can make suitable allocations to major and other heads
of the expenditure on State Departments from out of the allotment of
Rs 5 lakhs.

With kindest regards,

Yours sincerely,
Vallabhbhai Patel

Maharaja Hari Singh to Vallabhbhai Patel

Dehra Dun Camp
1 June 1949

My dear Sardar Patelji,
Kindly accept my best thanks for your letter of 18th May 1949 wherein
you have cleared some points mentioned by me in my letter dated
6th May 1949. I have also received a letter from Mr V.P. Menon
enclosing copy of a letter which the Ministry for States have addressed
to Sheikh Abdullah regarding certain financial issues relating to my
State. This last communication from Mr Menon makes mention of
certain matters which need further consideration before they are
finalized and there are some others about which we must have further
elucidation if misunderstandings and complications are to be avoided
in the future.

2. I am therefore writing to you to ask for your further help which
you have always ungrudgingly given to me, in clearing the way for a
complete understanding between my Government and myself.

3. I am grateful to you for the appreciation you have expressed for
my desire to adjust myself to the changed circumstances and for my
doing so in, what you call, 'a spirit of resignation to the superior
dictates of events.' I must however say that this has been possible for
me only because of my implicit faith in you and because of a feeling
that even when I consider that things don't look very bright at their
face value, you as my friend and guide with your undoubted foresight
have seen a long way ahead and are quite sure that it is all in my best
interest.

4. I am indebted to you for setting at rest all speculations by interested persons about my abdicating and making this position quite clear to Sheikh Abdullah and for telling him that he should stop indulging in such talk and other derogatory language about me. I however feel sure that he will not desist from doing so. In order to undo the mischief that has already been done and prevent rumours which are sure to be spread during my temporary absence from the State, it seems necessary that a statement may be issued by the Ministry for States deprecating all talk of abdication and use of improper and intemperate language about me and the Ruling Family.

5. I hope I shall have your protection in case any Press campaign in favour of my abdication or derogatory to me is again started with or without inspiration from Sheikh Abdullah's party. Frankly speaking, in the light of what has gone before I cannot be certain that the understanding now reached on this point would mark the end of this campaign; hence my concern over this matter. Should any such instances come to my notice I shall immediately draw your kind attention to it and I hope I shall then have the States Ministry's active help in putting a stop to or counteracting it.

6. As regards victimisation, I know that certain persons have been detained because of their sympathy towards me and my dynasty though for purpose of legal formalities and outward appearances, different reasons may exist on paper. Lest it should compromise their own chances or disturb the present understanding reached, I should not like to revive that issue but would only express the hope that such cases would receive the attention of the States Ministry if they come to their notice.

7. In Mr V.P. Menon's letter of 18th May to Sheikh Abdullah a copy of which has been sent to me, it is stated that it will be open to the Indian Government to reduce the strength of the Jammu and Kashmir Forces to such extent as the Indian Army authorities may consider necessary. In this connection I wish to invite attention to my letter of the 30th August 1948 to your address and Mr Menon's reply thereto dated the 30th September 1948. In this correspondence the Government of India accepted the position that I shall remain the Commander-in-Chief of the Jammu and Kashmir Forces and that my position as such shall be fully safeguarded. If, therefore, any change in the strength of Jammu and Kashmir State Forces is ever considered necessary, it should be made after full consultation between General Cariappa and myself and with my formal consent.

8. Regarding the suggestion about Her Highness' stay outside the State for a while it is understood that there is no sort of ban on her entry into the State and if Her Highness acts upon this suggestion and stays out for a while it will not be made the basis of a demand for her longer stay out. I hope you will kindly ensure that the period of her absence from the State is as short as possible.

9. I am surprised, I must confess, to find from the enclosure to Mr Menon's letter referred to above that the Ministry for States have already advised Sheikh Abdullah in regard to my Civil List and have fixed the very inadequate sum of Rs 15,00,000 for all of us i.e., Her Highness, the Yuvaraj and myself. It is a personal matter and I would not like to dwell on it at any great length but I feel that I would not be fair to my family or to myself if I failed to bring to your notice some very significant points in connection with this matter. You will agree that the matter of my Civil List is not a matter that affects my person alone. It has important bearing on the well-being of my son, my wife and a large number of my subjects who are employed in my Private Service. Besides there is the question of maintaining the privilege and prestige of the family and several other important and practical considerations have to be taken into account if a fair and just decision is to be arrived at about this question.

10. The Civil List which was fixed at 23.5 lacs in 1939 is being arbitrarily reduced to 15 lacs. This amount is wholly insufficient to meet the essential expenditure which will be necessitated by me and Her Highness being out of the State and by the Yuvaraj acting as Regent. In all probability three establishments at different places will have to be maintained.

11. In previous years I never insisted upon the Civil List being fixed according to any hard and fast rule of percentage. The Civil List was voluntarily reduced by me when the State Revenue fell, but when the Revenue increased I never demanded any enhancement to it. I merely claimed as much as was necessary to meet my reasonable needs and that has been my main criterion all along.

12. It is important to bear in mind that in 1930 with a view to augment the State income and to make available additional Revenue for the well-being of the People I surrendered my private *Jagirs* of Bhadarwah and Langet which I had inherited from my father (Raja Amar Singhji) and not from the last ruler of the State. The arrangement at that time was that a sum of Rs 8.5 lacs would be included in the Civil List in lieu of my private *Jagir* which comprised some of the

richest and most productive areas of the State. The income from these areas enormously increased after their amalgamation but I never claimed any enhancement on this account. During the last so many years the income from only one of the items of Revenue from my private *Jagir* viz. Bhadarwah and Langet Forests alone has been about 9 lacs a year.

13. Large sums have been spent out of my Privy Purse for giving relief to refugees and other sufferers of present upheaval.

14. I may mention that the Civil List of some Rulers of much smaller States have been more liberally fixed.

15. You have yourself said (vide para 7 of your last letter) that Yuvaraj will obviously require a larger allowance as he will be living more independent life and will therefore require a larger establishment etc. I am afraid that this may not be possible unless the suggested Civil List of 15 lacs is suitably increased.

16. The drastic reduction proposed in the Civil List will entail great suffering for some of my old and loyal servants whom I will have to throw out of employment to reduce expenditure.

17. A further fact to be noticed in this connection is that from S.V. 2001 to 2004 (April 1944 to March 1948) the full amount of the Civil List (at 5% of the total revenue) was not paid. The arrears for that period aggregate to Rs 38,21,673. During these years I had to incur usual expenditure which came to Rs 1,51,72,952 against Rs 1,08,73,051 received from the State as Civil List and *Jagir* compensation thereby leaving net deficit of about 43 lacs to be met from other sources. Of this amount no less than 17,00,000 is due to building contractors who are clamouring for payment. Early steps should be taken for the payment of the arrears to do so that I may be able to clear these liabilities.

18. I should also like to say that I have not received any amount from the State towards my Civil List since Baisakh 2005. Since then I have been meeting expenditure out of my slender private resources and I hope you will concede that in doing so I must have restricted the expenditure to the essential minimum. The expenditure already brought to account during the period Baisakh 2005 to end Chet 2005 comes to Rs 16,41,064. Her Highness has spent Rs 68,169 and the Yuvaraj has spent Rs 41,686 on his Staff and Establishment etc. alone. He was under treatment in America for whole of the year in question and his expenses in America have not yet been booked. In light of all these facts the Civil List should be fixed at least 20 lacs till such times

as the Revenue of the State increases. The allotment of allowances to Her Highness and the Yuvaraj would depend on the allotment for my Civil List. I shall let you know my views on this after I hear from you about your final decision on the question of the Civil List.

19. With reference to para of your letter I am sending herewith list of my private estates etc. I hope you will now settle as quickly as possible with Sheikh Abdullah the question of protection of these properties from encroachments. I am also sending herewith a list of Privileges and Amenities which I and the Ruling Family have been enjoying and which will have to continue. I thought I would place the list on record so that there is no unnecessary trouble later.

20. I must apologise for this very long letter inflicting on you so many details regarding the points involved but as the decisions that are now being taken are of a very radical character and have very far reaching effect and should be taken after full appreciation of the reasons and facts involved, I thought I must apprise you of all the facts and figures relating to the matters under consideration.

Thanking you again for your kind thoughts and your solicitude for me and my family.

With kind regards,

Yours very sincerely,
Hari Singh

Vallabhbhai Patel to Maharaja Hari Singh
Camp Doon Court, Dehra Dun
9 June 1949

My dear Maharaja Sahib,
I have received Your Highness' letter of the 1st June 1949, in which you have raised certain points arising out of our recent discussions.

2. Your Highness has asked that, in order to prevent further speculation and propaganda, a statement should be issued by the Ministry of States deprecating all talk of abdication and the use of improper and intemperate language against Your Highness and the Ruling Family. As Your Highness knows, I am most anxious, and will do all in my power, to prevent such propaganda; but a statement of the kind suggested by Your Highness would at the present juncture do more harm than good. An assurance has been received from Sheikh Abdullah that he considers the past controversy a closed chapter and

does not wish to raise it again. I suggest therefore that we may leave matters alone for the present.

3. As regards the Jammu and Kashmir State Forces the present position is that the Government of India have assumed the entire operational, administrative and organizational control over these forces and also the liability to meet all expenditure in connection with these Forces. Your Highness may well leave it to the discretion of the Government of India to decide about the strength of these Forces, and to undertake such consultation with you as they may consider necessary.

4. Regarding the point raised about Her Highness, V. P. Menon has already had a discussion with Her Highness and yourself and it has been agreed now that Her Highness will not remain with the Yuvaraj during this period.

5. As regards Your Highness' privy purse, it is true that the amount fixed for Your Highness is less than that fixed for the Rulers of similar status; but we have to take into account the grave financial position of the State. At the present time it will not be right for the Government of India to enhance this amount or for Your Highness to ask for it.

6. Your Highness has mentioned that, for the period from April 1944 to March 1948, a sum of Rs 38 lacs is due to Your Highness as arrears of privy purse. Here also I feel doubtful whether in the grave financial position in which the State finds itself at present, it is possible for its finances to pay this sum. I shall, however, consider whether I can do anything to meet Your Highness' wishes in this direction.

7. The Government of India accept Your Highness' list of private property. Menon would, however, go to Srinagar to settle any details arising from it. As regards Your Highness' personal privileges and perquisites, Your Highness would continue to enjoy it as you are the Ruler of Kashmir State, even while you are away from it.

8. I trust I have answered the points raised by Your Highness. We are still in a period of conflict and I am no less aware than Your Highness that it has not been possible to meet Your Highness wishes as fully as I should have liked, but we have to make a realistic approach in tackling the problems before us, and in a situation like the present compromises are inevitable. In your own interests no less than in the interests of the State, these compromises have to be accepted in a spirit of goodwill and cooperation.

Yours sincerely,
Vallabhbhai Patel

Maharaja Hari Singh to K.N. Katju

Poona
29 June 1952

Dear Dr Katju,

With reference to the statements made by the Prime Minister of India at a recent Press Conference and in the House of the People regarding the decisions taken by the Constituent Assembly of the State of Jammu and Kashmir with respect to the Headship of the State in the proposed Constitution which vitally affects my position and that of my dynasty. I am constrained to communicate to you my feelings in the matter.

2. The statement regarding the attitude of the Government of India in this matter seems to have been arrived at without regard to the assurances repeatedly given to me that nothing would be done in the matter unless my interests and the interests of my dynasty were effectively secured by appropriate agreement.

3. I must confess that the reported attitude of the Government of India ignores integral aspects of the question which affect me and my dynasty and is not in conformity with the assurances and the understanding between the Government of India and myself when at the insistent advice of the Government of India accompanied by their definite assurances I permitted the Yuvaraj to sign the Proclamation setting up the Constituent Assembly.

4. The Ministry for State is fully aware of the circumstances and the political context in which I agreed to raise the ban put by me on the Yuvaraj from signing the Proclamation setting up the Constituent Assembly. At the time of the setting up of the Constituent Assembly I had certain apprehensions which I communicated to the then Minister for States, Shri Gopalaswami Ayyangar. In his letter dated the 5th April 1951 in reply to my letter the Minister for States (Shri Gopalaswami Ayyangar) stated: 'On neither of the two matters about which I can understand your entertaining apprehensions, namely the continuance of the accession of the Jammu and Kashmir State or part thereof to India and the connection of the Headship of the State with your dynasty no final decision could be taken by the Constituent Assembly to be convened. They are essential matters which could be decided only as a matter of agreement between the Government of India and Parliament on the one side and the Government of Jammu and Kashmir State, Constituent Assembly or Legislature on the other. The Government of India will, no doubt, at the proper time take the

decision on these matters which, I need hardly assure you, would be essentially just from the standpoint both from dynasty and the people of the State. You have obviously to put your trust in the people of the State and the Government of India in respect of this matter. I hope, therefore, you will immediately lift the ban which you have placed on Shri Yuvaraj affixing his signature to the Proclamation and which naturally has placed him in great embarrassment.'

5. It was on this assurance and promise of the Government of India through the Minister for States that I authorized the Yuvaraj to affix his signature to the Proclamation setting up the Constituent Assembly.

6. On the basis of such assurance and promise I all the while believed that the question of the connection of the Headship of the State with my dynasty will not be dealt with by the Constituent Assembly without an agreement between the Government of India and Parliament on the one side and the Government of Jammu and Kashmir on the other. I believed that such an agreement would make adequate and effective provision for the Privy Purse and all other matters effectively securing my interests, rights and privileges and those of dynasty.

7. With this background you will appreciate with what feeling of surprise and resentment I read the following passage in the report of the Press Conference held by the Prime Minister on 21st June 1952 as appearing in the *Times of India*.:-

'In his first public reference to the Kashmir Constituent Assembly's decisions to abolish hereditary rulership and have an elected head, Mr Nehru said that the principle of abolishing dynastic rule in Kashmir had been stated repeatedly by the Kashmir Government and the Government of India had accepted it. The question that arose now was what to do in the present circumstances, so that it may be in keeping with the Indian Constitution and at the same time give effect to the wishes of the people of Kashmir.'

8. The Ministry of States is fully aware of the circumstances under which I acceded to the Dominion of India on 26th October 1947 and the circumstances and the reasons and the purposes for which I agreed to stay out of the State and appoint the Yuvaraj as the Regent. Fully

appreciating the political situation in the context and having regard to the larger interests of the State as well as of India in the larger context, I agreed to and carried out the suggestions made by the Government of India from time to time, with a view to create a situation which would secure full accession of the State of Jammu and Kashmir to the Indian Union and would facilitate the process of complete integration of the State of Jammu and Kashmir with India. Fully appreciating the internal situation in the State and the necessity of strengthening politically the hands of the Government of India at the UNO and to facilitate a favourable verdict in case plebiscite is taken in the State I readily cooperated with the Government of India in all the necessary steps which were required to be taken to achieve the double object on the assurances given by the Government of India from time to time that in the ultimate decision my interests and the interests of my dynasty would be safeguarded while giving effect to the wishes of the people of the State. Realizing the necessity of establishing responsible Government to meet the criticism at the UNO to prepare a ground for a favourable plebiscite to move with the progressive trends and to establish a Government in accordance with the wishes of the people and to enable the people of Jammu and Kashmir to draw up their own Constitution. I have all the while followed the policy and the suggestions made by the Government of India, who were mostly instrumental in my decision for the establishment of responsible Government in the State and the Constituent Assembly to achieve the desired objects. I did not stick to the legal aspects of the various steps which were taken, I realized that the occasion was not for indulging in legal niceties, but for facing the inevitable pressure of events and making adjustments accordingly.

9. Having regard to the provision contained in Article 370 of the Constitution, I naturally assumed that my Headship of the State could not be altered unilaterally by the Constituent Assembly without amending the said Article, and without making adequate provisions for my Privy Purse and other rights and privileges in the Constitution itself. I feel that the significance of the fundamental law of the Union of which the State of Jammu and Kashmir is an integral part is not fully appreciated by the Constituent Assembly. I am greatly worried as I feel that the attitude disclosed renders the assurances and promises of the Government and even the provision of the Constitution of very little significance.

10. I wonder if it is realized that implementing the reported decision would mean giving a go by not only to the promises and assurances given to me but also to a specific provision of the Constitution of India.

11. May I therefore have a definite assurance and a clear statement as to how my rights are to be safeguarded.

Yours sincerely,
Hari Singh

Jawaharlal Nehru to Maharaja Hari Singh

New Delhi
5 July 1952

Dear Maharaja Sahib,
Our Minister of States, Dr Katju, has shown me your letter of the 29th June 1952 which you sent him.

In this letter you refer to certain statements made by me at a Press Conference and in the House of the People and also to assurances given to you by or on behalf of the Government of India. At the end of the letter you ask for a definite assurance and a clear statement as to how your rights are to be safeguarded.

The Minister of States will, no doubt, reply to your letter. But as this letter of yours has been occasioned chiefly by what I said, I think that I should also write to you and make it clear what our basic position is in this matter.

Your are, no doubt, aware that the whole Constitution of India is based on and is derived from the people of India. In the final analysis, it is the people and their wishes that count and all private and personal interests must give way to the larger interests of the people. In so far as the old States are concerned, it was our position, repeatedly stated, that, wherever necessary, the wishes of their people will be consulted and will prevail. This was in regard to the accession to India. In the great majority of these States the wishes of the people were well known and obvious and, therefore no question arose of a separate consultation with them. In regard to the Jammu and Kashmir State, we felt that the people there would prefer accession to India, but the matter was delicate and not beyond dispute. Hence, even before Partition, and when large numbers of other States were acceding to

India, we did not press for the accession of Jammu and Kashmir State. We suggested that this matter should be considered at a later stage when the people's wishes could be ascertained in some form or other. Our then suggestion was that some kind of a Constituent Assembly might be constituted in Jammu and Kashmir State to decide the question of accession as well as other questions. Meanwhile Standstill Agreements were proposed.

On the invasion of the State by tribal raiders and others late in October 1947, a crisis arose there. At the time of that crisis you left Srinagar at the dead of night for Jammu. Many of your officers followed your example and the State was left without leadership or means of defence, in so far as official authority was concerned. You asked us then for help and proposed accession of the State to India so that that help could be more easily given. At the same time the leading popular organization of the State, the National Conference, also sent us an urgent request for help in their hour of danger. It was suggested by them also that the State should accede to India. After long and anxious consideration we accepted these requests and took immediate steps to tender assistance to the people of Kashmir against the ruthless invaders who were bringing arson, loot and murder in their train. In accepting accession, however, we repeated our policy that the wishes of the people must prevail in the end. It was, indeed because your request had been powerfully supported by the National Conference, representing the people of Kashmir, that we decided to accept accession. Nevertheless, we stated even at that moment that the people of Jammu and Kashmir State would finally decide the fate of their State.

War developed in the State and India became more and more involved in it. There was danger of this war spreading to other areas. In order to avoid this danger and in pursuance of our general policy to pursue peaceful methods, we referred this matter to the United Nations. Again we laid stress on our policy and our desire that the people of Kashmir should decide about their future, whenever a suitable opportunity for this was given to them.

In the Security Council of the United Nations, it was later proposed that a plebiscite should be held in the State after a number of other steps had been taken and conditions created for the proper holding of such a plebiscite. We accepted that resolution. That has been our position in the Security Council ever since. The plebiscite has been delayed because of Pakistan's insistence on certain conditions which we could not agree to. The matter is still pending before the United Nations where our position has been clearly stated on many occasions.

You will observe that in this basic picture of the crisis of Kashmir you do not come in at all. The fact that emerges is that the people of Kashmir must decide their own future. We have pledged ourselves to this not only in the Security Council but directly to the people of Jammu and Kashmir State. If, as a result of the plebiscite, it was decided that Kashmir should not accede to India, we would naturally have to accept that decision. And, in that event, it is clear that your personal interests in the State would automatically disappear. If the people of Kashmir decided in favour of India, as we hoped and believed they would, then also it would be for them to say what, if any your position should be in future. India went to the help of Kashmir on the invitation of the people of Kashmir. We did not go there, as Pakistan falsely asserts, as an invading army to suppress the people. We do not propose to continue there for a day when we are no longer wanted by the people of the State.

It has been our policy all over India to settle the problems of the old States peacefully and with goodwill and the consent of the parties concerned. We were fortunate to gain that consent in a very large number of cases and so the radical changes that were brought about were done in a spirit of cooperation. But it is always to be remembered that those changes were necessitated by the fierce pressure of changing time and the demands of a revolutionary situation. Those changes would have taken place, whether consent came or did not come, because the will of the people has to prevail and no vested interests could come in its way. The Government of India softened the change and made generous settlement with the Princes. But the main thing was the demand from people and the vital necessity of that change. It was because you did not sense the spirit of the times and the revolutionary changes that were coming over India and the world that you and your then advisors pursued a mistaken policy that led to the grievous development of subsequent days. You will remember how you discarded our advice, repeatedly given in 1946 and 1947. We saw a situation developing there which was full of danger. But your advisors then led you along a wrong path, which undoubtedly, would have led to complete disaster for you and your dynasty if the Government of India had not come to your help. They came to your help, but on that major condition that the people's will must prevail.

It surprises me that even after all these terrible experiences you still fail to understand the true nature of events in Jammu and Kashmir State, in India and the world. Those Princes in India who had some understanding of these events and the new forces at work, adapted themselves to them and thereby, though they lost power and authority, they secured an honourable place for themselves. Kashmir was rent by war in which India poured her blood and treasure. The people of Kashmir suffered greatly. In this crisis, you still imagined that your personal claim had first importance. The Government of India sought to help you in spite of you, but they had to face on many occasions difficulty and obstruction from you. You refer to your permitting the Yuvaraj to sign the Proclamation setting up the Constituent Assembly. Even in doing so you delayed matters considerably and obstructed, to some extent, the natural course of events. You did not appreciate then, as you do not seem to appreciate now, that Constituent Assemblies do not ultimately derive their authority from a Ruler but base their sanctions on the People. Certain forms are observed and it is desirable to observe them where possible. But if those forms are not available, they are done away with and matters take their course. The Constituent Assembly would have met whether you agreed to it or not.

In view of the assurances given by us to the United Nations we made it clear that we would not consider a decision of the Constituent Assembly as binding upon us, if it went against those assurances. Even so, we could not come in the way of the Constituent Assembly in deciding in regard to accession or other matters. Indeed, it was made clear that they had full authority, derived from the people to draw up their internal Constitution. Naturally that Constitution had to be in keeping with the Constitution of India, if the accession to India was to endure.

In your letter to Dr Katju you refer repeatedly to what you consider your rights and the rights of your dynasty. There is little mention in this letter of the rights of the people. That is the basic difference between your outlook and that of the Government of India. We have tried here and elsewhere to adjust rights, as far as possible but there can be no doubt that no right can prevail if it comes in conflict with the right of the people. For our part we would welcome any decision taken by the people of the Jammu and Kashmir State which acknowledges any right of yours but it would be against our policy as well as against the dominating facts of the situation, for us to consider your rights as overriding public rights. Indeed, whatever your theoretical position might be, you have no authority of position left now to influence the future of Kashmir. Because of various considerations, however, we have tried to maintain for you an honourable position, though that is devoid of authority. But if you claim rights which in reality you do not possess and if you come in the way of changes which are inevitable, then even that formal place that you occupy will be endangered. That place would ultimately be made secure only if you had the confidence and the affection of your people. Since you have lost this confidence and affection, the right also goes.

You will have appreciated that the people of Kashmir have gone through fire and suffering during these past four and a half years. I have seen no evidence of any great sympathy on your part for these people, no desire to help them in their distress. Kashmir became an international problem and the people there lived in fear and doubt, facing day-to-day perils, but you only laid stress from time to time on what you called your rights and privileges, on your Privy Purse and the like. You can imagine that this did not enhance your prestige or lead your people towards you.

You ask for a definite assurance and a clear statement as to how your rights are to be safeguarded. The only assurance I can give you is that the first place will be given always to the rights of the people and to the wishes of the people. If you fall in with those rights and wishes, then we shall endeavour to help you to the best of our ability. If you do not do so, then events will take their natural course.

Yours sincerely,
Jawaharlal Nehru

K.N. Katju to Maharaja Hari Singh

New Delhi
30 July 1952

My dear Maharaja Sahib,
Some weeks ago, I received your letter and I should like to apologise for not acknowledging it formally earlier, but I thought it was not necessary for me to write forthwith because I understood that the Prime Minister had already sent you a fairly long letter with reference

to the points to which you referred.

During the last few weeks, I have had the pleasure of discussing the whole situation in Jammu and Kashmir with Shri Yuvarajji, in all its aspects. Three days ago on his way to Bombay, he very kindly came again and, in the course of our conversation with regard to the statement made by the Prime Minister in Parliament the other day, on the recent negotiations. I expressed to him my own view on the matter and I requested him to communicate the same to you. You are fully aware of the intricacies of the present situation. At the present moment the relations between India and Jammu and Kashmir are regulated by Article 370 of the Indian Constitution and we can only move within that ambit.

It is not necessary for me to enlarge upon this topic at any great length. I am sure that you will of your own wisdom give due weight to all the implications of the present position and act in the interests both of your family and the people of Kashmir.

With kind regards,

I am,
Yours sincerely,
K. N. Katju

Maharaja Hari Singh to K.N. Katju

Poona
8 August 1952

My dear Dr Katju,
Thanks for your letter of 30th July.

I must confess I have looked in vain in this and Honourable Prime Minister's letter for a reply to the points I raised. The Honourable Prime Minister in his letter dated 5th July had stated that you would reply to my letter. In your letter you say that you did not think it necessary for you to write because the Honourable Prime Minister had already sent to me a fairly long letter with reference to the points I had referred to.

Honourable Prime Minister's letter so far I can see just gives us the ideals that we may have in view and nobody can seriously contest the theories he has referred to. But I have to point out that even theories must have reference to facts if they are to be worked to the best of advantage of those concerned. If the people's will is to prevail we have to have the people first and know what their will is of course, by suitable democratic methods. We have therefore to apply and work these theories not with a view to satisfying certain political exigencies but to meet the freely expressed genuine will of the people as a whole, and even so the method of fulfilling the will of the people has to be one of evolution if the object is to be achieved. It cannot be denied that in most other spheres the Government of India is working on this principle. The hon'ble Prime Minister seems mainly to rely on the principle that the present time are against the continuance of hereditary Rulership in any form even when it is combined with a democratic constitution wherein the will of the people finds expression is recognized and fully worked. This view is inconsistent with the recognition of hereditary Rajpramukhs in the B Class States and even hereditary Rulers in the C Class ones. It is not I hope the object of the Government of India to make an exception in the case of the Jammu and Kashmir State. Hereditary Rule can stay with advantage in a completely democratic setup, as we know so well is the case in the UK with which we are a member of the Commonwealth and the hereditary Ruler whereof we have accepted as the head of the comity of nations in the Commonwealth.

We could certainly think and justify a complete wiping out of the hereditary Rule only when the clearly expressed will of the people expressed in a free democratic manner required it. I would suggest the Government of India seriously consider if this condition does really exist or what they imagine is the will of the people is only the demand of a section of the people led by those whom for political exigencies we have decided to support.

Curiously enough, I referred to Article 370 of the Constitution of India and you have also referred to the same. You don't seriously suggest that what is now being done with regard to the Jammu and Kashmir State in relation to the Government of India is in consonance with Article 370. It cannot be gainsaid that the Article 370 will have to be amended to fit in with the scheme agreed to by and between Hon'ble Prime Minister and Sheikh Abdullah.

Yuvaraj saw me some days ago. Just as I am not interfering with him in any manner as he is his own master and is old enough to decide as to his future I am entitled to believe that if he held a view as a result of this conversation with you it does not preclude me from thinking independently. From his conversation with you I do not see how the Government of India can hold the views they do in relation to myself except on grounds of expediency.

If I understand the last sentence of your letter correctly it means that I should have the wisdom to see how best I can fit in with the position the Government of India find themselves in with UNO on one hand and Sheikh Abdullah on the other and not be a spoke in the wheel. Realizing what was in the offing my Secretary under my direction wrote to Mr Venkatachar in response to the letters and telephonic message giving the terms on which I was prepared to leave the field open to the Government of India. These terms were not newly set and had been the subject of talk with your predecessor in office and you will find if you enquire from the quarter mentioned that the only point on which the Government of India had any difficulty in meeting my wishes was the quantum of the Privy Purse to be allowed jointly to me and the Yuvaraj.

I am preparing a full representation and expect to send it within the next few days. In the meantime I thought I might write to tell you of my reaction to your letter.

I have written the letter in the same frank spirit in which the Honourable Prime Minister and you have written to me and I trust it will not be taken amiss.

I did not write to the Honourable Prime Minister in reply to his letter as I was waiting for yours.

With kindest regards,

Yours sincerely,
Hari Singh

Note by Jawaharlal Nehru to Mehr Chand Mahajan
26 October 1947

The Defence Committee of the Cabinet of the Government of India considered the situation in Kashmir and the request made by the Government of Jammu and Kashmir State for help against the raiders who had entered their territory and caused great loss. The suggestion that the Kashmir State should accede to the Indian Union was also considered. The Committee came to the following conclusions, which were subsequently confirmed by the Cabinet:-

(1) In view of the request made by the Kashmir Government for help against raiders who have entered their territory,

the Government of India have decided to give such help. In furtherance of this decision they are sending troops by air tomorrow morning to Srinagar. They intend reinforcing these troops by air as well as by the land route via Jammu, as the defence of Kashmir has become their responsibility now and they intend to discharge it to the best of their ability;

(2) His Highness, the Maharaja, in accordance with his wishes and the wishes of a large number of his people, will agree to Jammu and Kashmir State acceding to the Indian Union. The Government of India will accept this accession provisionally subject to their declared policy that such matters should be finalized in accordance with the will of the people. Any reference to the people can only take place when law and order have been fully established;

(3) H.H. the Maharaja will invite Sheikh Mohammad Abdullah to form an Interim Government after the Mysore pattern.

Jawaharlal Nehru to Mehr Chand Mahajan

New Delhi
26 October 1947

My dear Mr Mahajan,

I gave you a hurried note today just before you left. I have not even got a copy of it. I have therefore drafted a slightly fuller note and I am enclosing it. There is no essential difference between this and the previous note.

I think, it is important for Sheikh Mohammad Abdullah to go to Srinagar immediately as the situation there requires urgent handing and his presence will be helpful. I am suggesting to him therefore to go straight to Srinagar tomorrow morning. He will come to Jammu whenever the Maharaja so desires.

We have decided to send more troops to Srinagar tomorrow as at first intended. Probably, we shall be able to send 400 by air tomorrow I am quite sure that our troops will render a good account of themselves. Apart from other officers we are sending one of our senior and experienced officers, namely Brigadier Hiralal Atal to accompany the troops. He knows Kashmir and his presence ought to be of great help.

Yours sincerely,
Jawaharlal Nehru

Jawaharlal Nehru to Mehr Chand Mahajan

New Delhi
27 October 1947

My dear Mr Mahajan,
Thank you for your letter. I am glad indeed that the Maharaja Sahib has signed the Instrument of Accession and the Standstill Agreement, also that he has invited Sheikh Abdullah to form an Interim Government. I am sure this is a wise decision which will do good to Kashmir and to India. I hope that this decision will be given effect to in a spirit of the fullest trust and cooperation.

2. I am writing to His Highness separately and as, no doubt, you will see that letter, I shall not repeat it here.

3. We have decided for the present to issue to the press only the letter of the Maharaja to the Governor-General and the Governor-General's reply. These two state the facts clearly and briefly. Tomorrow your statement will be issued. No further information has been given to the press at present. We shall decide about this from day to day.

4. I am sending my secretary, Dwarknath Kachru, to Srinagar with these letters. He will remain there for some days and return when he can. It is my own wish to visit Srinagar for a day. But just at present it is impossible for me to leave Delhi. As soon as I can manage it, I shall go there.

Yours sincerely,
Jawaharlal Nehru

Jawaharlal Nehru to Maharaja Hari Singh

New Delhi
27 October 1947

My dear Maharaja Sahib,
Shri V. P. Menon returned from Jammu this evening and informed

me of his talks there. He gave me the Instrument of Accession and the Standstill Agreement which you had signed, and I saw also your letter to the Governor-General of India. Allow me to congratulate you on the wise decisions that you have taken. I earnestly hope that they will lead not only to the effective protection of the Kashmir State in the present, but also to the freedom and well-being of Kashmir and India as a whole.

2. I am sending you separately the Governor-General's reply to your letter. As you know, we sent Indian Army troops by air to Srinagar today. The decision to send them was made yesterday afternoon. Our resources in aircraft are limited. Nevertheless, we strained every nerve and got all the available planes and sent a considerable body of men to Srinagar today. I must express my great satisfaction at the manner in which this difficult piece of organizational work was done at this end. It involved working hard nearly the whole night. Soon after arrival in Srinagar the troops proceeded on the Baramulla Road and came in contact with the enemy raiders and held them at Baramulla. To have been transported from Delhi to Srinagar and to be in action within a few hours has been a remarkable achievement.

3. Tomorrow morning we shall send more troops by air and we propose to continue sending reinforcements by air and road. By road we would like to send them to Jammu, but we are not quite clear about the state of the road and I suggest that every effort might be made to put this road in proper conditions within the next two or three days. This road is going to be the chief life line for our troops and for supplies. It is essential and urgent, therefore, that the road be in good condition and the river that has to be crossed should be bridged. Naturally, there is no time for any permanent arrangements. Something should be done temporarily to make the road and the river passable.

4. I trust that there are enough motor vehicles in Jammu to take our troops and supplies to Srinagar from Jammu whenever necessary. Motor transport should also be made available to our troops in Srinagar. It is impossible to send it there. We shall try, of course, to send petrol.

5. It is our intention to use some aeroplanes in the Valley. For this it is necessary to have some kind of aviation petrol depot in Srinagar. We shall try to send the aviation petrol there.

6. I am sorry we have been unable to send relief to the pockets of Kashmir State troops which have been isolated in Jammu Province.

We felt that we must use every aircraft available for transport of troops to Srinagar. Tomorrow also we want to use every plane for troop transport. Day after tomorrow we shall endeavour to send food supplies to these isolated pockets in Jammu Province.

7. The arrival of our troops in Srinagar undoubtedly saved the situation at the very last moment. Probably, a day or two's delay would have been fatal. But the task is still very difficult and we have to put all our strength and energy into it. We propose to do so.

8. The way the people of Kashmir, Muslim, Hindu and Sikh, are facing the situation and preparing to defend their country is most heartening. I trust that in this defence we shall give a demonstration to all India and to the world how we can function unitedly and in a non-communal way in Kashmir. In this way this terrible crisis in Kashmir may well lead to a healing of the deep wounds which India has suffered in recent months.

Yours sincerely,
Jawaharlal Nehru

Maharaja Hari Singh to Lord Mountbatten

Jammu
26 October 1947

My dear Lord Mountbatten,
I have to inform Your Excellency that a grave emergency has arisen in my State and request immediate assistance of your Government.

As Your Excellency is aware the State of Jammu and Kashmir has not acceded to either the Dominion of India or to Pakistan. Geographically my State is (a) contiguous to both the Dominions. It has vital economical and cultural links with both of them. Besides my State has a common boundary with the Soviet Republic and China. In their external relations the Dominion of India and Pakistan cannot ignore this fact.

I wanted to take time to decide to which Dominion I should accede or whether it is not in the best interest of both the Dominions and my State to stand independent of course with friendly and cordial relations with both.

I accordingly approached the Dominions of India and Pakistan to enter into a Standstill Agreement with my State. The Pakistan

Government accepted this arrangement. The Dominion of India desired further discussion with representatives of my Government. I could not arrange this in view of the developments indicated below. In fact, the Pakistan Government under the Standstill Agreement are operating Post and Telegraph system inside the State.

Though we have got a Standstill Agreement with the Pakistan Government, that Government permitted steady and increasing strangulation of supplies like food, salt and petrol to my State.

Afridis, soldiers in plain clothes, and desperadoes, with modern weapons, have been allowed to infilter into the State at first in Poonch area, then in Sialkot and finally in a mass in the area adjoining Hazara district on the Ramkote side. The result has been that the limited number of troops at the disposal of the State had to be dispersed and thus had to face the enemy at several points simultaneously that it has become difficult to stop the wanton destruction of life and property and looting. The Mahora Power House which supplies the electric current to the whole of Srinagar has been burnt. The number of women who have been kidnapped and raped makes my heart bleed. The wild forces thus let loose on the State are marching on with the aim of capturing Srinagar, the summer capital of my Government as a first step to overrunning the whole State.

The mass infiltration of tribesmen drawn from the distant areas of the NWF Province coming regularly in motor trucks using Mansehra-Muzaffarabad road and fully armed with up to date weapons cannot possibly be done without the knowledge of the Provincial Government of the NWF Province and the Government of Pakistan. Inspite of repeated appeals made by my Government no attempt has been made to check these raiders or stop them from coming to my State. In fact, both the Pakistan Radio and Press has reported these occurrences. The Pakistan Radio even put out a story that a Provisional Government has been set up in Kashmir. The people of my State both Muslims and non-Muslims generally have taken no part at all.

With the conditions obtaining at present in my State and the great emergency of the situation as it exists I have no option but to ask for help from the Indian Dominion. Naturally, they cannot send the help asked for by me without my State acceding to the Dominion of India. I have accordingly decided to do so and I attach the Instrument of Accession for acceptance by your Government. The other alternative is to leave my State and my people to free-booters. On this basis no civilized Government can exist or be maintained. This alternative I will never allow to happen so long as I am the Ruler of the State and

I have life to defend my country.

I may also inform Your Excellency's Government that it is my intention to at once set up an Interim Government and ask Sheikh Abdullah to carry the responsibilities in this emergency with my Prime Minister.

If my State has to be saved immediate assistance must be available at Srinagar. Mr Menon is fully aware of the situation and he will explain to you if further explanation is needed.

In haste and with kindest regards,

Yours sincerely,
Hari Singh

Lord Mountbatten to Maharaja Hari Singh

New Delhi
27 October 1947

My dear Maharaja Sahib,

Your Highness's letter dated the 26th October has been delivered to me by Mr V. P. Menon. In the special circumstances mentioned by Your Highness, my Government have decided to accept the accession of Kashmir State to the Dominion of India. Consistently, with their policy that, in the case of any State where the issue of accession has been the subject of dispute, the question of accession should be decided in accordance with the wishes of the people of the State, it is my Government's wish that as soon as law and order have been restored in Kashmir and her soil cleared of the invader, the question of the State's accession should be settled by a reference to the people. Meanwhile, in response to Your Highness's appeal for military aid, action has been taken today to send troops of Indian Army to Kashmir to help your own forces to defend your territory and to protect the lives, property and honour of your people.

My Government and I note with satisfaction that Your Highness has decided to invite Sheikh Abdullah to form an Interim Government to work with your Prime Minister.

With kind regards,

I remain
Yours very sincerely,
Mountbatten of Burma

N. Gopalaswami Ayyangar to Maharaja Hari Singh

New Delhi
24 December 1947

My dear Maharaja Sahib,
I am most grateful to Your Highness for your letter of the 17th December. We have given anxious consideration to all the points mentioned in that letter and during the last two days we have had the advantage of further discussion of several of those points with Sheikh Abdullah.

2. I have set out below our considered conclusions. In our opinion they are in the best interests of the Jammu and Kashmir State, its Ruler and its people. I earnestly hope that you will find yourself able to accept and give effect to all of them.

3. The Government of India do not desire that you should deviate from the Mysore model except in respect of matters which are considered minor and which are necessitated by the different conditions, which ordinarily, and particularly now, prevail in Kashmir. For the Interim Government which you are anxious to set up immediately, the model should undoubtedly be the Mysore one but, in adopting that model to the present situation in your State, its peculiar conditions and the provisions of its existing constitution deserve to be taken into account. These have been kept fully in view by us.

4. You have laid stress on the reservation of subjects listed in Schedule II of the Mysore Proclamation dated 24th of September 1947 as being its most important essential. Most of the items in this schedule are reserved matters under the Jammu and Kashmir Constitution Act. Items 1, 2 and 4 are reserved from the cognizance of the Praja Sabha under Section 24 of the Jammu and Kashmir Constitution Act, 1896, though the description is not identical. They can be included in the list of subjects in the administration of which you are not bound to obtain the advice of your ministers. The powers of the Ruler under item 3 in regard to the High Court are to be found in Section 48 and 49 of that Act. In addition, similar powers are reserved to the Ruler in Section 71 as regards the Board of Judicial Advisers. The Ruler's powers to summon and dissolve the Legislature (item 6 of the Mysore model) are provided for in Section 15 of the Act. The residuary and emergency powers (item 8 of the Mysore

Schedule) are reserved to the Ruler under Sections 4 and 5 of the Jammu and Kashmir Act. The only matters in the Mysore Schedule which do not find specific mention in the Jammu and Kashmir Act are:

    a)   protection of legitimate interests of minorities; and

    b)   superintendence, direction and control of elections.

(a) may be reserved in the Proclamation to issue. It seems unnecessary to reserve (b) also. The matter referred to therein is one which could well be left to the Council of Ministers.

5. The Interim Ministry will, as suggested in your letter function as a Cabinet with a Prime Minister at its Head, and with such number of other Ministers as may be fixed by you in accordance with the provisions of Section 6 of the Constitution Act.

6. There may be a Dewan in addition to the Council of Ministers. It is desirable that he should have the right to attend meetings of the Cabinet, so that he might be closely associated with the work of the Cabinet, and might function as an effective Liaison Officer between the Cabinet and the Ruler, interpreting the one to the other and aiding and advising the Ruler in the transaction of business connected with reserved subjects. Not only does Section 6 of the Constitution Act require that the Prime Minister should preside over the Council of Ministers, but it is on the merits essential that he should do so. To direct that a person other than the Prime Minister should preside over the Cabinet would not make for that perfect understanding and intimate association between the Ruler and his Prime Minister, which are so essential for efficiency of administration.

7. I agree entirely that the person to be selected for the post of Dewan should be a man who enjoys your full confidence. It is, however, at the same time desirable that man should not be one to whom the leader of the Government has any violent objection. The two have to get on with cordiality and good understanding if Your Highness' Government of the State is to achieve the maximum beneficial results for the people that it ought to achieve. There can be no question of anybody attempting to sabotage your selection of the proper man for the Dewan's post. I am in a position to assure you that Sheikh Abdullah himself is only too anxious to have, as liaison between him and you, a Dewan who enjoys your fullest confidence, so that his relations with you might be of the smoothest possible description.

Should Yours Highness so desire, I shall be glad to be of assistance in selecting a Dewan who will be the best possible choice from all points of view.

8. We and in 'we' I include myself, Pandit Jawaharlal Nehru and Sardar Vallabhbhai Patel are convinced that it is not possible for Sheikh Abdullah and Mr Mehr Chand Mahajan to work together in the same Government hereafter and that it is best in the circumstances that Mr Mahajan should be allowed to terminate his present connection with the State. I have already informed you that I have good reason to think that Mr Mahajan would probably himself be glad to be relieved from the embarrassment of Your Highness asking him to stay on in the State.

9. In ordinary circumstances I should certainly have agreed in your view that six Ministers should be adequate for a State like Kashmir. The State is, however, in great turmoil. The invader has to be expelled, rebellion has to be quelled, law and order have to be established and normal economic life revived. For a considerable time to come, the burden of Government in Kashmir will be much heavier than in ordinary times. I have discussed this question with Sheikh Abdullah. He considers that there is more than enough work for each of 12 or 14 Ministers and he urges that this number need not scare anybody, as the salaries that will be taken by them will be very much smaller than the salaries you have been paying your Ministers hitherto the pitch of the salaries is not wholly relevant in this connection. It is desirable to avoid a crowd of Ministers. Responsibility will get too scattered and unity of policy and close collaboration in administration might not be fully achieved if the number of Ministers is too large. Taking all circumstances into consideration, I should recommend for the Interim Government, which will function only till the new Constitution is fashioned and comes into force, a strength of 9 Ministers. This would incidentally provide room for adequate representation, in the Ministry of Minorities and the different areas of the State. On this latter matter, namely, representation of Minorities and province, Sheikh Abdullah is as keen as you yourself are. His immediate object is so to constitute his Government that he will be able to rally to his support the maximum proportion of the population, especially in view of the threatened plebiscite.

10. On the question of the Army I thought I had made it clear to Your Highness that there was no need to fix proportions for the recruitment of the different communities in the Army. I am glad that

you are prepared to take Kashmiris, both Hindus and Muslims, into the Army provided that suitable material offers for recruitment. For the rest, no more is necessary than to apprise all sections of population in the State of the policy of Your Highness and Your Government to provide opportunities of service, whether civil or military, to members of all creeds and communities in the State on their merits. I agree, and I am in a position to assure you that Sheikh Abdullah agrees, that, for sometime to come and until things have completely settled down and normal life has been in full swing for a considerable period, we should hardly think of recruiting any large number of Muslims from the Jammu Province (including the Poonch area) which has contributed the largest number to the rebel ranks in the present disturbances. The populations of these areas have first to be won over and their loyalty to the State proved beyond cavil before recruitment to the Army from their ranks can be safely allowed to take place. It is, however, important that, in order to win them over, they should have the expectation from now that, if they become and remain loyal to the State, opportunities for service to the State, whether in a civil or military capacity, will not be denied to them.

11. The Mysore Proclamation dated 24 September 1947 laid upon the Dewan the duty of framing a Constitution Bill and directed that, in doing so, he should obtain the advice and counsel of a committee elected by the Legislature and of such other experts and expert bodies as might be found suitable and desirable. There was some controversy on this matter in Mysore State and, in the final understanding that was arrived at between the Dewan and the President of the Mysore Congress and embodied in the Mysore Maharaja's Proclamation dated 29th of October, the direction in this respect was that the Interim Ministry should set up a Constituent Assembly composed of elected representatives of the people and entrust to it the task of framing a Constitutional Bill providing for Responsible Government under the aegis of the Maharaja. I think that, so far as Kashmir is concerned, it would be sufficient if the Proclamation that will be issued by Your Highness gives the direction that the Interim Ministry should submit to you, as soon as possible, proposals for bringing into existence a Constitution making body composed of elected representatives of the people for the purpose of framing, for your approval and promulgation, a Constitution for the Jammu and Kashmir State. The Constitution of the present Praja Sabha provides for a large fraction of nominated members and will therefore not be accepted either to the

National Conference or even to other political bodies in the State. It would seem, therefore, best to ask the Indian Ministry itself to submit for your consideration proposals as regards the composition of the Constitution making body and the method of choosing the members.

12. This letter has become longer than I originally intended, I hope, however, I have met all the points raised in your letter.

13. With a view to saving time, the States Ministry is being asked to prepare a draft of the Proclamation and to send it on to you as early as possible for your consideration. If you desire, in the meantime, to give any instructions in connection with such drafting, will you kindly have them communicated to that Ministry direct by telegram or by letter?

14. The actual personnel of the Ministry has to be proposed by Sheikh Abdullah for your acceptance. If, in connection with this matter or for the purpose of further discussion of what I have said in this letter, my services should be required, they are always at your disposal.

With kindest regards,

Yours sincerely,
N. Gopalaswami

INDEX